MAKING THE MOST OF PERENNIALS IN THE GARDEN

An easy-to-use plant listing section, and over 450 plant portraits, make it simple to choose perennials, care for them, and enjoy them at their best

A comprehensive visual directory and practical guide to growing perennial plants to suit all garden styles and every kind of outdoor space

Richard Bird

southwater

Dedicated with love to Jenny Cline, for all her help and inspiration in the garden

This edition is published by Southwater

Southwater is an imprint of Anness Publishing Ltd
Hermes House, 88–89 Blackfriars Road, London SE1 8HA
tel. 020 7401 2077; fax 020 7633 9499

www.southwaterbooks.com; www.annesspublishing.com

If you like the images in this book and would like to investigate using them for publishing, promotions or advertising, please visit our website www.practicalpictures.com for more information.

UK agent: The Manning Partnership Ltd
tel. 01225 478444; fax 01225 478440; sales@manning-partnership.co.uk
UK distributor: Grantham Book Services Ltd
tel. 01476 541080; fax 01476 541061; orders@gbs.tbs-ltd.co.uk
North American agent/distributor: National Book Network
tel. 301 459 3366; fax 301 429 5746; www.nbnbooks.com
Australian agent/distributor: Pan Macmillan Australia
tel. 1300 135 113; fax 1300 135 103; customer.service@macmillan.com.au
New Zealand agent/distributor: David Bateman Ltd
tel. (09) 415 7664; fax (09) 415 8892

Publisher: Joanna Lorenz
Editorial Director: Helen Sudell
Editors: Ann Kay and Elizabeth Woodland
Designer: Michael Morey
Cover Designer: Nigel Partridge
Production Controller: Claire Rae

Ethical Trading Policy

At Anness Publishing we believe that business should be conducted in an ethical and ecologically sustainable way, with respect for the environment and a proper regard to the replacement of the natural resources we employ.

As a publisher, we use a lot of wood pulp to make high-quality paper for printing, and that wood commonly comes from spruce trees. We are therefore currently growing more than 500,000 trees in two Scottish forest plantations near Aberdeen – Berrymoss (130 hectares/320 acres) and West Touxhill (125 hectares/305 acres). The forests we manage contain twice the number of trees employed each year in paper-making for our books. Because of this ongoing ecological investment programme, you, as our customer, can have the pleasure and reassurance of knowing that a tree is being cultivated on your behalf to naturally replace the materials used to make the book you are holding. Our forestry programme is run in accordance with the UK Woodland Assurance Scheme (UKWAS) and will be certified by the internationally recognized Forest Stewardship Council (FSC). The FSC is a non-government organization dedicated to promoting responsible management of the world's forests. Certification ensures forests are managed in an environmentally sustainable and socially responsible basis. For further information about this scheme, go to www.annesspublishing.com/trees

Previously published as part of a larger volume, *A Gardener's Guide to Annuals and Perennials*

Main front cover image shows *Monarda* 'Scorpion'
Note: Bracketed terms are intended for American readers

MAKING THE MOST OF PERENNIALS IN THE GARDEN

CONTENTS

INTRODUCTION

In spite of a modern tendency for television personalities to create gardens with few or no plants, there is no doubt in most people's minds that without plants a garden is simply not a garden. There is something about the presence of plants – their colour, shape and fragrance – that lifts the spirits in a very special way. Perennials are one of the most popular types of flowering plants, offering a vast selection of ways to add that vital colour and stimulus to every kind of garden.

Perennials in this timber flower bed thrive under the shelter of the tall hedge behind it.

An elegant conifer lifts the eye above transient summer herbaceous perennials.

Enjoying plants

Plants give pleasure to people in many different ways. The majority of gardeners enjoy filling space with colour, shape and texture as well as planning a garden to make the most of their chosen plants' strong points. There are others for whom it is the plant itself that is of principal interest. They are less interested in how the plant fits into the overall picture of the garden, or indeed how the garden looks as a whole, and are more absorbed by growing a particular type of plant to absolute perfection. These gardeners may only grow plants in order to show them, or simply because they enjoy the challenge of growing rare and difficult types.

There are others still who garden simply because they enjoy working in the open air and get a real joy from cultivation. For them it is the process as well as the results that matter. The huge variety of perennials that are available, and the many ways in which they can be grown, can easily cater to all these different approaches.

Starting out

Tackling a large bare patch may seem a rather daunting task to somebody who has not done any gardening before, but it is nothing like as difficult as some experts would have you believe.

Gardening is rather like decorating a room: naturally a certain amount of time and effort is involved, but if you are not satisfied with the result you can always change it.

A lovely cottage garden effect is created along this informal path using both annuals and perennials. The lush foliage helps to provide bulk.

Working with colour

Many beginners are worried about combining colours, but the key is simply to go for plants and effects that you like without worrying about what other people do.

Remember that we all have some ability where colour is concerned: we choose what goes with what when we get dressed each day and we choose colours for decorating and furnishing our homes. Planning a garden is really no different. In the same way that there are fashion magazines to help you choose your style, so there is no shortage of different kinds of gardening magazine to browse through for inspiration, and there is nothing more enjoyable than wandering around other people's gardens in search of good ideas.

In this attractive and colourful bed, arching, swordlike leaves are almost as important a feature as the bright blue agapanthus and orange crocosmia flowers.

Choosing your plants

Plants form the basis of all good gardens and we have produced this detailed directory which will introduce you to the very best perennial plants.

There are far more perennials available than we could hope to include in this book, but the directory has been specially devised to act as a comprehensive basis. As you develop your garden you will become more interested in certain plants rather than others. You will then be able to create your own database of information from nursery catalogues, magazines, books and the internet. Soon you may even find that you have turned into one of those gardeners for whom studying plants is as fascinating as actually growing them.

In this subtle scheme (left), Two black pines protect the flowering perennials at their feet.

Perennials and their role

When a dream garden springs into our minds, the linchpins of the borders will usually be the perennials, with their great wealth of colours, textures and forms. They provide an enormous selection of plants that will fit in with any style of gardening and will satisfy both the keen and lazy gardener.

What is a perennial?

Perennials are just what they say – perennial – though the description must be modified slightly, as it could apply to any plant that lasts more than a year. In fact, it generally applies to herbaceous material that is grown in general borders. In other words, it excludes trees, shrubs and plants that are grown in rock gardens or in greenhouses, even though these all might be long-lived. Most perennials die back in winter and then regenerate the following year, though some remain green right through the winter. From the gardening point of view, perennials are generally considered hardy – that is, they are able to withstand at least a certain amount of frost.

Changing scene

Most perennials have a relatively short flowering season. This may be seen as a disadvantage, but in fact it can be a great asset because it means that the garden is never static, it never becomes boring. It allows the borders to be planned in such a way that they present an ever-changing scene. It is possible, for example, to have a spring border of blue and yellow that transforms itself over the months into a pink and mauve border in the summer and then perhaps to hot colours for the autumn. Such coordination needs careful planning, of course, but that is half the fun of gardening.

Use vivid, exciting colours to create a "hot" border. Just like beds of annual plants, herbaceous borders of perennials can be colour themed in all kinds of creative ways.

Foliage effect

Perennials are not only about flower colour. Many have interesting foliage in a wide range of colours, from greens, silvers and purples to yellows and creams. All these help to create a backdrop against which the flowers can be seen to advantage. Longer lasting than flowers, foliage forms the main structure of the borders throughout the growing season.

Herbaceous borders

Perennials can be used in many ways. One of the most effective is creating a herbaceous border entirely from perennials. These are usually planted in drifts, creating a sumptuous tapestry of colours through summer and autumn. Traditionally, herbaceous borders were found in large gardens, but smaller versions can easily be created to great effect.

This mixed border of perennials, annuals and shrubs shows the effects that can be achieved by combining a variety of different shapes, colours and textures.

Mixed borders

Many gardeners prefer to use a mixture of plants, perhaps using shrubs as the backbone and main structure of the garden and mixing in other plants to give differing colours throughout the year. Perennials are perfect for this role, particularly as there are a large number that like to grow in the light shade that is provided by being planted under or close to shrubs. Although shrubs form the structure, the perennials usually provide the majority of the plants. In some cases these may be a single large clump, but drifts of the bigger plants and carpets of the lower growing ones look better than scattering the plants around at random.

Potted perennials

It is often thought that the only place for perennials is in a large garden, but perennials are suited to all sizes of garden. They can be grown in a patio garden or even on a balcony or roof garden. As long as you are prepared to water them, they may be grown in containers, which can then be placed anywhere, including in gardens that are paved over and have no native soil at all.

Hardy perennials

Hardy perennials, as their name implies, are those that will tolerate frost and will reappear every year. Some tender perennials may be killed by frosts, although sometimes the frost will just kill off the exposed foliage, and the plant will regenerate from the roots. Although it is mainly temperature related, hardiness can be affected by soil conditions, and often a borderline plant will be more hardy in a free-draining soil than in a heavy damp one.

Many perennials, such as this lily, are ideal for tubs. Just move into position when in flower.

Plant-lovers

There are more varieties of perennial plants than any other type of plant available to the gardener. Some gardeners make a virtue of this and indulge their love of plants by creating special collections. Others collect a particular species, pinks (*Dianthus*) or hostas, for example, or favour broader groups – variegated plants are a very popular subject. There are also gardeners who seek out rare and difficult-to-grow plants, just to test their skills, and others who might make a collection of plants mentioned in, for example, the works of Shakespeare. The possibilities are almost endless.

Perennials are not dependent on their flowers for their attraction. Many earn their keep as foliage plants, with the shapes and colour providing plenty of interest, as seen here.

How plants are named

All living things are classified according to a system based on principles that were devised by the 18th-century Swedish botanist, Carl Linnaeus. This system states that a particular plant genus (plural: genera) is a group of plants containing similar species. Beyond that there may be plants that are simply a slight variation of a species, or are a hybrid (cross) of different species or variations.

Scientific names

Under this system, plants have botanical names – often Latin but also derived from other languages – that consist of the genus name (for example, *Verbena*), followed by the name that denotes the particular species (for example, *hastata*). Some genera contain a huge number of species that may include annuals, perennials, shrubs and trees, while others contain just one species. Although all members of a genus are assumed to be related to each other, this is not always visually obvious. It is useful to keep in mind that a species is defined scientifically as individuals that are alike and tend naturally to breed with each other.

Despite this system, botanists and taxonomists (the experts who classify living things) often disagree about the basis on which a plant has been named. This is why it is useful for a plant to retain its synonym (abbreviated to syn. in the text), or alternative name. Incorrect names often gain widespread usage, and in some cases, two plants thought to have separate identities, and with two different names, are found to be the same plant.

A well-known example of naming confusion is the genus *Pelargonium*. Until the 19th century, pelargonium plants were included in the genus *Geranium*, and despite being classified separately for over a century, they are still popularly known as geraniums.

Variations on a theme

Genetically, many plants are able to change over time to adapt to a changing environment. In the wild, individuals within a species that are not well adapted will not survive, so all survivors will look the same. The average garden is a more controlled environment, so gardeners can choose to encourage and grow on variations within a species that have small but

This is *Centaurea hypoleuca* 'John Coutts'. John Coutts is the name that has been given to a dark pink form of the pink knapweed species, *Centaurea hypoleuca*.

pleasing differences such as variegated leaves and double flowers. The terms for these variations are subspecies (abbreviated to subsp.), variety (var.), form (f., similar to variety and often used interchangeably) and cultivar. A cultivar is a variation that would not occur in the wild but has been produced and maintained solely by cultivation. Variations are given names in single quotes, for example *Papaver orientale* 'Allegro'.

Hybrids

When plant species breed with each other, the result is a hybrid. Rare in the wild, crossing is very common among plant-breeders, done specially in order to produce plants with desirable qualities such as larger or double blooms, variegated foliage and greater frost resistance. A multiplication sign (x) is used to indicate a hybrid, and the name often gives a clear idea of the hybrid's origins.

Plant Groups

A Group of plants is a group of very similar variations. Their names do not have quotation marks around them – for example *Tradescantia* Andersoniana Group.

The geranium is a well-known case of naming confusion, as many plants that actually belong to the genus *Pelargonium* are very commonly referred to as geraniums.

How to use the directory

Plants are arranged alphabetically, by genus. Each main entry features a general introduction to that genus, plus specific useful information such as tips on propagation and

which hardiness zone the genus belongs to. This is followed by a selection of plants from that genus, also arranged alphabetically according to their most widely accepted names.

One of these entries might be a species, a hybrid (or group of hybrids), a variety, form or cultivar. Each is given a useful description that may include height and spread.

Caption
The full botanical name of the plant in question is given with each photograph.

Genus name
This is the internationally accepted botanical name for a group of related plant species.

Common name
This popular, non-scientific name applies to the whole of the plant genus.

Cultivation
This section gives the level of sun or shade that the plants described in the selection either require or tolerate, advice on the best type of soil in which they should be grown, and any other helpful tips that might be appropriate.

Propagation
This section gives essential information on how and when to increase the plant – from seed, by dividing plants or by taking various types of cutting. Many annuals entries also give the best temperature at which to propagate a plant, often with specific centigrade (and Fahrenheit) figures given.

Individual plant entry
This starts with the current botanical name of the plant in bold, and this can refer to a species, subspecies, hybrid, variant or cultivar. If a synonym (syn.) is given, this provides the synonym, or synonyms (alternative names) for a plant. A common name may be given after the botanical name.

Plant description
This gives a description of the plant, along with any other information that may be helpful and relevant.

Paeonia lactiflora 'Bowl of Beauty'

PAEONIA
Peony

One of the most popular of all perennial species, these beautiful plants suit almost any type of garden, from old-fashioned cottage gardens to modern formal ones. There are only about 30 species of peony, most of which are in cultivation, but hundreds of cultivars have been bred from them. The typical peony has a bowl-shaped flower in varying shades of red, pink or white. There are also some rather fine yellows. The foliage of peonies is also very attractive.

Cultivation Peonies need a deep rich soil, so add plenty of well-rotted organic material. They will grow in either sun or a light shade. They often take a while to settle down after being disturbed so try not to move them once established. Z3–5.

Propagation They can be divided in spring but this is not easy and they will take a while to settle down. Root cuttings taken in early winter is the easiest method.

Paeonia lactiflora '**Bowl of Beauty**'
Deep rose-red petals and a large central boss of yellow make this a superb peony. H 75cm (30in) S 1m (3ft).

Photograph
Each entry features a full-colour photograph that makes identification easy.

Genus introduction
This provides a general introduction to the genus and may state the number of species within that genus. Other information featured here may include general advice on usage, preferred conditions, and plant-care, as well as subspecies, hybrids (indicated by an x symbol in the name), varieties and cultivars (featuring names in single quotes) that are available.

Additional information

This page shows a basic entry from the directory. Other information supplied includes:

Other plants (both directories): if given, these sections provide brief information about common types that are available and other recommended (often rarer) plants to look out for.

Plant hardiness zone
A plant hardiness zone is given at the end of this section. Zones give a general indication of the average annual minimum temperature for a particular geographical area. The smaller number indicates the northernmost zone it can survive in and the higher number the southernmost zone that the plant will tolerate. In most cases, only one zone is given. (See page 256 for details of zones and a zone map.)

Size information
The average expected height and spread of a genus or individual plant is frequently given, although growth rates may vary depending on location and conditions. Metric measurements always precede imperial ones. Average heights and spreads are given (as H and S) wherever possible and appropriate, and more consistently for perennials, although it must be noted that dimensions can vary a great deal.

A directory of perennials

This directory provides a highly illustrated listing of the many perennials that are now available. It demonstrates very clearly just how versatile these long-lasting plants can be – providing every conceivable colour of bloom, structural shape and foliage type to help create wonderful effects in any style or size of garden.

English (common) names are given throughout but increasingly the majority of plants are becoming known by their Latin or botanical names. Thus although *Agapanthus* was previously (and still is occasionally, particularly in books) known as African blue lily, it is referred to by most gardeners simply as agapanthus in the same way that *Hosta* has become hosta and *Iris* iris.

The hardiness zones given in the text refer only to the selected main plants featured and not to the whole genus. The height and spread given for each of the plants is an indication only. The dimensions will vary depending on the growing conditions and the vigour of the individual plants. The spread is particularly difficult to predict since many plants go on increasing their width throughout their lives.

One of the best geraniums for the front of a border is the colourful *Geranium cinereum* 'Ballerina', which flowers over a long period.

ACANTHUS
Bear's Breeches

There are about 30 species in this wonderful genus of which only four or five are commonly grown. The joy of these plants is their tall, architectural shapes. They are clump-forming, and produce spikes of smoky-coloured, hooded flowers. The large leaves are deeply divided and in some species are tipped with spines. These plants are ideal focal points for borders or elsewhere in the garden. They also make excellent cut and dried flowers.

Cultivation They will grow in any garden soil that is reasonably fertile in either full sun or partial shade. Z8.

Propagation From seed sown in pots in autumn or spring, or from root cuttings taken in early winter. Self-sown seedlings can also be transplanted while they are still young. Division is also possible but it can be heavy work to divide large plants.

Acanthus hungaricus
(A. balcanicus)

The flowers of this plant are pinkish-white with purple hoods, while the large leaves are dark green with narrow spineless leaflets. H and S 1.2m (4ft).

Acanthus mollis

Tall spikes of purple-hooded white flowers are carried over a clump of soft, dark green leaves with broad, spineless leaflets. H 1.5m (5ft) S 60cm (24in).

Acanthus spinosus

This produces very tall spikes of striking white flowers with purple hoods. The leaves are deeply cut

Acanthus mollis

with softish spines on the tips of the leaflets. H 1.5m (5ft) S 60cm (24in). There is a shorter form, *A. spinosissimus*, which has very deeply divided leaves with sharp spines. The leaves make this a dramatic plant, but it can be difficult to weed around.

Other plants For the keen gardener, *A. dioscoridis* (pink flowers with green hoods) and *A. hirsutus* (yellow flowers, green hoods) are well worth exploring.

ACHILLEA
Yarrow

There are 85 species of yarrow as well as a considerable number of cultivars. Not all the species are of interest to the gardener, indeed

Achillea 'Fanal'

some are weeds, but amongst their number are some first-class plants that most gardeners will appreciate. Many have a wonderful calm quality; their flat plates of flowers often seem to float above the other plants, creating a sea of tranquillity in the hurly-burly of the border. The predominant colour is yellow, but there are a number of white species and a few reds and terracottas among the cultivars. They make very good dried flowers.

Cultivation Yarrows prefer a sunny position and any reasonable garden soil. Some species need staking as they flop over. Z2–5.

Propagation Nearly all the main species and varieties can easily be increased by division or from basal cuttings taken in spring.

Achillea 'Fanal'

An attractive cultivar with brilliant red flowers. H 75cm (30in) S 60cm (24in).

Achillea filipendulina

A tall, elegant species with large flat heads of golden yellow floating 1.2m (4ft) above the ground. S 60cm (24in).

Achillea 'Moonshine'

Achillea millefolium

The species is best avoided (except in a spacious wild garden) since it is invasive, but there are a number of excellent cultivars suitable for flower beds and borders. They include 'Cerise Queen' (cerise), 'Fire King' (bright red), 'Lilac Beauty' (lilac), 'Paprika' (orange-red). H 60cm (24in) S 60cm (24in).

Achillea 'Moonshine'

This is an excellent cultivar with pale yellow flowers over soft grey foliage. However, it is not the strongest of plants and needs renewing every two or three years. H and S 60cm (24in).

Achillea ptarmica

A tall spreading plant with small heads of white flowers. It is normally grown in the attractive form 'Boule de Neige' which has double flowers. H 60cm (24in) S 1.2m (4ft).

Acanthus hungaricus

Acanthus spinosus

Achillea filipendulina

Achillea 'Taygetea'

Achillea 'Terracotta'

Achillea 'Taygetea'

This clump-forming plant has wide heads of sulphur yellow flowers carried on 60cm (24in) stems. The feathery leaves are greenish grey. S 60cm (24in).

Achillea 'Terracotta'

The best of the terracotta-coloured varieties. It has large flat heads floating 60–75cm (24–30in) above the ground and forming clumps. S 60cm (24in).

ACONITUM
Monkshood

This is a genus of about 100 species and 50 cultivars. They are very beautiful plants but unfortunately beneath this beauty is hidden poison – most parts of the plant are toxic if eaten. Avoid planting these if young children are likely to visit your garden, and in any case be careful where you site them. The plants are related to delphiniums and they have the same type of flower spikes carrying mainly bright blue flowers. The flowers are hooded, hence the plant's name, and also come in white and yellow.

Cultivation Aconitum prefer cool, partially shaded conditions but they will tolerate full sun if the soil is kept moist. They like a soil made rich with well-rotted organic material. Z3–6.

Propagation Sow seed in pots, preferably in autumn. The plants can also easily be divided in spring although they may take a while to settle down.

Aconitum 'Bressingham Spire'

A cultivar of proven track record with spikes that reach up to 1m (3ft) in height. The flowers are a rich violet blue. It flowers in late summer and into the autumn. S 30cm (12in).

Aconitum × cammarum 'Bicolor'

This is an intriguing plant with blue and white flowers that appear towards the end of summer. H 1.2m (4ft) S 50cm (20in). 'Grandiflorum Album' has large white flowers.

Aconitum carmichaelii

A long-used garden species with a number of valuable cultivars. It is a tall species, up to 1.8m (6ft), with deep blue flowers that appear from midsummer onwards. S 30cm (12in). 'Arendsii' is one of the best-known cultivars; it flowers slightly earlier than the species. 'Kelmscott' is another excellent cultivar; it has lighter blue flowers.

Aconitum hemsleyanum

This is different from the other species in that it is a climber that twines up supports or through shrubs. It has deep violet blue flowers from midsummer onwards. H 2–2.5m (6–8ft) S 1–1.2m (3–4ft).

Aconitum 'Ivorine'

One of the best of the non-blue monkshoods, this plant has beautiful pale creamy-yellow flowers that appear from spring into early summer. H 1m (3ft) S 60cm (24in).

Aconitum napellus

Aconitum 'Stainless Steel'

Aconitum napellus

A good species that has produced a number of excellent cultivars. The species has deep blue flowers but there is a cultivar 'Albiflorus' with pure white spikes. H 1.5m (5ft) S 30cm (12in).

Aconitum 'Spark's Variety'

A tall variety up to 1.5m (5ft) high with large spires of deep blue flowers that are carried from mid-summer onwards. S 60cm (24in).

Other plants Other pleasing cultivars worth checking out include *Aconitum* 'Eleonara' and *A.* 'Stainless Steel'.

ACTAEA
Baneberry

Actaeas have been grown for generations, mainly for their coloured berries. However, what most gardeners have known as *Cimifuga* has now been added to the genus, giving it a group of spectacular flowering plants. The original actaeas are relatively short, clump-forming plants with little, white tufts of flowers that are followed by white, black or red berries. The cimifugas are much taller (up to 2m/6ft) and have striking, tall spikes of white flowers over attractive foliage.

Cultivation All actaeas like a woodland-type, moisture-retentive soil. The original actaeas are true woodlanders and like partial shade.

The cimifugas like partial shade, but will tolerate more sun if the soil is not dry. Z3.

Propagation The easiest method of increase is by division in spring. Actaeas can also be grown from seed as long as it is sown fresh.

Actaea pachypoda
(syn. A. alba)

An actaea that flowers in the spring and then produces a head of white berries in the late summer, when it is at its best. H 1m (3ft) S 50cm (20in).

Actaea racemosa

One of the tallest cimifugas with good green foliage and white flower spikes that resemble fire-works going off. The flowers appear in summer. H 2.5m (8ft) S 50cm (20in).

Actaea rubra

Similar to *A. pachypoda* except that it has red berries in autumn. An excellent woodland plant. H 50cm (20in) S 30cm (12in).

Actaea simplex

An excellent cimifuga type with tall white spikes of flowers in autumn and green foliage. H 1.2m (4ft) S 60cm (24in). The leaves are deep purple in some of the cultivars; 'Brunette' is a fine example of this. 'Elstead' is another attractive cultivar in which the buds are pink before they open to white flowers.

Actaea racemosa

ADIANTUM
Maidenhair fern

A romantic name for a romantic fern. The great attraction of this fern is its delicately cut fronds. They are usually carried on black or deep purple stems which set off the fresh green of the leaves perfectly. They are deciduous and when the new fronds first uncurl in spring they have a delightful pinkish tinge. These plants are best placed in a choice position where they can be easily seen.

Adiantum is a large genus of around 250 species of which 20 or so are in general cultivation. Many are frost tender but those listed below are hardy.

Cultivation These are delicate plants and so should be sited out of direct midday sunlight. They like a cool, moist root-run with plenty of leaf mould in the soil. Remove the old foliage in the late winter before the new growth begins to unfurl. Z5–8.

Propagation The plants can be grown from spore but division in spring is the easiest method.

Adiantum aleuticum

Individual leaflets are arranged in columns on either side of the black wiry midribs, giving the appearance of a long, deeply cut leaf. H 30cm (12in), slowly spreading to form a small clump (30cm/12in). The form 'Japonicum' has beautiful browny-red fronds when they first open.

Adiantum pedatum

This has similar fronds to the previous species, except that they are larger and more upright. H 45cm (18in), slowly spreading into a small clump (45cm/18in).

Adiantum venustum

The gem of the genus. It has deeply divided, filigree fronds, with the black midribs showing up in beautiful contrast to the green of the foliage. H 23cm (9in) S 30cm (12in).

Other plants In frost-free areas or for conservatory or greenhouse use try *Adiantum raddianum* or one of its many cultivars.

AGAPANTHUS
African blue lily

A very attractive genus of about ten species. There are many cultivars, at least one of which no garden should be without. The flowers are tubular, usually blue and carried in a globe, up to 20cm (8in) across, at the top of a tall, leafless stem. The foliage is strap-like and erupts from the base of the plant like a fountain. Agapanthus make excellent plants for the border or for containers. They flower in summer and make good cut flowers. The majority are hardy.

Cultivation They will grow in any reasonably fertile soil in full sun. Although they prefer a moist soil they will tolerate a degree of dryness. In cold areas they will appreciate a warm mulch during the winter. Z7.

Propagation Although they can be grown from seed sown in autumn they are more reliable grown from divisions taken in spring.

Agapanthus 'Castle of Mey'

Agapanthus africanus

A late-summer species with deep blue flowers. The flower stems reach 1m (3ft) tall S 50cm (20in). 'Albus' has white flowers.

Agapanthus 'Blue Giant'

Excellent blue-coloured flowers carried on tall (1.2m/4ft) stems. S 50cm (20in).

Agapanthus campanulatus

A fine species that has produced a number of popular cultivars. It produces large (up to 20cm/8in) heads of variable blue or white flowers in mid to late summer. H 60–120m (2–4ft) S 50cm (20in). 'Isis' is one of the most popular cultivars with deep blue flowers in late summer. The variety *albidus* has white flowers.

Agapanthus 'Castle of Mey'

This is a shorter variety that carries lovely deep blue flowers. It blooms in mid to late summer,

Agapanthus 'Dorothy Palmer'

and is excellent placed in a position at the front of a border. H 60cm (24in) S 30cm (12in).

Agapanthus 'Gayle's Lilac'

This has lilac flowers so it is good for those who want a paler form. H 60cm (24in) S 30cm (12in). *A.* 'Golden Rule' has yellow edges to its strap-like leaves. The flowers are light blue and appear mid to late summer. H 60cm (24in) S 30cm (12in).

Agapanthus Headbourne hybrids

This term covers a collection of hybrids of varying blues, originally selected by Lewis Palmer for their hardiness. 'Loch Hope' is an excellent tall variety. It has deep blue flowers which appear from late summer into autumn. H 1.5m (5ft) S 50cm (20in). 'Peter Pan' is a short form, suitable for small pots. H 60cm (24in) S 30cm (12in).

Other plants There are many more cultivars to explore, including 'Dorothy Palmer'. Nearly all are worth considering.

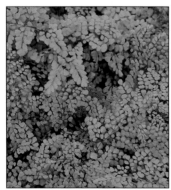

Adiantum venustum

Agapanthus campanulatus

Agapanthus 'Loch Hope'

Agastache foeniculum

Agastache 'Honey Bee White'

Alchemilla mollis

AGASTACHE
Mexican bergamot

This genus is not seen as often as it deserves to be. This is probably because the plants are short lived in moist soils. However, they self-sow and once you have them you are rarely without them. There are about 30 species but only a few are cultivated. The foliage is aromatic making this a pleasant plant to weed around. Another joy is the delightful spikes of flowers, which bloom from midsummer into autumn. Each plant sends up plenty of upright stems, the top of which is covered in whorls of bright blue, white, pink or red flowers. They are excellent for gravel gardens.

Cultivation These are plants from dry hills and so they like a well-drained soil in full sun. Z8.
Propagation They can readily be grown from seed, sown inside or scattered where the plants are to grow. They will self-sow if the conditions are right. Basal cuttings can be taken in spring.

Agastache foeniculum
(syn. *A. anisata*)

This can be a tall species when grown in a reasonably rich soil. The mint-like leaves smell of aniseed, and the flowers are a wonderful dusky dark blue. H 1.5m (5ft) S 50cm (20in). There are a number of cultivars the most popular being 'Alabaster' with white flowers. 'Blue and White' is also often grown.

Agastache mexicana

This is the other main hardy species in cultivation. It has pink to dark red flowers over a long period in late summer and often beyond. H 1m (3ft) S 30cm (12in). There are several cultivars including 'Mauve Beauty' with lilac-mauve flowers. 'Champagne' has fine fizzy spikes of creamy-white flowers.

Other plants These are the main species but it is worth exploring *Agastache rugosa* and *A. urticifolia* among others. 'Honey Bee White' is another cultivar to try.

ALCHEMILLA
Lady's mantle

A large genus of 250 species of which a number are in cultivation. Their attraction is that they are good both as flowering and foliage plants. The flowers are small but grouped in clusters; in some cases they form tight clusters, in others airy sprays. The flowers are a yellowy lime-green. This contrasts well with the green foliage which is rounded and pleated. In some species the foliage is more deeply cut. Alchemilla is a perfect plant for growing along paths or on the banks of ponds.

Cultivation Any reasonably fertile soil will do for this plant. It will grow in either full sun or partial shade. Cut back to the ground after flowering to prevent seeding and to promote new foliage. Z6.
Propagation Self-seeds, but it can be propagated from seed sown in spring or from divisions.

Alchemilla conjuncta

A mat-forming plant with very distinctive foliage. The deeply lobed leaves are green but edged with silver. It is low-growing, only reaching about 20cm (8in) unless it is scrambling through another plant. S 30cm (12in)

Alchemilla mollis

A common but excellent plant. It is floppy but reaches about 45cm (18in) in height. It has a lovely scent when you are up close. The flowers appear in early to midsummer and the plant should then be cut back. S 45cm (18in).

Other plants The above are the main species but there are plenty more that are worth growing, especially the low, mat-growing ones. Try *Alchemilla alpina*, *A. elizabethae*, or *A. ellenbeckii* with its red stems.

Agastache foeniculum 'Blue and White'

Alchemilla conjuncta

Alchemilla elizabethae

Perennials for seaside gardens

Artemisia
Centranthus
Crambe maritima
Crocosmia
Echinops
Erigeron
Eryngium
Geranium
Kniphofia
Lathyrus
Limonium
Linaria
Origanum
Osteospermum
Papaver
Perovskia
Persicaria affinis
Phormium
Sisyrinchium
Yucca

Allium cristophii

ALLIUM
Ornamental onions

This very large genus of bulbs (more than 700 species) has a deservedly popular place in hardy borders. Alliums are very decorative and are best placed so that they pop up between or through other plants. Although some have lax heads the majority of popular species have round globes of flowers, 25cm (10in) or more across.

Most have purple flowers but there are others with blue, white, pink or yellow heads. There are species that flower at all times between spring and autumn. Most have strap-like foliage. However, this can be rather ugly since it is often dying back just as the flowers are coming into bloom. Hide the plants amongst other plants in the middle of the border so that the dying leaves will not be visible.

Cultivation Alliums will grow in most soils except extremely wet ones. They are perfect for dry soils such as gravel borders. They like full sun. Z3–8.

Propagation Alliums generally increase with little help from the gardener. They can be grown from seed or from the bulbils that often appear in the flower heads. The easiest way is to divide off the little bulblets that develop around the main bulb.

Allium roseum

Allium carinatum subsp. pulchellum
A beautiful flower with a shower of drooping pink to purple flowers that appear over a long period in the autumn. The grass-like foliage can be confused with weeds early in the year. H 45cm (18in) S 8–10cm (3–4in).

Allium cristophii.
Very impressive purple flowers that are large and globe-like. They make good dried flowers. H 60cm (24in) S 20cm (8in).

Allium hollandicum
A medium-sized spherical-headed onion for the spring border. The flowers are purple. This plant is best known in its form 'Purple Sensation' which has an almost luminous quality. H 1m (3ft) S 10cm (4in).

Allium roseum
A charming allium which is best grown so that it peeps up through other plants. It has lax heads of only a few flowers, but these are of a most delicate pink. They appear in summer. The plant has bulbils and can be slightly invasive. However, it rarely causes problems especially if the bulbils are removed before they ripen. H 1m (3ft) S 10cm (4in).

Allium schoenoprasum
This is the humble chive. It flowers briefly but profusely in the early summer, when it is a perfect choice for lining paths. The flowers are purple but in the form 'Forescate' they are brighter and more rosy-pink. Shear to the

Allium schoenoprasum

ground after flowering to encourage new foliage. H 30cm (12in) S 10cm (4in).

Allium sphaerocephalon
This allium has bright reddish flowers that are compressed into a tight ball. It flowers in summer and is excellent planted amongst other plants. H 75cm (30in) S 10cm (4in).

Other plants There are many, many more species of allium to choose from and it is worth making a note of any pleasing ones that you see as you go round gardens. Be aware that some of the smaller ones can become a little invasive.

ALSTROEMERIA
Peruvian lily

Alstroemeria are known mainly as cut flowers, but increasingly, they are becoming popular as a garden plant. There are 20 species and about 100 garden-bred cultivars.

The plants are summer-flowering, producing masses of funnel-shaped flowers. They vary in colour from yellows and oranges to pinks and reds, with most having a mixture of two or more colours. The throats are distinctively streaked or spotted. As well as being suitable for growing in the greenhouse for cutting, most make good garden plants. They are ideally placed in the middle of the border.

Cultivation Alstroemerias like a moist soil with plenty of organic material added to it. They should be in full sun, although they will tolerate a little shade. Slugs can be a nuisance. Z7.

Propagation These plants can be grown from seed, but the most usual method of propagation is by division.

Alstroemeria aurea

Alstroemeria ligtu hybrids

Alstroemeria aurea
These are the most commonly seen Peruvian lilies in gardens and possibly the hardiest. The flowers are bright orange, streaked with reddish brown. They get up to 45cm (18in) high. S 60cm (24in). There are several cultivars: 'Lutea' has flowers of bright yellow with brownish spots.

Alstroemeria ligtu
A pink-flowered hardy species that is mainly grown in the form of ligtu hybrids which come in a variety of colours. H 75cm (30in) S 60–100cm (2–3ft).

Alstroemeria psittacina
The flowers are not so flared as on other species, but they are intriguingly coloured in shades of green and red. H 1m (3ft) S 60cm (24in).

Other plants There are many other highly coloured cultivars to explore. The best way to choose between them is to go to a specialist nursery which has plenty to offer.

ANEMONE
Anemone

This is a large genus of garden plants offering several distinct forms from tall Japanese anemones to low wood anemones. There are 120 species in the genus and most are in cultivation. For the keen gardener it is a good genus to collect since it presents interesting and varying flowers from early spring through to autumn. Most are simple open flowers but there are some lovely doubles. There are anemones of all colours except black.

Cultivation All need a moisture-retentive soil, except for the bulbous species, such as the

Anemone blanda

Anemone hupehensis 'Prinz Heinrich'

Anemone nemorosa

Anthemis punctata subsp. *cupaniana*

coronarias which need a well-drained soil. Shade is preferred by the small woodlanders and full sun by the bulbs. All the others like sun or partial shade. Z5–6.
Propagation All can be grown from seed preferably sown after it has ripened. Division is the other main method of increase.

Anemone blanda
A lovely woodland flower for early spring, with discs of blue, white or pink petals. It dies back after flowering and seeding. H 5–10cm (2–4in) S 10–15cm (4–6in).

Anemone coronaria
A tuberous anemone with bright red, blue or white spring flowers. Good for the front of a border or containers. H 5–25cm (2–10in) S 10–15cm (4–6in). The most common group of cultivars are the De Caens which are

delightful. *A.c.* 'Lord Lieutenant' is also an attractive cultivar. Other bulbous species worth considering are *A.* × *fulgida* and *A. pavonina*, which have bright red forms.

Anemone × hybrida
(Japanese anemone)
Few gardens can wish to be without Japanese anemones which embrace several species including this hybrid. Although tall (up to 1.5m/ 5ft) they are wiry and do not need staking. The colours are various shades of pink and white; the white look good against green hedges. They flower from midsummer onwards. S 60cm (24in).
There are lots of good cultivars including 'Honorine Jobert' (white) and 'Königin Charlotte' (semi-double flowers).

Anemone hupehensis
(Japanese anemone)
This species is often confused with the previous one. The summer flowers are very similar in shape and colour (pinks and whites). H 1m (3ft) S 1m (3ft).

Again there are plenty of good cultivars including 'Hadspen Abundance' and 'Prinz Heinrich', both with deep pink flowers.

Anemone nemorosa
(Wood anemone, windflower)
A dainty white flower that grows well under deciduous trees and shrubs. It dies back after flowering and seeding. H 5cm (6in) S 30cm (12in). There are blue forms, such as 'Blue Bonnet'. There are also similar species (*A.* × *ranunculoides*) which have bright yellow flowers.

Other plants For the enthusiast there are plenty of other species, such as *AA. polyanthes, rivularis, sylvestris* and *trullifolia*.

ANTHEMIS
Anthemis
This genus provides some of the mainstays of the summer border: fresh-looking daisies in a range of colours from white through cream to yellow and orange. All have a yellow or golden central disc. The flowers are carried on wiry stems up to 1m (3ft) high. The foliage is generally deeply cut and in some cases very attractive. Many have a tendency to reflex (curl back) their petals at night so they are not good plants to choose if you see your garden only in the evening. For the daytime border, however, their bright cheerfulness is indispensable.
Cultivation Anthemis need a fertile, moisture-retentive soil in full sun. Some will need support unless the garden is fairly wind-free. They resent disturbance so transplant young. Z4–8.
Propagation The species can be grown from seed but cultivars are best reproduced from basal cuttings in spring.

Anthemis punctata subsp. cupaniana
A delightful species with white daisies which float above a mat of silver foliage in early summer. Cut the flower stems off after flowering so that you can appreciate it as a foliage plant for the rest of the summer. The leaves are almost ground hugging, but flower stems reach up to about 30cm (12in) or so in height. S 30cm (12in).

Anthemis sancti-johannis
This has striking orange flowers in summer. The plants are short lived, so be sure to take cuttings each year. H 60cm (24in) S 60cm (24in).

Anthemis tinctoria
A good species with a superb group of cultivars, whose flowers vary from golden-yellow to palest cream. H and S 1m (3ft). Cultivars worth looking out for are 'E.C. Buxton' (lemon-yellow), 'Sauce Hollandaise' (pale cream) and 'Wargrave' (pale yellow), but all are good.

Other plants Cultivars worth growing include *AA.* 'Beauty of Grallagh', 'Grallagh Gold', 'Susanna Mitchell' and Tetworth'.

Anemone coronaria 'Lord Lieutenant'

Anemone hupehensis

Anthemis tinctoria 'E.C. Buxton'

Aquilegia 'Bunting'

Aquilegia 'Dove'

Artemisia ludoviciana 'Silver Queen'

AQUILEGIA
Aquilegia, columbine, granny's bonnet

Whichever of the various English names you prefer, these are delightful plants. The flowers resemble a female ballet dancer standing on tip-toe with her arms above her head. They vary from the typical blue through to different shades of white, pink, red, yellow and even greenish-brown.

These are plants of the late spring and early summer, and they look delightful when scattered among the other plants of that time of year. There are about 70 species and many cultivars from which to choose.

Cultivation Aquilegia will grow in most reasonably fertile soils. They can be grown in full sun or partial shade. Cut off the flowering stems after flowering as the foliage can still be enjoyed. Z3–6

Propagation They can easily be grown from seed, too easily perhaps as they will self-sow

abundantly if the seed pods are left on. Self-sown seedlings may not come true, but you can get some interesting results.

Aquilegia canadensis
A delicate, relatively small-flowered variety with yellow and red blooms. H 1m (3ft) S 30cm (12in). Another attractive red and yellow species is *A. formosa*.

Aquilegia fragrans
This species produces soft pinkish-white flowers that are occasionally tinged with blue. They have a sweet fragrance that you can smell when you get close to them. The plants can become hybridized with other species and the scent lost. H 45cm (18in) S 10cm (4in).

Aquilegia longissima
This is a good yellow species with largish flowers distinguished by their very long spurs. H 1m (3ft) S 50cm (20in).

Aquilegia McKana Group
A group of hybrids with large, mixed coloured flowers that have long spurs. H 60cm (24in) S 30cm (12in).

Aquilegia viridiflora
A delightful low-growing species with unusual greenish-brown flowers. It is best grown in groups at the front of a border or on a raised bed. H and S 30cm (12in).

Aquilegia vulgaris
The granny's bonnet
The typical plant as it grows in the wild has blue flowers but there are many cultivars with blooms in a mix of colours such as the wonderful white 'Nivea'. H 1m (3ft) S 50cm (20in). There are also double-flowered forms such as 'Nora Barlow' with green and red flowers.

Other plants The range above is fairly wide but there are still plenty of other plants that the enthusiast could look out for. They include *A. flabellata* (blue) and its wide range of cultivars, *A.* 'Hensol Harebell', *A.* 'Bunting', *A.* 'Dove' and *A. alpina*. A related genus with similar flowers but without the spurs is *Semiaquilegia*.

ARTEMISIA
Wormwood

A genus of about 300 species, many of which are weedy and certainly to be avoided in the garden. However, a number of species have some excellent cultivars that no garden should be without. Many of these are considered to be foliage plants, with most gardeners removing the flower spikes as they appear. The appeal of the foliage is firstly the

colour, which is often a beautiful silver, and secondly the cut, often a delicate filigree. These are good plants for any sunny border. They work well with soft colours, but can also be useful as foils between stronger colours.

Cultivation Artemisias are sun-loving plants and do not do well in shade. The soil should be fertile but well-drained, except for *A. lactiflora* which likes a moist soil. Z3–8.

Propagation Most are spreading forms, which are easy to increase by division. One or two are difficult to divide and are therefore best propagated by taking cuttings in spring.

Artemisia alba 'Canescens'
A silver-leaved artemisia with very fine foliage that can look rather like unruly coils of silver wire. The flowers are a dirty brown and should be removed when they appear in summer. H 45cm (18in) S 30cm (12in).

Artemisia lactiflora
The odd man out since it is grown for its flowers. This plant has tall upright stems with dark green leaves. The sprays of flowers in late summer are creamy

Aquilegia vulgaris

Aquilegia vulgaris 'Nora Barlow'

Artemisia lactiflora

Artemisia ludoviciana 'Valerie Finnis'

white and very attractive. H 1.5m (5ft) S 50cm (20in). It has a popular cultivar in 'Guizhou' which is prized for its foliage and stems which are purple in the early summer.

Artemisia ludoviciana

Another silver-leaved species, this time with more solid, spear-shaped leaves. The flowers are dirty yellow and are usually removed when they appear in summer. The plant can be tall, but tends to flop as it ages so it should be discreetly supported if possible. H 1m (3ft) S 60cm (24in). There are two extremely good cultivars: 'Silver Queen' and 'Valerie Finnis', either or both deserving of a place in the garden.

Artemisia 'Powis Castle'

To many gardeners this is the ace in the pack. It has deeply cut, filigree leaves that are an intense sparkling silver. The yellowish flowers tend to spoil the effect and should be removed. H 60cm (24in) S 1m (3ft).

Artemisia schmidtiana

Yet another excellent plant with very narrow silver foliage. It is a lowish carpeting plant. H 45 (18in) S 60cm (24in). It has a delightful cultivar 'Nana' which only grows 10cm (4in) high.

Other plants Artemisia arborescens, *A. caucasica* and *A. stelleriana* 'Boughton Silver' are worth exploring if there is space.

ARUNCUS
Goatsbeard

These plants are probably suitable only for large gardens since their flowering season is brief and they take up space. That said they are very attractive and are well worth growing if you have space near a pond or other area where the soil is reasonably moist. The flowers are creamy-white and held in large, loose pyramidal spikes in summer for about a week or so before they start to turn brown.
Cultivation Sun or partial shade in a moisture-retentive soil. Cut back in autumn. Z3–8.
Propagation Goatsbeards should be divided in spring.

Aruncus dioicus

Aruncus aethusifolius

A dwarf form that does not get taller than 30cm (12in). Useful for small gardens. S 20cm (8in).

Aruncus dioicus

The most commonly grown goatsbeard. This is a tall, clump-forming plant that can look truly magnificent when in flower. H 2m (6ft) S 1.2m (4ft). Out of flower it makes a moderate foliage plant. It has an excellent cultivar 'Kneiffii', which is shorter (1.2m/4ft) and has very attractive, deep-cut leaves for which it is mainly grown.

ARUNDO
Giant reed

A small genus of which only one species is of interest to the general gardener. This can grow to

Arundo donax

dizzy heights, up to 5m (15ft). It makes a bold focal point in a large garden, and an excellent feature in a border if it is big enough. However, for many gardens it is most effective when used as a summer screen. This is a tall grass with strong vertical stems and broad, strap-like leaves.
Cultivation The giant reed prefers a fertile, moisture-retentive soil but it will grow in any reasonable garden soil. Like most grasses it likes full sun but needs protection from winds. It should be cut back to the ground in spring before new growth starts. Z7.
Propagation Divide the clumps in spring just before growth begins. The giant reed can also be grown from seed sown in pots.

Arundo donax

This is the only species normally grown in gardens. It is tall with green leaves and stems, and purply plumes of flowers in autumn. H 3m (10ft) S 1m (3ft). Its variety *A.d. versicolor* is shorter (up to 2m/6ft) and has creamy stripes running down the length of its leaves. The cultivar 'Macrophylla' has very broad (up to 7.5cm /3in) leaves which are bluish-green in colour.

ASPLENIUM
Spleenwort

This is an enormous genus of some 700 species of evergreen and semi-evergreen ferns, and there are also a number of cultivars. Only a few species are in general cultivation so the gardener does not have too much of a problem deciding which to grow. They vary from those with typical triangular, fern-like fronds to those with wide, strap-like foliage. They are splendid plants for growing in a woodland setting or in shade and generally provide interest throughout the year.
Cultivation These plants need to be planted in a shady area, and in a moisture-retentive, but free-draining, soil.
Propagation The best method of increase is by dividing existing plants in spring. The species can also be increased by sowing spore as they ripen.

Asplenium bulbiferum
Hen and chicken fern

This plant gets its common name because it produces young plants along its fronds. The fronds are typically fern-shaped; triangular with deeply divided segments. It prefers acid soils. In really good conditions it can grow up to 1.2m (4ft) high. S 30cm (12in).

Asplenium scolopendrium
Hart's tongue fern

The most popular species with the most cultivars. As its name implies the strap-like fronds taper towards the top, like tongues. The margins are slightly wavy. It prefers alkaline soils. H 60cm (24in) S 45cm (18in).
There are a number of interesting cultivars. The Crispum Group have wavy margins to the foliage, while the Cristatum Group have crests at the top of the fronds.

Asplenium trichomanes
Maidenhair spleenwort

So called because it resembles the delicate maidenhair fern in that it has small dark green, elliptic leaflets arranged either side of a dark midrib. This plant prefers alkaline soils. H 15cm (6in) S 15–30cm (6–12in).

Other plants There are a number of other species that are more suitable for the conservatory or heated greenhouse, as well as other cultivars of *A. scolopendrium* which the enthusiast can explore.

Asplenium scolopendrium

ASTER
Aster

This is a large genus of about 250 species and at least as many cultivars. It is a popular genus and many of the species are in cultivation although most gardeners grow only a few, in particular the Michaelmas daisies. Asters have daisy-like flowers with a colourful outer disc of petals and a central one of yellow. The petals cover a wide colour range from white and pink to blue and purple. Most produce multiple heads and are a mass of colour when in bloom, often for a very long time. They make very good border plants.

Cultivation Any good garden soil, preferably in sun. Many asters can suffer from mildew, but unless this is unsightly it can be ignored. Many of the floppier forms need staking, but the Michaelmas daisies are usually self-supporting, except in exposed areas. Z4–8.

Propagation Most asters are extremely easy to divide in the spring. A few like *A. × frikartii* are difficult to divide and basal cuttings is then the best method.

Aster alpinus

These are low, spreading plants which are excellent for the front of a border. The species has blue flowers which appear from the early summer onwards. H 25cm (10in) S 30–45cm (12–18in). There are a number of very good cultivars to try, including 'Dunkle Schöne' (deep blue) and 'White Beauty' (white).

Aster amellus 'Blue King'

Aster amellus

Most of the numerous cultivars make splendid plants. They have relatively large daisies, up to 5cm (2in) across. The colours are many variations on pink and blue. Flowers appear from late summer and continue well into autumn. H and S 50cm (20in). Cultivars to look out for include 'Blue King' (blue), 'Brilliant' (pink), 'King George' (violet blue), 'Rosa Erfüllung' (pale pink), 'Rudolph Goethe' (lavender) and 'Veilchenkönigin' (violet).

Aster cordifolius

This has floating sprays of small flowers on stems up to 1.5m (5ft) high. S 1m (3ft). It is best grown in one of two cultivars: 'Silver Spray' (pale pink) or 'Sweet Lavender' (lavender-blue).

Aster ericoides

Beautiful, delicate sprays of small blue or pink flowers in autumn. H 1m (3ft) S 50cm (20in). Some superb cultivars, including 'Blue Star' (blue), 'Golden Spray' (pinkish white), 'Pink Cloud' (pink) and 'Snow Flurry' (white).

Aster × frikartii

An excellent hybrid of which 'Mönch' is the gem. This has large (7.5cm/3in) blue heads that

Aster lateriflorus

continue from midsummer right through to the end of autumn. Its 75cm (30in) stems often need some support. S 45cm (18in). 'Wunder von Stäfa' is similar.

Aster novae-angliae

These rather coarse Michaelmas daisies make excellent tall plants for the back of the border. There are many good cultivars including 'Andenken an Alma Pötschke' (rose-pink), 'Barr's Violet' (violet blue), 'Harrington's Pink' (pink) and 'Herbstschnee' (white).

Aster novi-belgii
Michaelmas daisies

More refined and shorter than the previous species, these are suitable for the middle of the border. H 1.2m (4ft) S 60–75cm (24–30in). There are hundreds of excellent cultivars; look at them in flower to choose your favourites.

Other plants There are many other excellent species, including *AA. divaricatus, lateriflorus, sedifolius* and *tongolensis*.

ASTILBE
Astilbe

A small genus of only about 12 species, but supplemented with many additional garden forms. Astilbes are characterized by their flat tapering flower heads and deeply divided leaves. The colours of the flowers vary from pink to red by way of purple, and with a few whites and creams. They flower in summer. Although they grow well in full sun they are also good plants for lightly shaded areas. They are particularly good for growing next to ponds and other water features.

Cultivation Astilbes like moisture-retentive soils that should preferably remain damp all

Astilbe × arendsii 'Fanal'

through the summer. They will grow in either full sun or light shade. Z4–7.

Propagation The plants can be divided in spring.

Astilbe arendsii

A wonderful selection of cultivars from Germany. H 1m (3ft) S 60cm (24in). Among the many excellent plants on offer are 'Brautschleier' (white), 'Bressingham Beauty' (pink), 'Erica' (bright pink), 'Fanal' (dark crimson-red), 'Irrlicht' (white), 'Snowdrift' (white) and 'Venus' (bright pink).

Astilbe chinensis

This is a relatively short astilbe (up to 60cm/24in) with pink flowers. The variety *pumila* is dwarf (25cm/10in) high, making it an excellent choice for the front of a border. It has purplish-pink flowers. S 20cm (8in).

Other plants There are a large number of garden cultivars, which vary in height and flower colour.

Aster alpinus

Aster × frikartii

Astilbe × arendsii 'Venus'

Astilbe 'Aphrodite'

Astrantia major 'Rubra'

Good examples to try include *A.* 'Aphrodite', *A. × crispa* 'Perkeo' (pink), *A.* 'Red Sentinel' (bright red), and *A.* 'Rheinland' (pink).

ASTRANTIA
Masterwort
Astrantia is a small genus of about 10 species. Only two of them are in general cultivation, but they are excellent plants and there are a number of garden cultivars. The flowers are basically greenish-white but they are generally flushed with pink or varying intensity, some dark enough to be red. They resemble pincushions surrounded by bracts. These clump-forming plants tend to reach up to 1m (3ft) in good conditions. Although they will grow in sun they are excellent plants for lightly shaded positions and flower over a long period from early summer onwards.
Cultivation Masterworts prefer moisture-retentive soil but generally do well in any reasonable garden soil. If the soil is on the dry side then a shaded position is required. Z5–8.
Propagation These plants are easy to divide in the spring. They will also grow readily from seed, but the cultivars are unlikely to come true if you use this method.

Astrantia major
This is the main species grown with most of the cultivars derived from it. The flowers of the species have a pinkish tinge, but some of the cultivars are much stronger in colour, some even a dark red. H 60cm (24in) S 45cm (18in). Although the species is worth growing in its own right, one of the cultivars will generally give a better effect. There are many good ones to try, including 'Hadspen Blood' (deep blood-red), 'Primadonna' (pink), 'Rosensinfonie' (deep pink), 'Rubra' (red), 'Ruby Cloud' (ruby red), 'Ruby Wedding' (ruby red), 'Shaggy' (greenish white with very long surrounding bracts) and 'Sunningdale Variegated' (creamy variegations on the leaves).

Astrantia maxima
This is mainly grown as the straight species, and is well worth tracking down for its delightful shell-pink colouration. H 60cm (24in) S 30cm (12in).

ATHYRIUM
Lady fern
This is a large genus consisting of about 180 species of ferns and a number of garden cultivars. It got its English name because of

Autumn-flowering perennials

Anemone x hybrida
Aster
Boltonia
Chelone
Chrysanthemum
Cimifuga
Helianthus
Kirenshonga
Liriope
Leucanthemella
Nerine
Ophiopogon
Rudbeckia
Schizostylis
Sedum
Solidago
Tricyrtis
Vernonia

the delicacy of the lacy, elegant fronds of the main garden species *A. filix-femina*. The plants are deciduous ferns whose fronds turn brown in autumn. They grow up to 1.2m (4ft) when they are well suited.

Like most ferns they prefer a shaded position and are ideal for growing in a woodland setting or in another shady position, such as in a border on the north side of the house.
Cultivation Lady ferns require a moisture-retentive soil such as you would find in a woodland. They do not like an alkaline soil, and need to be grown in light

shade. Cut back the old leaves in spring before the new growth begins. Z3–5.
Propagation Division in the spring is the easiest method. Plants can also be grown from spores.

Athyrium filix-femina
An attractive species which has a number of cultivars and is also worth growing in its own right. H 60–120cm (2–4ft) S 30–100cm (1–3ft). Among the best cultivars are the Cruciatum Group with crested fronds, the intriguing 'Frizelliae' in which the leaflets (pinnae) have been reduced to alternate, single round leaves on either side of the main rib, and the 'Minutissimum' with its smaller 30cm (12in) stems.

Athyrium niponicum
The species is in cultivation but it is the variety *pictum* which is usually seen. This is a lowish plant with the most beautifully coloured fronds. They are a metallic greeny-silver flushed with purple. H and S 30cm (12in).

Other plants There are several tender lady ferns that can be grown in a conservatory or heated greenhouse as well as a few more hardy cultivars that would make a welcome addition to the garden if you get hooked on ferns.

BAPTISIA
Baptisia
A genus of some 20 species of which only one is in general cultivation. This is *B. australis* which has a loose, lupin-like head of bright blue flowers. These appear in early summer and are set off against fresh green foliage. H 1.5m (5ft) S 60cm (24in).
Cultivation A rich, moist soil in sun or partial shade. Z5.
Propagation This is easily increased from freshly collected seed. It can also be propagated by division.

Astrantia major

A. major 'Sunningdale Variegated'

Athyrium niponicum

Baptisia australis

Bergenia 'Bressingham White'

Bergenia 'Sunningdale'

Brunnera macrophylla

Brunnera macrophylla 'Dawson's White'

BERGENIA
Elephant's ears

The English name is an apt description of plants in this genus of about eight species with its numerous cultivars. The key feature of the plants is the large oval leaves, which make an excellent ground cover on all types of soil and in conditions of sun or shade.

Most have shiny, evergreen leaves that glint in the sun, and many of them also turn a wonderful liverish-red during the winter. The flowers, which are produced in spikes in the early summer, are also attractive. The plants usually grow up to 45cm (18in) or sometimes a little more. S 60cm (24in).
Cultivation Bergenias prefer a moist but well-drained soil. However, they will also grow in dryish, but not drought-ridden, soils. They suit a sunny or partially shaded position. Z3–5.
Propagation You can increase these plants by division. Alternatively, place 2.5cm (1in) sections of budded rhizome in cutting compost (soil mix) until they have rooted.

Bergenia 'Ballawley'
This is a good form for winter use as the glossy green leaves take on a superb glossy purple-bronze tint throughout the winter. The spring flowers are bright red.

Bergenia 'Bressingham White'
This plant has deep green foliage surmounted by a spike of white flowers in spring.

Bergenia cordifolia
Crinkle-edged leaves that tint slightly during the winter. The flowers are an excellent magenta colour. There is a form 'Purpurea' which has darker winter leaves.

Bergenia 'Silberlicht'
Grown mainly for its flowers which are a brilliant white when newly opened but which fade to pink as they age.

Bergenia 'Sunningdale'
This is a very good winter-coloured variety with attractive carmine-coloured flowers.

Other plants There are many others to look at if you have the space. *B. ciliata* (hairy leaves) and the cultivars 'Schneekönigin' (white flowers), 'Morgenröte' (deep pink) and 'Wintermärchen' (almost red) are good choices.

BRIZA
Quaking grass

Most of the 15 species that make up this genus are annuals but there is one good perennial *B. media*, the common quaking grass or trembling grass. The English name comes from the fact that the hanging, heart-shaped heads move in the slightest breeze, giving the impression that the whole plant is trembling. The spikelets are purple changing to a golden-yellow as they ripen. The grass can grow up to 60cm (24in) high, with a spread of 10cm (4in). This plant is attractive in the garden and also works well in dried arrangements.
Cultivation Any well-drained garden soil in full sun. Z4
Propagation Can be divided in early spring just as growth begins. It can also be grown from seed.

BRUNNERA
Brunnera

A small genus of three species of which one, *B. macrophylla*, is in general cultivation. This is a gem for a lightly shaded position, either under shrubs or trees, or on the shady side of a building or fence. It has fairly large, oval leaves that are slightly coarse. The blue flowers are similar to forget-me-nots but they are carried on airy stems above the leaves. They appear in spring but the foliage continues to provide interest for most of the summer.
Cultivation A moisture-retentive soil is needed in a partial shaded position. Z3
Propagation Brunnera is easy to increase by division in spring.

Brunnera macrophylla
The species is attractive in its own right and it is certainly well worth growing. H 50cm (20in) S 60cm (24in). However, there are several cultivars with variegated leaves which makes

Bergenia 'Silberlicht'

Briza media

Brunnera macrophylla 'Jack Frost'

Winter-flowering perennials

Adonis amurensis
Crocus
Cyclamen coum
Eranthis hyemalis
Euphorbia rigida
Galanthus
Helleborus niger
Helleborus
   orientalis

Helleborus
   purpurascens
Hepatica nobilis
Iris ungicularis
Primula vulgaris
Pulmonaria rubra
Ranunculus ficaria
Vinca difformis
Viola odorata

Caltha palustris 'Alba'

Caltha palustris 'Flore Pleno'

them even more desirable. 'Dawson's White' has wide, irregular, white margins to the green leaves. 'Hadspen Cream' is similar except that the margins are narrower and a creamier white. 'Jack Frost' has silver foliage that looks as though the leaves have frost on them. 'Langtrees' is an intriguing cultivar which has silver spots in the middle of each leaf.

CALAMAGROSTIS
Reed grass

Calamagrostis is a large genus of grasses. It includes some species that were classed as Stipa until recently. They are all decorative grasses which can be used either as a prominent feature in a border or simply mixed in to enhance the general effect.

Cultivation Reed grasses will grow in any reasonable garden so long as they are planted in full sun. Cut back the old stems in late winter before the new growth starts. Z5

Propagation This is best carried out by division in spring just as growth is beginning.

Calamagrostis × acutiflora

A tall grass with narrow leaves and plumes of purplish flowers that turn silver. H 2m (6ft) S 50cm (20in). It has a couple of very good cultivars: 'Karl Foerster' has pinkish flowers that fade to beige, and the slightly shorter 'Overdam' has leaves with yellow margins that fade to white.

Calamagrostis arundinacea

This plant forms a clump of arching foliage, soon topped with masses of fine-stemmed drooping flowers that create a lovely hazy effect. H 1m (3ft) S 1.2m (4ft).

Calamagrostis brachytricha

A splendid grass with green leaves that are often tinged with bronze in spring and autumn. The flowers are pinkish-grey. H 1.2m (4ft) S 75cm (30in)

Other plants C. emodensis and *C. epigejos* are two more interesting species that grass enthusiasts might like to look at.

CALAMINTHA
Calaminth

A small genus of about eight species, of which only two are in general cultivation. They are relatively low plants, only reaching about 45cm (18in) in good conditions. Their glory is the mass of thyme-like flowers that are produced over a long period in the summer. The flowers are mainly pink but can also edge towards mauve. The leaves are aromatic when crushed or bruised. These are excellent plants for placing at the front edge of borders or along paths.

Calamintha nepeta subsp. nepeta

Cultivation Plant in any good garden soil in full sun. Z6.

Propagation Divide plants in spring, or sow seed, also in spring.

Calamintha grandiflora

This is a larger plant, which has flowers of a bright pink. H 45cm (18in) S 45cm (18in).

Calamintha nepeta

About the same size as *grandiflora*, this has flowers that are a paler lilac-pink, sometimes almost white. H 45cm (18in) S 60cm (24in). *C.n.* subsp. *nepeta* is often called *C. nepetoides*. It is a shorter plant and has tiny lilac-white flowers that cover the plant in a cloud – perfect for the edge of a path or patio. *C.n.* 'Blue Cloud' has, as its name suggests, many flowers with a distinct blue tinge.

CALTHA
Marsh marigold

There are about ten species of caltha, but only one of them, *C. palustris*, with its several

Caltha palustris

varieties and cultivars, is in general cultivation. This plant with its delightful large golden buttercup-like flowers is one of the glories of spring.

It does best when grown beside water but it will also grow in bog gardens and even in borders if the soil is kept sufficiently damp. Marsh marigolds are sprawling plants but they can reach 45cm (18in) in height and 30cm (12in) in width.

Cultivation The soil must be moist and, unlike many plants, the roots can be in mud or shallow water. Caltha flourishes in a sunny position but it will also grow in light shade, under deciduous trees, for example. Z3.

Propagation Increase is easily carried out by division in spring or from seed that is sown as soon as it is ripe.

Caltha palustris

Although there are good cultivars, the species is well worth growing in its own right – it makes a superb addition to any pond. 'Alba' is not quite as striking as the species, but this white-flowered form still has a lot of charm and looks particularly attractive growing along side the golden form. 'Flore Pleno' is a smaller plant than the species but its worth lies in its exquisite double flowers with their concentric rows of petals.

Caltha palustris var. *palustris*.

This is sometimes known as *C. polypetala*. It is a giant form of the species with large flowers. There is also an attractive double form of this larger plant with the name 'Plena'.

Camassia leichtlinii subsp. *leichtlinii*

CAMASSIA
Quamash

This is a small genus of bulbs that are frequently grown as part of a herbaceous border. They have also become popular for naturalizing in a meadow or wild garden. Camassias are tall-growing plants which produce tall spikes of striking, star-like flowers, usually in blue or white. The foliage is lush but not attractive; it is a good idea to plant them in the middle of the border so that the foliage is hidden but the flower spikes stand proud of surrounding vegetation. H 1m (3ft) S 20–30cm (8–12in).
Cultivation Camassias like good moist, but free-draining soil in full sun or just a light shade. Plant in autumn at a depth of about 10cm (4in). Z2.

Camassia leichtlinii subsp. *suksdorfii*

Campanula carpatica

Propagation Increase by dividing the bulbs in summer or by sowing seed while it is still fresh.

Camassia leichtlinii subsp. leichtlinii

This plant used to be known as *C.l.* 'Alba', the 'Alba' referring to its white flowers. These have a touch of green in them and are really very beautiful.

Camassia leichtlinii subsp. suksdorfii

Being the commonest form, this was and still often is referred to simply under the species name *C. leichtlinii*. It has blue flowers which vary in intensity from pale to very deep blue-violet. There are several cultivars to explore.

Camassia quamash

This plant is similar to the above with blue flowers. It is excellent for naturalizing.

CAMPANULA
Bellflower

This is a much loved genus of some 300 species of which many are in cultivation. They vary from ground-hugging plants to ones

Campanula 'Loddon Anna'

with tall spires of flowers. The typical bellflower is blue but there are also plenty of white and pink variants. The flowers vary from classic bell-shapes to flat, wide-open stars. The majority flower in summer, and most are excellent at forming large clumps. They should be placed anywhere from the front to the back of a border, depending on their height.
Cultivation Most bellflowers need a rich, moist, but well-drained soil. The majority also prefer full sun but there are a number that like a little shade. Z3–6.
Propagation Seed can be sown in the spring, and many of the plants can also be divided at the same time of year. Basal cuttings can also be taken from many species in spring.

Campanula carpatica

A low-growing (25cm/10in) species that is perfect for edging the path or border. The flowers are an open-dish shape and come in varying shades of blue as well as white. S 30cm (12in). There are a number of excellent cultivars including 'Weisse Clips' (white) and 'Blue Clips (blue).

Campanula punctata

Campanula glomerata

A medium bellflower that carries its flowers in a cluster at the top of the flower stem. Excellent for borders or for naturalizing in meadow gardens. H 45cm (18in) S 60cm (24in).

Campanula lactiflora

A tall border plant with many flowers carried in loose heads. H 1.2m (4ft) S 60cm (24in). The type is well worth growing but there are also a number of very good cultivars including 'Loddon Anna' (lilac-pink), 'Prichard's Variety' (violet blue) and 'White Pouffe', which is a dwarf form with white flowers.

Campanula latifolia

A tall species with large tubular bells of intense blue. H 1.2m (4ft) S 60cm (24in). The variety 'Alba' has beautiful white flowers that brighten up a lightly shaded

Campanula lactiflora

Campanula portenschlagiana

Campanula poscharskyana

spot of the garden. 'Brantwood' (deep violet) is another excellent cultivar to try.

Campanula latiloba

This bellflower has dense heads of open bell-shaped flowers with lavender blue flowers H 1m (3ft) S 45cm (18in). Again there are several very good cultivars.

Campanula persicifolia

An attractive medium height bellflower which often needs staking to keep its upright stance. The flowers are large open cups in blue or white. H 1m (3ft) S 30cm (12in). There are some beautiful double forms, such as 'Boule de Neige'.

Campanula portenschlagiana

A low-growing campanula with bright violet purple flowers. It is excellent for edging paths. H 15cm (6in) S indefinite.

Campanula poscharskyana

A spreading campanula that will scramble up through shrubs and other plants. The pale-blue flowers are star-shaped and are carried over a long period from early summer well into autumn. This plant makes good ground cover. H 10–15cm (4–6in) S indefinite.

Other plants There are so many other campanulas that are worth pursuing, such as *C. punctata* or the similar *C. takesimana* with their large pink tubular bells. Virtually any campanula you come across in a nursery will be worth growing, and it can be fun to experiment.

CARDAMINE
Bittercress

A delightful genus of plants whose numbers have been increased by the addition of species that were in the genus *Dentaria*. There are some weeds – hairy bitter cress being one that gardeners especially hate – but the majority of cardamines are garden plants with great charm. They flower in spring. Since they are suited to partial shade, they are excellent for growing under deciduous shrubs or in the shade of a building.

Cardamine heptaphylla

Cultivation Most prefer a moist, woodland-type soil with plenty of added leaf mould. They will grow in sun as long as the soil is kept moist, but prefer a light shaded position. Z5–6.
Propagation Most cardamines are easy to divide in the spring. They can also be grown from seed or, in some cases, from the small reddish bulbils that are carried in the leaf joints.

Cardamine enneaphyllos

A spreading plant with clusters of creamy white flowers held above mid-green leaves. It needs to be grown in partial shade. H 30cm (12in) S 60cm (24in).

Cardamine heptaphylla

Clusters of simple white, and occasionally pink, flowers. It reaches 30cm (12in) tall, and sometimes double that. Does best in partial shade. S 30cm (12in).

Cardamine pentaphyllos

An attractive plant with clusters of pinkish-purple flowers, sometimes white. H 30cm (12in) but sometimes double that. S 60cm (24in). This plant requires a partially shaded position.

Cardamine pentaphyllos

Cardamine pratensis

This is the much-loved cuckoo flower or milkmaid. It has loose heads of delightful lilac flowers. H 45cm (18in) S 30cm (12in). There are various interesting double forms.

CARDIOCRINUM
Giant Lily

Although there are three species in the genus, only one of them, *C. giganteum*, is in general cultivation. It is a tall plant, reaching up to 2m (6ft), with large white trumpet flowers, creating a very striking picture. It likes a cool shaded position but the head can be in sun – making it ideal for growing amongst shrubs or at the back of borders. The dried seed capsules are amongst the most desirable of dried flowers. S 1m (3ft)
Cultivation It must have a rich soil with plenty of humus in it. Plant in partial shade. Z6.
Propagation It is best to buy bulbs. It can be grown from seed but you will have to wait seven years or more before it flowers. Established bulbs will produce offsets (offshoots) which can be divided but even these take up to five years to flower.

Cardiocrinum giganteum

A tall plant with lily-like trumpet flowers that are angled downwards. They are white and highly scented, and appear in

Cardiocrinum giganteum

summer. There is also a variety *yunnanense* which has shiny brown stems and flowers that are tinged with green.

Other plants Keen gardeners should look out for the similar but less frequently seen species *C. cordatum*, which is worth finding a supplier for.

CATANANCHE
Cupid's dart

A small genus of five species of which only one is in general cultivation. These are for the border rather than for containers and are best used in association with other plants. Catananche are perfect for gravel gardens. The buds have a curious paper-like quality and even the cornflower-like petals feel dry and papery. The flowers are carried on slender, wiry stems in summer and into the autumn. They are ideal for dried arrangements.
Cultivation These are short-lived plants but their life can be prolonged by growing them in a free-draining soil. They must have a sunny position. Z4.
Propagation Catananche are best increased from seed sown in spring. They can be divided but care is needed as they have thick tap roots. These roots can be used as cuttings, taken in the winter.

Catananche caerulea

This is the main species in cultivation and the form that one usually sees. The flowers are blue with a darker centre. H 45cm (18in) S 30cm (12in). The form 'Major' is a popular one but it often looks the same as the main species. A good alternative is the cultivar 'Bicolor' which has a violet-purple centre and white petals. The all-white form is 'Alba', which is also very attractive.

Catananche caerulea

CENTAUREA
Knapweeds

For the serious perennial gardener this is a "must-have" genus: there are many top-class plants in it. It is a large genus, containing about 450 species with about 40 being in general cultivation. They have thistle-like heads which are often quite large. They come in a variety of colours: reds, purples, blues, yellows and whites. The flowers usually appear in summer and rarely last more than a few weeks. They provide good colour for the border.

Cultivation Most will grow in any good garden soil. They prefer a sunny position. Z3–7.

Propagation The most common method of increase is by division in spring, although most species can also be grown from seed sown at the same time of year.

Centaurea dealbata

An appealing clump-forming perennial with purple-pink flowers with white centres. H 1m (3ft) S 60cm (24in). The cultivar 'Steenbergii' has deeper pink flowers and is even more attractive than the species.

Centaurea hypoleuca

Another clump-forming centaurea which is somewhat similar to the previous one, but with larger flowers. The flowers are again pink with a paler centre. H 60cm (24in) S 45cm (18in). The cultivar 'John Coutts' has dark pink flowers.

Centaurea hypoleuca 'John Coutts'

Centaurea macrocephala

This is a clump-forming plant with upright stems. These carry large heads with a papery, dark brown bud that contrasts beautifully with the bright yellow flowers. A truly wonderful plant. H 1.5m (5ft) S 60cm (24in).

Centaurea montana

A favourite of the late spring to early summer garden. A somewhat sprawling plant whose bright blue flowers each have a purple centre. H 45cm (18in) when staked, S 60cm (24in). There is a good white form *alba* and several good colour varieties.

Centaurea pulcherrima

An attractive plant with very good silvery foliage that earns it a place in the garden as a foliage plant when it is not in flower. The

Centaurea montana

exquisite flowers are pink with a creamy centre. H 75cm (30in) S 60cm (24in).

Centaurea 'Pulchra Major'

Strictly speaking, this is now called *Leuzea centauroides*. It is similar to *C. pulcherrima* but is on a much larger scale with huge flowers up to 7.5cm (3in) across. H 1m (3ft) S 60cm (24in).

Centaurea simplicicaulis

A mat-forming plant with large pink flowers. H 25cm (10in) S 60cm (24in).

Other plants There are many more for the gardener to try. *C. bella* (pink) has good foliage, *C. cheiranthifolia* (cream and purple) is exceptionally good, and *C. ruthenica* (yellow) is another cultivar worth considering.

CENTRANTHUS
Red valerian

A genus of a dozen or so plants of which one, *C. ruber*, is in general cultivation. It forms clumps of stems, which carry dense heads of tiny purplish-red flowers. The colour varies, sometimes it is redder, sometimes pinker and occasionally it is white. These are excellent plants for growing in gravel gardens, and in spite of their height they are also good for walls and banks. H 1m (3ft) S 45–60cm (18–24in).

Cultivation Red valerian will grow in any garden soil, even impoverished ones. It likes a well-drained position in full sun. Z3.

Propagation The simplest method is from seed sown in spring. One plant will usually provide enough self-sown seedlings for most uses.

CEPHALARIA
Cephalaria

A genus of plants of which only one is in general cultivation. This is *C. gigantea* which is a clump forming plant. It forms a very tall, open plant with airy stems, each carrying soft yellow, almost creamy-yellow, flowers. The flowers are similar to those of the scabious to which it is related. It is eye-catching, especially when planted against a dark green hedge and it is a valuable border plant. H 2.5m (8ft) S 1.2m (4ft). There is a shorter (2m/6ft) species, *C. alpina*, which has similar yellow flowers, but this is less common and not quite so long lived.

Cultivation It likes a well-drained but fertile soil. Plant in a sunny position if possible, although it will take a little light shade. Cut back after flowering or it will self-sow prodigiously. Z6.

Propagation This plant is easy to grow from seed sown in either autumn or spring.

Centaurea dealbata

Centaurea macrocephala

Centranthus ruber

Cephalaria gigantea

Ceratostigma plumbaginoides

CERATOSTIGMA
Ceratostigma

A small genus that consists mainly of shrubs but there is one notable perennial, *C. plumbaginoides*. It is a spreading plant up to 45cm (18in) high and 20cm (8in) wide. The joy of it is the bright blue periwinkle-like flowers, which sparkle out of the late summer and autumn garden. The leaves take on reddish autumn tints. This is a good plant for interspersing with others towards the front of the border. The shrubby ceratostigmas fulfil the same function and have very attractive flowers that are also blue. In particular, have a look at *C. griffithii* and *C. willmottianum*.

Cultivation Ceratostigmas thrive in any good garden soil with plenty of organic material. They need a sunny position. Prune the shrubs in early spring. Z6.

Propagation Increase your stock of these plants by taking cuttings in spring or summer.

CHELONE
Turtlehead

This is a small genus of which only one species is in general cultivation. The name refers to the strange turtle-like shape of the flowers. These are dark pink and carried in a short terminal spike from late summer into autumn. The main species is *C. obliqua* which grows to about 60cm (24in) in height and has a spread of 50cm (20in). These are good plants for providing autumn colour in the middle of the border. The other species worth looking at if you can find them are *C. glabra* and *C. lyonii*.

Cultivation Turtleheads need a rich, fertile soil that is moist. They can be grown in sun or light shade. Z4.

Propagation Division is the easiest method of increase but they can also be grown from seed sown in spring or from cuttings taken at the same time of year.

CHRYSANTHEMUM
Chrysanthemum

This genus needs little introduction since it is familiar as both a cut flower and garden plant. The familiar florist chrysanthemums are perennials, but they are treated as annuals because they are tender and need to be renewed each year. However there are a number of species and cultivars that are truly hardy and can be left outside all year. Most have a very long flowering time and will last from late summer and sometimes right into winter. Some – such as *C. rubellum* (syn. *C. zawadskii*) and its cultivars – are very similar to the single florist chrysanthemums and make good cut flowers.

The list of plants classified under the genus *Chrysanthemum* have gone through several changes. Many were moved to *Dendranthema*. They have now been

Chrysanthemum rubellum

moved back to *Chrysanthemum* but you may still come across them under the previous name.

Cultivation The hardy plants will grow in any reasonably fertile garden soil, preferably one that is well-drained. They prefer a sunny position but they will grow in light shade so long as they receive some sun. Z4.

Propagation Taking basal cuttings in spring is a reliable method of increase. The plants can also be divided at the same time of year.

Chrysanthemum rubellum

Strictly speaking, this species is now called *C. zawadskii* but it is still generally referred to as *C. rubellum*. H 75cm (30in) S 45cm (18in). The species is occasionally grown, but its many cultivars are more common. They have single, semi-double or double, daisy-like flowers in a variety of colours. Some of the best include 'Clara Curtis' (pink), 'Emperor of China' (double pink), 'Mary Stoker'

Chrysanthemum rubellum 'Clara Curtis'

(apricot-yellow), 'Mrs Jessie Cooper' (red) and 'Nancy Perry' (dark pink).

Chrysanthemum hosmariense

This is now *Rhodanthemum hosmariense* but is still often referred to by its former name. It is a delightful little plant with silver foliage and white daisy flowers that are in bloom from spring to autumn. Perfect as an edging plant in a well-drained sunny position. H 15cm (6in) S 30cm (12in).

Chrysanthemum uliginosum

Now known as *Leucanthemella serotina*, this is a wonderful plant for autumn. It is tall with white daisy flowers that appear from mid-autumn through until winter. The flowers have a habit of tilting and facing the sun, which they follow throughout the day. A good plant for the back of a border, but make sure it will face into the garden when flowering. H 2m (6ft) S 60cm (24in).

Chelone obliqua

Chrysanthemum rubellum

Chyrsanthemum hosmariense

CLEMATIS
Clematis

Most people think of this genus purely in terms of woody climbing plants. The majority of the 200 species and hundreds of cultivars are just that, but there are also a number of herbaceous species that die back each year. They do not have the big blowsy quality of some of the climbers but they are still very attractive. Most need some form of support but even with this, they rarely grow very tall. Some can be left to sprawl over the neighbouring plants, perhaps covering a spring plant that has lost its freshness.
Cultivation A rich moisture-retentive soil is required. The roots should be in shade with the plant in sun, although some will tolerate a little light shade. Most need some form of support, such as pea-sticks. Cut to the ground each spring. Z3.
Propagation Take basal cuttings in spring. Most perennial clematis can also be divided, with care.

Clematis × durandii
One of the largest flowered herbaceous clematis with indigo-blue blooms. Grow through a shrub or over pea-sticks. H 1–2m (3–6ft) S 45–150cm (1½–5ft).

Clematis heracleifolia var. davidiana
A late-summer flowering species whose blue flowers have reflexed (turned back), strap-like petals. An added bonus is that this plant is highly scented. H 1m (3ft) S 75cm (30in). There are a number of cultivars of varying shades of blue.

Clematis recta

Clematis integrifolia
This has intriguing nodding flowers that hang attractively from upright stalks. They are usually blue, but there are also several forms that produce flowers in other colours, including 'Rosea' (pink) and 'Alba' (white). 'Hendersonii' has extra large flowers. The plants are sprawling and can be left to clamber over other plants; they can also be supported. H and S 75cm (30in).

Clematis × jouiniana
It is the sheer number of flowers that makes this clematis attractive: it is a mass of small mauve-blue flowers. It requires support on pea-sticks. H 1m (3ft) S 1–2m (3–6ft).

Clematis recta
Although the species is often grown in its own right it is usually the form 'Purpurea' that is

Clematis integrifolia 'Hendersonii'

grown. This has wonderful purple foliage in spring; in early to midsummer it produces masses of small white flowers. H 1–2m (3–6ft) S 50cm (20in).

Other plants There are a few more species that can be explored including *C. texensis*, *C. addisonii* and *C. stans*. There are also myriad woody ones to grow; plants in the *C. viticella* group, in particular, go very well with herbaceous plants.

CONVALLARIA
Lily-of-the-valley

A small genus of which one species, *C. majalis* – the much-loved lily-of-the-valley – is regularly grown. This low plant is ideal for shady positions under shrubs or for growing on the shady side of a building. It spreads to form a mat of leaves surmounted in spring by short arching stems carrying fragrant white bells. In warm weather the scent can spread widely. The flowers are good for cutting for display or bouquets. H 23cm (9in) S indefinite. There is a pink form *rosea* which is identical except for the colour of the flowers. There is also 'Albostriata' in which the flowers are the same but the leaves have narrow yellow stripes running down them. In the cultivar 'Fortin's Giant' everything is doubled in size.
Cultivation A shady position in rich moist soil although it will survive drier soils. Z2.
Propagation Divide in the autumn or early spring. Plants can be grown from seed sown in spring, but the seed is not easy to find.

COREOPSIS
Tickseed

A useful genus of plants which add welcome splashes of gold to a border. It is a large genus of around 100 species but only a handful are in cultivation. They have daisy-like yellow or gold flowers, double in some cultivars, which bloom in summer. They work well towards the front or in the middle of the border where their colour stands out.
Cultivation Tickseed will grow in any reasonable garden soil. It needs a sunny position. Z3.

Convallaria majalis

Coreopsis verticillata 'Moonbeam'

Propagation To increase, divide plants in spring, or take stem cuttings in summer.

Coreopsis lanceolata
Tall flower stems carry single flowers of bright gold. H 60cm (24in) S 30cm (12in). There are various forms: some have brown centres ('Sterntaler') and others are much shorter ('Baby Gold').

Coreopsis verticillata
The most widely grown of the perennial species. It is a fine plant with masses of shining gold flowers floating above delicate, narrow foliage in summer. H 75cm (30in) S 30cm (12in). There are some good cultivars: 'Grandiflora' (also known as 'Golden Shower') has warm yellow flowers, 'Moonbeam' has wonderfully soft yellow blooms and 'Zagreb' is golden yellow.

CORTADERIA
Pampas grass

A small genus of grasses of which a couple of species with their cultivars are generally grown.

Coreopsis verticillata 'Zagreb'

Cortaderia selloana 'Pumila'

These are stunning: they have fountains of narrow leaves that are surmounted by tall stems carrying great tufts of white flower heads. Unfortunately, most are so large (up to 3m/10ft tall and 2m/6ft across) that you need a large garden to do them justice. There are some dwarf forms for smaller gardens, but these seem rather to miss the point. Pampas grasses make excellent focal points, especially if they are placed so that they can be seen against the blue sky. They last well into winter before they start to look untidy.

Cultivation They will grow in any reasonable garden soil, but require a sunny position. Cut down flowering stems in late winter and shear off the leaves every three years. Do not plant pampas grass near areas where children run or play as the edges of the leaves are very sharp. Z7.

Propagation Divide off part of the plant in late winter or early spring just before growth begins.

Cortaderia richardii

A lesser-grown species than the following. It comes from New Zealand rather than South America, but looks similar. The flowering stems tend to be more arching, but they too carry huge feathery plumes.

Cortaderia selloana

This is the main species grown and it is fabulous: tall and stately with feathery flower heads. The form 'Aureolineata' (also known as 'Gold Band') has golden stripes on the margins of the leaves. 'Albolineata' is similarly variegated but with silvery-white stripes; it is slightly smaller. 'Pumila' grows to only 1.5m (5ft). 'Pink Feather' has silvery-pink flower heads. 'Sunningdale Silver' has glistening silvery-white feathers.

CORYDALIS
Corydalis

This is a large genus of 300 or more species. It is much beloved by alpine gardeners, but there are

Corydalis flexuosa

a couple that are large and robust enough for the perennial gardener to consider. These have curious tubular flowers which look rather like swarms of tiny fish, floating above the ferny leaves. They are good for naturalizing along the edge of woodland gardens, or under deciduous shrubs and trees in smaller gardens. H 30cm (12in) S 30cm (12in).

Cultivation The corydalis listed here require a moist soil in either sun or partial shade. Z5–6.

Propagation Grow from seed, which should sown while it is still fresh. Many self-sow.

Corydalis cava

This plant has white or purplish flowers which appear in the spring. It grows well in woodland type soil in partial shade.

Corydalis flexuosa

Brilliant blue flowers in spring and early summer. This species should be grown in a moist, fibrous soil in a lightly shaded position. There are several good cultivars to explore.

Corydalis lutea

One of the easiest of the corydalis to grow, this has yellow flowers. It is excellent for growing on old walls. Flowers all year.

Corydalis ochroleuca

Good for damp positions. This has a long flowering season, with creamy white and yellow blooms.

Corydalis solida

This plant produces a range of different coloured flowers, based on mauvish purple but including red especially in the fine form 'George Baker'. Spring flowering.

COSMOS
Cosmos

A small genus of annual and perennial plants of which few, mainly annuals are in cultivation. The one perennial that is commonly grown is C. atrosanguineus. This has deep crimson flowers, so deep and velvety that they appear almost brown. In addition, the plant actually smells of chocolate when the weather is warm. The flowers are dish-shaped, rather like a daisy with wide petals. They are carried on wiry stems up to 75cm (30in) high. The plants are excellent for placing in a front-of-border position where they can easily be smelt. S 45cm (18in).

Cultivation Cosmos need a rich, moist soil and a warm, sunny position. They are late in appearing in spring, so hold off digging them up if you think they have died. Z7.

Propagation Increase by taking basal cuttings as soon as the plants are big enough.

Cortaderia selloana 'Sunningdale Silver'

Cortaderia selloana 'Aureolineata'

Corydalis lutea

Cosmos atrosanguineus

Crambe cordifolia

Crepis incana

CRAMBE
Crambe

Two plants in this small genus are in general cultivation. They can be spectacular but the most popular one, *C. cordifolia*, is not often seen outside large gardens because of its size. With care, though, it can be accommodated in smaller areas. The glory of this plant is the flowers which form a wonderful haze of white.

Cultivation These plants need rich, well-drained soil in full sun. They can be prone to slugs when the leaves first appear; you must control these pests at this point, or you will lose the plant. Z7.

Propagation Division is possible but awkward because of the size of the plants. The best option is to take root cuttings in winter.

Crambe cordifolia

A large plant with a great dome of white flowers, 2m (6ft) high and across in summer. It is ideal for a large herbaceous border. The multi-branching flower stems are excellent for dried arrangements if you can get them through the door. The leaves are rather coarse but since this is a plant for the middle or rear of the border, they are rarely seen, whereas the flowers float mistily above the surrounding plants.

Crambe maritima

This is a much smaller plant, growing only about 45cm (18in) high with a spread of 60cm (24in). It also produces a mass of flowers, but not quite as delicately as its larger relative. The main reason for growing it is the foliage, which is a wonderful powdery blue. It is an excellent foliage plant for the front of border. It needs a well-drained soil and does particularly well in gravel gardens.

CREPIS
Hawk's Beard

A large genus of dandelion-like plants that includes 200 or more species. Only a handful of them are generally grown in cultivation. Some are annuals or treated as annuals (see page 117) but others are true perennials. They are clump-forming plants that are suitable for the front of a border or for naturalizing in short grass. The flowers are multi-petalled, in the manner of a dandelion. They are carried on wiry stems that reach up to 30cm (12in) above rosettes of ground-hugging leaves. S 10cm (4in)

Cultivation Hawk's beard will grow in any reasonable garden soil, as long as it is well-drained. They need a position in full sun. Z7.

Propagation Increase by sowing fresh seed. The plants often produce self-sown seedlings.

Crepis aurea

This has typical dandelion-like flowers in a rich orange-yellow; they are carried from late summer onwards. These plants are good for the front of a hot-coloured border or for growing in short grass in a meadow garden.

Crepis incana

This is a short-lived perennial that is sometimes treated as an annual. It carries a large number of sugar-pink flowers. This form is usually just used in the border where it is an ideal plant for a frontal position. It looks particularly good when planted with blue veronicas.

CRINUM
Crinum

This is a large genus of tender bulbs, most of which are suited to growing in a conservatory. There is one that is not only hardy but also very attractive. This is *C. × powellii*. It has large strap-like leaves that arch outwards, framing the tall flowering stems that carry lily-like, trumpeted flowers. These are generally pink but there is also a glistening white form 'Alba'.

Crinums are best planted behind other plants so that the leaves are hidden but the gorgeous trumpets show above their surroundings. These appear in late summer and autumn and grow to 1m (3ft) high and 60cm (24in) across.

Cultivation These plants need a rich, free-draining soil in full sun. Plant the bulbs so that the neck is above the soil level. Z7.

Propagation Increase by dividing off the offsets (offshoots) from around existing bulbs.

CROCOSMIA
Montbretia

These plants form a small genus of popular bulbous plants. They include the common montbretia (*C. × crocosmiiflora*) – which seems to occur in most gardens.

Most bulbs seem to have rather ugly foliage, but the crocosmia has long, ribbed, tapering leaves that stand upright, making a good contrast to other foliage around them. In late summer tall arching stems carry a spray of red, orange or yellow flowers, which look good against with the foliage. These plants are excellent for growing in clumps or drifts in the middle of the border or for planting in odd corners.

Cultivation Plant in any reasonable garden soil, preferably in full sun, although they will also tolerate a little light shade. Divide the plants every few years as they can get congested. Z7.

Propagation The plants are very easy to propagate: divide off the new corms in late winter or early spring, before they start to grow.

Crambe maritima

Crinum × powellii

Crocosmia × crocosmiiflora

Crocosmia 'Lucifer'

Cynara cardunculus

Crocosmia × crocosmiiflora

This is the main species cultivated. It grows up to 60cm (24in) tall and has dull-orange flowers held on upright stems. S 15–20cm (6–8in).

There are plenty of cultivars to explore. The flowers vary from the subdued, soft apricot-tinted yellow of 'Solfatare', with its soft bronze foliage, to the striking 'Emily McKenzie' which has large flowers with brown centres surrounded by a bright orange. 'Jackanapes' is another bicolour cultivar; its flowers come in yellow and rich orange. 'Star of the East' is an excellent orange form, paling towards the centre. 'Lady Hamilton' is similar but has deep yellow flowers. The many cultivars are generally much better than the species and it is worth acquiring several different ones, for a hot-coloured border.

Crocosmia 'Emberglow'

A good border plant with bright red flowers that always create a splash of colour.

Crocosmia 'Honey Angels'

This is a fine crocosmia whose appealing yellow flowers have creamy throats.

Crocosmia 'Lucifer'

One of the most spectacular of the crocosmias. It is tall, reaching up to 1.2m (4ft). The flower stems are arching and carry sprays of large bright crimson flowers that stand upright like flames. They are superb against the green foliage. S 20–25cm (8–10in)

Crocosmia masoniorum

This is similar to the previous one, but its flowers contain more orange and are not so bright. H 1.2m (4ft) S 15cm (6in).

Other plants There are many cultivars for the enthusiast to look at, all with subtle variations

on the basic type. Since they are easily grown, they make ideal plants to collect.

CYNARA

Cynara

Two plants in this genus are generally grown in gardens, one for decoration (although it can be eaten) and the other for eating (although it can also be used for show). The main border plant is *C. cardunculus*. This is a statuesque plant: tall with silver foliage and huge purple thistle-like heads. It looks good planted singly as a focal point or in a group.
Cultivation These plants need a fertile, well-drained soil. Place in a sunny position, away from strong winds. Z7.
Propagation To increase, divide off "slips" (rooted cuttings) in spring.

Cynara cardunculus

A superb giant "thistle". It produces fountains of silver foliage surmounted by tall silver

stems carrying thistle-like flowers in summer. They are excellent for drying. The base of the stems and leaf stalks can be cooked when young – when the plant is known as a cardoon. H 2m (6ft) S 1m (3ft). Occasionally you can find dwarf forms on offer which are useful for small gardens. 'Florist Cardy' is a form specially bred for use as a cut flower, but it is not a great deal different from the type.

Cynara scolymus

Now officially, but cumbrously, known as *C. cardunculus* Scolymus Group. This is the globe artichoke of the vegetable garden. It is the large flower bud that is eaten. It can be used in the border as a lesser version of the above. The leaves are not so attractive in shape, nor so silver, but it still makes a good foliage plant, especially early in the season. H 1m (3ft) S 60cm (24in).

Crocosmia 'Honey Angels'

Bee and butterfly plants

Anchusa	Helenium
Aster	Lythrum
Centaurea	Mentha
Delphinium	Monarda
Doronicum	Nepeta
Echinacea	Origanum
Echinops	Scabiosa
Eryngium	Sedum
Eupatorium	Solidago
Foeniculum	Trifolium

Cynara scolymus

CYNOGLOSSUM
Hound's tongue

A genus of about 55 species. Most of those with garden interest are annuals or biennials. However, there is one, *C. nervosum*, which is perennial and worth growing in the border. This is a medium-sized plant with bristly stems and leaves. It is the flowers that are principally of interest since they are a wonderful bright blue colour. The individual flowers are quite small but they are carried in uncurling spikes – much in the same way as forget-me-nots, to which they are related. The plant flowers in early summer and is very useful for adding bright blue colour to the middle of the border at that time of year. H 60cm (24in) S 50cm (20in).
Cultivation Plant in any garden soil that is not too rich. Choose a sunny position. This plant is short lived and needs replacing every three years or so. Z5.
Propagation The best way to increase this plant is by sowing seed in spring.

DELPHINIUM
Delphinium

These plants are much-loved, but few gardeners know the full range of them: the flowers come in yellow and red as well as the most commonly seen blue ones. This is a fairly large genus of some 250 species of which a surprising number are in cultivation. The most popular are those that produce tall spires covered in

Delphinium 'Fenella'

flowers, but there are also shorter species whose flowers are held in loose airy clusters. Many of these are not as robust as the taller ones, but they make good garden plants if renewed every few years.
Cultivation A deep, rich but free-draining soil is required. Delphiniums should be placed in full sun. Tall ones with heavy spikes may need staking, unless the garden is very sheltered. Watch out for slugs in the early stages of growth. Z3.
Propagation The best way of increasing most cultivars is to take basal cuttings in spring. The species should be grown from seed, sown as soon as it is ripe.

Delphinium Belladonna Group, Elatum Group and Pacific Hybrids

These are the main groups of tall, heavily flowered delphiniums. Many are grown for cutting rather than for border display, but they can also be used in such situations. They flower in early summer and grow up to 1.5m (5ft) tall. S 60cm (24in). There is a vast range of named cultivars with flowers varying in colour from pale to dark blue, purple and white. Many have double flowers, often with white or black centres, known as "bees". They include: 'Bruce', a semi-double with deep purple flowers and brown eyes; 'Butterball', another semi-double, this time with creamy-white flowers and deeper eyes; 'Fenella', a semi-double with bright blue petals and a black eye. 'Giotto', a semi-double whose flowers are two-toned blue with light brown eyes; 'Sandpiper', a semi-double with white petals and a brown eye; and 'Tiddles', which has double mauve flowers.

Delphinium 'Sandpiper'

Delphinium 'Elizabeth Cook'

Delphinium 'Alice Artindale'

A wonderful double for the border. The little button flowers are a light blue; when dried, they retain their colour for years. H 1.2m (4ft) S 60cm (24in).

Delphinium cardinale

This unusual delphinium has bright red flowers with yellow centres. The flowers are carried in a loose spike. H 1–2m (3–6ft) S 60cm (24in).

Delphinium cashmerianum

This perennial is short lived, but it is still worth growing for its loose heads of bright blue flowers. H 45cm (18in) S 30cm (12in).

Delphinium grandiflorum

A delightful delphinium with gracefully floating bright blue flowers. It is good for the front of a border, especially if planted

Delphinium 'Southern Countryman'

Delphinium 'Clifford Sky'

in a group of three. However, it is short lived. H 45cm (18in) S 30cm (12in).

Delphinium nudicaule

Another short-lived plant, this time with loose spikes of yellow, orange or red flowers. It likes a well-drained soil. H 20cm (8in) S 5–10cm (2–4in).

Delphinium semibarbatum

Still known to many gardeners as *D. zalil*, this has loose spikes of yellow flowers. H up to 1m (3ft) in good conditions; S 30cm (12in). However, it is short lived and needs replacing regularly.

DIANTHUS
Pinks

Dianthus is a large genus of about 300 species. Many are in cultivation, and they are often grown by alpine enthusiasts. Border use is almost exclusively confined to one species, *D. caryophyllus*, or rather to the many cultivars that have been derived from it. These are known collectively as pinks. They can be roughly divided into two groups: the old-fashioned varieties which generally flower only once in the summer and are often scented; and the modern varieties which have the advantage of flowering, often continuously, throughout the summer but are in most cases scentless. Old-fashioned varieties have flowers that can be single, semi-double or double, while most modern ones are doubles. The flowers grow on stiff stems

Dianthus deltoides

Dianthus 'Garnet'

Dianthus 'Whatfield Ruby'

that emerge from a clump of narrow, silver foliage. The tallest grow to about 45cm (18in) but most are shorter. They are excellent plants for the front of borders and for lining paths. S 25cm (10in).
Cultivation Pinks need a well-drained soil that is neutral or alkaline. Full sun is essential. Z7.
Propagation Since most pinks are cultivars only vegetative methods can be relied upon. Of these, taking cuttings in summer is by far the easiest.

Dianthus deltoides
A choice plant for edging a path. The foliage is narrow and dark green, while the flowers are like tiny jewels in pink, red or white. This species is grown from seed. H 20cm (8in) S 25cm (10in).

Dianthus 'Doris'
One of the best old-fashioned pinks – a double with pink petals and a darker pink centre. It is very long-flowering and well scented.

Dianthus 'Garnet'
A low-growing pink for the rock garden or front of border with single carmine flowers with a darker centre. The foliage is compact and a good silver colour.

Dianthus 'Mrs Sinkins'
Another fine old-fashioned pink. It is a rather untidy double (the calyx which holds the petals together splits), but it is a good white and it has the most amazing scent. It is very easy to grow and will tolerate heavy soils.

Dianthus 'Musgrave's Pink'
Also known as 'Charles Musgrave'. An excellent single, old-fashioned variety with single, creamy-white flowers that have a pale green centre. It is scented.

Dianthus 'Rose de Mai'
This is a wonderful old-fashioned pink with pale mauve-pink flowers. It is fragrant and is one of the earliest to flower. The plant is rather sprawling.

Dianthus 'Whatfield Ruby'
This small, single-flowered pink produces brilliant ruby-coloured flowers. It is best placed at the front of a border.

Other plants There are about a thousand cultivars from which to choose, most of which make excellent plants. Go to a specialist nursery in summer so that you can see them in flower before making your choice.

DIASCIA
Diascia
These plants have been grown in gardens since at least Victorian times, but it is only relatively recently that they have achieved the popularity they deserve. They have a very long flowering season, producing spikes of mostly pink flowers over low-growing mounds of green, heart-shaped foliage. They grow on average to about 25cm (10in) high with a spread of 60cm (24in) and are perfect for creating mats in the front of borders. They are also excellent plants for growing in containers.
Cultivation Diascias need a moist but well-drained soil that is not too wet in winter. They prefer a position in full sun, although they will tolerate a little light shade under tall trees or shrubs. Shear occasionally to keep the plants compact. Z4–7.

Propagation These plants are easy to root from cuttings, which can be taken at any time of the year.

Diascia 'Blackthorn Apricot'
This is a good modern cultivar with apricot-pink flowers.

Diascia rigescens
One of the oldest species in cultivation. It is larger and coarser than most others but produces large spikes of deep pink flowers.

Diascia 'Ruby Field'
This is an excellent form, which produces deep pink flowers.

Diascia 'Rupert Lambert'
Another fine form. Like the previous one, it produces blooms of a deep pink.

Diascia 'Salmon Supreme'
A good modern form which has salmon pink flowers.

Diascia vigilis
One of the longest-lived forms, with soft pink flowers. It is best grown in the form 'Jack Elliott'.

Dianthus 'Doris'

Dianthus 'Rose de Mai'

Diascia 'Rupert Lambert'

Diascia vigilis

DICENTRA
Dicentra

A genus of much-loved cottage garden plants. Their main characteristic is the locket-shaped flowers that hang like jewels from arching stems. They are set against foliage which is also attractive, usually being finely cut and fern-like. There are a good number of species and cultivars around, allowing keen gardeners to make an interesting collection. All dicentra like a bit of shade making them very useful for growing under shrubs or on the shady side of buildings or fences. Some will spread, making them useful ground cover for the earlier part of the summer.

Cultivation Dicentra are basically woodland plants and so they like the type of moist soil found there. They also require a lightly shaded position. Z2–4.

Propagation Division in spring is the easiest method of increasing dicentra. The species can also be propagated by sowing seed in autumn or spring.

Dicentra 'Bacchanal'

This beautiful plant forms a large mat of green ferny foliage that is surmounted by pendants of deep crimson flowers in early summer. When given the right conditions it can grow to 45cm (18in) high. Spread starts at about 10cm (4in) but the plant continues increasing indefinitely.

Dicentra 'Brownie'

This delightful plant forms large spreads of silvery grey foliage with pearly-white flowers appearing in early summer. H 30cm (12in) with an ever-increasing spread.

Dicentra 'Brownie'

Dicentra 'Bacchanal'

Dicentra formosa

A popular species with several cultivars, each forming spreading mats of green leaves and pink lockets. H 45cm (18in) with an ever-increasing spread.

The species is worth growing in its own right but there are also several interesting forms including *alba* with white flowers. The subspecies *oregana* has pink flowers and is the parent of many of the dicentra cultivars.

Dicentra 'Langtrees'

Another spreading form, with good, silvery grey foliage and pinkish-white flowers in early summer. H 30cm (12in) with an ever-increasing spread.

Dicentra 'Luxuriant'

This cultivar has bluish foliage and bright red flowers. H 35cm (14in); again the plant continues to spread until removed.

Dicentra scandens

This is an unusual, summer-flowering dicentra. Not only does it have yellow or whitish-yellow flowers, but it is also a climber. It will scramble though or over low shrubs and other plants. H and S up to 1m (3ft).

Dicentra spectabilis

Bleeding hearts or Dutchman's breeches are both apt descriptions of the flowers of this plant. The large flowers are carried on long arching stems in spring. In the species they are rose-pink tipped

Dicentra spectabilis

with white and in the form *alba* they are pure white. This is also different from the preceding forms as it is a bigger and more robust form that forms a clump rather than a spreading mat. H and S 60cm (24in) when given good conditions.

Dicentra 'Stuart Boothman'

A very good form with beautiful blue-grey foliage that sets off well the rose-pink flowers. It flowers in early summer and reaches about 30cm (12in) or so in height and spread.

DICTAMNUS
Burning bush

A genus of which *D. albus* is the only species, although its little-grown subspecies *caucasica* is sometimes considered a separate

Dictamnus purpureus

species. It is a splendid border plant, with spikes of white flowers held high above its deeply divided, ash-like leaves (its old name was *D. fraxinella* – meaning 'resembling ash'). In the form *purpureus* they are purplish-pink, striped with darker pink. The flowers appear in the summer.

This plant is known as the burning bush because on a hot day the seed pods release gases which can be ignited with a match. The white and purple forms grow up to 1m (3ft) with a spread of 60cm (24in). Both certainly deserve their place in middle of a border.

Cultivation Any reasonable garden soil as long as it is well-drained. It is best in a sunny position, although it will also tolerate a little light shade. Z4.

Propagation The easiest method of increase is sowing fresh seed. Plants can be divided in spring but this can be tricky since they do not like to be disturbed.

DIERAMA
Angel's fishing rod

This is a beautiful genus of plants that ought to be more widely grown. There are 44 species altogether, but most gardeners only know one or two. The strange English name is derived from the fact that the flowers are hang from very slender arching stems, much in the manner of bait from a fishing rod. The flowers are bell-shaped and come in variations of pink and purple.

Dierama dracomontanum

They appear in summer. The stems emerge from a fountain of strap-like foliage.

The flowers need space to hang so dieramas should not be surrounded by tall plants: the edge of a border is ideal or, even better, overhanging water.
Cultivation These need a moist, but well-drained soil and they should be placed in full sun. Z8.
Propagation The best method of increase is from seed sown fresh, although it may take several years to get a flowering plant. They can also be divided in spring but they will take a while to settle down.

Dierama dracomontanum
This is a short form, so it is suitable for small gardens. It has light pink flowers. H 60cm (24in) S 45cm (18in).

Dierama igneum
A short-stemmed version with unusually bright red flowers. H 60cm (24in) S 45cm (18in).

Dierama 'Merlin'
A new form with beautiful rich purple flowers that are a deep blackberry colour. H 1m (3ft) S 75cm (30in).

Dierama pulcherrimum

Dierama pendulum
One of the taller species when it is grown in good conditions. It has purplish-pink flowers. H 2m (6ft) S 15–20cm (6–8in).

Dierama pulcherrimum
This is another tall form, with attractive flowers of varying shades of pink and purple. H 2m (6ft) S 1m (3ft). There is also a white form *album*.

Other plants There are a surprising number of other species and cultivars waiting to be discovered by the keen gardener. *D.* 'Guinevere', *D. latifolium, D. medium, D. pauciflorum, D.* Slieve Donard hybrids and many others are certainly worth looking at.

DIGITALIS
Foxglove
Everyone knows the foxglove, but many gardeners grow only the common purple one which is in fact a biennial. There are a surprising number of other species that are far less well-known. While most of these are perennial they tend to be short lived and so need to be replaced every two or three years. However, they are easy to propagate from seed. The flowers all have the same basic foxglove shape except some are smaller and more squat. The flowers vary considerably in colour from yellow and cream through to differing shades of soft brown, purple and pink.

Digitalis ferruginea

Digitalis lutea

They are carried in tall spikes. Foxgloves can either be dotted around amongst other plants in a cottage garden style, or you can grow them in a drift for a more organized effect.
Cultivation Foxgloves will grow in any reasonable garden soil and will tolerate either sun or light shade, making them versatile plants. Z3–5.
Propagation These plants all come readily from seed, which should be sown in spring.

Digitalis ferruginea
A distinguished-looking plant with upright stems carrying masses of rust-brown flowers over dark green leaves during summer. H 1.5m (5ft) S 45cm (18in).

Digitalis grandiflora
A shorter plant, up to 1m (3ft) high, which produces pale yellow blooms with a slightly flattened appearance in early summer. H 1m (3ft) S 45cm (18in).

Digitalis lanata
Extremely beautiful, soft white foxgloves with brown veining. H 60cm (24in) S 30cm (12in).

Digitalis × mertonensis

Digitalis lutea
Another yellow-flowered foxglove. This one produces narrow tubes in early summer. H 60cm (24in) S 30cm (12in).

Digitalis × mertonensis
This is a hybrid with large, slightly flattened foxgloves. They are a purple-pink with a touch of light brown in them. This makes a good border plant. It reaches 1m (3ft) in height, with a spread of 45cm (18in).

Digitalis parviflora
As the botanical name implies, this foxglove has small flowers, but a lot of them. They are a wonderful rusty-brown colour. H 60cm (24in) S 30cm (12in).

Other plants There are many interesting foxgloves that are just as good as those listed above. Try, for example, *DD. davisiana, dubia, obscura, stewartii, thapsi* and *viridiflora*.

Spring-flowering perennials

Ajuga reptans	*Lamium orvala*
Anemone blanda	*Meconopsis cambrica*
Anemone nemorosa	*Myositis*
Bergenia	*Primula*
Cardamine	*Pulmonaria*
Dicentra	*Ranunculus ficaria*
Doronicum	*Symphytum*
Euphorbia polychroma	*Trillium*
Helleborus	*Veronica peduncularis*
Lamium maculatum	*Viola*

Doronicum 'Spring Beauty'

D. affinis 'Polydactyla Mappleback'

Dryopteris affinis 'Cristata'

Echinacea purpurea

DORONICUM
Leopard's bane

This genus can be easily overlooked as "yet another daisy", but they are very good daisies, especially as they appear in spring when their golden flowers are most welcome. This is a grouping of about 25 species of which only a few are in cultivation. They are simple plants with large yellow flowers that float above the mid-green foliage. They look best when planted in a large clump, rather than individually, so that they shine out from the dappled spring shade.

Cultivation Any reasonable garden soil, but preferably a moist one. Most require a light shade. Z4.

Propagation They are very easy to increase by division.

Doronicum 'Frühlingspracht' (or 'Spring Beauty')

This is a double that is beautiful but lacks the elegance of the singles. Golden-yellow flowers are carried on stems up to 45cm (18in) high. S 30cm (12in).

Doronicum 'Miss Mason'

One of the best with large (8cm/3in) heads that appear in early summer. H 45cm (18in) S 60cm (24in).

Doronicum orientale

This is a taller species with large yellow flowers. It has a particularly good form called 'Magnificum', which is slightly taller and has larger flowers. H 60cm (24in) S 1m (3ft).

Other plants There are several others worth checking out including 'Little Leo' (dwarf) and *D. pardalianches* (tall).

DRYOPTERIS
Buckler fern

A huge genus of some 200 species of ferns of which quite a number are in cultivation. These are excellent ferns for use in shady areas such as under tall shrubs or in the shade of a house or wall. They look especially good filling odd dark corners. They are deciduous but in milder areas they

may stay evergreen throughout the winter. They form fountains of typical fern-like fronds. The fanatic might want to collect all the variations but to the general gardener just one or two is likely to be sufficient since the variations between cultivars are not that great.

Cultivation Like many ferns these like a moist, rich, woodland-type soil in partial shade. Z3–5.

Propagation The easiest method is to divide the plants in spring just before growth resumes. They can also be grown from fresh spore.

Dryopteris affinis

This is one of the three main species. It has fronds that are very similar to those of *D. filix-mas*: lance-shaped and about 1m (3ft) long. There are a large number of cultivars, such as 'Cristata' and

'Polydactyla Mappleback', to explore. Most of them have distorted fronds of some kind. S 1m (3ft).

Dryopteris dilatata

Similar to the above but with broader fronds. It is taller growing to about 1.5m (5ft) when happy with the conditions. Again there are a number of cultivars. S 45cm (18in).

Dryopteris filix-mas

This is the male fern. It is very similar to the *D. affinis*. An excellent garden plant with lots of poise. H 1.2m (4ft) S 1m (3ft). There are a large number of variants, including the popular 'Crispa Cristata' from which to choose.

ECHINACEA
Coneflower

A small genus of which one species, *E. purpurea*, is widely grown both as a species and in its various cultivars. It is a moderately tall plant which is

Doronicum 'Miss Mason'

Dryopteris filix-mas 'Crispa Cristata'

Echinacea purpurea 'Green Edge'

Echinops ritro

grown for its flowers. These are like large daisies with a single fringe of petals around a central cone. Being large they stand out in the border and mix well with both other herbaceous plants and with grasses. H 1.2m (4ft) S 45cm (18in).
Cultivation This plant needs a soil rich in well-rotted organic material, but it should be well drained. It can be grown in full sun or a little light shade. Z3.
Propagation The species can be grown from seed sown in spring, but the cultivars need to be increased by division in spring.

Echinacea purpurea
The flower has a cone which is a bronze colour while the petals are a deep purple-pink. The flowers are up to 12cm (5in) across and larger in some cultivars. They flower in summer and continue into autumn.

The forms 'Alba', 'White Lustre' and 'White Swan' all have white flowers; the white petals of 'Green Edge' have a delicate green edging. Other cultivars include the dwarf form 'Kim's Knee High', the large-flowered 'Magnus' and 'Rubinstern', a very good dark purple form.

Other plants There are other species which are available for the keen gardener to hunt down. *E. angustifolia* has similar flowers except that the petals are much narrower and longer. *EE. pallida* and *paradoxa* are good plants to include in a collection.

ECHINOPS
Globe thistle
A large genus of more than 100 species of which only a few are worthy of general cultivation. Most of those are very similar, mainly varying in the colour of the thistle. This flower is spherical and held on stiff stems above slightly spiny foliage. Most of these plants are best grown in the middle of a border; their foliage is not particularly attractive and is best hidden behind surrounding plants.
Cultivation These will grow in any reasonable, well-drained garden soil. They prefer a sunny position, but tolerate light shade. Z3.
Propagation The species come readily from seed and will often produce self-sown seedlings. It is possible to divide the plants but it is not easy. Root cuttings can be taken in winter.

Echinops bannaticus
This has blue heads above a greyish-green foliage. The heads are up to 5cm (2in) across and are in flower from midsummer onwards. H 1.2 (4ft) S 1m (3ft).

There are some good cultivars of which 'Taplow Blue' is the best, although 'Blue Globe' and the white form 'Albus' are also well worth growing.

Echinops ritro
This is the most popular species. The flowers are slightly smaller than those of the previous one; it is also a shorter plant. H 1.2m (4ft) S 75cm (30in). The subspecies *ruthenicus* and cultivar 'Veitch's Blue' are also very good.

Echinops sphaerocephalus
A tall plant for the back of the border. The flowers are an off-white. It self-sows vigorously. H 2m (6ft) S 1m (3ft).

ELYMUS
Wild rye
This is a large genus of grasses, of which a couple are of interest to the general gardener. Their main attraction is the unusual blue or silvery-blue leaves, which make them very useful for adding foliage interest to gravel beds. The plants form low hummocks

Elymus magellanicus

of arching blades surmounted by flower spikes which are not particularly attractive. H 20cm (8in) S 15cm (6in).
Cultivation Any garden soil that is well-drained will be suitable. Place in full sun. Z4.
Propagation The easiest method of increase is to divide existing plants just before growth begins in spring. They can also be grown from seed which should be sown at the same time of year.

Elymus hispidus
The foliage of this species grows erect and is an attractive silver-blue colour.

Elymus magellanicus
This is considered the best plant since the short blades are of an intense blue.

EPILOBIUM
Willow herb
The name willow herb strikes terror into most gardeners' hearts because the genus contains some of our worst weeds. However, it also contains a few very pleasing garden plants. They vary from tall ones that reach 1.5m (5ft) or so to very low ones. With such a variation in height their uses obviously vary, but in general they make good border plants.
Cultivation Grow in reasonable, well-drained garden soil. They do well in full sun or light shade. Z7.
Propagation Increase can be from seed sown in spring or by division at the same time of year.

Epilobium angustifolium album

Epilobium angustifolium
This is one of the worst of weeds, but the form *album* is worth growing if you have a very large wild garden where it can be kept out of harm's way. It produces tall spikes of white flowers. Since it will form attractive drifts but is not so rampant as the species, it is an excellent plant to include in a white colour scheme. H 1.5m (5ft) with an infinite spread.

Epilobium glabellum
A perfectly safe little willow herb, this forms a mat of dark green leaves which offsets perfectly the creamy flowers. Grow in partial shade at the front of a border. H 20cm (8in) S 15cm (6in).

Epilobium hirsutum
This is another species to avoid unless you have a large wild gardens where it would be welcome. It has a variegated form 'Well Creek' that is liked by some gardeners. H 2m (6ft) and an infinite spread.

Epilobium glabellum

EPIMEDIUM
Barrenwort

A genus of 30 or so species which has become quite popular of late, especially with several new species coming in from China. These are generally dual-purpose plants since they have attractive flowers and also have good foliage for the rest of the year. The spring flowers are small and hang airily from arching stems. Many are evergreen and the foliage is an elongated heart-shape with a leathery and often glossy appearance. Epimediums are essentially woodlanders and like to grow in a shady position. They are good either under shrubs or in the shade of buildings or walls, where they make the perfect, spreading ground cover.

Cultivation Best grown in a moist, typical woodland soil. These plants should also be positioned in partial shade although some will grow in full sun. Z4–5.

Propagation All the species can be grown from fresh seed, but the easiest method of increase is to divide them in spring.

Epimedium grandiflorum

The flower stems are up to 35cm (14in) high and have yellow, pink, purple or red flowers dangling from them. The foliage is often tinged with bronze or even red. S 30cm (12in).

There are many good cultivars including 'Crimson Beauty' (crimson flowers), 'Nanum' (dwarf with white flowers) and 'White Queen' (white flowers).

Epimedium × perralchicum

The floating flowers are yellow in this species, and hang from 45cm (18in) stems. The evergreen

Epimedium × perralchicum

Epimedium × rubrum

leaves are a shiny dark green with a bronze tinge. S 30cm (12in). 'Fröhnleiten' is a good form that produces large flowers.

Epimedium × rubrum

The leaves are tinged with red and bronze, while the flowers are a wonderful mixture of yellow and bright red. H 30cm (12in) S 20cm (8in).

Epimedium × versicolor

A dainty-flowered plant: the outer parts of the flowers are pink and the inner are yellow. The foliage is tinted with reddish-brown. H and S 30cm (12in). There are several good cultivars including the yellow-flowered 'Sulphureum'.

Other plants Plants in this genus are such an interesting bunch that many gardeners collect them. Other species to check out include *EE. acuminatum, alpinum, davidii, diphyllum, leptorrhizum, perralderianum, × warleyense* and many more.

EREMURUS
Foxtail lily

It would be a strange gardener who was not immediately struck by these plants, with their huge, colourful spikes of flowers. There are more than 40 species, of which half a dozen plus a few cultivars are in cultivation.

They are all splendid and very eye-catching. In late winter thick shoots emerge from the fleshy roots and tall stems up to 2m (6ft) develop. The large flowering spikes begin to bloom from the bottom and seem to fizz away like giant fireworks. There is a good range of colours from white and yellow to pink of various shades. These plants are excellent for a position in the middle or back of the summer border.

Eremurus himalaicus

Eremurus × isabellinus 'Oase'

Cultivation These need a well-drained soil that is rich in well-rotted organic material. Place in a sunny position, sheltered from wind. Protect the emerging buds from severe frosts. Z4–6.

Propagation The easiest method is to dig up the fleshy roots and divide into individual crowns once flowering is over.

Eremurus himalaicus

This stunning plant produces long heads of pure white flowers. H 1m (3ft) S 1.2m (4ft). 'Himrob' has flowers of pale pink.

Eremurus × isabellinus

This is a group of very interesting cultivars with a good range of colours including 'Cleopatra'

Eremurus stenopyllus

(orange), 'Feuerfackel' (flame red), 'Moonlight' (pale yellow) 'Oase' (apricot), 'Obelisk' (white) and 'Pinokkio' (orange). H 1.5m (5ft) S 60cm (24in).

Eremurus robustus

A slightly shorter plant at 1.2m (4ft) or so. It produces spikes of pale pink flowers. S 1m (3ft).

Eremurus stenophyllus

A 1m (3ft) high plant with spikes of dark yellow flowers. Excellent. S 45cm (18in).

Other plants There are a number of other species and cultivars that will repay the effort spent seeking them out from specialist catalogues and nurseries. However, don't fill the whole garden with them as this will overdo the dramatic effect they create.

ERIGERON
Fleabane

Daisies may not be as exotic as, say, lilies, but they do form the backbone of many of our borders. Erigeron is a large genus with a large number of daisy-like species and their commonly grown cultivars. They are clump-forming plants, usually of low stature, making them ideal for carpeting the front of a border. The tall ones are good for mid-border situations. The flowers come in a range of colours and often appear over a very long season.

Erigeron glaucus

Cultivation Any reasonable garden soil is suitable but one that has been enriched with well-rotted organic material will suit these plants best. A sunny position is required, although many will tolerate a little light shade. The taller varieties may need support as they can be floppy. Z3–6.

Propagation The clump-forming varieties are best divided in the spring. Seed can be sown for the species and basal cuttings can be taken from some in spring.

Erigeron aurantiacus

A clump-forming plant whose bright orange flowers have a yellow central disc. H 30cm (12in) S 30cm (12in).

'Azurfee' is a taller form reaching 45cm (18in), this time with light blue, semi-double flowers with yellow centres. 'Dignity' has purple daisies with a yellow centre; again it grows to 45cm (18in) or more. 'Dimity' is a semi-double with bright pink flowers; H 30cm (12in) S 45cm (18in). 'Dunkelste Aller' is a very

Erigeron karvinskianus

good semi-double form with deep violet-blue flowers which have yellow centres. It is one of the taller forms, growing to 60cm (24in) S 60cm (24in). 'Foerster's Liebling' is another excellent form with pinkish-purple, semi-double flowers. It grows to 45cm (18in). S 60cm (24in).

Erigeron karvinskianus

This is a superb, airy plant for growing on banks, in walls or in crevices in paving or containers. It produces masses of small white and pink daisies on thin wiry stems over a very long season from spring until winter. It grows in clumps. It deserves a place in almost any garden. H 30cm (12in) S 45cm (18in).

Erigeron 'Quakeress'

This is a taller form which produces pale bluish-pink flowers. H 45cm (18in) S 60cm (24in).

Other plants There are several other species and cultivars, including *E. glaucus* to investigate. All produce a good number of flowers and are easy to grow.

ERYNGIUM
Sea holly

No garden should be without at least one of these wonderful plants. The foliage and flowers generally have a bluish tinge to them, although some also have a silvery appearance. The flowers form tight domed heads, which are surrounded by blue, silver or greenish bracts, rather like a collar. They retain their colour for a long time and are very useful for drying. These flower heads are often very spiky. The leaves can also be spiky and are usually attractive in their own right.

There are around 200 species, many of which are in cultivation. They are very good border plants, usually best sited in a middle position, and they are especially good in gravel beds.

Cultivation Most sea hollies grow in any garden soil so long as it is free-draining. It is important to plant them in full sun. Z3–7.

Propagation Species will come quite readily from seed sown fresh. They can also be divided,

Eryngium alpinum

although this is not easy since most are tap-rooted. Taking root cuttings in winter is usually easier.

Eryngium agavifolium

A tall plant with stems carrying clusters of pale green flower heads. The leaves that spring from the rosette at the base are spiny. An eye-catching plant but the spines mean that you need to take care when weeding nearby. H 2m (6ft) S 60cm (24in).

Eryngium alpinum

Large heads of silvery blue, which are touched with purple and surrounded by narrow, soft bracts. *E. × oliverianum* is similar except that the stiff bracts are prickly. H 1m (3ft) S 60cm (24in).

Eryngium × oliverianum

Eryngium bourgatii

This much-branched plant has masses of small blue heads. The leaves are dark green, veined with silver. It is a good foliage plant. H 45cm (18in) S 30cm (12in).

Eryngium × tripartitum

A splendid plant with a haze of small violet-blue flower heads. If well treated it can grow to nearly 1m (3ft). This is an excellent plant for mid border but it is often short lived. S 50cm (20in).

Other plants There are many other wonderful eryngiums, including *EE. amethystinum, eburneum, horridum, maritimum, pandanifolium* and *planum* with all its wonderful cultivars.

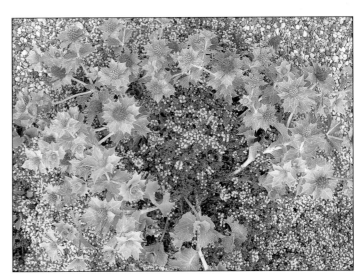

Eryngium maritimum

ERYSIMUM
Wallflowers

A large genus related to the cabbage family – but don't let that put you off since they are superb garden plants and every garden should include several of them. The most commonly grown wallflowers are treated as biennials but there are also a selection of excellent plants that, although short lived, are grown as perennials. The small, flat flowers are carried in loose spikes or clusters in early summer, often well into summer and even beyond. Most colours are represented except for blue. They are usually bright and cheerful-looking plants, making them good for the front of a border. Most grow from 45–75cm (18–30in) S 45cm (18in).
Cultivation Any garden soil will do, but the plants will last longer in a well-drained soil. A sunny position is required. Z3–6.
Propagation The species can be grown from seed, but most cultivars are best increased by cuttings taken in early summer.

Erysimum 'Bowles' Mauve'
What a wonderful plant this is. A great dome of airy stems carries purple flowers from spring through to autumn. Up to 1m (3ft) in height.

Erysimum 'Bredon'
This is a shorter form (up to 30cm/12in or less) with bright yellow flowers.

Erysimum 'Bowles' Mauve'

Erysimum 'John Codrington'

Erysimum 'Constant Cheer'
A lovely mixture of colour: the flowers open a brownish-orange and then slowly change to purple.

Erysimum 'John Codrington'
Another excellent form. This time the flowers come in a mixture of yellow, soft purple and brown creating a tapestry of colour.

Erysimum 'Moonlight'
This is a low-growing cultivar that forms a mat some 25cm (10in) high. The pale yellow flowers open from red buds.

Erysimum 'Rufus'
This has flowers of a good rusty brown colour. However, it isn't very strong and needs replacing every or every other year.

Erysimum 'Wenlock Beauty'
'Wenlock Beauty' is possibly the best of the bunch. It carries masses of sparkling flowers in a mixture of reds, mauves, browns and apricots. It grows to 45cm (18in) or so.

Other plants Other wallflowers worth considering include *E. linifolium*, which can be grown from seed. It produces a number of cultivars, basically with a lilac or purple base colour. *E. mutabile* is similar with mixed colours. Other cultivars include 'Butterscotch' (yellowish-orange), 'Jacob's Jacket' (mixed colours), 'Golden Jubilee' (golden yellow) and 'Golden Gem' (golden yellow).

EUPATORIUM
Hemp agrimony

A large genus of which only a handful of plants are widely grown in gardens. They are valued

Eupatorium p.m. 'Album'

for their late summer and autumn flowering. Many are large and they create a good block of colour at that time of year. They are also attractive to butterflies and bees. The main species and cultivars produce flattish heads of pink flowers, while others have loose heads of small button-like white flowers. They can be invasive, so they are usually only grown in large borders. There are some smaller versions that are suitable for smaller gardens.
Cultivation These plants need a moisture-retentive soil. They do best in sun although they will take some light shade.
Propagation The easiest method of propagation is to divide the plants in spring.

Eupatorium cannabinum
This is not the most attractive of the eupatoriums, but it is good for attracting butterflies and insects. Place in a damp site in a wild garden. H and S 1.2m (4ft).

Eupatorium purpureum
This is the main plant for border use. It is tall at 2m (6ft) or more. Again it is very attractive to butterflies. It is probably most frequently grown in the form *E.p. maculatum* 'Atropurpureum' which has good purple colouration both

Eupatorium purpureum

in its flowers and stems. S 1.5m (5ft). Its companion *E.p.m.* 'Album' has white flowers. The form *E.p.* 'Purple Bush' is lower-growing, reaching up to around 1m (3ft), so it is better suited to smaller gardens.

Eupatorium rugosum
This is species with flattish heads of up to 30 round, white flowers. It looks good in the evening light. H 1.5m (5ft) S 30cm (12in). A similar white-flowered species is *E. perfoliatum*.

EUPHORBIA
Spurge

An enormous genus of over 2,000 species, which vary from trees to ground-hugging plants. Fifty or more herbaceous species are in regular cultivation. The flowers are insignificant, but they are surrounded by colourful bracts, usually in yellowish-green. These last longer than the flowers giving the plants greater staying power. They make good border plants, planted singly or in groups. Some of the bigger ones make good focal points. The sap can be irritating to the skin and eyes.
Cultivation Any good garden soil is suitable, but preferably one that is not too dry. They do best in sun but most tolerate light shade.
Propagation Sow seed in spring. Some self-sow, producing enough seedlings for most purposes. Some spreading species can be divided. Those that grow from one basic stem can be increased by taking basal cuttings in spring.

Euphorbia amygdaloides
The species is best grown in a wild woodland garden. Its variety *robbiae* is an excellent plant for shady areas, even quite dense and dry ones. The short-lived form 'Purpurea' has good purple foliage and bracts in spring and is more suitable for the border. H 60cm (24in) S 30cm (12in).

Euphorbia characias
A tall rounded clump of radiating stems each topped with a club-shaped spike of yellowish-green "flowers". There are many forms, of which *wulfenii* is the most important. This is similar to the

Euphorbia characias wulfenii

species but the flower heads are often larger and yellower. Both the species and *wulfenii* have a lot of cultivars, with only marginal differences between them. They make superb border plants and a large clump makes an eye-catching feature when planted on its own. H and S 1.5m (5ft).

Euphorbia griffithii
A spreading, single-stemmed plant with reddish stems, leaves and bracts. The forms 'Dixter' and 'Fireglow' are excellent. It can be rampant in light soils. H 1m (3ft) S 50cm (20in).

Euphorbia polychroma
An excellent species that forms a rounded hummock 45cm (18in) high. It has bright yellow "flower" in spring. S 50cm (20in).

Other plants There are many species from which to choose. Good ones to consider include *EE. dulcis* (especially 'Chameleon'), × *martinii, mellifera, myrsinites. nicaeensis, palustris* and *sikkimensis*.

FILIPENDULA
Meadowsweet
This is a small genus with a few worthy garden plants. Their attraction comes from the sprays of white, pink or purple flowers, held on strong purple stems above attractive, deep-cut foliage. Many are good border plants; others are perfect for the wild or meadow garden. Some filipendulas are moisture-lovers and they are therefore good for growing next to water features or in bog gardens. They generally grow to about 1m (3ft) although some

Euphorbia dulcis 'Chameleon'

reach double that height. They flower from midsummer onwards. S 1m (3ft).
Cultivation A soil with plenty of well-rotted organic material is ideal, although it should be free draining. Plant in either full sun or partial shade. Z2–3.
Propagation Division is by far the easiest method of propagation for all of them.

Filipendula camtschatica
A tall plant with large, divided leaves and sprays of white or pinkish flowers. H 2m (6ft) S 1m (3ft).

Filipendula 'Kahome'
This is a smaller (45cm/18in) form, ideal for the small garden. It has pink flowers suspended above a bronze foliage. An excellent plant. S 30cm (12in).

Filipendula purpurea
A fine plant with several very good cultivars. It has sprays of magenta flowers. H 1.2m (4ft)

Filipendula rubra

S 60cm (24in). The cultivar 'Elegans' is worth considering since it is a more refined version. The form *albiflora* has beautiful white flowers.

Filipendula rubra
A good garden form, especially in the variety 'Venusta' which produces bright cerise flowers that become pink as as they age. It grows to about 2m (6ft) or even higher under good conditions. S 1.2m (4ft).

Filipendula ulmaria
The species can be grown in a border but it is not a top-class plant. However, it is perfect for naturalizing in a meadow garden, especially in damper areas or along a ditch. H and S 30cm (12in). The form 'Aurea' has yellow foliage that changes to a yellowish green with age. It is often placed in borders as a foliage plant.

Euphorbia polychroma

Euphorbia × *martinii*

Filipendula ulmaria

Foeniculum vulgare

FOENICULUM
Fennel

For some gardeners fennel is something confined to the vegetable garden, but *F. vulgare* is a splendid plant for the border. It is usually grown in the form 'Purpureum'. It is mainly grown as a foliage plant, but the flat heads of tiny yellow flowers are beautiful in their own right especially when seen floating above the delicately cut foliage. The plant is very upright-growing and gets up to 2m (6ft) tall. The foliage is very fine and feathery. When freshly opened the leaves are a dark bronze colour, becoming purplish-green as they age. This is a superb plant, grown either by itself or in groups, for the middle or towards the back of a border. S 75cm (30in).

Francoa sonchifolia

Cultivation Any good garden soil will do, but moister and richer soils produce better plants. A sunny position is needed. Fennel can self-sow prodigiously so cut back the flowering stems before seed is produced. Z4.
Propagation The easiest and best method of increase is from seed sown in autumn or spring. There are usually enough self-sown seedlings for most uses but move them into position while they are still small as they are tap-rooted.

FRANCOA
Bridal wreath

A quiet and relatively unassuming plant that always adds a touch of quality to a border. *Francoa* is a small genus of plants of which only three are regularly grown in gardens. Their attraction is the arching stems that are topped with cylindrical spikes of small, star-like, pink flowers with reddish markings. In good conditions these spikes will reach 1m (3ft) but they are usually less. There is little to choose between the species except in the density of the pink colouration. They make excellent plants for the first or second row of the border, placed so that the stems arch over other plants that have already flowered or have yet to flower. S 45cm (18in).
Cultivation These plants prefer a humus-rich soil that is well-drained but they will grow in most reasonable garden soils. Sun is preferable but they tolerate a little shade. They may need winter protection in cold areas. Z7.
Propagation Francoas come readily from seed sown in spring.

Francoa appendiculata
This plant has pale pink flowers with darker makings.

Francoa ramosa
Very pale pink, almost white flowers with deep pink markings.

Francoa sonchifolia
Pink flowers with purplish-pink markings. There is an almost pure white form, 'Alba', of this. There is also 'Rogerson's Form' in which the flowers are much darker, appearing almost purple.

Fritillaria imperialis

FRITILLARIA
Fritillary

A large genus of bulbs of 100 species. Most are of interest to the alpine enthusiast, with only a handful being suitable for the perennial garden. They vary in size from a few centimetres to 1.2m (4ft). They have pendant bell-shaped flowers in many colours, including green and almost black. True blue is the only colour missing. Some are worthy of the spring border but others are better in a wild garden.
Cultivation Conditions vary and are given under individual species below. Z3–6.
Propagation Seed is readily produced and this is an easy if lengthy method of reproduction. Division of the small bulblets, or "rice" is also very easy.

Fritillaria acmopetala
A small-belled form suitable for choice spots at the front of a border where it will not get swamped. The bells are green

Fritillaria meleagris

Fritillaria persica

suffused with purple. It needs a well-drained soil that does not get too wet in winter. H 30cm (12in) S 5–8cm (2–3in). *F. graeca* is similar but with bigger bells.

Fritillaria imperialis
A very impressive plant. It has clusters of orange or yellow flowers at the top of each tall stem just beneath an upright tuft of green leaves. It needs similar conditions to the previous plant, and is good for the middle of the border where its dying foliage will be covered by summer plants. H 1.2m (4ft) S 30cm (12in).

Fritillaria meleagris
A beautiful plant with large bells hanging from thin stems. The flowers are checkered purple and white, although there are also white forms which have a light chequering of green. These can be grown in a border but are also ideal for naturalizing in grass, particularly if the soil is damp. H 30cm (12in) S 5–8cm (2–3in).

Fritillaria verticillata

Green-flowered perennials

Alchemilla mollis	Hemerocallis 'Lady Fingers'
Anemone nemorosa 'Viridiflora'	Iris 'Green Halo'
	Iris 'Green Spot'
Aquilegia viridiflora	Kniphofia 'Green Jade'
Dianthus 'Charles Musgrave'	Kniphofia 'Percy's Pride'
	Lilium 'Limelight'
Euphorbia	Primula auricala (several)
Galtonia viridiflora	Ranunculus 'Green Petal'
Helleborus argutifolia	Zantedeschia aethopica
Helleborus foetidus	'Green Goddess'

Gaura lindheimeri 'Siskiyou Pink'

Gentiana acaulis

Fritillaria persica

This plant is another tall form. It produces clusters of very dark purple, almost black flowers. It needs dry conditions and a hot place to do well. *F. persica* often does not live long in borders but it is so beautiful that it is worth trying to grow. H 75cm (30in) S 10cm (4in).

Fritillaria verticillata

A delightful plant with pale green and white flowers. It soon forms a large clump. It is best planted near shrubs to which its tendrils can cling. It will grow in most well-drained borders. H 45cm (18in) S 10cm (4in).

GALEGA
Goat's rue

A small genus of herbaceous plants of which four are in general cultivation. These are tall, open plants with many branches, the tips of which carry short, upright spikes of small, pea-like flowers. The colours are generally white, blue or pinkish-purple, and the pretty flowers are often bicoloured. Galegas flower in early summer when they produce

Galega × hartlandii

a good mound of blooms for the back of the border. H 1.5m (5ft) S 1m (3ft).
Cultivation Any good garden soil will do, but a richer, moister soil will provide the best results. These plants do best in full sun, but they will also tolerate a little light shade. They may need some form of support.
Propagation Galegas can be divided in spring, although this is not easy. They can also be grown from seed sown at the same time.

Galega × hartlandii

This is one of the better plants, most commonly represented by two of its cultivars. 'Alba', as its name suggests, has white flowers. The other is 'Lady Wilson', which is a bicolour whose flowers come in white and mauvish-blue.

Galega officinalis

There is not much to choose between the two species. Again this has bicoloured flowers in white and pale blue. It also has an all-white form 'Alba'. The form 'His Majesty' has white and mauve-purple bicoloured flowers.

GAURA
Gaura

A genus of about 20 species of which only one is in general cultivation. This is *G. lindheimeri*. It has several cultivars but the species itself is as good as any of them. It has tall, thin stems from which dance delightful butterfly-like flowers. These are white with a touch of pink. H 1.2cm (4ft) S 1m (3ft). 'Siskiyou Pink' is the most popular cultivar. Here the flowers are a dark pink, but they

are less effective than the white and the plant is not very robust. 'Corrie's Gold' has gold-edged leaves which do little to increase the attraction of the plant.
Cultivation Gaura will thrive in any reasonable garden soil as long as it is well drained. It must have a sunny position. Z5.
Propagation They can be divided with care in the spring, but this is not the easiest of tasks. It is easier to take basal cuttings at the same time of year. The species can also be grown from seed, which is sown in spring.

GENTIANA
Gentian

The 400 species of gentians provide some of the bluest plants in nature. There are a number that are of interest to the alpine gardener, but there are only one or two that are suitable for use in the perennial garden. The flowers are trumpet-shaped. The majority of gentians are ground-hugging plants that like moist, even boggy conditions. The taller border varieties are more accommodating and will grow in any soil that has humus in it. They are ideal plants for shady areas in the garden.
Cultivation Grow in rich moisture-retentive soil. They prefer partial shade, although full sun will be tolerated if the ground does not dry out. Z5.
Propagation Divide gentians in spring or sow the seed as soon as it is harvested.

Gentiana acaulis

This is not the easiest plant to grow but when it is happy, it is wonderful. Very large, upward-

facing trumpets appear in late spring and early summer. H 10cm (4in) S 10cm (4in).

Gentiana asclepiadea

This is the willow gentian, a tallish plant that produces long arching stems, the tips of which often touch the ground. They carry blue, upward-facing flowers on either side. A perfect plant for a choice position in the shady garden. It flowers in late summer. H 1m (3ft) S 60cm (24in).

Gentiana lutea

This is an unusual yellow gentian. It is a tall, upright plant which carries whorls of bright yellow, starry flowers in midsummer. Ideal for naturalizing in grass, such as in a meadow garden. H 1.2m (4ft) S 60cm (24in).

Gentiana sino-ornata

A ground-hugging plant with brilliant blue trumpets facing upwards. There are many cultivars and similar species, all of which are suitable for moist ground in light shade where they will not get swamped by other plants. H 5cm (2in) S 30cm (12in).

Gentiana asclepiadea

Geranium 'Ann Folkard'

Geranium clarkei 'Kashmir White'

Geranium 'Johnson's Blue'

GERANIUM
Hardy geraniums

Many people get confused between these plants and the pelargoniums, the red-flowered plants that are still commonly referred to as geraniums more than 100 years after their name was changed. Geranium is a large genus with more than 300 species. Some are tender but a surprising number of the remainder are in cultivation. There are many gardeners who have been bitten by the collecting bug and have a large number in their garden. Even if you don't collect them it can be surprising how quickly the number of different geraniums that you own increases, which shows how good and versatile they are.

They have open, dish-like flowers in a variety of colours, mainly based on pink and purplish-blue colour schemes. They vary in height from ground-hugging to 1.2m (4ft). Most flower in early summer but some are later and others flower over a long period. Geraniums are very versatile: there is a geranium for every position in the garden in both sun and shade.

Cultivation Most geraniums grow in any reasonable garden soil, but they prefer it laced with plenty of well-rotted organic material. Some are sun lovers, others prefer shade. Cut early-blooming forms after flowering to the ground to get fresh foliage. Z2–6.

Propagation Species can be grown from seed sown in spring. Cultivars can be divided or cuttings taken in spring.

Geranium 'Ann Folkard'
A sprawling plant that clambers between and over other plants. The foliage is yellowish early on, while the flowers are magenta with a dark eye. This geranium has a long flowering season. H 60cm (24in) S 1m (3ft).

Geranium × cantabrigiense
An excellent carpeting geranium that makes perfect ground cover. The leaves are slightly shiny and set off the pink flowers perfectly. 'Biokovo' has flowers of such a pale pink as to be almost white. 'Cambridge' is another good pink form. H 15cm (6in) with an infinite spread.

Geranium cinereum
This is a dwarf plant that is usually grown as one of its cultivars such as 'Apple Blossom' (pale pink flowers) or 'Ballerina' (purple-veined pink flowers). Both have a long flowering season and are perfect for placing at the edge of borders. H 15cm (6in) S 30cm (12in).

Geranium clarkei
This species is grown only in the form of its cultivars. These make excellent plants although they only flower once. 'Kashmir Purple' has perfect mauvish-pink flowers with reddish veins, while 'Kashmir White' has white flowers with paler veins. They grow in a rounded hummock, and make excellent border plants. H and S 45cm (18in).

Geranium himalayense
A good border plant. The flowers are a light purple, darker towards the middle and with a whitish centre. There are several good forms. 'Plenum' ('Birch Double') has attractive double flowers and 'Gravetye' has larger flowers with more purple in them. H 30cm (12in) S 60cm (24in).

Geranium magnificum
A good old-fashioned cottage-garden plant with soft leaves and blue flowers. It tolerates some shade. H and S 60cm (24in).

Geranium 'Johnson's Blue'
A good single form, this has blue flowers with whitish centres. H 45cm (18in) S 60cm (24in).

Geranium macrorrhizum
A superb plant for shade (although it will also grow in sun). The leaves are aromatic when crushed and are semi-evergreen. The pink flowers are produced in early summer. There are several good forms with flowers of varying pinks. H 38cm (15in) S 60cm (24in).

Geranium oxonianum
This and its many cultivars make excellent ground cover in either sun or shade. The clump-forming plant will scramble up through shrubs given a chance. The flowers are bright pink. H and S 75cm (30in).

Geranium phaeum
Another excellent clump-forming plant. This time the flowers are relatively small with reflexed (bent back) petals held in airy sprays on thin stems. The flowers vary from

Geranium cinereum 'Ballerina'

Geranium phaeum

Geranium psilostemon

Geranium sanguineum striatum

Geum rivale

Gillenia trifoliata

pink to purple to white. There are many good cultivars including 'Samobor' which has large chocolate blotches on the leaves. H 75cm (30in) S 45cm (18in).

Geranium psilostemon
A superb plant that forms a large round hummock of airy stems bearing magenta flowers with dark centres. Perfect for larger borders. H and S 1.2m (4ft).

Geranium sanguineum
This is a superb species with lots of cultivars, many of which flower over a long period. It has purple-red flowers over a hummock of foliage. The variety *striatum* and its cultivars have pink rather than red flowers, with prominent veins. H and S 30cm (12in).

Other plants There are many, more species and cultivars to explore including all the forms of *G. pratense* and *G. sylvaticum*.

GEUM
Avens
A genus of about 50 species, a number of which make good garden plants. Although several species are grown it is mainly

their cultivars that grace our borders. Geums are low clump-formers with thin, wiry stems that carry brightly coloured flowers well above the foliage. The flowers are flat discs, usually with a golden central boss. Some forms are double. The colours are mainly reds, oranges and yellows although there are some with more subtle colours. They mainly flower in early summer although some are repeat flowering.
Cultivation Geums will grow in most reasonable garden soils as long as they are free-draining. They need a sunny position. Z5.
Propagation The species can be increased from seed sown in spring, but division is the easiest method and an essential one for the cultivars.

Geum 'Borisii'
This is a wonderfully bright plant with vivid orange-red flowers that are produced over a long season. H 45cm (18in) S 30cm (12in). Another excellent cultivar is 'Coppertone', a lowish-growing (30cm/12in) geum with soft coppery-coloured flowers which are more bell-shaped. 'Lemon Drops' has lemon-yellow flowers

which look particularly good planted near blue violas.

Geum rivale
A plant with pinkish-orange flowers which are bell-shaped rather than disc-shaped. The species is attractive but the cultivars are more often grown. H 45cm (18in) S 20cm (8in). 'Leonard's Variety' is the most famous. It is a more refined plant than the species with lots of reddish-apricot flowers. 'Album' has greenish-white flowers.

There are lots of other cultivars to explore including 'Mrs Bradshaw' (large, semi-double red), 'Georgenberg' (flame orange), 'Prinses Juliana' (orange) and 'Rubin' (semi-double flowers in flame-red).

GILLENIA
Gillenia
A small genus of two, of which one, *G. trifoliata*, is in general cultivation. This is a shrubby perennial with a mass of wiry stems carrying very delicate, butterfly-like flowers. These are pure white with red bud sheaths. It makes a delightful plant, which is not seen as frequently as perhaps it should be. The flowers last throughout the summer. H 1m (3ft) S 60cm (24in).
Cultivation Any reasonable garden soil except alkaline ones. It needs a sunny position lightly shaded at the hottest time of day. Z4.
Propagation Grow from seed sown in spring. The plants can be divided at the same time, although this is not that easy.

GLADIOLUS
Gladiolus
This is a large genus of bulbs that is well known to gardeners. Most are tender and are treated as annuals, but there are a few exceptions which are of interest to the perennial gardener. One in particular, *G. byzantinus*, is hardy and commonly grown. This has not got the big blowsy flowers of the annuals; its blooms are simpler and in many ways much more refined. Gladioli are excellent plants for a late-spring border. Plant in-between emerging summer plants so that the gap

left when flowering is over is covered by the new foliage.
Cultivation Any reasonable garden soil will do. Site in full sun; they can tolerate light shade. Z7–8.
Propagation Dig up the corms and divide off the new ones. They can also be grown without much problem from seed sown in spring. They do not need staking.

Gladiolus communis subsp. byzantinus
This is still known mainly as *G. byzantinus* by most gardeners. It has vivid magenta flowers down one side of a slightly arching stem. It has long sword-like leaves. H 1m (3ft) S 15cm (6in).

Other plants There are a few other gladiolus that can be grown in the open garden although they may be a problem in colder areas. *G. papilio* is probably the best of these with wonderful smoky yellow flowers. *G. × colvillei* has some good cultivars in particular the white 'The Bride'.

Geum 'Lemon Drops'

Geum 'Rubin'

Gladiolus communis subsp. *byzantinus*

Gunnera manicata

Gypsophila paniculata 'Bristol Fairy'

Gypsophila repens 'Fratensis'

GUNNERA
Gunnera

This is a genus consisting of about 45 species. Several of them are of interest to the gardener but only a couple are cultivated to any extent. Although these have similarities in terms of their leaf and flower shape, they are very different in form and size: one is ground-hugging and grows only to 10cm (4in) or so, while the other towers to at least 2m (6ft) and sometimes double that across. It is the latter that is usually of most interest to most gardeners.
Cultivation Gunneras, particularly the larger ones, require a deep, rich soil with plenty of well-rotted organic material. You need to protect the crowns over the winter. Z6–8.
Propagation Division is the easiest method for smaller species. However, their sheer size makes this impractical for the large ones, although small rooted pieces can be detached. Instead, take basal cuttings from the buds that emerge in spring.

Gunnera magellanica
A low creeping plant with rounded leaves. The flowers are green but are given colour when the flame red berries are formed. They are held in upright heads, only a few centimetres high. These plants are not really suitable for the perennial border but can be grown over a rock garden or down a bank. They need covering in winter. S indefinite.

Gunnera manicata
This is the main species grown. It is a giant with leaves that can reach more than 2m (6ft) across. They look like giant rhubarb leaves and are tall enough for children to shelter under. The stems are rough with coarse prickles. These rub in the wind producing a rasping sound. Although these plants are mainly for the large garden it has been known for them to be used as ground cover in a small suburban front garden. They are best sited next to medium to large ponds. The flowers would be insignificant if it wasn't for the size of the flower head. They are green and are carried on a thick clumps below the leaf canopy. H and S at least 2m (6ft).

Gunnera tinctoria
This plant is less frequently seen than the previous one, but is becoming more popular. It is similar but slightly smaller and more compact. It is not so hardy and will require winter protection. H and S 1.5m (5ft).

GYPSOPHILA
Gypsophila

It is hard to image any plant that differs so much from the heavy presence of the Gunnera above. These plants are lightness itself, with large airy sprays of small flowers that create a misty effect. This is a large genus with around 100 species. A handful of these are in cultivation, providing the gardener with plants that are not only beautiful in their own right but contrast well with many of those around them Some are annuals.
Cultivation Any good garden soil will do so long as it is not too acid. It should have plenty of grit incorporated so that it is very free-draining. Z3.
Propagation Increase stock by sowing seed in spring. These plants are difficult to divide so take root cuttings in early winter.

Gypsophila cerastioides
This is really the province of the alpine growers. However, it can be used on the edge of raised beds or next to paths so long as it is not swamped by larger neighbours. It is mat-forming, and the flowers are white with pinkish centres. H 7.5cm (3in) S 10cm (4in).

Gypsophila paniculata
This is the main plant for the border. In summer it forms a cloud of small white flowers and is often called baby's breath because of this. The mass of wiry stems form a mound up to 45cm (18in) high or so. It needs a position towards the front of the border. S 1m (3ft).

There are several cultivars of which 'Bristol Fairy' is still the best. This has larger flowers than the species. There is a smaller plant with double flowers: 'Compacta Plena'.

Gypsophila repens
This is much shorter than the previous plant. It tends to be more spreading and is ideal for planting on the edge of a raised bed so that it can spill over the edge. The flowers are white, or

Gypsophila cerastioides

Gypsophila tenuifolia

white tinged with pink. H 25cm (10in) S 30cm (12in). The best known form is 'Dorothy Teacher' which is more compact with pink flowers that darken as they age. Another is 'Fratensis'.

Gypsophila 'Rosenschleier'

Also known as 'Rosy Veil', this plant is one of the best gypsophilas for the border. It forms a large, rounded haze of pale pink flowers that are white when they first open. H 45cm (18in) S 45cm (18in).

Gypsophila tenuifolia

A tufted plant forming a mat over which float plenty of small white or pink flowers. It grows up to 20cm (8in) high and 60cm (24in) across.

HAKONECHLOA
Hakonechloa

This is just one species in this genus. It is *H. macra*, which is sometimes grown in gardens but it is usually as one of its two main cultivars that it is grown. It forms a clump with arching stems. The plant reaches about 45cm (18in) high and 60cm (24in) across. 'Aureola' is the form most commonly seen. It is variegated, with alternating bright golden and green stripes running down the length of the leaves. 'Alboaurea' is similar but has touches of white.

Cultivation These plants will grow in most reasonable garden soils but they do best in richer soils so

Hakonechloa macra 'Alboaurea'

long as they are free-draining. They will grow in either sun or light shade, but the colour is best in the latter. Z6.

Propagation Increase is by division which should be carried out in spring as the new growth begins.

HEDYCHIUM
Ginger lily

A genus of around 50 species, which in spite of their tenderness have become increasingly popular for use in the border as well as in containers. The plants have a tropical appearance with large, shiny green leaves and a terminal spike of butterfly- or orchid-like flowers which add to their exotic appearance. One of the attractions is their sweet scent. These plants generally grow to between 1 and 1.5m (3–5ft) but some of the more vigorous ones can reach 3m (10ft) if they are given the right conditions. These are plants for exuberant colourful borders, especially those with a tropical feel about them – mix them in with other large-leaved and colourful plants. S 1m (3ft).

Cultivation These need a rich soil with plenty of well-rotted organic material. It should be well-drained. The position can be in either sun or partial shade. Plant the rhizomes just below the surface of the soil. Mulch deeply in the autumn to protect them from the frosts. Z8.

Propagation Ginger lilies should be propagated by dividing the rhizomes in spring.

Hedychium coccineum

This is one of the most colourful of the ginger lilies. The flowers are about 5cm (2in) long, and they may be white, pink, coral red

Hedychium densiflorum

or orange with red stamens. In good conditions, the plant can grow to 3m (10ft) but it usually reaches only half this height. It has a very good form 'Tara', which has orange flowers. S 75cm (30in).

Hedychium densiflorum

This species has yellow or orange flowers. It is one of the tallest but rarely grows to its full potential height, usually reaching only 2m (6ft) with a spread of 60cm (24in). It is reasonably hardy. There are number of good cultivars including 'Assam Orange', which has bright orange flowers, and 'Stephen' (primrose yellow with red anthers).

Hedychium gardnerianum

This is a spectacular plant, producing clear yellow flowers with red stamens. It is tender and can only be grown in frost-free positions unless it is grown inside in containers and moved out after frosts have passed. H 2m (6ft) S 75cm (30in).

Hedychium gardnerianum

Other plants There are a number of other species and cultivars that are widely grown but their hardiness is doubtful. If you want to try, they are best grown in a warm, sheltered position or they can be cultivated under glass.

HEDYSARUM
Hedysarum

This is a large genus of around 100 species. Only one is in general cultivation, although there are a couple of others that are worth looking out for. They are members of the pea family and have spikes of small pea-like flowers, which provide a good splash of red in the spring or summer borders.

Cultivation Grow in any reasonable garden soil that is well-drained. A sunny position is needed. Once in position, avoid disturbing. Z7.

Propagation They come readily from seed sown in spring. They can be divided at the same time of year, but this is not easy.

Hedysarum coronarium

This is the species most commonly seen in gardens. It has bright red flowers which appear in the spring and early summer. H and S 1m (3ft).

Hedysarum hedysaroides

Similar to the previous plant but it is a bit smaller and the flowers are more purple. The blooms are produced in the summer. H 60cm (24in) S 60cm (24in).

Hedysarum multijugum

This is a bigger plant with erect spikes of red-purple flowers throughout the summer. H 1.5m (5ft) S 60cm (24in).

Hedysarum coronarium

Helenium 'Moerheim Beauty'

Helenium 'Waldtraut'

Helianthemum 'Henfield Brilliant'

HELENIUM
Sneezeweed

A genus of about 40 or so species of which only two or three are in cultivation. There are a large number of cultivars and these are most welcome since they add colour to our borders from summer onwards. They are upright, clump-forming plants that reach between 1–1.2m (3–4ft) in height. The flowers are daisy-like with red, yellow, orange or brown outer petals and a brown or gold inner disc.
Cultivation Heleniums do best in full sun and in a soil that does not dry out too much; add plenty of well-rotted organic material. Slugs can be a nuisance when new shoots are emerging. Z3.
Propagation The simplest method of increasing heleniums is to divide them in spring.

Helenium autumnale
This plant is parent to many of the cultivars. However, it is still worth growing in its own right.

The flowers have yellow petals and a brown central disc. H 1.5m (5ft) S 45cm (18in).

Helenium bigelovii
This is the other plant that is responsible for many of the colourful hybrids. It is shorter than the previous, getting up to about 60cm (24in). It has yellow petals and a brown or yellow central disc. S 30cm (12in).

Helenium 'Bruno'
This has bright reddish brown petals and a brown disc.

Helenium 'Butterpat'
A plant with bright butter-yellow petals and a golden disc.

Helenium 'Moerheim Beauty'
One of the most attractive of the heleniums. It has brownish-red flowers touched with yellow, with brown discs.

Helenium 'Riverton Beauty'
This plant has petals of a lovely soft yellow with a reddish-brown central disc.

Helenium 'Rotgold'
Distinctive colouring features red flowers streaked with yellow, and a brown disc.

Helenium 'Waldtraut'
A plant with mahogany and yellow petals and a brown central disc.

Helenium 'Wyndley'
'Wyndley' has flowers that are yellow streaked with red. It has brown disc florets.

HELIANTHEMUM
Rock roses

These are really shrubs but they have always had a place in the perennial border and so are included here. This is a large genus of more than 100 species but it is the many cultivars that are of interest to gardeners. These form rounded hummocks of grey or green foliage against which round, flat flowers are displayed. The blooms come in many shades of red, pink, orange, yellow and white. They have a yellow centre. There is a quiet simplicity about these flowers that makes them perfect for the edge of a border, or grown to hang down a wall or sprawl onto a path or patio. They flower in early summer; some, especially the doubles, last into late summer. H 30cm (12in) S 45cm (18in).
Cultivation Any garden soil as long as it is free-draining. A sunny position is important. Sheer over the plant once it has flowered to keep it compact. Z5.

Propagation Helianthemums are increased by cuttings taken in either spring or early summer.

Helianthemum 'Amy Baring'
A superb form with deep golden flowers and orange in their centres.

Helianthemum 'Butterball'
'Butterball' is double-flowered form with buttery yellow flowers as its name implies.

Helianthemum 'Cerise Queen'
This plant carries double flowers which look like powder puffs of cerise petals.

Helianthemum 'Chocolate Blotch'
A delightful plant whose orange petals have chocolate brown blotches at the base.

Helianthemum 'Henfield Brilliant'
This gorgeous cultivar has flowers of such a bright red that they can seem to hit you between the eyes with their brilliance.

Helenium 'Riverton Beauty'

Helianthemum 'Wisley Pink'

Helianthemum 'Raspberry Ripple'

One of the brashest of the rock roses. The flowers are white with splashes of raspberry red and with a yellow boss of stamens.

Helianthemum 'Wisley Pink'

Strictly speaking, this is now called 'Rhodanthe Carneum' but it is still generally known as 'Wisley Pink'. It is a wonderful plant with soft pink petals set off against soft grey foliage. Possibly the best of the bunch.

Helianthemum 'Wisley Primrose'

Another superb plant whose primrose-yellow flowers look charming against soft grey foliage.

Helianthemum 'Wisley White'

An excellent plant which has wonderful white flowers touched with yellow.

HELIANTHUS
Sunflower

Most people are aware of the large sunflowers that are grown as annuals (see page 132) but many do not realise that there are also a number of perennial species. These might not be as big and brazen as the dinner-plate-sized annuals, but they still make a good splash of bright colour, especially during the autumn. They have daisy-like flowers, with an outer ring of bright yellow petals surrounding an inner disc of similar colour. Some of the cultivars are double forms where the disc is replaced by a pompom of petals. The flowers are carried on stiff, upright stems, which vary in height from 1m (3ft) or so up

Helianthus 'Loddon Gold'

to 2.5m (8ft). They soon make a decent-sized clump. Most are best sited at the back of the border and look particularly good against a dark green hedge.
Cultivation Add plenty of well-rotted organic material to the soil before planting in a sunny position. The taller varieties may need staking in exposed positions.
Propagation Division in spring is by far the easiest method of propagation.

Helianthus atrorubens

In late summer this vigorous sunflower produces yellow flowers with a deep red central disc. H 1.5m (5ft) S 1m (3ft).

Helianthus × laetiflorus 'Morning Sun'

Helianthus 'Capenoch Star'

A good plant which has large yellow-petalled flowers with a yellow centre. H 1.2m (4ft) 60cm (24in).

Helianthus × laetiflorus

A popular hybrid that has produced some good cultivars. It has yellow flowers with yellow disc. H 2m (7ft) S 1.2m (4ft). 'Miss Mellish' is a semi-double form with yellow petals and a more golden-coloured disc. 'Morning Sun' is similar.

Helianthus 'Lemon Queen'

A fine variety with lemon-yellow petals and a yellow centre. It is a tall variety that needs to be grown at the back of the border where it can peep over the other plants. H 1.8m (6ft) S 60cm (24in).

Helianthus 'Loddon Gold'

A old variety that has stood the test of time. It is a double with a mass of golden-yellow flowers. H 1.5m (5ft) S 60cm (24in).

Helianthus 'Monarch'

A tall plant with semi-double flowers with narrow yellow petals and green-brown centre. H 2.5m (8ft) S 60cm (24in).

Helianthus salicifolius

Before the flowers appear in autumn this can be a difficult plant to identify: its upright stems carry a large number of narrow leaves which droop down, looking just like those of a tall lily. But the idea of a lily is quickly dispelled when the bright yellow flowers appear. This is a tall plant growing to 2.5m (8ft), S 60cm (24in).

Other plants There are a number of other species and cultivars to explore, although most are variations on the same theme.

HELICHRYSUM
Helichrysum

A very large genus of over 500 species, which like the last genus is mainly known for the plants grown as annuals. However, there are a number of perennials that are worth growing. They are perhaps not in the top league

Helianthus salicifolius

of plants but they do add unusual colour combinations to the border, mainly through their grey foliage. The felted leaves do not like wet climates, especially winter wet. They do well in gravel beds.
Cultivation Helichrysums grow in any reasonable garden soil but it must be really well drained. A sunny position is essential. Z6–8.
Propagation Division is possible in spring. Alternatively, cuttings can be taken in summer.

Helichrysum splendidum

This is a shrubby plant with upright stems carrying narrow grey leaves. They are topped with small yellow flowers in late summer. H and S 1.2m (4ft).

Helichrysum 'Schwefellicht'

Also known as 'Sulphur Light', this is one of the best helichrysums for the perennial border. The foliage is an attractive grey-green overlaid with white. The bunches of upward-facing flowers are bright sulphur yellow fading to orange or brown as they go over, which creates a delightful two-toned effect. They flower in late summer. H 40cm (16in) S 30cm (12in).

Other plants There are several other species and varieties worth checking out if you like to include plenty of grey in your borders.

Helichrysum 'Schwefellicht'

Helleborus foetidus

Helleborus × hybridus Double

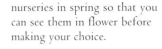

Hemerocallis 'Stafford'

HELLEBORUS
Hellebore

This is an extremely popular genus. There are about 15 or so species, most of which are in cultivation, along with a host of cultivars. Their popularity may be partly due to the fact that they flower in late winter when not much else is around. At that time of year they certainly brighten up the garden. They have flat or cup-shaped flowers which come in a wide variety of colours. Doubles and picotee varieties with flowers edged in a different colour have extended the range available. These are mainly woodland plants. Place where they can be seen in winter and spring, but hidden during the rest of the year.
Cultivation A soil kept moist with plenty of organic material is required for most species. Partial shade is preferable. Z4–6.
Propagation Species can be grown from seed, which should be sown as soon as it is ripe. Species and cultivars can also be divided in spring after flowering.

Helleborus argutifolius
These are tall plants that often need support. The dark green leaves are noticeably toothed and

the flowers are cup-shaped and a delicate pale green. H 1.2m (4ft) S 45cm (18in).

Helleborus foetidus
A leggy plant with narrow leaves and bell-shaped flowers. The flowers are green, often with a purple lip. H and S 45cm (18in). 'Wester Fisk' is a good form.

Helleborus × hybridus
These plants used to be known as the oriental hybrids. The flowers are flat and dish-shaped and there is a wide mixture of colours; some are spotted and others are doubles. There are many named varieties from which to choose. All are good, so try to see them in flower before you buy. H 45cm (18in) S 45cm (18in).

Helleborus niger
The Christmas rose produces flat flowers which are white, but usually infused with a little pink. It is not the easiest plant to grow and it can be a martyr to slugs. H and S 30cm (12in).

Other plants There are a great number of other species and cultivars that are worth exploring, such as *H. × sternii*. Visit specialist

nurseries in spring so that you can see them in flower before making your choice.

HEMEROCALLIS
Daylily

A genus of around 15 species, but it is the thousands of cultivars that are of most interest to the perennial gardener. This vast quantity is well beyond the needs of even the keenest, but there is a surprising amount of variation between them. The basic plant is a clump of strap-like leaves arching out in a fountain, from which emerge stiff stems carrying a mass of buds. These open a few at a time but only for a day (hence the plant's English name). The flowers are shaped like flaring trumpets and are coloured in mainly yellow, orange or red as well as occasional pinks and whites. They are one of the mainstays of the summer border. H 75cm (30in) S 60cm (24in).
Cultivation Plant in any reasonable garden soil that has been enriched with organic material. A sunny position is best but most will take some light shade. Staking is not usually required. Z2–4.
Propagation Although they are heavy plants to dig up, division is the best method of increase.

Hemerocallis 'Catherine Woodberry'
This is a very beautiful plant which produces flowers of an unusual lilac-pink.

Hemerocallis 'Corky'
One of the most refined of the daylilies. It produces small trumpet-shaped flowers that are

mahogany on the outside and bright golden yellow on the inside. A superb plant to grow.

Hemerocallis 'Golden Chimes'
This has quite open trumpets with reflexed (turned back) petals of clear gold. It is good against a background of green foliage.

Hemerocallis 'Lark Song'
The flowers of this cultivar are a delightfully clear yellow with distinctive green throats.

Hemerocallis 'Red Rum'
This produces yellow-throated flowers of a lovely flame-red. They are quite startling.

Hemerocallis 'Stafford'
The flowers are deep red, almost mahogany, with yellow in the throat and up the centre of petals.

Hemerocallis 'Stella de Oro'
Here the broad petals that make the flower are more circular. They are a good golden-yellow colour.

Other plants There are hundreds of other excellent daylilies, including 'Eenie Weenie' (short, yellow), 'Frans Hals' (mahogany red), 'Green Flutter' (yellow and

Helleborus niger

Helleborus × sternii

Hemerocallis 'Lark Song'

Hemerocallis 'Wind Song'

green), 'Marion Vaughn' (clear yellow), 'Prairie Blue Eyes' (lavender blue), 'Wind Song' (creamy yellow) and many more.

HEUCHERA
Coral flower

A genus of 55 species and an increasing number of cultivars. The plants used to be grown for the erect, airy stems of tiny flowers, but they are now often cultivated as foliage plants as more plants with attractive leaves have been bred. The leaves are basal and circular. They are green or purple and often have silver markings. The spikes of flowers are green, white pink or red and usually appear in early summer. They are perfect at the front of the border. H 60cm (24in) S 45cm (18in).
Cultivation Any reasonable moisture-retentive soil in sun or shade will be suitable. Z4.
Propagation Heucheras should be propagated by division in the autumn or spring.

Heuchera cylindrica
Green leaves with a silverish, mottled effect. The spikes of flowers are cream. It is best grown in the form of one of its cultivars: they include 'Chartreuse' (yellow-green flowers), 'Greenfinch' (green flowers) or 'Hyperion' (pink and green flowers).

Heuchera 'Firefly'
This plant produces wonderful spikes of bright scarlet flowers.

Heuchera 'Helen Dillon'
One of the best, this has silvery-grey leaves with green veins. The spikes of flowers are red.

Heuchera micrantha 'Palace Purple'
This attractive foliage plant has purple leaves with a metallic sheen. The flowers are buff.

Heuchera 'Pewter Moon'
Another good foliage plant. The leaves are purple with silver markings. Pinkish-buff flowers.

Heuchera 'Rachel'
This plant has purple leaves similar to those of 'Palace Purple' but the flowers are pink.

Other plants There are many other cultivars, which are mainly variations on the above themes.

HOSTA
Hosta

A genus of about 40 species and many thousands of cultivars. They are grown mostly for their foliage, but they also have spikes of attractive small lily-like flowers in white, blue, or pale purple. The green leaves are generally heart- or spear-shaped. There are many variations: some are heavily pleated or puckered; some have cream or yellow variegations; some are golden and others are blue. This gives the gardener tremendous scope when adding foliage to the borders. Hostas will grow in full sun or partial shade so long as the soil is moist. They will often make dense drifts. The foliage usually reaches about 30–45cm (12–18in) with the flower spike reaching twice that height. S 1m (3ft).
Cultivation Plant hostas in an organic-rich soil which retains moisture well. They can be placed either in sun or partial shade. They are very susceptible to slugs, so will need protection.
Propagation The cultivars are increased by division, which can be hard work if clumps are large.

Hosta 'Big Daddy'
Large, puckered leaves that are a good bluish-green. White flowers.

Hosta crispula
Wavy-edged leaves are green with white variegations round the margins; the flowers are pale blue.

Hosta fortunei
An attractive species with many excellent varieties. The species has pointed, dark green leaves and lavender flowers. The leaves of the variety *albopicta* have pale yellow centres and green margins; in *aureomarginata* they are green with golden-yellow margins; *hyacinthina* has grey-green leaves edged in white and dark blue flowers.

Hosta 'Frances Williams'
An old favourite and still considered one of the best. The leaves are puckered and a bluish-green with a wide, irregular margin of creamy-white or yellow. The flowers are pale lavender.

Hosta 'Halcyon'
This is a choice plant which has superb leaves of a dusty blue. The flowers are also blue.

Hosta 'Honeybells'
Large, pale green leaves with wavy margins. The fragrant flowers are white, streaked with lavender.

Hosta 'Hydon Sunset'
The leaves are small, opening a fresh yellow-green and then going to a darker green. The flowers are deep purple.

Hosta 'Sum and Substance'
This has very large leaves that are lime green and can be yellow when the plant is sited in full sun. The flowers are very pale lavender.

Other plants The plants listed above make up only a fraction of those available. The only way to see anything approaching the whole-range is to find a specialist nursery or its catalogue.

Hosta 'Frances Williams'

Heuchera micrantha

Hosta crispula

Hosta 'Halcyon'

Hosta 'Hydon Sunset'

Houttuynia cordata 'Chameleon'

HOUTTUYNIA
Houttuynia

The only species in this genus is *H. cordata*. This is widely grown in gardens, but it is more frequently seen in either its variegated or double forms. The species is low growing, and its heart-shaped leaves make good ground cover, especially for shady areas. The flowers are four white bracts (petal-like leaves) with a central flower cone, which show up well against the leaves. H 25cm (10in) S indefinite.

The variety 'Chameleon' has similar flowers but variegated foliage which is green with creamy-yellow margins touched with red. 'Flore Pleno' has green leaves and double flowers. Houttuynias are excellent for woodland areas or under shrubs. They are also very good for growing in bog gardens or around water features.
Cultivation Any reasonable garden soil although it prefers moist conditions. It is best in the shade but will grow in sun. Z5.
Propagation The best way to propagate houttuynias is to divide them in spring.

HUMULUS
Hop

Only one hop is grown in the decorative garden. This is *H. lupulus* 'Aureus', the golden form of the one used for brewing beer. It is a climber that ascends by twining around its host. It dies back to the ground each winter so it has to climb its 5m (16ft) or so from scratch each year, which it normally does by midsummer. The leaves and stems are very rough in texture and can cause burns on the skin if heavily brushed against. The foliage is golden yellow. The female plants

Humulus lupulus 'Aureus'

produce 'hops', which are the green flowers, in early autumn. Hops are good for growing over frameworks or up through trees.
Cultivation Grow in any reasonable garden soil, although the plants will do better in richer conditions. They are best grown in full sun and will need some support: a framework, trees, or strings or wires attached to poles. Z6.
Propagation Divide the plant carefully in spring.

INULA
Inula

A large genus of daisy-like plants. Of the 100 or so species, only a handful are in cultivation, but these provide some stunning plants. They vary from low-growing plants of only 15cm (6in) to towering giants of 2.5m (8ft) or more. The foliage is generally quite coarse but the flowers are more refined. They are golden-yellow or light orange, with slender petals and central golden disc. Most appear from late summer onwards.

Depending on the plants' height, they can be used at any point from the front to the back of a border.
Cultivation Inulas like a rich soil with plenty of well-rotted organic material. They also like a sunny position. Z5.
Propagation The easiest method of increase is to divide in the spring, although the species can also be readily grown from seed sown at the same time of year.

Inula ensifolia

Inula ensifolia

This is a short, clump-forming plant that is perfect for the front of a border. H 45cm (18in) S 30cm (12in). It has a few cultivars, of which 'Goldstar' is the best. 'Compacta' is only 15cm (6in) high.

Inula helenium elecampagne

This is excellent for naturalizing in a wild or meadow garden. H 1.2m (4ft) S 60cm (24in).

Inula hookeri

The best of the bunch, with wonderful buds that open to flowers whose petals look like threads of gold. The flowers are carried singly at the tip of each stem. The plant may be cut back by late frosts but recovers. H 75cm (30in) S 45cm (18in).

Inula magnifica

This is a taller species suitable for growing in the middle to the back of the border. The flowers are carried in heads of up to 15 blooms. H 2m (6ft) S 1m (3ft).

Inula orientalis

A medium-height species for the middle of a border. The flowers are carried singly. H 1m (3ft) S 60cm (24in).

Inula hookeri

Inula magnifica

Inula racemosa

The tallest of the garden varieties reaching up to 2.5m (8ft) in good conditions. It may need support in exposed positions. The flowers are pale yellow and are carried singly up the tall stems, often effectively forming a spike. Best grown at the back of a border or as an impressive clump at the end of a path. S 1.2m (4ft).

Inula royleana

A medium-height plant for the middle of the border. The leaves are large and coarse. The orange flowers are carried singly. H 1m (3ft) S 60cm (24in).

IRIS
Iris

A very large genus of about 300 species, of which many are in cultivation. They are a diverse collection since they vary from dwarf to tall plants. They flower at almost all seasons of the year including winter and they like conditions from dry soil to standing in water. However, the flowers all bear a close resemblance to each other: they have three "standard" petals that stand upright and three "falls" that hang or arch downwards. Standing up in the centre of all these are three small "stigma flaps". Most colours are represented in one cultivar or another. They are wonderful plants for a border; their one disadvantage is that they flower only once in a season. On the

Iris 'George'

Iris pallida

Iris unguicularis

Iris 'Purple Sensation'

other hand, their sword-like leaves make them into an effective foliage plant for the remainder of the time. There are many specialist irises, which are grown under glass by alpine growers.

Cultivation The majority like a well-drained garden soil that is not too rich but not too spare either. They need a sunny position, especially the *germanica* ones which like to have the tops of their rhizomes exposed to the sun. Plant in late summer or autumn. Z3–5.

Propagation For all species the easiest method of increase is to divide them after flowering.

Iris chrysographes

A delicate iris with small dark purple, almost black, flowers with gold markings. It prefers a moist soil. H 45cm (18in) S indefinite.

Iris danfordiae

A small bulbous iris that flowers in late winter. It has yellow flowers. H 15cm (6in) S 5cm (2in). There are several other dwarf bulbous species worth growing such as *I. histrioides* (blue) and *I. reticulata* (blue, purple). There are also lots of named varieties such as 'George' (purple), 'Harmony' (blue and

yellow) and 'Joyce' (blue). They are all about the same height and flower in late winter.

Iris ensata

This species and its more than 100 cultivars like a damp position that never dries out. They can be grown in borders with plenty of moisture-retaining material in the soil. H 1m (3ft) S indefinite. The flowers are variations on purple, although there are white forms such as 'Alba' and 'Moonlight' as well as some blues.

Iris foetidissima

A useful iris for shady places and woodland. The flowers are purple suffused with yellow. They have prominent red seeds in winter. H 30–100cm (1–3ft) S indefinite.

Iris germanica

A portmanteau name that covers an extremely large number of cultivars such as 'Chantilly'. These are the border irises with thick rhizomes. The flowers are generally large and come in many colours. Specialist dealers or their catalogues are the only way to find your way around these plants if you are interested. Most gardeners are content with one or two chosen at random. H 60–120cm (2–4ft) S indefinite.

Iris laevigata

This is similar to *I. ensata* in both its appearance and preferred conditions. There are plenty of cultivars from which to choose, the colours mainly based on purple or white. H 60–120cm (2–4ft) S indefinite.

Iris pallida

A very beautiful species with pale grey-green leaves that set off beautifully the misty blue flowers. It has two variegated cultivars: 'Argentea Variegata' with silver-

striped leaves and 'Variegata' with gold stripes. H 70–100cm (2½–3ft) S indefinite.

Iris sibirica

A clump-forming iris with narrow leaves. The flowers are based on the violet-blue of the species. There are many good cultivars from which to chose. H 50–120cm (1½–4ft) S indefinite.

Iris unguicularis

A must in every garden. This is a winter-flowering iris with delicate soft mauve flowers and a lovely scent. It is good for picking but beware: slugs love it. There are several cultivars with flowers of varying degrees of purple. It likes poor soil conditions and a sunny spot. H 20cm (8in) S indefinite.

Other plants Each of the above species has masses of cultivars and there are also many other species including *II. douglasiana, innominata, japonica, setosa, xiphium* (Spanish irises and Dutch irises such as *I.* 'Purple Sensation').

Iris germanica

Iris sibirica

Iris 'Chantilly'

Knautia macedonica

KNAUTIA
Knautia

A small genus of about 60 species of which only one is in general cultivation. These plants are related to the scabious. They have flowers that look like miniature pincushions, carried on tall airy stems. They tend to have a long flowering period, which makes them useful although the flowers at the end of the year are noticeably smaller than those in midsummer. They are very good plants for the middle of the border, especially if you like the effect of one clump of plants merging with the next since they tend to be a bit floppy.

Cultivation Knautia can be planted in any good garden soil and in a sunny position. Z6.

Propagation These are easy to increase either from basal cuttings in spring or seed sown at the same time of year.

Knautia arvensis
This is not frequently seen, but it is still a delightful plant with lavender-coloured flowers. It is good for the meadow garden. H 1.2m (4ft) S 45cm (18in).

Knautia macedonica
This is the most commonly grown plant in the genus. Its great virtue is the deep crimson flowers, a colour that is not often seen in herbaceous plants. This was the only colour available until recently when pastel-coloured varieties were introduced. These are generally referred to as Melton Pastels. It is a floppy plant that can be staked, but this must be done at an early stage of growth. H 75cm (30in) S 60cm (24in).

KNIPHOFIA
Red hot poker

A very distinctive genus of flowering plants, of which there are about 70 species and many cultivars. The plants form dense clumps of narrow, sword-like foliage that arches out like a fountain. Erect stems rise out of the foliage, each carrying a dense club-like spike of flowers. Initially most garden forms were flame-red, hence the English name, but variations on red, orange, yellow and green are now being grown.

When in full flower the plants are stunning, but they can look tatty once they start to go over; at this point it is best to remove the flower stems. They vary in height from dwarf forms of about 45cm (18in) to tall ones that reach about 1.5m (5ft). Most flower in summer, and some last into the autumn.

Cultivation Kniphofias need a deep, free-draining soil to which plenty of well-rotted organic material has been added. They prefer a sunny position although they will tolerate a little light shade. Z7.

Propagation The best way of propagation is by division.

Kniphofia 'Alcazar'
This is a flame red poker of medium height. H 75cm (30in) S 45cm (18in).

Kniphofia 'Bees' Sunset'
Soft orange flowers bloom from mid to late summer. H 1m (3ft) S 60cm (24in).

Kniphofia 'Buttercup'
Yellow flowers are produced by this cultivar in early summer. H 75cm (30in) S 60cm (24in).

Kniphofia 'Candlelight'
This is a short form. There is green tip to the flower head, which turns greenish-yellow as the flowers open. H 60cm (24in) S 60cm (24in).

Kniphofia 'Little Maid'
This is a superb small kniphofia with pale yellow flowers that turn cream as they age. H 60cm (24in) S variable.

Kniphofia 'Percy's Pride'
A good kniphofia for the autumn garden. The flowers are yellowish-green. H 1m (3ft) S 50cm (20in). Another good green is 'Green Jade'.

Kniphofia 'Prince Igor'
Perfect for the hot border, the poker of this tall variety is a wonderful rich orange. H 1.5m (5ft) S 60cm (24in).

Kniphofia rooperi
This is a late-flowering species which produces its poker in the autumn, often late autumn. The flower heads are much fatter and rounder than usual. They are a flame-orange that ages to golden

Kniphofia 'Candlelight'

yellow. These plants are taller than most others. H 1.2m (4ft) S 75cm (30in).

Kniphofia 'Royal Standard'
A typical poker with an orange tip and yellow base where it is ageing. H 1.2m (4ft) S 60cm (24in).

Kniphofia 'Sunningdale Yellow'
A good all-yellow kniphofia. H 1m (3ft) S 60cm (24in).

Kniphofia 'Toffee Nose'
An intriguing form with flowers of a toffee colour that fades to an attractive cream further down the flower head. H 45cm (18in) S 30cm (12in).

Kniphofia 'Wrexham Buttercup'
A rich golden-yellow poker that illuminates a border. H 1.2m (4ft) S 60cm (24in).

Kniphofia 'Alcazar'

Kniphofia 'Prince Igor'

Kniphofia 'Toffee Nose'

Lamium maculatum 'Roseum'

Lamium maculatum 'Beacon Silver'

LAMIUM
Dead nettle

The leaves of some species may worry gardeners as they look like those of stinging nettles, but they are harmless. There are about 50 species in all. Most of them are weeds but a few make good garden plants. In some the leaves are marked or mottled in silver while in others it is the cluster of large thyme-like flowers in white, purple or yellow that are the attraction. Most flower early on, from spring to early summer, but those with attractive leaves can double as foliage plants for the rest of the season. Most are spreading, making them good ground cover for the front of the border, where they will weave their way between other plants.
Cultivation Lamium should grow well in any reasonable garden soil so long as it does not dry out completely. They can be grown in either sun or light shade. Z3–4.
Propagation They can easily be divided in spring. If you do not want to disturb the plants, basal cuttings can be also taken at the same time of year.

Lamium galeobdolon

The yellow archangel of the woodlands. A tall species with mid-green leaves that are often splashed with silver and with spikes of yellow flowers. It is attractive but it can become a nuisance so it is best suited to wild plantings; plant one of its cultivars in more regulated areas. H 60cm (24in) S indefinite. 'Hermann's Pride' is a more compact plant. It has dark green leaves with prominent silver markings. 'Silberteppich' ('Silver Carpet') is a popular variety with leaves that are greyish-green but so overladen with silver that the green can hardly be seen. The flowers are yellow. 'Silver Angel' is another well-loved silver variety worth trying.

Lamium maculatum

This is a delightful old-fashioned, cottage-garden plant. It produces spreading carpets of green foliage, usually with white or silver markings. From these arise short spikes of pink flowers. After flowering the plants tend to get a bit straggly; they are best cut back to regenerate the foliage and induce second flowering. H 20cm (8in) S 1m (3ft).
There are a number of very good forms. 'Roseum' is an old one with darker, purplish flowers. A white-flowered form is 'Album' but this has been superseded by 'White Nancy' which not only has white flowers but very silver leaves, touched with green around the margins. 'Pink Pewter' is a pink-flowered version of this, while 'Beacon Silver' is similar but with pale pink flowers. 'Aureum' and 'Cannon's Gold' both have pink flowers and golden foliage, the former with silver patches.

Lamium orvala

This is a delightful plant that is not seen as often as it should be. It flowers in spring, when it forms a well-rounded clump of stems. Peering from the large nettle-shaped leaves are smoky purple-pink flowers. The plant dies back once its flowering season finishes. H 60cm (24in) S 30cm (12in).

LATHYRUS
Everlasting pea

Although not as well known as the annuals, the perennials in this genus are very pretty. Some are climbers, while others are scramblers and yet others form a bushy plant. They all produce pea-like flowers of differing sizes. Their colours are all generally are based on purple. They can be used in the border or on the edge of shrubby areas.
Cultivation These plants will do best in a soil that has had plenty of organic material added to it.

Lathyrus tingitanus

They prefer a sunny position, but many everlasting peas will grow in light shade. Z5.
Propagation Grow from seed sown in the spring. Those that spread underground can be divided.

Lathyrus grandiflorus

One of the best, this has large rounded flowers in two-tone pink. It scrambles through shrubs. H 1.2m (4ft) S 60cm (24in).

Lathyrus latifolius

This everlasting pea is a bit coarse but it produces a show of pink or white flowers. Let it sprawl or tie it to supports. H 1.5m (5ft) S 2m (6ft).

Lathyrus vernus

A wonderful clump-former, which blooms in early spring. H 45cm (18in) S 30cm (12in).

Other plants Look at *L. aureus* (orange flowers), *L. nervosus* (blue) and *L. tingitanus* (pink).

Some purple perennials

Aster (various)	Lythrum salicaria
Centaurea montana 'Parham'	Lythrum virgatum
Echinacea purpurea	Penstemon 'Burgundy'
Erigeron 'Dunkelste Aller'	Penstemon 'Russian River'
Erodium manescavii	Phlox 'Le Mahdi'
Erysimum 'Bowles' Mauve'	Salvia viridis
Geranium (various)	Senecio pulcher
Liatris spicata	Stachys macrantha
Linaria purpurea	Thalictrum delavayi
Lobelia × gerardii 'Vedrariensis'	Verbena bonariensis

Lamium orvala

Lathyrus vernus

Lavatera thuringiaca

Lavatera cachemiriana

LAVATERA
Mallow

This is a genus of about 25 species of which a few are perennial. There are also some shrubs that are often thought of as perennials in the border context. What distinguishes this group of plants is the funnel-shaped flowers, which usually come in soft, delicate shades of pink. The most popular species tend to be quite tall. They add bulk to a border and often bring continuity since they flower for a long time.

Cultivation Mallows will grow in any reasonable garden soil so long as it is well drained. They should have a sunny, sheltered position protected from winds. Z6–8.

Propagation Species can be grown from seed sown in spring. Cultivars need to be propagated from cuttings taken in summer.

Lavatera cachemiriana

This is a true perennial. It has tall, upright stems from which grow delicate pink flowers. These are flatter and not so funnel-shaped as some other varieties. It is not a long-lived plant but it is easy to increase from seed, of which it produces masses. H 1.5–2m (5–6ft) S 1m (3ft).

Lavatera × clementii

A collection of shrubby hybrids that make good background plants or centrepieces in a border. H 2m (6ft) S 2m (6ft). One of the best known of these hybrids is 'Barnsley' which has white flowers, each with a prominent blotch of red in the centre. 'Bredon Springs' is another popular variety. This has purplish-pink flowers with prominent purple veins. 'Kew Rose' is similar with bright pink flowers with purple veining. 'Candy Floss' has very pale pink funnels.

Lavatera maritima

This is a true perennial. It naturally grows near the sea but it can be also used to good effect in inland gardens. It has pink or white flowers with prominent carmine veins. H 1.5m (5ft) S 1.5m (5ft).

Lavatera thuringiaca

This is a shrubby plant which will fill a large space. It produces bright purple-pink flowers. H and S 2m (6ft). In the form 'Ice Cool' the flowers are a wonderful pure white.

LEUCANTHEMUM
Shasta daisy

A genus of 25 species that were once known as *Chrysanthemum* and indeed they resemble those plants. There are only a couple of species that are grown regularly in the garden, both having typical daisy-like flowers with a ring of outer white petals and a central yellow disc. They are not refined plants, and look their best in a cottage-garden setting. Shasta daisies are very tough. In a neglected garden, they will be virtually the last cultivated plants to disappear.

Cultivation These will grow in any reasonable garden soil, but they do best if it has been enriched with well-rotted organic material. They need a sunny position. Z5.

Propagation The easiest method of increase is to divide these plants in the spring.

Leucanthemum × superbum

The shasta daisies are rather coarse plants growing to about 1m (3ft) high, and eventually making a large clump. They need staking at an early stage. The white flowers are large, up to 10cm (4in) or more across and are often rather untidy looking, especially in the doubles. All this makes them sound undesirable but in fact they create a very

Leucanthemum × superbum 'Sonnenschein'

pleasing splash of white in the border and are easy to look after. S 60cm (24in).

There are a number of cultivars including several doubles: 'Horace Read', 'Esther Read', 'Fiona Coghill', 'Cobham Gold', 'T.E. Killin' and 'Wirral Supreme'. 'Aglaia' is an excellent semi-double. There are also plenty of very good singles including 'Phyllis Smith', 'Silberprinzes-schen', 'Alaska', 'Mount Everest' and many more. The flowers all have subtle differences. The cultivar 'Sonnenschein' has primrose-yellow flowers, and is worth growing.

Leucanthemum vulgare

This is the ox-eye daisy or marguerite of the roadside and meadow. It is a much more delicate plant than the above, with flowers that are usually about 5cm (2in) across. It is not particularly brilliant in the border but it is a must for a wild or meadow garden. H 45cm (18in) S 60cm (24in).

Lavatera × clementii 'Barnsley'

Leucanthemum maxicum

Liatris spicata

LIATRIS
Gayfeather

A genus of 35 species of which only a few are in cultivation. The difference between the various species in cultivation is botanical rather than visual and so there is little difference between them from a gardener's point of view. Liatrises are readily available from nurseries but they are not as widely grown as perhaps they ought to be. Their beauty is in the dense spikes of purple flowers that rise above a mass of narrow leaves: they look a bit like bottle brushes. A clump of these plants is always most colourful and makes a welcome addition to any border, so it is worth tracking them down.

Cultivation A moisture-retentive soil is needed for these plants, so make sure that there is plenty of well-rotted organic material in the soil. The soil should also be well-drained. A place in full sun is required. Z3.

Propagation The easiest method of increase is to divide the plants in spring. However, they can also be grown from seed sown at the same time of year.

Liatris aspera
This species has pinkish-purple flowers that are further apart in the spike. It flowers in summer. H 1m (3ft) S 30cm (12in).

Liatris pycnostachya
A tall species. The long-lasting flower heads are long, often over 30cm (12in). They are a reddish-purple and occasionally white. The plant blooms from summer into autumn. H 1.5m (5ft) S 30cm (12in).

Liatris spicata
This can also grow up to 1.5m (5ft) but does not usually reach this height in gardens. The flower spikes are pinkish-purple. This plant flowers from late summer onwards. S 30cm (12in).

There are several garden cultivars. 'Alba', as its name suggests, has white flowers as has the popular 'Floristan Weiss'. 'Floristan Violett' is similar but with violet-purple flowers. 'Kobold' is another popular form, especially in smaller gardens since it is a much more compact plant. It has violet-purple flowers.

LIGULARIA
Ligularia

This is a large genus of 180 species. About 20 are in cultivation, although only a few are generally available. They vary in appearance from plants with large orange, daisy-like flowers to those with tiny flowers held in a

Ligularia dentata 'Desdemona'

large airy spike. Most of the garden forms are tall. Many are rather coarse and are best placed in wild areas of the garden; others are more refined and make good border plants.

Cultivation Ligularia generally like a moist soil, so plenty of well-rotted organic material should be added before planting. They will grow in sun or partial shade. Some are susceptible to slugs. Z3.

Propagation Division in spring is the easiest method of increase, although species can also be grown from seed sown at the same time of year.

Ligularia dentata
One of the shorter species. It has orange daisies from late summer onwards. H 1.2m (4ft) S 60cm (24in). It is grown mainly as one of two cultivars: 'Desdemona', which has deep orange flowers and large, heart-shaped leaves that are purple underneath; and 'Othello' which is similar except that the leaves are also purplish on the top. Both are grown as foliage plants as well as for their attractive flowers.

Ligularia 'Gregynog Gold'
A tall species that bears heads of deep golden flowers, each with a browner centre. H 2m (6ft) S 60cm (24in).

Ligularia × palmatiloba
A medium height species with yellow flowers and lobed leaves. H 1m (3ft) S 75cm (30in).

Ligularia przewalskii
Tall spikes of small yellow flowers rise on black stalks from attractive divided foliage. This makes a good border plant. H and S 1m (3ft).

Ligularia 'The Rocket'
One of the best ligularias, this is similar to the previous one. The flower spikes resemble a rocket with trail of golden sparks. It is excellent for the back of a border since it is very tall. It also looks very impressive when grown as a large clump or drift. H 2m (6ft) S 1m (3ft).

Other plants If you have a large garden, especially with wild areas, then you might consider looking at some of the other species such as: *L. hodgsonii*, *L. sibirica*, *L. veitchiana*, and *L. wilsoniana*.

Ligularia 'The Rocket'

Flowers with good heads for drying

Acanthus	Humulus
Achillea	Liatris
Allium	Limonium
Anaphalis	Miscanthus
Catananche	Persicaria
Cortaderia	Rheum
Delphinium	Scabiosa
Eryngium	Solidago
Gypsophila	Stipa

Lilium auratum

Lilium 'Cover Girl'

Lilium regale

LILIUM
Lily

Everybody knows the lilies. This is a magnificent genus with more than 100 species and innumerable cultivars. They are bulbous plants. Most reach about 1m (3ft) in height but they are often much taller. They have a spread of up to 30cm (12in). The flowers vary in shape from trumpets, flared funnels and bowls to pendulous turkscaps and bells. There is also a wide range of colours with pure blue being about the only one missing. Many are fragrant. Lilies are excellent plants for the border, with different varieties growing in sun and shade. They can also be grown in containers. They are very good for cutting.

Cultivation A soil enriched with organic material is ideal for lilies, but it must be free-draining. Species vary: most like the sun and a few prefer shade. Slugs can be a nuisance and increasingly the scarlet lily beetles are becoming a real pest. It is important to check daily and kill these pests whenever they are seen or you will lose the plants. Z3–7.

Propagation There are several ways of increasing lilies. For the amateur the easiest method is simply dividing off the new bulbs that form around the old. Seed can be sown from the species. The brown or black bulbils that form on the stem can also be "sown".

Lilium auratum
A species which has wide-open, flared flowers. They are white with a golden centre and usually spots. This plant is the parent of several cultivars and a number of hybrids. H 1m (3ft).

Lilium candidum
This is the Madonna lily. It is a choice plant with pure white trumpets. H 1.5m (5ft).

Lilium lancifolium
Also known as *L. tigrinum*, or the tiger lily, this has orange turkscap flowers with reddish-brown spots. H 1m (3ft).

Lilium longiflorum
Long trumpet flowers in pure white. Prefers light shade. A good cut flower. H 1m (3ft).

Lilium martagon
A delightful turkscap lily for a woodland or shady setting. The flowers dangle airily from the stem and are purple. There are also white forms. H 1.5m (5ft).

Lilium pyrenaicum
A superb turkscap lily with masses of very narrow, bright green leaves and pendant yellow flowers with brown spots. Unfortunately the flowers smell of foxes, so they should not be planted near seating areas. Excellent plants in shade or sun. H 30–120cm (1–4ft).

Lilium regale
The doyen of the cottage garden, this has trumpet flowers. They are white in colour, but flushed with pinkish-purple on the outside. This species is very fragrant. H 1–1.2m (3–4ft).

Lilium speciosum
This large lily has white turkscap flowers with crimson spots. They have a delightful fragrance. The plant requires a shady position. H 1.5m (5ft).

Other plants Most species are in cultivation and there are many elegant cultivars – including 'Chinook', 'Cover Girl' and 'Enchantment'. Go to specialist nurseries to see the full range.

LINARIA
Toadflax

This large genus of more than 100 species has several that are garden-worthy. The attraction is the small antirrhinum-like flowers which are carried in erect spikes. These vary in colour from yellow to purple; some are bicoloured. Linaria are not in the top league of plants but they fill the spaces between other plants with a certain charm. Another advantage is that they are easy to grow.

Cultivation Any reasonable garden soil that is free-draining. They prefer a sunny position. Z7.

Propagation By far the easiest method of increase is from seed, although some of the linarias that run can be divided.

Linaria dalmatica
This plant carries spikes of large yellow flowers in summer. It creates a good drift. H 1m (3ft) S 60cm (24in).

Linaria purpurea
A good plant that self-sows but does not become a nuisance. The stems can rise to 1m (3ft) but are often shorter. They carry spikes of tiny purple flowers over a long period. There is a superb pink form, 'Canon Went' and a

Lilium 'Chinook'

Lilium 'Enchantment'

Lilium pyrenaicum

Lilium lancifolium

Linaria purpurea

white one, 'Springside White', both of which usually come true from seed. S 60cm (24in).

Linaria triornithophora

A slightly ungainly plant with large yellow and purple flowers. Good for the general border. H 1m (3ft) S 60cm (24in).

Linaria vulgaris

This is rather like a smaller and paler version of *L. dalmatica* except that it runs vigorously. It can become invasive in a border but earns its keep in a wild garden. H 75cm (30in) S 10cm (4in).

LINUM
Flax

A very large genus of more than 200 species of which only a few are in general cultivation. Those that are, however, are well worth

Linum narbonense

Linum perenne

their place in the garden. Some are annuals. The flowers are usually funnel-shaped, although some are so flared as to be almost flat. They come in yellow, red or blue; the blues being a good intense colour. The flowers often only last a day and the ground is frequently covered in colourful petals where they have dropped. The stems are rather thin but they are wiry and do not usually need support. Linums are excellent border plants.
Cultivation These plants will grow in most garden soils but they are longer lived if the soil is free-draining. A sunny position is essential. Z5.
Propagation The easiest method of increase is from seed sown in spring. Tip cuttings can also be taken from some species.

Linum narbonense

This is one of the two main border flaxes. It is a plant of great beauty: hundreds of blue flowers float on very thin stems in a hazy cloud. It is not long lived so it is worth propagating some spares every other year. H 45cm (18in) S 45cm (18in).

Linum perenne

This is very similar to the previous plant, except that it is even shorter-lived. Although it is a perennial, winter damp often kills it off, so have some spares. H 30cm (12in) S 15cm (6in).

LOBELIA
Lobelia

Most gardeners are familiar with the blue annual lobelia that is seen hanging from baskets and other containers. However, few realize just how many lobelia there are to choose from: there are 370 species in the genus. Many are tropical. These are very tall and cylindrical, with some resembling the rotating brushes found in car washes. However, there are also a handful of perennials that are a welcome addition to temperate gardens. These include some that produce the reddest of all garden flowers. Most need damp conditions and are most at home near water features.
Cultivation A humus-rich soil that doesn't dry out is required for most perennials. They prefer a sunny position but also grow well in shade. Most are on the tender side and suffer in damp winters so give them some protection in colder, wetter areas. Z2–3.
Propagation Most of the perennial lobelias should be propagated by division in spring.

Lobelia 'Bees' Flame'

A superb plant. It has rich purple foliage and tall spikes of the most brilliant scarlet flowers. A clump of them makes a stunning sight. H 75cm (30in) S 30cm (12in).

Lobelia cardinalis

This is similar to the previous plant, except that it is taller. The foliage is not quite so dark, except in some of the cultivars. H 1m (3ft) S 23cm (9in).

Lobelia 'Cherry Ripe'

Spikes of cherry-red flowers are set off against dark green foliage that is suffused with purple. H 1m (3ft) S 23cm (9in).

Lobelia 'Dark Crusader'

Another deep red-flowered variety with deep purple-red foliage. H 1m (3ft) S 23cm (9in).

Lobelia × gerardii 'Vedrariensis'

A wonderful border plant, this lobelia is upright, with a loose spike of purple flowers. The flowering season is long, and starts in the summer. H 1m (3ft) S 30cm (12in).

Lobelia 'Pink Elephant'

This has sugary pink flowers and green foliage. H 1.5m (5ft) S 30–35cm (12–14in)

Lobelia cardinalis

Lobelia 'Queen Victoria'

One of the best of the red forms, this carries bright scarlet flowers above purple leaves and stems. H 1m (3ft) S 23cm (9in).

Lobelia siphilitica

This plant produces a tall spire of blue flowers. Although it will grow in the sun, it is perfect for a shady position. H 1m (3ft) S 23cm (9in).

Lobelia tupa

This is a more tender (Z8) plant but it is well worth growing in warmer areas. It can be very tall and has a loose spike of red flowers that have an exotic quality about them. The foliage is unlike the other forms in that it is slightly furry. This plant needs a well-drained soil and a warm position. H 2m (6ft) S 1m (3ft).

Lobelia 'Cherry Ripe'

Lupinus polyphyllus

LUPINUS
Lupins

There is something tranquil about a clump of lupins. They are the quintessential plant of herbaceous borders and a vital ingredient in the cottage garden. There are more than 200 species, of which a handful are grown in gardens. The flowers are dense spires of pea-like blooms in either one or two colours. They have a gorgeous peppery fragrance. The leaves are also attractive; they are deeply divided, like fingers on a hand.
Cultivation A deep humus-rich soil is ideal, but it should be well-drained. A sunny position is needed. Modern lupins do not seem to last long and need replacing every two or three years to perform satisfactorily. Watch out for the grey lupin aphid. Z4.

Lupinus Russell hybrids

Propagation The simplest way to propagate is to grow lupins from seed, but for specific cultivars it is best to take cuttings in spring.

Lupinus 'Chandelier'
A delightful bicolour with dark and light yellow flowers. H 1m (3ft) S 60cm (24in).

Lupinus 'The Chatelaine'
This is a bicolour with rose-pink and white flowers. H 1.2m (4ft) S 45cm (18in).

Lupinus 'The Governor'
This is a bicolour with flowers of deep blue and white. H 1m (3ft) S 60cm (24in).

Lupinus 'My Castle'
This is a single-coloured, rose-pink lupin. A very satisfying plant when at its peak. H 1m (3ft) S 60cm (24in).

Lupinus 'The Page'
A single-coloured form whose blooms are a lovely carmine. H 1m (3ft) S 60cm (24in).

Lupinus polyphyllus
The species from which many garden hybrids have been bred. It is interesting to grow but the numerous cultivars derived from it are much better. H 1m (3ft) S 60cm (24in).

Lupinus Russell hybrids
Originally introduced in 1937, these are a wonderful selection of cultivars. Many of those currently available may not be descended from the original stock but they are still very good. H 1.2m (4ft) S 75cm (30in).

Other plants There is a similarity between many cultivars, with the main difference being the colour. So it may simply be a matter of choosing a strain that fits in with your colour scheme, rather than trying to obtain particular plants.

LYCHNIS
Lychnis

A small genus that is related to the garden pinks. There are a dozen or so species available for garden use. They are quite a diverse collection of plants, the

Lychnis × arkwrightii

majority being pink or white with a few being orange or flame-red. All the garden forms make good border plants and are especially good for informal or cottage-garden style borders.
Cultivation Any reasonable garden soil will do. However, the better the soil, the better the plants will do. Most prefer it to be well-drained. Place in full sun or light shade. Z3–4.
Propagation Most come readily from seed sown in the spring, but many of the clump-formers can also be divided in spring. Basal cuttings can be taken at the same time of year.

Lychnis × arkwrightii
A lowish plant with large flat flowers that are a superb bright orange. The foliage is brownish-purple and sets off the orange beautifully. This is a perfect plant for the hot border. It flowers in early to midsummer. H 45cm (18in) S 25cm (10in). There is a good cultivar, 'Vesuvius'.

Lychnis chalcedonica

Lychnis coronaria 'Alba'

Lychnis chalcedonica
Flat heads of flame-red are set off against a brightish green foliage. This plant grows tall but it needs support. An early to midsummer species. H 1m (3ft) S 45cm (18in). There are also a dirty-white form *albiflora* and muddy-pink form 'Rosea'; neither are as stunning as the species.

Lychnis coronaria
A frequently seen lychnis with furry silver stems and foliage, and the most vivid magenta flowers which appear during summer. There is a white form, 'Alba', and a white form with pink centres known as the Oculata Group. H 1m (3ft) S 45cm (18in).

Lychnis flos-cuculi
The ragged robin. It is not a good border plant since the flowers are too slight but it is excellent for damp areas such as bog gardens or areas beside natural streams, especially in meadow gardens. Flowers in early summer. H 45cm (18in) S 20cm (8in).

Lychnis flos-jovis
A small version of *L. coronaria*, except that the flowers are more refined and the plant more

Lychnis flos-jovis

compact. The main flower colour is a rose-pink to red but there are also white forms. H 75cm (30in) S 45cm (18in).

Lychnis × haageana

Another orange-flowered species, this time of moderate height. It flowers in early to midsummer but it is not long lived. H 75cm (30in) S 30cm (12in).

LYSICHITON
Skunk cabbage

Only two species make up this genus, both of which are grown in cultivation. These are not plants for small gardens (unless you like things on a grand scale). They both flower in early spring when there is not much else around. The flowers are relatively modest in size, but as the leaves get bigger the plant increases rapidly until it reaches 1m (3ft); it looks rather like a giant cos lettuce. One would be enough for most gardens, but they spread quite freely and soon create a grove of such monster lettuces. However, they are spectacular plants and if you have the space and the right conditions where they can grow alongside a stream or in a bog garden, then they are certainly worth having.
Cultivation A damp, rich soil, preferably near water. Plant in sun if possible but they will tolerate a little light shade. Z6.
Propagation The easiest method of increase by division of the small side growths. Alternatively sow the fresh seed in a compost (soil mix) that is kept wet, or directly into mud.

Lysichiton americanus

The most popular of the two species. This has bright yellow spathes or hoods, enclosing a spike of small yellow flowers on 30cm (12in) stems. The spathe adds another 15–20cm (6–8in) to the height. They have an unpleasant smell. S 75cm (30in).

Lysichiton camtschatcensis

Similar to the previous in shape and size but the spathe is pure white and the flower spike greenish-yellow. A sweetish scent. H 75cm (30in) S 60cm (24in).

Lysichiton americanus

LYSIMACHIA
Loosestrife

This is a large genus of about 150 species, a number of which are in cultivation. It should not be confused with the next genus, *Lythrum*, which is also commonly known as loosestrife. Plants in this genus have yellow or white flowers that are carried in tall spikes. They generally like moist conditions but as long as the borders have plenty of organic material they can be successfully grown there. They look most effective when grown in drifts. Most gently spread, forming large clumps. However, they are not difficult to control if they exceed their allotted space. The flowers consist of a shallow cup of five petals forming a star-shape. The plants vary in height from ground-hugging mats which are suitable for winding between plants at the front of a border to tall, 1.2m (4ft) ones, which are best placed at the middle or back.
Cultivation Lysimachia like a humus-rich soil in full sun or partial shade. Z3–5.
Propagation By far the easiest method of increase is to divide the plants in spring.

Lysimachia ciliata

A tall plant with loose spikes of slightly hanging, lemon-yellow flowers. It flowers in summer. H 2m (6ft) S 60cm (24in). There is an extremely good cultivar called 'Firecracker'. It has

Lysimachia ephemerum

brownish-purple foliage which sets the yellow off wonderfully. It also makes a good foliage plant, especially in spring.

Lysimachia clethroides

This species has curious crooked spikes of small white flowers from midsummer onwards. It is a beautiful plant. H 1.2m (4ft) S 60–100cm (2–3ft).

Lysimachia ephemerum

Tall plants with spikes of small white flowers with pinkish centres in summer. The leaves are bluish-green. H 1m (3ft) S 30cm (12in).

Lysimachia nummularia

This is normally grown in its golden-leaved form 'Aurea'. It is a running, mat-forming plant that

Lysimachia nummularia 'Aurea'

makes excellent ground cover, especially between other plants. The yellow flowers are individual rather than held in spikes, and appear through summer. This is a good foliage plant. H 2.5–5cm (1–2in) S indefinite.

Lysimachia punctata

This plant carries spikes of deep yellow flowers which are carried tightly against the stems and nestle amongst the leaves. It is very attractive but can be aggressive so it should be planted either where it can be controlled or in a wilder area, where it can rampage at will to make a large drift. H 60–75cm (24–30in) S 60cm (24in).

Lysimachia vulgaris

This plant is very similar to the last species but its flowers grow in loose spikes that arise from the axils (joints) of the leaves. It spreads and is best used in the wild garden. H 60-75cm (24–30in) S 60cm (24in).

Lysimachia punctata

Lythrum salicaria 'Feuerkerze'

LYTHRUM
Purple loosestrife

A genus of about 40 species, of which only one or two are deemed garden-worthy. Those that are grown make excellent border plants since they form clumps of bright pink-purple flowers over a long period. The flowers are carried in long spikes and the plants grow up to 1.2m (4ft) high. They can be placed in any border but they are particularly useful for planting in a bog garden, or beside a water feature.

Lythrum salicaria 'Robert'

Cultivation Lythrums need a moisture-retentive soil, so dig in plenty of well-rotted organic material before planting. They like a position in full sun. Z3.
Propagation The simplest way to increase your stock is to divide the clumps in spring. It is also possible to take basal cuttings, also in spring.

Lythrum salicaria
This plant gets its name from its narrow, willow-like leaves. It is one of the main border plants that is grown extensively in its own right but also in the form of a wide number of cultivars. It grows to about 1.2m (4ft) high and has tall spikes of pinkish-purple flowers from midsummer onwards over a long period. S 45cm (18in).

The cultivars are all variations on the same theme, the intensity of the pink or purple being the main varying factor. Good forms include 'Blush', 'Feuerkerze', 'Lady Sackville', 'Morden Pink', 'Robert' and 'Zigeunerblut'.

Lythrum virgatum
This is very similar to the previous species, except that it is not quite so tall and the flower spike is generally shorter. The flowers are purple, with those of some cultivars paler and others darker. H 1m (3ft) S 60cm (24in).

Again there are several cultivars. 'Dropmore Purple', 'Rose Queen', 'Rosy Gem' and 'The Rocket' are all worthy of a place in the border, but one or two of them would be enough for most gardeners.

MACLEAYA
Plume poppy

A small genus of which all three species are in cultivation. These are wonderful plants for the back of a large border. They can rise up to 2.5m (8ft) when given the right conditions, so they are not plants for a small garden. Another problem for the small garden is that macleayas tend to run and can become invasive, so they do need to be given plenty of room. However, there is no doubt that these plants are beautiful enough to earn their place in the large garden, because of both their

Macleaya cordata

foliage and flowers. The flowers are tiny and petalless. They are carried in airy sprays, creating an off-white or pinkish-coral haze. This is set off by the unusual greyish-green foliage, the colour of which is almost impossible to describe. The leaves are heart-shaped and lobed.
Cultivation Macleayas will grow in any reasonable garden soil, so long as it is well-drained. They require a sunny position. Watch out for slugs, which can be a problem with this plant. Another

Macleaya × kewensis

M. microcarpa 'Kelway's Coral Plume'

hazard is late frosts, which will cut them back although they will reshoot. Z3.
Propagation These plants can be divided in spring but they take a while to settle down again and do not always take. Alternatively use the thick roots as cutting material in early winter.

Macleaya cordata
A tall species, with whitish flowers that create a dangling haze. The flowers appear from midsummer onwards. This is possibly the least invasive of the macleayas. H 2.5m (8ft) S 60cm (24in). There is a very good cultivar, 'Flamingo', in which the flowers are pinker.

Macleaya × kewensis
This plant is similar to the above except the flowers are cream or buff in colour.

Macleaya microcarpa
A slightly short form but it is also the most invasive. The species is sometimes grown, but it is mainly cultivated as 'Kelway's Coral Plume', probably the most popular of all the plume poppies. It has coral-pink flowers which are carried throughout the summer. H 2–2.5m (6–8ft) S 1–1.2m (3–4ft). A more recent cultivar, 'Spetchly Ruby', has darker coloured flowers.

Malva moschata alba

MALVA
Mallow

This genus contains around 30 plant species, and is closely related to the genus *Lavatera*. This relationship is evident in the similar shape of the flowers, but mallow blooms are nowhere near as brash as those of their near-relations. Although still funnel-shaped, they are flatter and more open. The *Malva* genus also offers gardeners a wider range of colour, which not only includes pink and white but also purple and blue.

The plants are shorter and more herbaceous. They tend to grow between 45cm (18in) and 1.2m (4ft). They make good border plants and some are also perfect for naturalizing in the meadow garden.
Cultivation Mallows will grow in any reasonable garden soil. They prefer a place in full sun. Z3.
Propagation These are not easy plants to divide but they can be increased from basal cuttings in spring. Alternatively the species can be grown from seed which should be sown in spring.

Malva moschata

This, the musk mallow, is one of the gems of the genus. When happy with its conditions it will grow up to 1m (3ft) but it is often shorter. It produces masses of candy-pink flowers, which always seem to have a freshness about them. The plant continues producing flowers from the early summer right on into the autumn. It can be naturalized in grass. S 60cm (24in). It has an equally delightful form – *alba* – with white flowers.

Malva sylvestris

This is the other main garden species. It can grow a bit taller than the previous, up to 1.2m (4ft), but often flops rather than growing upright. The flowers are a pinkish-purple, usually with deeper coloured veins, and, again, are produced over a very long

Malva sylvestris 'Primley Blue'

season. S 1.2m (4ft). There are several cultivars, the most famous of which is 'Primley Blue' in which the flowers, as the name suggests, are blue, with pronounced darker veins. It tends to be prostrate rather than upright. Another excellent form, this time very upright, is the subspecies *mauritanica*. This has large, dark purple flowers. 'Brave Heart' is very similar.

MALVASTRUM
Malvastrum

There are number of species in this genus but only one of them, *M. lateritium*, is generally in cultivation. This plant is somewhat tender and so it is usually only grown in frost-free areas. It will last longer if the soil drainage is good, and makes an ideal candidate for the gravel or Mediterranean garden.

M. lateritium is a prostrate, sprawling plant that grows as tall as 25cm (10in) and up to 1m (3ft) across. It carries 5cm (2in) saucer-shaped flowers which are white with a narrow pink ring surrounding the yellow centre. The fresh-green leaves are shaped like those of the maple.
Cultivation This plant needs a well-drained position in full sun. It needs winter protection in colder areas. Z8.
Propagation Increase by taking softwood cuttings in summer. Malvastrum can also be grown from seed sown in spring.

MATTEUCCIA
Matteuccia

This is a small genus of ferns, of which only one species is frequently grown in our gardens. This is *M. struthiopteris*, the ostrich fern. It is so called because its large fronds resemble the tail feathers of the ostrich. Another name is the shuttlecock fern because the whole plant with its ring of fronds looks like a shuttlecock. When it is growing well, the plant reaches up to 1.5m (5ft) in height, with a spread of 75cm (30in). A space in a woodland area is the ideal setting. *M. orientalis* is occasionally also grown. This is similar but it only grows to H 60cm (24in) S 45cm (18in), making it more suitable for smaller gardens.
Cultivation Matteuccias grow well in moist, humus-rich soil in sun or partial shade. Z2.
Propagation The simplest method is division of the small plants that form around the main one. It can also be grown from spore.

Grasses and ferns

Grasses	Pennisetum
Arundo	*Phalaris*
Briza	*Stipa*
Calamagrostis	**Ferns**
Cortaderia	*Adiantum*
Elymus	*Asplenium*
Hakonechloa	*Athyrium*
Milium	*Dryopteris*
Miscanthus	*Osmunda*
Molinia	*Polystichum*

Matteuccia struthiopteris

Meconopsis cambrica

Meconopsis grandis

Mentha × piperita f. *citrata*

MECONOPSIS
Meconopsis

This is a genus of some 45 species of poppy-related plants. This relationship can be seen in the tissue-paper-like petals. Most of the flowers come in one of a range of wonderful blues, while others are yellow. There are also a few reds. Most of the species are in cultivation, but the majority are tricky to grow and are really the province of specialist growers.

With one exception, *M. cambrica*, these plants need a moist, buoyant atmosphere and so are best grown in damp, maritime areas where they do not dry out. They are most difficult in dry, hot areas. They are among the most beautiful of garden plants and look especially good in a woodland setting or planted amongst shrubs.

Cultivation Meconopsis need a deep, rich soil that remains moist and, if possible, a moist atmosphere around them. They like a partially shaded position. A special plot with plenty of well-rotted organic material that is regularly sprayed with water but which does not contain sitting water is necessary in dry, hotter areas. Z5–7.

Propagation They can be grown from seed sown as soon as it is ripe. Some species can be divided.

Meconopsis betonicifolia

The best-known of the blue poppies. It grows to a magnificent height and has large blue flowers, which appear in early summer. This is a really stunning plant when grown well. Unfortunately it is not long lived and so it is best to propagate it every year from seed to ensure its continuance. There are white forms. H 1.2m (4ft) S 45cm (18in).

Meconopsis cambrica

The Welsh poppy is the easiest meconopsis to grow. It is an attractive plant with yellow or orange flowers. They appear mainly in spring and early summer but continue sporadically throughout the summer. The plant will grow in sun or shade; the brightly coloured flowers look especially effective in a shady area. It needs deadheading regularly since it self-sows. H 45cm (18in) S 30cm (12in).

Other plants The above species are the two most popular plants, although *M. grandis* and *M. × sheldonii*, which are similar in appearance to *M. betonicifolia*, are also widely grown. If you have the right conditions and like meconopsis, there are plenty of other wonderful plants that you can search out.

MENTHA
Mint

The one thing most gardeners know about mint is that it runs. However, there is quite a bit more to them than that. There are about 25 species in the genus and quite a number of these are in cultivation. Many are for the herb garden and are of no real interest to the perennial gardener, but others are suitable for the border. They are mainly grown for their foliage, which adds flavour and fragrance to cooking, but the scents can also be appreciated in the garden. The flowers are not conspicuous but they attract bees and butterflies, which are a welcome addition to any garden.

Cultivation Any reasonable garden soil will do. Choose a sunny position. Most mints are inclined to be invasive so be careful with your choice of position. Either restrict their root run by planting in a pot or dig round them each year and remove questing roots.

Propagation Mints are very easy plants to increase by division at any time of year.

Mentha × gracilis

The species, ginger mint, is not of interest in the border but the form 'Variegata' is more attractive. This has darkish green foliage with bright gold markings, making it a useful foliage plant. H 45cm (18in) S 60cm (24in).

Mentha longifolia

This is one of the best border mints, although it is still invasive. It has greyish-silver foliage which can be very attractive, and spikes of lilac flowers. H 1.2m (4ft) S indefinite. A good form for border use is the so-called Buddleia Mint Group. There is also a variegated form.

Mentha longifolia Buddleia Mint Group

Mentha × piperita f. citrata

A special mint that smells of eau de cologne. H 20cm (15in) S indefinite.

Mentha suaveolens

This plant has quite large, round, hairy leaves. The form 'Variegata' is a good foliage plant: pale green leaves with nicely contrasting creamy blotches. H 30–45cm (12–18in) S 60cm (24in).

MILIUM
Milium

A small genus, of which only the marvellous *M. effusum*, in its golden form 'Aureum', is of interest. Known as Bowles' golden grass, this plant reaches just 30cm (12in), with a spread of 30cm (12in), but it has arching leaves in a lovely shade of yellow. Arising from the spring foliage are stems with delicate flower spikelets, both of which are also yellow. Use it to add a splash of sun to shady areas.

Cultivation Bowles' golden grass will grow in any good garden soil, but it prefers a woodland-type

Milium effusum 'Aureum'

soil with plenty of leaf mould. It also likes a lightly shaded position. Z5.

Propagation It will grow easily from seed and can also be divided in early spring as new growth gets under way.

MIMULUS
Musk

Mimulus is a large genus of some 150 species, some of which are perennials and are regularly grown in our gardens. They have tubular flowers that flare out at the end. The inner parts of the tubes are usually heavily spotted, sometimes resembling a monkey's face; monkey flower is another common name for the plant. The flowers are yellow, red, pink or orange and often a mixture of these. The plants generally like moist conditions and are ideal for lightening the edges of ponds or streams, or in a bog garden.

Cultivation Grow in a moist, humus-rich soil that never dries out. Some will thrive in shallow water. They like full sun or just a little light shade. Z3–7.

Propagation Most mimulus are easy to divide and cuttings can also be taken.

Mimulus 'Andean Nymph'

A wonderful plant with rose-pink tubes diffused with cream. The inside is lightly spotted red. It has a long flowering season. H 23cm (9in) S 25cm (10in).

Mimulus lewisii

This is a very good border plant that can be grown away from water. It forms a loose clump which is speckled with rose-pink flowers with pale throats over a long period. H 60cm (24in) S 45cm (18in).

Mimulus guttatus

Mimulus aurantiacus

Mimulus luteus

A yellow-flowered monkey flower with red spots in the throat. It spreads to make a dense mat and is perfect for the side of streams or ponds. H and S 30cm (12in).

Other plants There a many more attractive species and cultivars. Those in bright reds and oranges, such as 'Wisley Red', 'Fire Dragon' (gold and red), 'Western Hills' and 'Whitecroft Scarlet' as well as the taller *M. cardinalis*, are very good for hot borders, as are the red and orange forms of *M. aurantiacus* and *M. guttatus*.

MISCANTHUS
Miscanthus

This is an important genus of grasses to the gardener. It consists of about 20 species of which a number are in cultivation. They are grown mainly for their size and stunning appearance. Most are tall, up to 3m (10ft) or more when in flower. Then, they make a fountain of narrow leaves and

Miscanthus sinensis 'Gracillimus'

are topped with tall stems carrying elegant silky tufts of flowers. They are excellent plants for creating a focal point, either in a border or by themselves. They look particularly good next to water.

Cultivation These plants are usually happy in any reasonable garden soil, but they need a sunny position. Cut down the old foliage and flower stems in late winter. Z5.

Propagation Miscanthus need to be increased by division in early spring as new growth begins.

Miscanthus floridulus

A giant plant. The arching leaves are light green and rough along the margins. The flowers are white, but are only reliably produced in warmer areas. H 2.5m (8ft) S 1.5m (5ft).

Miscanthus sacchariflorus

This is very similar to the previous species, except that it is taller and produces its white

Miscanthus sinensis 'Variegatus'

flowers more reliably. It can be slightly invasive. H 3m (10ft) S indefinite.

Miscanthus sinensis

This is the species that is usually of most interest to gardeners. *M. sinensis* is widely grown in its own right but there are now more than 100 cultivars all varying by a small degree. H 3m (10ft) S 45cm (18in). Some of the cultivars are much smaller than the species, providing those with small gardens a welcome opportunity to grow these graceful plants. Some of the best cultivars are 'Flamingo', 'Gracillimus', 'Kleine Fontaine' (dwarf), 'Pünktchen', 'Silberfeder', 'Variegatus' and 'Zebrinus' (variegated), but there are many others to check out.

Miscanthus sinensis 'Flamingo'

Miscanthus sinensis 'Kleine Fontaine'

Miscanthus sinensis 'Zebrinus'

Molinia caerulea

Molina caerulea 'Edith Dudszus'

Monarda 'Cambridge Scarlet'

MOLINIA
Molinia

A tiny genus of two species of which only one, *M. caerulea*, is of interest to gardeners. However, there are also a large number of cultivars so the keen gardener does not go short of choice.

The main species has thick clumps of narrow arching leaves from which arise stiff stems carrying an airy array of upright flowers. They look particularly effective when covered with rain drops or dew. The top of the flower stems reach to about 1.5m (5ft), while the clump of leaves is about 60–75cm (24–30in). This versatile plant looks good in a border or in a lone position, especially by water.

Cultivation Molinia grows in any reasonable garden soil and, like most grasses, it needs a sunny position. Cut to the ground in late winter before the new growth begins. Z4.

Propagation The species can be grown from seed while the cultivars should be increased by division in spring, just before growth begins.

Molinia caerulea

This has been described above. The cultivars vary mainly in height and colour and all belong to one of the two subspecies described below. H 3m (10ft) S 60cm (24in).

Molinia caerulea subsp. arundinacea

This subspecies is generally taller and more airy than the next. The main cultivar is undoubtedly the magnificent 'Karl Foerster'. It can grow to 2.2m (7ft) and has delicate open flower heads. Both these and the leaves turn a wonderful golden-yellow in autumn. S 60cm (24in). Other cultivars that are worth looking at include 'Fontäne', 'Transparent' and 'Windspiel'.

Molinia caerulea subsp. caerulea

There are several cultivars here that are well worth checking out. They include 'Edith Dudszus' (dark flowers), 'Heidebraut' (yellow flowers), 'Moorhexe' (black stems),

Molinia caerulea subsp. *arundinacea*

'Strahlenquelle' (arching stems) and 'Variegata', which has variegated foliage.

MONARDA
Bergamot

This is a small genus of around 15 species. About half of them are in cultivation, and their number is greatly exceeded by the many cultivars available. One of the first things you notice about monardas is the strong scent that the bruised foliage gives off: it is a real pleasure weeding near them. The next is the curious shape of the flowers. They look like large thyme flowers and are arranged in dense whorls around the stem. The colours of the flowers vary from bright red to softer pinks

Monarda 'Prärienacht'

and purples and they appear in summer. These are perfect border plants and a large clump of them is always eye-catching. Some are quite tall, but the average height is about 1m (3ft), with a spread of 45cm (18in).

Cultivation These plants need a moist, humus-rich soil, otherwise they will dwindle and eventually die and they are also likely to suffer from mildew. They do best in a position in full sun. Z3.

Propagation The easiest method of increase is by division in spring, but basal cuttings can also be taken at the same time of year.

Monarda 'Beauty of Cobham'
This attractive plant has purplish-green foliage that nicely sets off the dense whorls of pale pink flowers held in purple bracts.

Monarda 'Cambridge Scarlet'
This is an old form, but is still one of the best. The flowers are bright scarlet.

Monarda 'Croftway Pink'
Another old cultivar. As its name suggests, it produces pink flowers.

Monarda didyma
One of the main garden species. It is from this that many of the cultivars are derived. The flowers are red or pink held with red-tinged bracts.

Monarda 'Petite Delight'
A lavender-rose form. It is short, reaching only half the height of most, at about 45cm (18in).

Monarda 'Petite Pink Supreme'
This is another short form, this time with red flowers and purple bracts. H 45cm (18in).

Monarda 'Prärienacht'
The flowers of this form are a wonderful clear purple.

Monarda 'Schneewittchen'
A good form with white flowers, which work well in a border with an all-white colour scheme.

Monarda 'Scorpion'
This one has purple flowers. It is a little taller than the others at about 1.2m (4ft).

Monarda 'Scorpion'

Monarda 'Squaw'

Another red-flowered form, but this has the advantage of being a little more mildew-resistant than the previous one.

Other plants There are quite a number of other species and cultivars that are well worth looking out for. Most are in the same colour range as those that have been listed above.

MYRRHIS
Sweet cicely

The only member of the genus is *M. odorata*. It was once widely used as a herb but it is now mainly grown for its decorative quality, although some cooks still use the leaves for flavouring fruit dishes. The delicate fern-like leaves are very finely cut. Above them in early summer are flat heads of tiny white flowers, much in the style of cow parsley, another hedgerow plant. The plant grows to about 60cm (24in) or more in

Myrrhis odorata

favourable conditions, with a similar spread. It looks good growing against a green hedge or against an old wall. Although it can be used to good effect in a border it makes an excellent plant for the wild garden.

Cultivation Any reasonable garden soil will suffice and a place in light shade seems to be best. It will self-sow if the seeds are allowed to be shed. Z4.

Propagation The simplest method of increase is from seed sown in spring. The plant can also be divided but this is not easy.

NEPETA
Catmint

A very large genus of around 250 species of which more than 40 are grown in gardens. However, there are only a few that are of specific interest to the general gardener. Most of these plants produce a haze of tiny, soft blue flowers carried on stiff arching stems; one produces blooms of pale yellow. The leaves are often aromatic.

Nepetas can be one of the mainstays of a romantic garden, and are at their best at the height of summer. Their pastel flower colours work very well with other soft shades, and can also be used to soften stronger neighbouring colours. Their love for well-drained soils makes the grey-leaved forms good for gravel or Mediterranean gardens. Generally nepetas grow no taller than about 1m (3ft) and they have a spread of 60cm (24in).

Cultivation Any good garden soil will do so long as it is free draining. Nepetas must have a sunny position. Cut them back after their first flush of flowers and then fresh foliage and more flowers will appear. Cats like the smell of some of these plants and will often lie on them crushing them to the ground.

Propagation Nepetas can be increased from basal cuttings in spring or by division at the same time of year.

Nepeta cataria

This is a coarser plant than the others. It has dirty-white flowers and greyish-green foliage. This species is the favourite for cats.

Nepeta clarkei

Nepeta clarkei

A nepeta with stiff upright stems and flowers of pure blue, which are accentuated by a white spot. H 80cm (32in).

Nepeta × faassenii

An excellent clump-forming plant with silvery-grey, aromatic foliage and pale blue flowers. It is a bit floppy but that adds to its hazy charm. H 45cm (18in).

Nepeta govaniana

The odd one out since it has pale yellow flowers carried loosely on stems up to 1m (3ft) high.

Nepeta nervosa

A much lower plant than other border species. It has upright stems containing spikes of blue flowers. It is a good front-of-border plant. H 45cm (18in).

Nepeta racemosa

This is similar (it is one of its parents) to *N. × faassenii* with the same soft blue flowers and ethereal appearance. However, it is a bit shorter. It is a good plant for flopping over the edge of paths. H 45cm (18in). 'Walker's Low' is a good compact variety. 'Snowflake', as its name suggests, has white flowers.

Nepeta govaniana

Nepeta racemosa 'Walker's Low'

Nepeta sibirica

A good plant for the mid-border. It has upright stems carrying pale blue flowers. H 1m (3ft).

Nepeta 'Six Hills Giant'

A cultivar with grey-silver leaves. It is similar to *N. × faassenii*, but the flowers are darker and it is much taller. H 1m (3ft).

Nepeta 'Souvenir d'André Chaudron'

This is similar to *N. sibirica*, but half the size. H 45cm (18in).

Nepeta subsessilis

A tall species with upright stems carrying bright blue flowers from midsummer. H 1m (3ft).

Nepeta 'Six Hills Giant'

Oenothera fruticosa

Oenothera fruticosa subsp. *glauca*

Oenothera speciosa

Origanum laevigatum

OENOTHERA
Evening primrose

A large genus containing 125 or so species, of which a number are in cultivation. Their main attraction is the flat saucer-like flowers that open mainly towards evening, which makes these plants ideal for commuters who only see their gardens at that time. Their colour is usually yellow although there are some white and pinks. Summer is their flowering time.

The plants vary considerably in their heights: there are prostrate ones whose stems crawl across the ground and tall ones that can reach 1m (3ft) or more. They are often short lived, especially in wetter soils.

Cultivation Evening primroses will grow in most garden soils so long as it is free draining – this is essential. They need a sunny position. Z4.

Propagation The species all come readily from seed but the cultivars generally need to be divided.

Oenothera acaulis

A plant for the front of a border or perhaps for a rock garden since it has quite prostrate stems. These carry flared funnel-shaped flowers that are white, turning to

pink as they age. This plant must have good drainage. H 15cm (6in) S 20cm (8in).

Oenothera caespitosa

Another low-growing species. It has white-cupped flowers that are fragrant. They also turn pink as they age – a feature of many oenotheras. They are short lived. H 12cm (5in) S 20cm (8in).

Oenothera fruticosa

This is the main perennial border species. It is an upright plant reaching up to 1m (3ft), although some of its cultivars are only half this tall. It has spikes of yellow or gold flowers. This plant will take a little light shade. S 45cm (18in).

'Fyrverkeri' is the best-known cultivar. The flowers open from red buds and the leaves are flushed with purple, making a beautiful plant. Another good cultivar is 'Yellow River'. There is a subspecies *glauca* (previously known as *O. tetragona*) which has pale yellow flowers.

Oenothera macrocarpa

This vibrant plant was previously known as *O. missouriensis*. It is a prostrate, species whose sprawling

stems produce flowers that are brilliant yellow. H 30cm (12in) S 40cm (16in).

Oenothera speciosa

This is a delightful species that tends to run among other plants. It is mainly prostrate. The flowers are white or pale pink with darker pink veins. H 30cm (12in) S 30cm (12in).

Oenothera stricta

A wonderful species with tall, gangling stems carrying yellow flowers opening from red buds. 'H 1.2m (4ft) S 30cm (12in). 'Sulphurea' is a delicate soft yellow. The flowers of both age to coral pink.

ORIGANUM
Marjoram

A genus with several species in cultivation, although many of the smaller ones are really only suitable for the alpine grower. The perennial ones have fragrant foliage and thin stems carrying sprays of purple flowers. They make excellent front-of-border plants but they do tend to spread by self-sowing. They can become a nuisance unless they are dead-headed before the seed is spread.

Cultivation These will grow in any reasonable garden soil. They prefer full sun, but will take a little light shade. Z7.

Propagation The species can be grown from seed sown in spring, and the cultivars are easily divided at the same time of year.

Origanum 'Kent Beauty'

A wonderful plant that will attract much attention. It is low in the ground, but it has flower heads that resemble very attractive hops.

The small pink flowers are tucked inside whorls of deep pink and green bracts. It likes a well-drained soil in a sunny position. Ideal for the front of a border. H 15cm (6in) S 30cm (12in).

Origanum laevigatum

Probably the main origanum for the perennial border. The flowers appear in sprays on the top of wiry stems. The flowers are pinkish-purple and have dark purple bracts around them, which make them appear to be in flower for a longer period than they really are. H 60cm (24in) S 20cm (8in). There are several good forms, of which 'Herrenhausen' is possibly the best.

Origanum vulgare

This is the wild marjoram. It is similar in many respects to the last, with sprays of pink flowers reaching up to 60cm (24in) in height but often less. It has several cultivars of which 'Aureum' is possibly the best. This has golden leaves and they remain golden for most of the season, making it a valuable foliage plant. This plant self-sows prodigiously so be sure to remove flower heads before it seeds. S 45cm (18in).

Oenothera fruticosa 'Yellow River'

Oenothera macrocarpa

Origanum vulgare 'Aureum'

Osmunda regalis

OSMUNDA
Royal fern

This is a genus of about 12 fern species of which only one, *O. regalis*, is in general cultivation. This splendid fern grows as high as 2m (6ft) when well suited but is often much shorter. The fronds are not as delicately cut as many garden ferns but still have a good shape and their vivid green sets off the central cluster of smaller flowering stems, which are covered with rusty brown spores. This fern likes a permanently damp position: a bog garden or a spot beside a stream or pond. S 1m (3ft).

O. cinnamomea and *O. claytoniana* are also worth checking out if you can find them.
Cultivation These need a damp position that does not dry out. The soil should contain plenty of humus. They grow in shade but will also grow in full sun if the situation is moist enough. Z2.
Propagation The easiest way to increase your stock of royal ferns is to divide the plants in the spring, just before the new growth begins. They can also be grown from spore.

OSTEOSPERMUM
Osteospermum

This is a delightful genus of roughly 70 species of which a number of the more hardy are in cultivation. Osteospermums are colourful daisies that always make a splash in the border. Colours of the outer petals include white, yellow and shades of pink through to purple, while the centres are yellow, purple or brown. They are wonderful plants for the front of a border or even for containers. Their only disadvantage is that they often shut up in dull weather and during the evening. Some are marginally tender so take cuttings each year to safeguard your stock.
Cultivation Any good garden soil as long as it is well drained. A sunny position is vital. Z8.
Propagation Take cuttings in spring or early summer.

Osteospermum 'Buttermilk'
As you would imagine from the name, the outer petals are very pale yellow, darkening towards the ends. The central disc is bluish-purple. This is a very good plant that flowers over a very long period. H 60cm (24in) S 30cm (12in).

Osteospermum 'Cannington Roy'
This is another gem. The outer petals are white with purple tips to them. As they age they become flushed with pink. The central disc is purple. This is shorter than the previous plant with a height of 25cm (10in). S 45cm (18in). There are several other Cannington hybrids covering the full range of colours.

Osteospermum jucundum
A very good plant with masses of flowers that have pinkish-purple petals and blue central discs. It is a late flowerer, producing blooms from late summer onwards. H 45cm (18in) S 30cm (12in). It has a number of cultivars. One of the best is the excellent 'Blackthorn Seedling', which has darker flowers in a rich purple.

Osteospermum 'Lady Leitrim'
This plant has white petals that fade to pink as they age. The central disc is blue. H 45cm (18in) S variable.

Osteospermum 'Nairobi Purple'
This is one of the lower-growing osteospermums. It carries flowers that have dark purple petals and a black central disc. It flowers over a long period from early summer onwards. H 25cm (10in) S 30–45cm (12–18in).

Osteospermum 'Whirlygig'
This cultivar is one of the most intriguing members of the genus.

Osteospermum 'Lady Leitrim'

The petals are pure white and the central disc is blue. Its attraction lies in the fact that the petals fold in half-way down their length. This makes the ends look like paddles, while the whole flower has the appearance of the ripples made in still water after a pebble has been dropped in – a truly wonderful shape. H 60cm (24in) S 30–45cm (12–18in).

Osteospermum 'White Pim'
The identification of this plant has still not settled down: it is still familiar to most gardeners as *O. eklonis prostratum* or to some as *O. caulescens*. This is one of the hardiest plants in the genus and it survives well in most gardens. The petals are white and the central disc varies but is often bluish. Flowers appear over a long season. H 60cm (24in) S variable.

Osteospermum 'Cannington Roy'

Osteospermum 'White Pim'

Paeonia lactiflora 'Bowl of Beauty'

Paeonia lactiflora 'Alice Harding'

Papaver orientale 'Curlilocks'

Papaver orientale 'Khedive'

PAEONIA
Peony

One of the most popular of all perennial species, these beautiful plants suit almost any type of garden, from old-fashioned cottage gardens to modern formal ones. There are only about 30 species of peony, most of which are in cultivation, but hundreds of cultivars have been bred from them. The typical peony has a bowl-shaped flower in varying shades of red, pink or white. There are also some rather fine yellows. As well as single flowers there are also semi-doubles and doubles. While the doubles are beautiful they do have the problem of being top-heavy, especially when filled with rain water, and they often sag miserably to the ground. The foliage of peonies is also very attractive, especially when it first emerges and some have very good autumn colour.

Cultivation Peonies need a deep rich soil, so add plenty of well-rotted organic material. They will grow in either sun or a light shade. They often take a while to settle down after being disturbed so try not to move them once established. Z3–5.

Propagation They can be divided in spring but this is not easy and they will take a while to settle down. Root cuttings taken in early winter is the easiest method.

Paeonia lactiflora

This white-flowered species is grown in its own right, but it is known mainly in the form of one of its hundreds of cultivars. There are far too many to mention but one exceptional one is given separately below and other ones to look out for include 'Adolphe Rousseau' (semi-double deep red flowers), 'Alice Harding' (pale pink double), 'Duchesse de Nemours' (double white), 'Félix Crousse' (double cerise), 'Festiva Maxima' (double white) and 'Monsieur Jules Elie' (double red).

Paeonia lactiflora 'Bowl of Beauty'

Deep rose-red petals and a large central boss of yellow make this a superb peony. H 75cm (30in) S 1m (3ft).

Paeonia mlokosewitschii

This is one of the most beautiful of peonies. It blooms in spring, making it one of the earliest to flower. The single flowers are

lemon-yellow. The foliage has reddish tints when it first appears and again in the autumn. As a bonus the plant also produces colourful seedpods in autumn. A great plant for any garden. H and S 75cm (30in).

Other plants There are so many other good peonies. Take a look at *PP. cambessedesii, mascula, tenuifolia,* and *veitchii,* as well as many of the other cultivars. If you get hooked, seek out a specialist nursery or get its catalogue.

PAPAVER
Poppy

This is another popular genus with many in cultivation, although many of these are annuals or short-lived perennials. The main perennial is *P. orientale,* which is one of the mainstays of the early summer border. The floppy coarse stems rise up to 1m (3ft) in height when supported. The flowers are great bowls of paper tissue in a variety of reds, pinks, oranges and white. They are not attractive once flowering is over, so place in the middle of the border where other plants will cover them or the gap they leave when cut back. S 1m (3ft).

Cultivars that are well worth growing include: 'Allegro' (scarlet with black basal markings on the petals), 'Black and White' (white with deep crimson basal markings), 'Cedric Morris' (pink with black basal markings), 'Curlilocks' (bright orange with frilled petals), 'Effendi' (orange), 'Goliath' (huge flowers, deep red, black basal marks), 'Khedive' (pale pink), 'Mrs Perry' (salmon-pink with black basal marks), 'Patty's Plum' (plum coloured), 'Perry's White' (white), 'Picotée' (white petals with an orange edge to them), 'Prinzessin Victoria Louise' (deep salmon-pink with black basal marks), 'Türkenlouis' (scarlet with black basal marks) and 'Turkish Delight' (soft pink).

Cultivation Choose a deep rich soil that is well drained and give them a sunny position. Give the plants some support in spring when they are about half-grown. Z2.

Propagation These plants can be divided with difficulty in spring but it is much easier to take root cuttings in the early winter.

PENNISETUM
Fountain grass

This is a large genus of grass, which has produced a number of very decorative plants for our gardens. The main characteristic as far as gardeners are concerned is the soft cylindrical flower heads, which look especially delightful when they have dew on them. These are flower heads to run your fingers through, so plant them near paths or at least at the front of a border. Pennisetums form rounded clumps from which the thin flowering stems arch. The flowers are buff or pink. They are not completely hardy so

Paeonia lactiflora 'Adolphe Rousseau'

Paeonia mlokosewitschii

Papaver orientale 'Effendi'

Pennisetum alopecuroides

Pennisetum villosum

Penstemon 'Sour Grapes'

Penstemon 'Russian River'

in colder areas it is important to propagate them regularly. Another problem is that they can look like grass weeds when they first appear in spring so take care not to weed them out.

Cultivation Pennisetums will grow in any reasonable garden soil as long as it is well drained. A sunny position is essential. Cut back the dead growth in early spring before the new growth appears. Protect in cold winters. Z6–8.

Propagation The easiest method of increase is from seed sown in spring. It is also possible to divide these plants just before the new growth starts in spring.

Pennisetum alopecuroides
A tall grass whose flower stems reach up to 1m (6ft) in height and 45cm (18in) in spread if conditions are favourable. The flowers are deep pink-purple and are held in long (20cm/8in) cylindrical spikes. They appear in late summer. This is a very attractive plant and there are also a number of cultivars. 'Hameln' is

interesting as it is a much shorter form (H 60cm/24in) and it flowers earlier. 'Little Bunny' is even smaller at H 40cm (16in).

Pennisetum orientale
This plant is similar to the previous one, but smaller with violet-pink flowers. H 45cm (18in) S 30cm (12in).

Pennisetum villosum
Another very attractive grass. It has arching stems carrying shorter and fatter cylinders of flowers that are a buff colour. H 45cm (18in) S 50cm (20in).

PENSTEMON
Penstemon
An invaluable genus for the garden. It contains more than 250 species. Many are of interest to the specialist grower, but only a few appeal to the perennial gardener. It is the many cultivars that make this such an important group of plants. The flowers are carried in loose spikes from early summer through to the frosts and beyond. They are tubular and often flared. The colour varies from pink to red and purple and also includes white. Most have at least two colours in them. The flowers of the species come in a wide range, including blue and yellow. These are excellent plants for growing singly or as drifts.
Cultivation Any reasonable garden soil will do, but better results will be achieved in a fertile soil. It should also be free draining. Penstemons need full sun. Z4–6.

Propagation The plants are easy to propagate from cuttings taken at any time of year, even winter.

Penstemon 'Alice Hindley'
This has widely flared tubes shaded in soft pinkish-blue and white. H 1m (3ft) S 30cm (12in).

Penstemon 'Andenken an Friedrich Hahn'
One of the hardiest, this produces wine-red flowers over a long period. Also known as 'Garnet'. H 1m (3ft) S 60cm (24in).

Penstemon 'Apple Blossom'
The flowers are large, with pink tips merging into a white throat. H 75cm (30in) S 60cm (24in).

Penstemon 'Burgundy'
This is a tall penstemon, carrying burgundy-red flowers. H 1.5m (5ft) S 60cm (24in).

Penstemon heterophyllus
A smaller-flowered plant with electric-blue flowers that are especially bright in the cultivar 'Heavenly Blue'. A superb plant. H 45cm (18in) S 25cm (10in).

Penstemon 'Hidcote Pink'
This has rose-pink flowers with crimson pencilling in the throat. H 1m (3ft) S 30cm (12in).

Penstemon 'Sour Grapes'
The flowers of this cultivar are tubes of purple. H 60cm (24in) S 60cm (24in).

Other plants Amongst others, look at 'Cherry' (red), 'Chester Scarlet' (scarlet), 'Pennington Gem' (pink), 'Russian River' (deep purple), 'Schoneholzeri' (scarlet) and 'White Bedder' (white), and the species *P. hirsutus* (white and mauve).

Pennisetum orientale

Penstemon 'Pennington Gem'

Penstemon hirsutus

Persicaria affinis (summer)

PEROVSKIA
Perovskia

This genus of seven species is little known, possibly because only one is in general cultivation. This is the delightful plant *P. atriplicifolia*. Strictly speaking it is classed as a sub-shrub rather than a perennial but it is usually treated as the latter by gardeners. From its shrubby base it throws up tall stems carrying airy spikes with soft violet-blue flowers. The small foliage is a soft grey and so the plant has a misty quality about it. It is perfect for a romantic setting, especially when mixed with other pastel colours. It grows to about 1.2m (4ft) with a spread of 1m (3ft), and the flowers appear from late summer onwards. The foliage is aromatic. There is a shorter cultivar, 'Little Spire', and a couple of other hybrids of which 'Blue Spire' is the most popular. It is essentially the same as *P. atriplicifolia*, except for the deeply divided leaves.

Perovskia 'Blue Spire'

Persicaria affinis (autumn)

Cultivation Any reasonable garden soil will do but it must be well-drained. It is important to plant in full sun. Prune each year's growth back to old wood near the base. Z6.
Propagation The easiest method of increasing perovskias is to take cuttings in summer.

PERSICARIA
Persicaria

This genus was until relatively recently part of what was known as *Polygonum*. About 70 species were moved to this genus, quite a number of which are worthy of cultivation. The flowers of most are small and carried cylindrical spikes, the majority being pink of one shade or another. They are normally held well above the foliage. This is dense, making good ground cover. The plants are useful for creating a mat between other plants, either in a border or in some odd corner where ground cover is needed simply to suppress weeds. The foliage of some species also has the advantage of producing good autumnal colours which in some cases continues well into the winter. These are easy, obliging plants and yet add colour to the borders at most times of the year.
Cultivation Persicarias will grow in any reasonable garden soil and they can thrive in either sun or partial shade. Z3–6.
Propagation The easiest method of propagating persicarias is by division in the spring.

Persicaria affinis
This is a wonderful ground-cover plant. It is low growing: up to 25cm (10in) to the top of the flowers with the mat of foliage reaching half that. The spikes of

Persicaria amplexicaulis

flowers are pink, and age to red then brown. The leaves similarly age to red and brown, and make good winter cover. S 30cm (12in). There are several good cultivars including 'Dimity', 'Donald Lowndes' and 'Superba'.

Persicaria amplexicaulis
A clump-forming plant, which is ideal for the middle or back of a border. It has large leaves, which are topped by a narrow cylinder of flowers on thin stems: these seem to whiz out of the foliage like fireworks. H and S 1.2m (4ft).

The main colour is red but there are cultivars with other colours such as 'Alba' (white), 'Firetail' (bright red, very thin spikes), 'Inverleith' (dark red) and 'Rosea' (pink).

Persicaria bistorta
Although this will grow in a border if the soil is moist enough, it is primarily a plant of damp places and so it does well in bog

gardens or beside water. The large leaves form a low (30cm/12in) mat above which the flower spikes rise. The flowers are a sugary pink and contrast well with the leaves below. They appear in spring. It makes excellent groundcover; and will spread gently without becoming a nuisance. S indefinite. There is a good form 'Superba', which produces bigger flower spikes.

Persicaria virginiana
Although the species is often grown in its own right, it is mainly found in the form 'Painter's Palette'. The attraction here is the large leaves, which are splashed with green, cream, brown, pink and red. As with the main species, the loose flower spikes are greenish, aging to red. H and S 60cm (24in).

Other plants Cast an eye over *PP. campanulata, capitata, milletii* and *vacciniifolia* if you can find them.

Persicaria bistorta

Phalaris arundinacea

Phlox divaricata 'Chattahoochee'

Phlox paniculata 'Mother of Pearl'

PHALARIS
Phalaris

This is a genus containing about 15 species of which the majority are far too weedy for the garden. The only one that is generally grown can also be considered a weed since it can become very invasive. It is so beautiful, however, that a special place should usually be found for it. It is *P. arundinacea* var. *picta*, which is known as gardener's garters. The attractive feature of this plant is the leaves which are pale green striped with silvery white and with occasional pink flushes. It does run, so be sure to contain it in some way or plant it where it can romp freely. The greenish flower stalks can reach 1m (3ft) but are often less. S indefinite. There is another form *P.a.* 'Feesey' which has pinkish-purple flushes and is not quite so rampant.

Cultivation Any garden soil will be sufficient for this plant, but it must have a sunny position. Plant it in a sunken bucket or surround in some other way to prevent it from spreading too far. Cut down old growth before the new starts in spring and trim it over again in early summer. Z4.

Propagation Its invasive habit means that this plant is very easy to propagate by division in spring.

PHLOX
Phlox

There are 67 species of phlox, a number of which are in cultivation. There are three different forms: the tall border phloxes, the low cushions for use on rock gardens and border edges, and an intermediate-height group which are good for woodlands and shady places. They all have the same shaped flowers. These consist of a disc of five petals, which are narrower in some species than others. They are all colourful, some intensely so. They range from soft pinks and mauves to bright reds, taking in purples and whites. The main border species is *P. paniculata* which has a large number of cultivars.

Cultivation The majority of these plants need a rich, moist soil, although it should be well drained. Most grow in full sun or light shade. Z4.

Propagation They can be divided or basal cuttings can be taken in the spring. However, the taller species can suffer from stem eelworm and so it is best to propagate them from root cuttings taken in early winter.

Phlox carolina

This is mainly grown in the excellent form of 'Bill Baker' which has pink flowers in early summer. It makes a very good plant for the edges of woodland gardens, or for areas of light shade with a woodland-type soil. H 45cm (18in) S 30cm (12in).

Phlox divaricata

Another woodlander growing in moist soil. This has pale blue or white flowers on stems growing up to 45cm (18in) high. There are a number of cultivars, the most spectacular of which is 'Chattahoochee' whose lavender flowers have a rose-pink centre. The plant is not long lived and needs regular replacement. H 45cm (18in) S 30cm (12in).

Phlox douglasii

A low mat-forming species with small flowers in spring. It is excellent for the front of the border. H and S 20cm (8in).

There are many colourful cultivars, including 'Crackerjack' (magenta) and 'Red Admiral' (bright crimson).

Phlox paniculata

This is the main border phlox. The elegant flowers are often subtly perfumed, and appear from midsummer onwards. H 1.2m (4ft) S 60cm (24in).

The many cultivars include 'Blue Ice' (pale blue), 'Bright Eyes' (pale pink with red eyes), 'Eventide' (pale blue), 'Fujiyama' (pure white), 'Hampton Court' (lilac-blue), 'Le Mahdi' (violet with darker eyes), 'Mother of Pearl' (pink-tinged white) and 'Norah Leigh' (variegated leaves and pale mauve flowers with dark centres).

Phlox subulata

Like *P. douglasii*, this is low growing and covered with masses of flowers in spring. H 10cm (4in) S 20cm (8in). A good variety is 'Marjorie' (deep pink).

Phlox douglasii

Phlox paniculata 'Hampton Court'

Phlox paniculata 'Norah Leigh'

Phormium tenax 'Variegatum'

PHORMIUM
New Zealand flax

The two species of this genus are important garden plants. They are clump-forming plants on a grand scale, producing a huge fountain of wide sword-like leaves and, occasionally, towering sprays of red or yellow flowers. There is a surprising number of cultivars, mainly with different coloured foliage. The flower stems can reach up to 5m(16ft) in height, and the clump of leaves are up to 2.5m (8ft) tall. These impressive architectural plants make ideal focal points either in a border or freestanding at some other point in the garden. Their size dictates that they are really only suitable for larger gardens, but there are some smaller cultivars that would suit those with less space. They are excellent for seaside gardens.
Cultivation These plants need a well-prepared free-draining soil and a sunny position.
Propagation Although it is a struggle with such a large plant, division is the best method of increase. Fortunately it is possible to break off a small piece without digging up the whole plant.

Phormium cookianum
This is the smaller of the two species with leaves that reach up to 1.5m (5ft) and flower stems that are a little taller. It has yellowish flowers. S 30cm (12in). The form *P.c.* subsp. *hookeri* 'Tricolor' is the most popular cultivar. Its green leaves have red and yellow stripes.

Phormium 'Sundowner'
This is a gem of a plant, which is about the same height as the previous one. It has erect bronze-coloured leaves attractively striped in pink and yellow. H 1.5m (5ft) S 1.2m (4ft).

Phormium tenax
This is the big one. Although some leaves are arching, the majority tend to stand up giving it a good shape. H 3m (10ft) S 1–2m (3–6ft). There are a number of cultivars of which the Purpureum Group, with its purple foliage, is the most popular. 'Variegatum' with cream stripes is also a good cultivar.

PHUOPSIS
Phuopsis

The only species of this genus, *P. stylosa*, is a low-growing spreading plant carrying beautiful balls of pink flowers over a long period in the summer. The spreading stems root as they go so it can be a nuisance in the wrong place. However, it is very attractive placed at the front of a border where it can weave between other plants. It has a slight foxy smell, to which some people object. H and S 30cm (12in).
Cultivation Any reasonable garden soil is suitable. It will grow in full sun or light shade. Cut back after flowering reduce spreading. Z6.
Propagation Phuopsis can easily be propagated by dividing the plants in the spring.

PHYGELIUS
Phygelius

Both species of this genus are in cultivation and there is also a hybrid between them. They are actually shrubs but they are

Phuopsis stylosa

usually considered perennials by gardeners. They are grown for their tall stems carrying loose sprays of pendant tubular flowers. These are red, pink or yellow, and appear over a long period, from early summer to autumn. The plants can get very tall, up to 3m (10ft) or more, but generally they are around 1–1.5m (3–5ft) tall, with a spread of 2m (6ft). They are not startling plants but more than earn their keep in a border.
Cultivation Phygelius need a reasonably rich soil which is free-draining yet moisture-retentive. They need a sunny position. Z8.
Propagation The best method of increase is to take softwood cuttings in early summer.

Phygelius aequalis
This plant has dusky-pink flowers. It has a few cultivars of which 'Yellow Trumpet' is one of the best, with pale yellow flowers.

Phygelius aequalis

Phygelius × rectus 'African Queen'

Phygelius capensis
This is a slightly bigger plant than the previous species, and has orange-red flowers.

Phygelius × rectus
This is the hybrid between the two species above. There are a number of interesting forms. 'African Queen' is one of the best known, with its red flowers. 'Moonraker' has pale yellow flowers. 'Pink Elf' is shorter at H 75cm (30in) and has pink flowers with deeper coloured tips. 'Salmon Leap' has salmony-orange flowers and 'Winchester Fanfare' has deep reddish-pink flowers.

PHYSOSTEGIA
Obedient plant

One species of this small genus is grown in the garden. *P. virginiana* is called the obedient plant because

Phygelius × rectus 'Moonraker'

Physostegia virginiana subsp. *speciosa* 'Bouquet Rose'

P.v. ssp. 'Variegata'

Platycodon grandiflorus

when the flowers are pushed to one side, they stay in position instead of springing back. The spikes of flowers are tubular and flared at the end, rather like those of antirrhinums. They are either pink or white and appear from midsummer onwards on stems up to 1.2m (4ft) high. The plant has a spread of 60cm (24in).

There are several cultivars. 'Alba', 'Crown of Snow' and 'Summer Snow' are white as their names suggest. *P.v.* subsp. *speciosa* 'Variegata' has whiter margins to the greyish leaves and cerise flowers. Another *speciosa* cultivar is 'Bouquet Rose', which has pale mauve-pink flowers. *P.v.* 'Vivid' has bright purple-pink blooms.
Cultivation Grow in any reasonable garden soil so long as it does not dry out too much; add plenty of well-rotted organic material. They like full sun or light shade. Z4.
Propagation Increase is by division in early spring. The species can be grown from seed.

PLATYCODON
Balloon flower

A genus with *P. grandiflorus* as its only species. The English name refers to the flower which inflates itself like a balloon just before it fully opens. It is closely related to the bell flowers and resembles them when open. The five petals form a shallow dish with the tips bent back. The colour is a wonderful violet-purple. These are not big plants, reaching only 60cm (24in) in height and with a spread of 30–45cm (12–18in) but they make excellent plants for the centre of a bed in late summer when the flowers open. There is a white form 'Alba' as well as pink forms such as 'Perlmutterschale' and 'Fuji Pink'. 'Apoyama' and 'Mariesii' are possibly the best blue forms, the latter being a more compact plant.
Cultivation Any well-drained garden soil will do, but it must be capable of retaining some moisture throughout the summer. Either a sunny or partially shaded position will suffice. Z4.
Propagation Taking basal cuttings in spring is probably the easiest method of increasing your stock.

Platycodons can also be divided but this can be tricky since they do not like to be disturbed.

PODOPHYLLUM
Podophyllum

A small genus of plants of which two or three are in cultivation, although they are not frequently seen. They are woodland plants and are best planted in such areas since they are not really border plants. The foliage has the curious habit of emerging through the ground like a folded umbrella before opening. At least one species hides its flowers beneath these leaves which is intriguing, but does not help its popularity. In spite of this shyness they make good shade plants and they do at least have attractive leaves. The flowers are followed by large, plum-sized coloured fruit. These are plants for those who want to grow something different. They will spread to form a large clump for those who have space.
Cultivation Podophyllums like a deep moist soil, such as a woodland soil with plenty of leafmould or other organic

material. They will grow in sun but are better suited to dappled shade under trees or amongst shrubs. Z3–7.
Propagation These plants spread by underground rhizomes so they can easily be divided. They can also be grown from seed, which should preferably be sown as soon as it is ripe.

Podophyllum hexandrum

This plant used to be known as *P. emodii*, a name which is still more familiar to many people than its new one. It produces solitary white flowers on each stem before the leaves unfold from their furled umbrella. When the leaves do open they are large and mid-green with brownish-purple mottling that makes them rather attractive. The ensuing red fruit are large and plum-shaped. H 45cm (18in) S 30cm (12in). There is a variety *chinense* which has pink flowers and deeper divisions in the leaves.

Podophyllum peltatum

This is the other major podophyllum grown in our gardens. In contrast to the previous one, the leaves open before the flowering. This is a shame since the 5cm (2in) cup-shaped flowers hang down and are obscured by the leaves. They are a rather attractive pale pink or white, and are followed by yellowish-green, or sometimes reddish, fruit. H 30–45cm (12–18in) S 30cm (12in).

Physostegia virginiana 'Summer Snow'

Red-hot perennials

Canna 'Assault'	*Lobelia tupa*
Canna 'Endeavour'	*Lychnis chalcedonica*
Crocosmia 'Lucifer'	*Mimulus cupreus* 'Whitecroft
Dahlia 'Bishop of Llandaff'	Scarlet'
Geum 'Mrs Bradshaw'	*Mimulus* 'Wisley Red'
Hemerocallis 'Berlin Red'	*Papaver orientale* 'Glowing
Hemerocallis 'Little Red Hen'	Embers'
Hemoracallis 'Stafford'	*Penstemon* 'Flame'
Kniphofia 'Prince Igor'	*Potentilla* 'Gibson's Scarlet'
Leonotis leonurus	*Tropaeolum speciosum*

Podophyllum hexandrum

Polemonium caeruleum

POLEMONIUM
Jacob's ladder

This genus of about 25 species includes 20 or so that are cultivated, although there are only a handful that are really popular. It is a delightful group; the flowers are generally blue or pink and have a decidedly fresh look about them. The majority are funnel-shaped blooms, with some being flatter than others. They flower in spring or early summer, making them perfect plants for the early border. Their foliage is often composed of leaflets on either side of the stem, resembling a primitive ladder, hence its English name.
Cultivation These will grow in any reasonable garden soil, but they do best in a moisture-retentive one. They will grow in either full sun or partial shade. Z4.
Propagation The species can be easily grown from seed (some will self-sow). Alternatively, they can all be divided in spring.

Polemonium carneum

Polemonium foliosissimum

Polemonium caeruleum
This is the species that best exhibits the Jacob's ladder foliage. It is a tall, upright plant topped with loose clusters of blue flowers. It flowers in early summer. H 1m (3ft) S 60cm (24in). The form *album* has white flowers as does 'Everton White'. 'Brise d'Anjou' has variegated foliage; *P. foliosissimum* is similar.

Polemonium carneum
This is a delightful plant with saucer-shaded flowers of the most delicate pink. It is a loose, clump-forming plant which flowers in early summer. It makes a good front-of-border plant. H 40cm (16in) S 45cm (18in). It has a variety 'Apricot Delight', which produces flowers of that colour.

Polemonium 'Lambrook Mauve'
A loose, clump-forming plant with masses of beautiful mauve flowers from late spring. A superb plant for the front of border. H 30cm (12in) S 30cm (12in).

Polemonium pauciflorum
This is the odd one out since it produces long tubular flowers that are pale yellow flushed with red and appearing in midsummer. It is a tallish plant making it suitable for mid border use. H 45cm (18in) S 15cm (6in).

Polemonium reptans
A low-growing, rather sprawling plant but one that is blessed with fine flowers especially in its numerous cultivars. Those of the species are blue. H 30cm (12in) S 30cm (12in). 'Blue Pearl' is a good blue form, while 'Virginia White' is white. 'Pink Dawn' is, as its name suggests, pink.

Polygonatum × hybridum

POLYGONATUM
Solomon's seal

These are graceful plants with an air of tranquillity about them. There are about 50 species in all but only a few are in general cultivation. They are characterized by arching stems from which dangle creamy-white bells, usually hanging in pairs; the pointed oval leaves are held stiffly above them like wings. Although these can be grown in sun they often do best planted in cool, dappled shade, such as under trees or shrubs. They are plants to look at individually rather than in a crowded border where their effect is lost.
Cultivation If possible, plant in a moisture-retaining, woodland-type soil. They do best in light shade, but full sun is all right if the soil is kept moist. Z4.

Polygonatum hookeri
This is a gem. It is also unusual owing to its bluish-pink flowers. It spreads between other plants. H 10cm (4in) S 30cm (12in).

Polygonatum × hybridum
This is probably the main garden species. It forms large clumps or drifts but is not invasive. The creamy-white flowers hang in fours. They appear in spring. H 1.2m (4ft) S 1m (3ft).

Polygonatum multiflorum
This is the other main garden species. It is similar to the previous except the flowers are possibly whiter and it is shorter growing. H 1m (3ft) S 30cm (12in). There is also a variegated form called 'Striatum'.

Other plants There are a number of other species worth looking at, especially *P. hirtum* with its broader leaves, *P. biflorum*, and the variegated form *P. odoratum* var. *pluriforum* 'Variegatum'. If you are interested in Solomon' seals then there is a closely related but little-known genus *Disporum* that you may want to check out.

POLYSTICHUM
Shield fern

This is a large genus of some 200 evergreen species of fern. About 20 of these are in cultivation although only a couple of these are seen with any frequency. These have a typical fern shape with lance-shaped fronds that arise from a central crown, reminiscent of a shuttlecock, and unrolling as they emerge. The fronds are deeply cut and make attractive plants for a shady position, either under trees or shrubs, or in the

Polygonatum odoratum var. pluriforum 'Variegatum'

P. setiferum 'Pulcherrimum Bevis'

shade of a house. Dappled shade is the best place to show them off. They add a cool tranquillity to the scene and make a good contrast to bright golden flowers of, say, *Meconopsis cambrica*.
Cultivation They need a deep woodland-type soil, well supplied with rotted organic material. They should be grown in the shade. Z5.
Propagation Shield ferns can be divided in spring, just before growth starts. Alternatively they can be grown from spore.

Polystichum acrostichoides
This fern has narrow fronds that are up to 60cm (24in) long with a spread of 45cm (18in).

Polystichum aculeatum
A popular polystichum, this is also called the hard shield fern. Its narrow, dark green fronds are up to 60cm (24in) long.

Polystichum munitum
This is rather different from the rest since the fronds are not soft but leathery and somewhat glossy, making them good for reflecting light in dull areas. They are narrow and up to 1m (3ft) long, with leaflets that are not subdivided. S 30cm (12in).

Polystichum setiferum
This is the most popular species and it has 30 or so cultivars, all varying slightly from the species, which has long fronds. These may be up to 1.2m (4ft) in ideal conditions but are more usually

around 1m (3ft). S 45cm (18in). There are various groups of cultivars that are worth considering. These include the Divisilobum Group, the Plumosodivisilobum Group and the Plumosum Group. Other attractive cultivars include 'Dahlem', 'Herrenhaussen' and 'Pulcherrimum Bevis'.

Other plants If you get hooked on ferns it is a good idea to visit specialist nurseries and browse through their catalogues.

POTENTILLA
Cinquefoil
This is a very large genus containing more than 500 species. The majority of garden-worthy plants fall into two camps, the shrubs and the perennials. The latter are of interest here, although it must be said that the shrubs are very useful in mixed borders. They have flat or saucer-shaped flowers with five petals (sometimes they are doubles) in various colours from white through to the most vivid of reds. They tend to be sprawling plants that wend their way pleasingly around and through other plants. They bring splashes of colour to the front and mid border.
Cultivation Cinquefoils will grow in any reasonable garden soil. They prefer a sunny position. Z4.
Propagation The best way of increasing your stock is to divide potentillas in spring.

Potentilla alba
A mat-forming plant with large leaves and loose sprays of white flowers in spring. H 10cm (4in) S 8cm (3in).

Potentilla 'Gibson's Scarlet'

Potentilla neumanniana

Potentilla atrosanguinea
The foliage often has silver hairs, especially on the underside. The flowers are red, orange or yellow. They appear over a long period in the summer. H 45cm (18in) S 60cm (24in).

Potentilla 'Gibson's Scarlet'
This is a real show-stopper. It carries flowers of the most brilliant scarlet throughout the summer. H and S 45cm (18in).

Potentilla nepalensis
One of the best, with excellent cultivars. It is loose and sprawling with masses of crimson, orange or pink flowers. H 50cm (20in) S 60cm (24in). Some of the cultivars are bicoloured. Among the best are 'Miss Willmott' (reddish pink flowers with a

darker centre), 'Ron McBeath' (carmine with a darker centre) and 'Roxana' (bright pink with a darker centre).

Potentilla neumanniana
Another mat-former for the front of a border. It has yellow flowers. H 10cm (4in) S 30cm (12in).

Potentilla recta
An erect plant that is good for scrambling through other plants. It has yellow flowers. H 60cm (24in) S 60cm (24in). 'Warrenii' is the best-known form, again with yellow flowers. *P.r.* var. *sulphurea* has beautiful soft yellow flowers.

Potentilla 'William Rollison'
This is a startling semi-double with bright orange suffused with yellow. H and S 45cm (18in).

Potentilla nepalensis 'Ron McBeath'

Potentilla 'Blazeaway'

Primula bulleyana

Primula japonica

Primula vialii

Pulmonaria saccharata

PRIMULA
Primula

One of the most delightful genera of all garden plants. It is surprisingly large with more than 400 species and innumerable cultivars. Most are in cultivation, but mainly with specialist growers. However there are still a large number that are grown in the general garden. They vary from those that are only a few centimetres high to tall candelabra types up 1m (3ft) tall. Most prefer shade and so they make excellent plants for under trees or shrubs. They are also good for damp positions beside streams or ponds and in bog gardens.
Cultivation All the perennial garden types need a moist soil. They prefer light shade but will grow in sun. Z4–7.
Propagation Most will come easily from seed and many can also be easily divided in spring.

Primula bulleyana
A candelabra primula with tall stems carrying whorls of red flowers that eventually fade to

orange. The flowers are produced in the summer. H 60cm (24in) S 30cm (12in).

Primula denticulata
Known as the drumstick primula. Its stems carry a terminal ball of purple flowers. Spring flowering. H 45cm (18in) S 30cm (12in).

Primula florindae
This is a very tall primula. Its stems carry a terminal cluster of flowers which hang down. They are yellow and appear in summer. H 1m (3ft) S 60cm (24in).

Primula japonica
A candelabra primula which carries whorls of red or white flowers in late spring and early summer. It is very easy to grow. H and S 45cm (18in).

Primula pulverulenta
A tall candelabra primula with stems carrying whorls of purple-red flowers in early summer. H 75cm (30in) S 45cm (18in).

Primula veris
The cowslip is a meadow plant and likes an open position. It is ideal for the wild garden. It flowers in late spring. H and S 15–20cm (6–8in).

Primula vialii
A orchid-like primula with stems carrying a pyramidal cluster of smaller flowers. They are mauve when open but the buds above them are crimson, giving a wonderful two-toned effect. The flowers appear in the summer. H 45cm (18in) S 30cm (12in).

Primula vulgaris
It seems impossible to imagine a garden without primroses growing in it. These ones are low, with stems that carry a single soft yellow flower in the spring. H and S 20cm (8in).

PULMONARIA
Lungwort

A small genus of about 15 species of which a number are in cultivation. These are late-winter and spring-flowering plants. They produce small funnel-shaped blooms in blue, pink, red and white. They are carried in clusters on top of stems which rise up to 30cm (12in) above the ground, with a spread of 30cm (12in). The foliage is rough with bristly hairs and in many cases has silver blotches. If the stems and leaves are cut to the ground after flowering new foliage appears. It remains fresh for the rest of the summer, and the lungwort earns its keep as a foliage plant. They will grow in sun but do best in light shade and are excellent for growing under shrubs.
Cultivation Pulmonaria need a fertile soil that does not dry out too much. As long as the soil is

kept moist they can be grown in full sun, otherwise a position in light shade is best. Z3.
Propagation The plants are easily divided in spring.

Pulmonaria angustifolia
This species produces attractive blue flowers and foliage that is a plain green but which is often edged in brown.

Pulmonaria 'Beth's Pink'
A excellent fresh-looking form with deep pink and blue flowers. There is a light silver spotting on the leaves.

Pulmonaria 'Lewis Palmer'
A fine-looking form with long spotted leaves and pink flowers that age to blue.

Pulmonaria rubra
This has plain, light green leaves that contrast well with the brick-red flowers. There are several good cultivars including 'Bowles' Red' and 'Redstart'. 'David Ward' has coral-red flowers and excellent cream-coloured variegations on the leaves.

Pulmonaria saccharata
Violet or red and blue flowers and spotted leaves. There are several excellent cultivars including 'Frühlingshimmel' (blue flowers) and 'Mrs Moon' (pink/blue).

Pulmonaria 'Sissinghurst White'
This is a very good white-flowered form, which has silver spots on the foliage.

Primula japonica

Primula vulgaris

RANUNCULUS
Buttercup

The buttercup family is a large one, covering 400 species. Many are weeds but there are also a number of excellent border plants as well as many smaller ones grown by alpine specialists. The general conception of buttercups is that they are yellow but there as many, if not more, white-flowered species. One thing that most have in common is the shallow, saucer-shape of the flowers, although there are also a number of button-like double-flowered cultivars. Ranunculus like varied conditions: there are some for the open border, others for the shade of trees and shrubs while still more prefer the moisture of a bog garden. On the whole the garden varieties are not as invasive as the more weedy species.

Cultivation Most buttercups that the perennial gardener will be concerned with require a fertile, reasonably moist soil, with plenty of well-rotted organic material. Plant in a sunny or partially shaded position. Z3–5.

Propagation Many buttercups can be divided. They will also come from seed, preferably sown as soon as it is ripe.

Ranunculus aconitifolius

Possibly the most important buttercup for the perennial gardener. It is a clump-forming plant, producing white flowers in early summer. H 60cm (24in) S 50cm (20in). The best known form is the double-flowered 'Flore Pleno'. It does best in shade.

Ranunculus acris

This is the meadow buttercup. It is not recommended for the normal border but it is excellent

Ranunculus amplexicaulis

in meadow gardens. 'Farrer's Yellow' (pale yellow) and 'Flore Pleno' (double) are sometimes grown in borders. It will grow in sun or shade. H and S 45–60cm (18–24in).

Ranunculus amplexicaulis

A delightful species with white flowers that are flushed with pale pink. It likes a gritty soil and should be planted at the front of a border. It produces its flowers in early summer. H 30cm (12in) S 10cm (4in).

Ranunculus ficaria

The lesser celandine can become invasive but its leaves are only above ground during the spring so it is not a real nuisance. It is very low-growing with shining yellow flowers. H 10cm (4in) S 20cm (8in). There are also forms with orange (*R.f.* var. *aurantiacus*) and near white ('Salmon's White') flowers as well as some with decorative foliage such as 'Brazen Hussy' (deep purple leaves). They are all excellent for growing under shrubs.

Ranunculus gramineus

This is a clump-forming species with large glistening yellow flowers and thin grass-like leaves.

Ranunculus gramineus

It flowers in spring and makes a good border plant. H 30cm (12in) S 8cm (3in).

RODGERSIA
Rodgersia

A small genus of plants with all six species in cultivation. The great thing about these is that they have both attractive foliage and flowers. In good conditions they will grow up to 2m (6ft) and they form quite large clumps (up to 2m/6ft), so they are plants for a larger garden. The foliage is palmate (like fingers on a hand), large, deeply veined and with a slight gloss on it. It is often purple or purple-tinged. The flowers are carried well above the leaves in clusters of white, cream or pink in summer.

Cultivation These plants need a soil that does not dry out, so add plenty of organic material to it. They do best in a lightly shaded position.

Propagation The simplest method of increase is to divide these plants in spring.

Rodgersia aesculifolia

The foliage of this species is palmate, and looks like that of a horse chestnut. The flowers are white or pink.

Rodgersia aesculifolia

Rodgersia pinnata

This is similar to the previous species, with palmate leaves and slightly darker flowers. The form 'Superba' is excellent. It has good purple foliage when it first appears, and bright pink flowers.

Rodgersia podophylla

This is slightly smaller than the previous, reaching about 1.2m (4ft). It has similar palmate foliage, although the leaflets are broader and divided at the tips giving a jagged appearance. It produces clusters of white flowers. Good autumn colour.

Rodgersia sambucifolia

This is the shortest species, at only 1m (3ft). The leaves are more pinnate, with leaflets arranged opposite each other as in an ash. The flowers are white or pink.

Ranunculus acris

Ranunculus ficaria, double form

Rodgersia pinnata

Rodgersia podophylla

ROMNEYA
Tree poppy

The only member of this genus, *R. coulteri*, is widely grown in gardens. It is a somewhat woody perennial, which runs below ground to form large clumps when it is happy with the conditions. It is related to the poppies and has the characteristic paper-tissue flowers. In this case they are glisteringly white with a wonderful golden boss of stamens in the middle. They are large, up to 20cm (8in) across. The flowers are set off well against the grey-green foliage. The plants are a bit untidy and sprawling but the quality of the flowers more than makes up for this. They are suitable for borders where there is space, otherwise they can be grown on their own. They grow up to about 2.5m (8ft) but are often less, especially when they are sprawling. Spread is 1m (3ft). There is a variety *trichocalyx* which in gardening terms is not much different from *coulteri* itself. However, its form 'White Cloud' is more free-flowering and the foliage better.

Cultivation Any reasonable garden soil will do but it must be well drained and in a sunny warm position. Z7.

Propagation Tree poppies can be divided but this is quite difficult. It is much easier to take basal cuttings in spring.

RUDBECKIA
Coneflower

This is a genus of about 20 species, of which a number are annuals. There are also a number of perennials, which are well worth growing in your autumn borders. They add a welcome touch of brilliant gold and have the habit of flowering over a long period, often starting in the summer and going on until the frosts arrive.

Coneflowers are daisies and get their name from the cone-like central disc in the flowers. This disc is usually a brown or green colour, while the outer ray petals are yellow or gold, sometimes verging on orange. The flowers measure 8cm (3in) or more across. The majority of these plants grow up to about 1m (3ft) but some that will reach 3m (10ft). S 60cm (24in).

Cultivation Rudbeckias do not like soil that dries out too much, so add plenty of well-rotted organic material. At the same time it should not be waterlogged, so add grit to keep it free-draining. Z3.

Propagation Most can easily be increased by division in spring. Species can be grown from seed sown at the same time of year.

Rudbeckia fulgida var. *deamii*

Commonly known as black-eyed Susan, this is a very popular plant for borders, especially hot-coloured ones. It has orange-yellow flowers that appear from midsummer onwards. H 75cm (30in). Another well-known and popular rudbeckia

Rudbeckia 'Herbstsonne'

is *R.f.* var. *sullivantii* 'Goldsturm' This grows to about 60cm (24in) and has very large flowers. The third variety that is commonly grown is var. *speciosa*.

Rudbeckia 'Goldquelle'

This is a popular cultivar with double flowers that are a bright lemon-yellow. H 1m (3ft).

Rudbeckia 'Herbstsonne'

This is a plant for the back of the autumn border since it grows to 2m (6ft). It produces flowers of bright gold. They are large, up to 12cm (5in) across. The central cone is green.

Rudbeckia laciniata

This particular species makes an excellent plant for the back of a border. It can grow up to 3m (10ft) in height when it is given the right conditions, although it is usually shorter than this, at about 2–2.5m (6–8ft). The flowers are a paler yellow than the previous species and are very wide, measuring up to 15cm (6in) – often the petals droop under their own weight. Like the other rudbeckias, this plant has a long flowering season – from midsummer right through to the end of autumn.

'Hortensia' is currently the best-known of this species' cultivars. It is a vigorous plant, and one that looks very similar to the species, except that its flowers are doubles.

Rudbeckia occidentalis

The species itself is not often grown but there are two cultivars – known as 'Black Beauty' and 'Green Wizard' – that are becoming increasingly popular with gardeners. Basically, these consist simply of the dark brown central cone, surrounded by green bracts or leaves. The effect is as though somebody has pulled off all of the petals. Although these are undoubtedly rather intriguing-looking flowers, few people could honestly describe them as being beautiful.

Romneya coulteri

R.f. var. *sullivantii* 'Goldsturm'

Rudbeckia fulgida var. *deamii*

SALVIA
Sage

This is a huge genus, of almost 900 species. The gardener is only concerned with about a tenth of these, which is still a lot of plants, especially since some species have plenty of cultivars. Sage grown as a garden plant is characterized by its tubular flowers, with an upper and lower lip. Their colour varies from bright red to bright blue, with lots of shades in-between. The flowers are carried in whorls, in spikes held well above the foliage, which can be aromatic. Generally these plants are grown for their flowers, although there are shrubby species (*S. officinalis*), with variegated foliage. Flowering starts in summer and continues into autumn. Some of the salvias are marginally tender and may need overwinter protection. They all make excellent border plants; some can be used in containers.
Cultivation Salvias like a fairly rich, well-drained soil and prefer a sunny position, although some will take a little light shade. Z5–8.
Propagation Species can be grown from seed sown in spring. Most can be grown from basal cuttings taken in spring and many can also be divided at the same time.

Salvia argentea
This is one perennial definitely grown for its foliage. It produces large woolly leaves that are a

Salvia sclarea

wonderful silver. It also produces spikes of pink or white flowers. It is not keen on winter wet. H 1m (3ft) S 45cm (18in).

Salvia buchananii
The large flowers produced by this sage are magenta. H 60cm (24in) S 30cm (12in).

Salvia cacaliifolia
An attractive plant which carries piercing blue flowers. H 1m (3ft) S 30cm (12in).

Salvia fulgens
Bright red flowers held in loose spikes. H 1m (3ft) S 1m (3ft).

Salvia guaranitica
This is a tall plant with deep blue flowers. H 1.5m (5ft) S 30cm (12in). There are several excellent cultivars including 'Blue Enigma' with large fragrant flowers.

Salvia involucrata
A good late-flowering plant for the border. It has purplish-red flowers. The form 'Bethellii' is the best with well-coloured flowers. H 75cm (30in) S 1m (3ft).

Salvia nemorosa
A regular plant in the garden border, with spikes of purple flowers. H 1m (3ft) S 45cm (18in). There are some excellent cultivars, which include 'Amethyst', 'Lubecca', 'Ostfriesland' and 'Pusztaflamme'.

Salvia involucrata 'Bethellii'

Salvia sclarea
This sage is normally grown in gardens as the variety *turkestanica*. It is tall, with dense spikes of white and pink flowers. It is an excellent plant but needs to be replaced regularly. H 1.2cm (4ft) S 30cm (12in).

Salvia sylvestris
A shrubby plant with purple flower spikes. H and S 45cm (18in). Its many superb cultivars include 'Blauhügel' (blue), 'Mainacht' (deep blue) and 'Rose Queen' (pink).

Other plants There are plenty more salvias for the interested gardener to discover and enjoy.

SANGUISORBA
Burnet

Sanguisorbas tend to be grown as specialist plants. There are about 18 species, most of which are in cultivation, but not often seen. They are mainly tall plants, with thin waving stems that carry the

Sanguisorba obtusa

flowers in terminal bottlebrushes. These vary in colour from white to deep red. They make good plants for the summer border. H 1.5m (5ft) S 45cm (18in).
Cultivation Any reasonable garden soil will do so long as it is not barren. Burnets like sun, but will tolerate a little light shade. Z4.
Propagation The plants will come readily from seed and can also be divided in spring.

Sanguisorba armena
This is grown mainly for its foliage which is a powdery blue-green, much in the mould of *Melianthus*. The flowers are pink. H 1.2m (4ft) S 45cm (18in).

Sanguisorba canadensis
Cylinders of white flowers are held 1.2m (4ft) or more above the ground. S 60cm (24in).

Sanguisorba hakusanensis
A beautiful plant whose terminal spikes of flowers are a deep pink colour with an underlying white. H 75cm (30in) S 60cm (24in).

Sanguisorba menziesii
These tall plants produce tight cylinders of deep red flowers. H 2m (6ft) S 60cm (24in).

Sanguisorba officinalis
Similar to the previous burnet, except that the flower cylinders are shorter, almost rounded. It is best grown in the wild garden. H 1.2m (4ft) S 60cm (24in).

Sanguisorba obtusa
Similar to the previous two species, but shorter at 60cm (24in). S 45cm (18in).

Scabiosa 'Blue Butterfly'

SCABIOSA
Scabious

A large genus of around 80 species, of which a number are grown in gardens both as annuals and perennials. They are delightful plants that deserve to be grown in all gardens. The flowers look like round pincushions and are carried above the foliage on wiry stems. They are in pastel colours, mainly mauves as well as creams and white, and flower over a long period through the summer.
Cultivation Scabious grow in any reasonable garden soil but they need a sunny position. Z3.
Propagation The simplest way to increase the perennials is to divide or take basal cuttings in spring.

Scabiosa 'Blue Butterfly'
This is a fine cultivar with lavender-blue flowers. H 45cm (18in) S 30cm (12in).

Scabiosa caucasica
A clump-forming plant with plenty of 'pincushions' that come in various shades of pale blue and lavender. The flowers are up to 8cm (3in) across. H and S 60cm (24in). There are also some excellent cultivars including 'Clive Greaves' (lavender) and 'Miss Willmott' (white).

Schizostylis coccinea

Scabiosa columbaria
This is similar to the above except that the flowers are about half the size. H and S 1m (3ft). It has a smaller form 'Nana' and a variety *ochroleuca* with wonderful creamy yellow flowers.

Scabiosa prolifera
A rarer scabious but one worth considering if you can find it. It has cream flowers which are surrounded by green bracts. H 60cm (24in) S 30cm (12in).

SCHIZOSTYLIS
Kaffir lily

This genus contains just one species, *S. coccinea*, with several good cultivars. It is a bulbous plant, producing narrow, strap-like leaves and tall spikes of cupped, star-like flowers in autumn. The flowers are shades of pink, white or flame-red. They are valuable plants for the autumn border or for odd corners. In the wild it is usually found growing next to water. H 60cm (24in) S 30cm (12in). Its variety *alba* has white flowers. Other plants include: 'Jennifer' (pink blooms); 'Maiden's Blush' (pink); 'Major' (large and red); 'Sunrise' (salmon-pink); 'Viscountess Byng' (the palest of pink); and 'Zeal Salmon' (salmon-pink).

Cultivation They grow in any reasonable garden soil, but prefer one that does not dry out completely. A sunny position is needed. Z6.
Propagation Kaffir lilies are very easy plants to lift and divide in the spring.

SEDUM
Stonecrop

This is a very large genus of some 400 species. A surprising number of these are in cultivation but there are only a handful that are of direct interest to the perennial garden. They vary considerably in size from ground-huggers only a centimetre or so high to border plants of 60cm (24in). They are all characterized by their succulent, fleshy leaves. The flowers are small and star-like and carried in clusters. There is a wide range of colours from yellows and oranges to pinks and reds. For the border types it is mainly the reds that are of interest. Their main flowering period is autumn.
Cultivation Any reasonable garden soil will do for sedums so long as it is well-drained. A place in the sun is to be preferred to get the best out of the plants. Z3.
Propagation The easiest method of increase is to root individual leaves in a cutting compost.

Sedum cauticola
This is a low-growing sedum that needs to be placed at the front of the border. The grey-green leaves set off well the pretty purplish-

Sedum middendorffianum

pink flowers which deepen in colour as they age. H 10cm (4in) S 20cm (8in).

Sedum 'Herbstfreude'
Better known as 'Autumn Joy', this is an old favourite for the border. It is one of the taller forms, and has flat heads of pink flowers that turn brownish-red as they age. The foliage is green, flushed with icy white. H 60cm (24in) S 30cm (12in).

Sedum middendorffianum
Another plant for the front of the border. It has dense heads of yellow flowers which rise above the glossy green foliage. H 15cm (6in) S indefinite.

Sedum 'Ruby Glow'
A superb front-of-border plant. The ruby flowers really do seem to glow and they are set off well by the purple-flushed foliage. H 25cm (10in) S 25cm (10in).

Sedum spectabile
This is the main border species with several excellent cultivars. It has flat heads of pink flowers. H and S 60cm (24in). Good cultivars include 'Brilliant' (bright pink flowers), 'Carmen' (bluish-pink), 'Iceberg' (white) and 'Septemberglut' (pink).

Scabiosa prolifera

Schizostylis coccinea 'Sunrise'

Sedum cauticola

S.t. maximum 'Atropurpureum'

Sedum telephium

This species has green leaves and pink flowers. It is mainly grown in the gorgeous form *S.t. maximum* 'Atropurpureum', which has dark purple stems and foliage as well as pink flowers. H 60cm (24in) S 30cm (12in).

SIDALCEA
Sidalcea

This is a genus of about 25 species. Although only a couple are grown in general cultivation they are important garden plants. They are related to the mallow and hollyhock and have the same saucer-shaped flowers. They are usually a shade of pink and appear in early and midsummer. The flowers grow on spikes carried on tall stems, up to 1.2m (4ft) when the plant is growing well. The leaves are rounded, and become more deeply lobed further up the stem. These are perfect plants for the middle of the border and the clear pink forms have a wonderful serenity about them. The darker purple-pinks are a bit more difficult to place, but they still make very good plants.
Cultivation Any reasonable garden soil will do for the sidalcea. A sunny position is preferred but it will grow in partial shade. Z5.
Propagation Species can be increased from seed, but cultivars need to divided in spring.

Sidalcea candida

This is a wonderful species, producing lovely white flowers that are often carried in a dense

Sidalcea malviflora

spike. It is not as tall as the following species, *S. malviflora*. H 1m (3ft) S 60cm (24in).

Sidalcea malviflora

This is the main species from which most of the cultivars have been derived. It has pink flowers, which vary in intensity from a pale to a purplish pink. There is also a white variety 'Alba'. The flowers are produced from early to midsummer. H 1.2m (4ft) S 30cm (12in).

These excellent cultivars are often listed directly under *Sidalcea*: 'Croftway Red' (reddish-pink flowers), 'Elsie Heugh' (a wonderful purplish-pink), 'Loveliness' (pale pink), 'Mrs Borrodaile' (another purplish-pink), 'Oberon' (rose-pink), 'Rose Queen' (dark rose-pink), 'Sussex

Beauty' (a really lovely shade of pink) and 'William Smith' (very deep pink).

SILENE
Campion

A very large genus with some 500 species. Almost 50 of these are available to gardeners, though not that many as garden perennials. They are related to the dianthus and many have the same flat-disc-like flowers, each with five petals, sometimes with a notch in the centre of the outer edge. They are good reliable plants rather than startling border features. Some are better in a wild or meadow garden.
Cultivation Any garden soil as long as it is reasonably moisture-retentive. Most will grow in either full sun or light shade. Z5.
Propagation Sow seed in spring or early autumn or take softwood cuttings in spring.

Silene acaulis

This is the moss campion, a low carpeting plant with delightful flowers carried on very thin stems in spring. This is really a plant for the alpine gardener, but they also make such excellent edge-of-border plants for a shady place. The flowers are pink, white or red. There are a number of cultivars worth exploring. H 5cm (2in) S 15cm (6in).

Silene alpestris

This is another rock-garden plant but, again, it is eminently suited to the front of a border so long as it is not swamped by larger plants.

Silene dioica

It produces masses of pure white flowers in the early summer. H 15cm (6in) S 20cm (8in).

Silene dioica

The red campion of hedgerows and open woodland. This is an attractive plant with rose-pink flowers. It can be grown in the border but it is better used in a wild garden, especially under light shrubs or in a damp meadow. H 75cm (30in) S 25cm (10in). The double forms 'Flore Pleno' and 'Rosea Plena' are more suitable for the border.

Silene schafta

Another rock-garden plant that is suitable for the edge of a border. This produces masses of magenta flowers from the late summer onwards, much later than most other silenes. H 25cm (10in) S 10cm (4in). There is a good cultivar 'Shell Pink', which has pale pink flowers.

Silene uniflora

A low-growing, mat-former that is ideally suited to the rock garden, but also does well on the edge of a border. This is the sea campion. It has white flowers and an inflated calyx (sheath round the base of the flower) with intricate veining. H and S 20cm (8in). The double form 'Robin Whitebreast' is especially popular. The excellent variegated form, 'Druett's Variegated', has greyish green leaves splashed with cream.

Sidalcea 'Elsie Heugh'

Sidalcea malviflora 'William Smith'

Sisyrinchium striatum

Smilacina racemosa

Solidago cutleri

Stachys byzantina

SISYRINCHIUM
Sisyrinchium

This is a genus of about 90 species. There is only one, *S. striatum*, which is of general use to the perennial gardener although there are several grown by alpine enthusiasts. These plants are related to the irises and this can be seen in the leaves, which are stiff and sword-like. From these fans of leaves erupt spikes of yellow or blue flowers in summer.

Cultivation Any reasonable garden soil will do but a free-draining one will see the best results. The plants self-sow prodigiously so deadhead after flowering. Z4.

Propagation These are extremely easy to divide in spring and they also come readily from seed sown at the same time of year.

Sisyrinchium 'Biscutella'
A rock-garden plant that can be used in the front of a border so long as it does not get swamped. It has yellow flowers diffused with brown and purple. Also good for gravel beds. H 30cm (12in) S 20cm (8in).

Sisyrinchium 'E.K. Balls'
Similar to the previous plant, except that it is slightly shorter with deep lilac flowers. H 25cm (10in) S 20cm (8in).

Sisyrinchium graminoides
This plant has deep violet-blue flowers with a yellow throat. It is good for the front of borders and gravel beds. H 45cm (18in) S 8cm (3in).

Sisyrinchium striatum
The main border plant. It has dull green foliage and masses of star-like creamy-yellow flowers. They

can be impressive in a drift. H 1m (3ft) S 30cm (12in). 'Aunt May' is a variegated form with soft grey foliage striped with creamy-white. This cultivar is not long lived and it is worth dividing each year to have some plants in reserve.

SMILACINA
Smilacina

A genus of 25 species of which only one is regularly grown in gardens, although others are occasionally seen. The main one is *S. racemosa*. It is related to the Solomon's seal (*Polygonatum*) but although the foliage is similar it is has more upright stems. The creamy-white flowers are carried in dense spikes at the top of each stem, and are set off well by the dark green foliage. This is an excellent plant for a lightly shaded position, but the flowers do not last long and soon go brown. H 1m (3ft) S 45cm (18in). *S. stellata* is the only other relatively common species. The flowers are smaller and it forms large clumps which are best sited in a wild woodland garden.

Cultivation A woodland-type soil with plenty of leaf mould or other organic material. A lightly shaded position is best. Z3.

Propagation This is easy to divide in spring, but can also be grown from seed.

SOLIDAGO
Golden rod

A genus of about 100 species, but most are too weedy for the garden. However, there are a few exceptions, which make excellent border plants. They carry golden-yellow sprays of small aster-like daisies, which appear from the late summer. They work well in mid to rear border positions, and

are especially useful for hot-coloured borders. H 1m (3ft) S 30cm (12in).

Cultivation Any reasonable garden soil, but it should be well-drained. Sun is best although some will take a little light shade. Z4.

Propagation Golden rods are very easy to propagate by division in the spring.

Solidago 'Crown of Rays'
A medium-height solidago with flattened heads of golden flowers. H 60cm (24in) S 25cm (10in).

Solidago cutleri
A shorter front-of-border plant. It reaches 45cm (18in) in good conditions. S 30cm (12in).

Solidago 'Golden Wings'
Another excellent form, this time with flattened sprays of golden flowers. It is a much taller plant. H 2m (6ft) S 1m (3ft).

Solidago 'Goldenmosa'
One of the best. It has upright sprays of golden flowers. H 75cm (30in) S 45cm (18in).

Solidago 'Goldenmosa'

Solidago 'Linner Gold'
An old favourite with conical heads rather than sprays of golden yellow flowers. H 1m (3ft) S 45cm (18in).

Other plants A hybrid between *Solidago* and *Aster* has produced × *Solidaster luteus*. These hybrids have clusters of flowers rather than sprays and are a fresh-looking mixture of gold and pale yellow. They grow to about 1m (3ft) with a spread of 45cm (18in) and are excellent border plants.

STACHYS
Stachys

A very large genus of plants, containing up to 300 species. Most are too weedy for the garden, but there are one or two excellent border plants. They have thyme-like tubular flowers, usually in variations of pink. The foliage in some is more important than the flowers, indeed some gardeners actually remove the flower-stems of *S. byzantina* as they feel it spoils the effect of the attractive silver foliage.

Cultivation Stachys will grow in any reasonable garden soil as long as it is free-draining. Choose a sunny position. Z4.

Propagation These clump-forming plants can easily be divided.

Stachys byzantina
This is the species that most gardeners grow. It has soft furry leaves with a silvery tinge, which gives it its English name of lamb's ears. The leaf stems are prostrate and creep gently across the surface of the soil. The flower stalks, which are also furry, are upright and carry tiny pink flowers. These are perfect for the foliage but many gardeners cut them off. The

Stachys byzantina 'Primrose Heron'

Stipa arundinacea

Stipa tenuissima

flowers stems reach up to 45cm (18in) with a spread of 60cm (24in). There are several cultivars. 'Big Ears' has extra large leaves. In 'Cotton Boll' the flowers are covered with silvery hairs. 'Primrose Heron' is a variegated form in which the silver is infused with yellow. 'Silver Carpet' is a good non-flowering form with intense silver foliage.

Stachys candida
Another silver-leaved plant. This one forms a more rounded shape and carries white flowers that are spotted with purple. It is short, so it is more suited to the front of the border or raised bed. H 15cm (6in) S 30cm (12in).

Stachys citrina
A second short form, it also has woolly leaves but carries spikes of pale yellow flowers. H 20cm (8in) S 30cm (12in).

Stachys macrantha
This species is an excellent early-summer plant which produces dense spikes of large, bright

purple flowers. It makes a good splash of colour. H 45cm (18in) S 30cm (12in).

Stachys officinalis
This is the wild betony. A midsummer flowerer which has smaller heads than the previous but is nonetheless still very noticeable. The flowers are deep reddish-purple. It can be grown in the border but it does self-sow rather viciously so it is best grown in the wild garden, possibly on a bank where it looks good. H 45–60cm (18–24in) S 30–45cm (12–18in).

STIPA
Stipa
A very large genus of some 300 grasses of which there are two or three that are of interest to the gardener. These are clump-forming plants that are well-behaved and do not spread too far. They are mainly grown for their flower heads rather than the foliage. The heads are carried on stiff, upright stems and form a hazy effect. These are excellent

plants to position where they catch the evening sun: they seem to sparkle and glow if placed with the sun behind them. Some are tall and statuesque and make an excellent feature. Others are humbler and fit well in a border.
Cultivation Stipas can be grown in any free-draining soil, but they should be given a sunny position. Cut back before the new growth begins in spring. Z6.
Propagation To increase, divide these plants in spring as soon as the new growth starts.

Stipa arundinacea
This produces a fountain of flowering heads from midsummer onwards. These are not carried on stiff stems but arch over, often touching the ground. Good for the front of a border, especially next to pathways. H 1m (3ft) S 1.2m (4ft).

Stipa calamagrostis
Arching sprays of flowers appear in summer. Their silvery colour makes them look rather like jets of water being sprayed out from the centre of the plant. Excellent. H 1m (3ft) S 1m (3ft).

Stipa gigantea
This is the one that every one knows. It can grow very tall and has stiff stems carrying open heads of straw-coloured flowers. These move in the slightest breeze and glisten in the sun. Give it sheltered position. H 2.5m (8ft) S 1m (3ft).

Stipa tenuissima
A much shorter grass. This is an erect grass with very fine flowers that create a beautiful hazy effect in the summer. H 60cm (24in) S 60cm (24in).

Stachys macrantha

Stipa calamagrostis

Stipa gigantea

Stokesia laevis 'Blue Star'

STOKESIA
Stokesia

This is a genus of only one species, *S. laevis*. It is not seen that often in general gardens but it is much more common in those of plant enthusiasts. As a result, it has gradually built up a number of cultivars, although the species itself is still well worth growing. It is not a very tall plant, 60cm (24in) at the most and often less as it can be rather sprawling. The foliage is noteworthy, but the flowers are even better. They are carried singly on the end of each stem and are about 10cm (4in) across. They face upwards and look rather like large cornflowers, with the outer florets being purple and the inner ones either darker or paler shade. These are plants for a position towards the front of the border. 'Alba' and 'Silver Moon' have white flowers. 'Blue Danube' is deep blue. 'Blue Star' is a light lilac blue. 'Wyoming' is an old form with good purple flowers.

Cultivation Stokesia prefer a neutral or acid soil which should be fertile and free-draining, especially during the winter. They should be sited in full sun. Z5.

Propagation The plants should be divided in spring, or take root cuttings in early winter.

SYMPHYTUM
Comfrey

This genus consists of about 30 or so species. Most of them are weeds, but in spite of this we still insist on growing them in our garden. They are rampant, but in the right place they can be magnificent. Generally the right place is not the border (unless you can contain the plants) but in a wild garden where they can rampage. They are grown both for their foliage and their flowers. The foliage is coarse and often bristly, but in some cultivars it is pleasantly variegated. The tubular flowers are carried at the ends of the stems in a coil which unfurls further as each flower opens. They are blue, red and white (and often a combination of these), as well as creamy-yellow. They flower mainly in spring or early summer.

Cultivation Any good garden soil will do but they do best in rich, fertile soils that do not dry out too much. They grow in sun or partial shade. They are invasive through underground rhizomes so give them plenty of space. Z3.

Propagation Comfreys can easily be propagated by dividing the plants in spring.

Symphytum asperum

This is a tallish plant with flowers that open pink and age to blue or a mixture of both. Invasive. H 1.2m (4ft) S indefinite.

Symphytum caucasicum

A medium-height plant of about 60cm (24in) with floppy stems. The flowers are a true blue and

Symphytum rubrum

appear over the summer. An invasive plant. H 60cm (24in) S indefinite.

Symphytum 'Goldsmith'

A good variegated form with red, white and blue flowers. H 30cm (12in) S indefinite.

Symphytum 'Hidcote Blue'

An excellent plant with very colourful flowers. These are multicoloured, containing red, white and blue. H 45cm (18in) S indefinite.

Symphytum 'Hidcote Pink'

This is similar to the previous plant, except that the flowers are pink and white. It is also known as *S.* 'Roseum'. H 45cm (18in) S indefinite.

Symphytum ibericum

A plant with cream flowers and a floppy habit. H 45cm (18in) S indefinite. It has several cultivars, including 'Blaueglocken' and 'Wisley Blue' (blue flowers).

Symphytum officinale

A tall plant, which does not have a lot to recommend it to general gardeners. However, its leaves can be used for making excellent compost or liquid fertilizer. The flowers are generally purple but they can also be cream. It is best grown in a wild garden where there is plenty of space. H 1.5m (5ft) S indefinite.

Symphytum rubrum

This is one of the better forms for gardeners. It can be used in the border so long as an eye is kept on its spread. It produces good red flowers. H 60cm (24in) S 1m (3ft).

Symphytum × uplandicum

This hybrid is the tallest of all the comfreys. It has flowers that start off pink and then age to blue and purple. H 2m (6ft) S 60cm (24in).

There are some good variegated forms: 'Variegatum' and 'Axminster Gold'.

Stokesia laevis 'Wyoming'

Symphytum ibericum

Pink perennials

Anemone H hybrida	Malva moschata
Aster	Monarda didyma 'Croftway
Astilbe	Pink'
Dianthus	Papaver orientalis 'Cedric
Diascia vigilis	Morris'
Dicentra	Penstemon 'Hidcote Pink'
Erigeron 'Charity'	Persicaria
Filipendula	Phlox paniculata
Lamium roseum	Sedum spectabile
Lychnis flos-jovis	Sidalcea

TELLIMA
Fringe cups

This is a genus with only one species, namely *T. grandiflora*. This is a good plant for the spring border. Its flowers are pale green at first, making the plant almost inconspicuous, although they age to red. They are carried in loose spikes on tall stems above lobed, rounded leaves. The plant has a fresh quality about it, making it well suited to the spring and early-summer garden scene. It looks good planted in the shade, from where the light green can shine out. Fringe cups are excellent plants for growing under shrubs or trees or in the shade of a house. H and S 1m (3ft).

The redness is brought out in some of the cultivars, such as 'Perky', which is a shorter plant with red flowers. Several have purple or purple-tinged foliage including 'Purpurteppich' and Rubra Group.

Cultivation Fringe cups can be grown in any reasonable garden soil but do best in a moisture-retentive one. If the soil is moist enough they will grow in sun but their preferred position is in a light shade. They self-sow, so either deadhead once flowering has finished or dig up the seedlings. Z4.

Propagation These plants come very easily from seed sown in spring. Larger plants can be divided, also in spring.

Thalictrum aquilegiifolium

THALICTRUM
Meadow rue

Thalictum is a large genus of around 130 species. About 50 or so of these are in cultivation, although not all are of direct interest for the perennial gardener. The fascinating thing about the thalictrum is that the flowers do not have any petals; the fluffiness of the tuft of stamens is what gives them their interest; fortunately this tuft is very prominent. There are a group of very colourful plants, with the flowers varying in colour from lilac and purple to creamy white and yellow, that bring a great deal of delight to our borders. They vary in height from just a few centimetres to 2m (6ft); however, the small ones are of little use in the general border.

Tellima grandiflora

Thalictrum flavum subsp. *glaucum*

Cultivation Any decent garden soil with a good humus content. They will grow in sun or in a light shade. Z4–5.

Propagation Sow seed as soon as it is ripe. The plants can be divided in spring, but this can be tricky.

Thalictrum aquilegiifolium

This is a spring-flowerer. The flowers are either creamy-white or purple and appear in wonderful fluffy clusters. The dangling seedpods are also very attractive. H 1m (3ft) S 30cm (12in). 'Thundercloud' is a good cultivar with darker purple flowers.

Thalictrum delavayi

An excellent border plant with a haze of purple flowers in summer. H 1.2m (4ft) S 60cm (24in). The superb 'Hewitt's Double' has no stamens; instead it produces a double purple flower of the sepals (the bud sheath).

Thalictrum lucidum

Thalictrum flavum subsp. glaucum

A tall plant with powdery blue-green leaves and clusters of bright yellow flowers in summer. H 2m (6ft) S 60cm (24in).

Thalictrum lucidum

Similar to the previous, with greenish yellow flowers but shining green foliage. Up to 1.2m (4ft) tall. S 30cm (12in).

Thalictrum rochebruneanum

An elegant plant with lavender or white flowers in the summer. H 1m (3ft) S variable.

TRADESCANTIA
Tradescantia

A large genus best known for its house plants. However, one group of cultivars, *T.* Andersoniana Group, is widely grown in gardens. Long, pointed leaves arch out of an untidy clump, and three-petalled brightly coloured flowers shine out like jewels from the leaf joints. The plants make good-sized clumps for the front of a border. H 45cm (18in) S 30cm (12in). Good cultivars include 'Iris Prichard' (white and blue), 'Isis' (dark blue), 'J.C. Weguelin' (light blue), 'Karminglut' (magenta), 'Osprey' (white and blue) and 'Purple Dome' (purple).

Cultivation Chose a moisture-retentive soil containing plenty of well-rotted organic material. They thrive in sun or light shade. Z7.

Propagation The simplest method of increase is to divide existing plants in spring.

Tradescantia Andersoniana Group

TRICYRTIS
Toad lily

These are intriguing plants which are more frequently grown by the specialist grower than the general gardener. This is a shame because they are attractive and are not difficult to grow. They are not showy at a distance but close up they are fascinating. The star-shaped flowers are either white or yellow, heavily spotted in purple and with a central column of stamens and stigmas. The flowers appear in late summer or autumn on plants that grow to about 1m (3ft) high and spread 45cm (18in). These plants are shade-lovers and should be grown under shrubs or tree, or in the shade of a house. They need to be grown in a drift to have any impact.

Cultivation A moist, woodland-type soil with plenty of organic material is required. Plant in a shady position. Z4.

Propagation The best method of propagation for toad lilies is by division in spring.

Tricyrtis formosana

White or pink flowers heavily spotted with reddish purple. The plants are fairly high and the dark leaves also have purple spotting. The Stolonifera Group is similar. H 80m (32in) S 45cm (18in).

Tricyrtis hirta

Another of the main toad lilies. They have white flowers with purple spots. H 80cm (32in)

S 45cm (18in). There are a number of cultivars including 'Alba' with white flowers, 'Albomarginata' which has variegated leaves and 'Miyazaki' which has light spotting on the white flowers and is a taller plant.

Other plants If you get hooked on tricyrtis there are a number of other species and cultivars to look at. *T. macrantha* has deep yellow pendant flowers and *T.* 'White Towers' has pure white flowers.

TRILLIUM
Wake robin

This is a genus containing about 30 species of woodland plant. They are grown mainly by specialist growers. However, they also have a lot to offer the general gardener so long as they are grown in a shady area. The main characteristic is that each stem carries three leaves as well as a flower that consists of three petals. The flower colour varies from white, through pink to red and purple as well as yellow. The plants vary in height from just a few centimetres to 60cm (24in). They flower in spring.

Cultivation Grow in a woodland-type soil with plenty of humus that does not dry out. These plants need a shady position under shrubs or trees. Z4.

Propagation Division is a method of increase but they are often slow to re-establish. Seed can be sown when still fresh.

Trillium grandiflorum

Trillium cuneatum

A tall plant, with tall mottled leaves and upright petals in a glossy deep maroon. H 60cm (24in) S 30cm (12in).

Trillium grandiflorum

These are one of the most beautiful of the trilliums. The flowers are upward-facing and have wide glistening white petals. The plant spreads slowly to form a clump. H and S 30cm (12in).

There is a beautiful double form 'Flore Pleno' and a rare pink form 'Roseum'.

Other plants Gardeners can become fanatical about trillium. If you like them it is worth finding specialist nurseries and seeking out the more unusual ones.

Trollius europaeus

TROLLIUS
Globeflower

A small genus of about 24 plants of which a couple are suitable for the perennial border. They are closely related to the buttercups as shown by the globe-like yellow flowers. Globeflowers flower in late spring and early summer. H 1m (3ft) S 45cm (18in).

Cultivation Globeflowers need a deep, humus-rich soil that retains plenty of moisture. They prefer sun but tolerate light shade. Z4.

Propagation Existing plants can be divided in spring, or seed can be sown as soon as it is ripe.

Trollius × cultorum

This is a collection of hybrids with 'Alabaster' being one of the best. Its flowers are a very delicate

Tricyrtis formosana

Trillium cuneatum

Trillium grandiflorum 'Roseum'

Veratrum nigrum

Verbascum 'Letitia'

Verbena bonariensis

shade of pale yellow. 'Feuertroll' and 'Orange Princess' have orange-yellow flowers. H 60cm (24in) S 30cm (12in).

Trollius europaeus
This is a little shorter than the previous plant and produces golden flowers. 'Canary Bird' is a pale yellow form. H 60cm (24in) S 45cm (18in).

VERATRUM
Veratrum
A specialist genus of 45 species which should be grown by more general gardeners. The plants take several years to reach flowering size, but during that time the pleated leaves provide great interest. Once flowering size is reached, a large stem up to 2m (6ft) rises up and its side branches are festooned with masses of star-like flowers in white or brownish-red. It is a truly remarkable sight, especially if seen against the sun. These are mainly plants for a woodland or shade garden.
Cultivation A deep, humus-rich soil is required and either a shady position, or a sunny one that does not dry out. Z6.
Propagation The quickest method is to divide in spring, but these plants can also be grown from seed sown when fresh.

Veratrum album
This veratrum produces white or greenish-white flowers in summer. H 2m (6ft) S 60cm (24in).

Veratrum nigrum
The choicest species, which has mahogany-red flowers in summer and superb pleated foliage. H 1.2m (4ft) S 60cm (24in).

Veratrum viride
This plant has plainer foliage than the above but it is still impressive. It grows to 2m (6ft) and has greenish flowers. S 60cm (24in).

VERBASCUM
Mullein
This is a glorious genus of about 45 species of annual and perennial plants without which many gardens would be impoverished. The attractive thing about them is the tall spikes, which are densely covered with flowers. Sometimes these spikes rise up 2.5m (8ft) or

Verbascum nigrum

more. The colours of the flowers are basically yellow, but there are also white, pink and purple cultivars. These plants add structure and shape to a border. Even the shorter ones are eye-catching when planted in drifts. They flower throughout the summer and into autumn.
Cultivation Any reasonable garden soil will do but it should be free-draining. A sunny position is best. Deadhead unless you want them to self-sow. Z5.
Propagation Mulleins all come easily from seed sown in spring. Root cuttings can be taken in early winter.

Verbascum chaixii
A plant producing several main stems. The flowers are yellow with red centres. H 1m (3ft) S 60cm (24in). There is a white form 'Album'.

Verbascum 'Cotswold Queen'
Spikes of yellow flowers with purple centres. The spikes are not so densely packed as those of the previous species. H 1.2m (4ft) S 30–60cm (12–24in).

Verbascum 'Gainsborough'
Similar to the previous plant but with softer yellow flowers. H 60–120cm (2–4ft) S 30–60cm (12–24in).

Verbascum 'Letitia'
This is a shrubby plant with lots of woolly, wiry stems carrying bright yellow flowers. H and S 30cm (12in).

Verbascum nigrum
Similar to *V. chaixii* with yellow and white forms. H 60cm (24in) S 60–120cm (2–4ft).

Verbascum olympicum
Although a perennial this dies after eventually flowering in its third year. It is an excellent foliage plant with glistening silver-white stems and leaves. The flowers are yellow. H 2m (6ft) S 1m (3ft).

VERBENA
Verbena
A very large genus of tender perennials (see annuals page 167) and perennials. Although there are

only a few of the latter, it is still an important genus for the general gardener, with at least three excellent species to choose from. All the plants listed below have very long flowering seasons, which mainly start in midsummer and last well into the autumn They all make very good border plants, needing little attention.
Cultivation Verbenas will grow in any good garden soil as long as it is free-draining. A sunny position is preferred. Z8.
Propagation They all come readily from seed and *V. corymbosa* can easily be divided.

Verbena bonariensis
This is superb plant with tall wiry stems carrying small clusters of purple flowers. Although tall, this is a "see-through" plant which can be placed anywhere in the border including the front. It is short lived but readily self-sows. H 2m (6ft) S 60cm (24in).

Verbena corymbosa
A lowish, floppy plant. It creeps gently to form a large clump. It has blue flowers, which seem to shine out in the twilight. H 1m (3ft) S 25cm (10in).

Verbena hastata
A delightful upright plant without the wiriness of the others and with more foliage. It has purple flowers. H 1m (3ft) S 30cm (12in). There is an excellent pink form ('Rosea') and a very good white one ('Alba').

V. austriaca subsp. *teucrium* 'Blue Fountain'

Veronica peduncularis

VERONICA
Speedwell

A large genus of some 250 species and many cultivars. This is an important genus in the garden, providing us with many valuable plants, especially blue-flowered ones. They vary considerably in height, so there are plants for all parts of the border; the taller ones provide excellent vertical emphasis in the middle or back. The majority of speedwells carry their flowers in distinct spikes. The flowers appear mainly during the summer and are various shades of blue with the occasional pink or white cultivar. They are very easy plants to grow and every border should include at least one.

Cultivation Veronicas like a moist, humus-rich soil and will immediately show distress if the ground dries out too much (a good early indicator of drought). They prefer a sunny position but will grow in light shade. Z4.

Propagation Most can be divided in spring and species also come readily from autumn-sown seed.

Veronica austriaca

The species is rarely grown, but its many cultivars make this a popular plant. They are all roughly 20–30cm (8–12in) high with a similar spread. They have dense spikes of blue flowers throughout summer. 'Ionian Skies' has sky-blue flowers. The subspecies *teucrium* contains most of the notable cultivars, most of which have dark blue flowers. They include 'Blue Fountain', the traditional favourite 'Crater Lake Blue', 'Kapitan', 'Shirley Blue' and 'Royal Blue'.

Veronica cinerea

A low prostrate species with silver woolly foliage and short spikes of blue flowers. It is ideal for the front of border. H 15cm (6in) S 30cm (12in).

Veronica gentianoides

A taller species which produces loose spikes of pale blue flowers. The forms 'Alba' and 'Tissington White' have white flowers. H and S 45cm (18in).

Veronica spicata 'Alba'

Veronica longifolia

A good border plant, forming large clumps of drift. The blue flowers are densely packed into spikes. This plant self-sows prodigiously so always deadhead once flowering is finished. There is a pink form 'Rosea'. H 1.2m (4ft) S 30cm (12in).

Veronica peduncularis

A spreading mat-former. It is mainly grown in the form 'Georgia Blue' which has purple foliage and deep blue flowers. H 12cm (5in) S 1m (3ft).

Veronica spicata

A good species for the front of border with lots of interesting cultivars. The subspecies *incana* is fantastic. It has very silvery foliage and stems topped with vivid blue flowers. H and S 45cm (18in). Other *V. spicata* cultivars worth looking at include 'Alba' (white), 'Heidekind (pink flowers), 'Icicle' (white), 'Rotfuchs' (dark reddish-pink) and 'Wendy' (bright blue).

VIOLA
Viola

For the gardener, the genus *Viola* can be split into three types. There are the species, then there are the pansies which are considered as annuals and finally there are the violas. The violas have larger flowers than those of the species, and are of most interest to the perennial gardener. However, do not write off the species since there are several excellent plants which carpet the ground in spring and are well worth growing. Violas are usually low plants. The flowers are carried on single stems arising from the foliage. The flowers are either single or multicoloured.

Cultivation Violas must have a moisture-retentive soil or they will die out. As long as they are moist enough they will grow in sun, but light shade is the best position. Z5.

Propagation The species can be grown from seed, but any perennial cultivar needs to be increased by taking basal cuttings in the spring.

Viola 'Ardross Gem'

This is, indeed, a real gem, with blue and yellow flowers. H 15cm (6in) S 20cm (8in).

Viola cornuta

A species that flowers from spring to autumn, producing lilac or blue flowers. It will scramble through low shrubs. There are several cultivars, all of which make excellent border plants. H and S 20cm (8in).

Viola 'Irish Molly'

An attractive plant with yellowy-bronze flowers. H 10cm (4in) S 20cm (8in).

Viola 'Jackanapes'

This plant produces cheeky gold and red-purple flowers. H 8–12cm (3–5in) S 20cm (8in).

Viola odorata

The sweet violet, which starts to flower in mid-winter. It is ideal for a shady spot under shrubs. The small flowers vary from violet

Veronica longifolia

Veronica spicata

Viola 'Ardross Gem'

Viola 'Elizabeth'

blue to pale blue, pink and white, and are highly scented. H 7cm (3in) S 15cm (6in).

Other plants There are hundreds of viola cultivars, including the delightful 'Elizabeth'. Check out the several nurseries that specialize in them if you become enthused and want more of them.

YUCCA
Yucca

A genus of about 40 species, of which half a dozen are in general cultivation. Some might argue that these are shrubs but they are widely included in perennial borders and so are included here. They have pointed, sword-like leaves coming either from the base or from a woody stem. Above these rise huge spikes of bell-shaped, cream flowers. These are plants for dry areas and they do

very well in gravel beds, They are always striking and can be grown in association with other plants or singled out by themselves as focal points in the garden. They can be grown in containers.
Cultivation Any garden soil will do as long as it is very well-drained. Add plenty of grit to wetter soils. Grow in full sun. Z5.
Propagation Take off the rooted suckers and transplant them. Alternatively, take root cuttings in early winter.

Yucca filamentosa
Known as Adam's needle, this stemless species has dark green leaves that grow directly from a rosette on the ground. Along the margins of the leaves are thin, curly threads – the filaments of its name. Tall spikes up to 2m (6ft) high carry nodding white bells from midsummer onwards.

S 1m (5ft). There are three variegated forms 'Bright Edge', 'Color Guard' and 'Variegata'.

Yucca flaccida
This plant is similar to the previous since it is almost stemless and the leaves again come from basal rosettes. It has thin threads on the margins of the leaves. Large bell-shaped, white flowers appear from midsummer onwards. H and S 1m (3ft). Again there is a variegated form, 'Golden Sword'. 'Ivory' has creamy-ivory flowers.

Yucca gloriosa
A stemmed species with pointed leaves that are arching rather than stiffly erect. It produces large amounts of flowers from late summer onwards. These are cream but may be flushed with purple. H 3m (10ft) S 2m (6ft).

ZANTEDESCHIA
Arum lilies

These are superb plants. Most people know the blooms but few realize that the plants can be grown in the garden. There are six species in the genus but only *Z. aethiopica* is grown in the open. This forms large clumps of shiny, dark green, arrow-shaped leaves. They set off beautifully the glistening white spathes (sheaths) that surround the true flowers, which are modest and are carried on a spike inside the spathe.

This plant must have moist soil. It is marginally tender and may need winter protection in some areas. The form 'Crowborough' is reputedly more hardy than others but most seem to come through most winters. Arum lilies can be grown in an ordinary border so long as it is kept moist, but they do best next to or in a water feature or bog garden. It grows well in shallow water up to 30cm (12in) deep; the water is likely to remain below freezing, protecting the plant. H 1m (3ft) S 60cm (24in).
Cultivation A wet or moist soil that does not dry out. A sunny position is required. Z8.
Propagation Increase your stock of arum lilies by dividing the plants in spring.

Zantedeschia aethiopica

ZAUSCHNERIA
Zauschneria

A small genus of plants. There is only one that is worth growing in the perennial border. This is *Z. californica* which is valuable because of its late flowering. This starts in the autumn, but continues right through to the first frosts. It is a spreading plant, which runs underground but it is not too difficult to prevent it from travelling too far. It has grey foliage and brilliant orange flowers, which certainly pep up the late border. In spite of coming from California, it is hardy. H and S 30cm (12in). The subspecies *cana* 'Dublin' has red flowers.
Cultivation This needs full sun and a well drained soil, but it need not be too fertile. Z7.
Propagation Zauschnerias can be increased by dividing existing plants in spring.

Yucca filamentosa

Yucca flaccida

Zauschneria cana 'Dublin'

Index

Monarda 'Cambridge Scarlet'

G

Ligularia dentata 'Desdemona'

100 IDEAS THAT CHANGED FASHION

Harriet Worsley

Laurence King Publishing

**100 IDEAS THAT
CHANGED FASHION**

Harriet Worsley

Introduction

Life's formative moments often come when one least expects them. As an unworldly 12-year-old, I was offered the chance to explore my grandmother's wardrobe, and an entirely new and dazzling world opened up before me: silks and furs and velvet, and, so it seemed to me, numerous excuses for dressing up. There were boxy 1960s silk shift dresses in every imaginable colour, neat tweed suits and long velvet evening gowns. I was utterly captivated – and have remained so ever since. Vintage clothes have a history, and stories. There is something magical about holding a 1920s beaded silk flapper dress and imagining who wore it and what secrets it has within its folds: forgotten dances at wild parties? Secret love affairs?

My grandmother's clothes not only opened my eyes to the richness and variety of women's clothing, but, importantly, to the enormous distance that fashion itself had travelled. Like human evolution, women's fashions had adapted through countless stages to become the clothing that she wore. It was evident, looking at the well-crafted but simple luxury of those clothes from the 1950s and 1960s, so far removed from the fusty Victoriana of just 50 years before, that something dramatic happened to fashion in the first half of the twentieth century; and the remaining years proved no less exciting.

The twentieth century was one rich in innovation. It gave life to hundreds of new ideas and inventions, many of which had an impact on women's clothing. The sartorial contrast between the beginning and the end of the century is extreme. From the corsets, sweeping dresses and chaperoned women of 1900 to nude sunbathing, miniskirts, air travel and Internet shopping just 100 years later, it hardly seems possible that so much changed, and so fast.

The aim of *100 Ideas That Changed Fashion* is to highlight and explain these revolutionary changes in womenswear from 1900 to 2010. The ideas are presented chronologically, and are positioned in the book's fashion timeline to mark a point of change. For example, the T-shirt was worn in the early twentieth century as men's underwear, and was a mainstream fashion item during the second half of the century, so it appears in the book at the point that it became worn as outerwear – during the 1950s. The book sets out to encourage the reader to look at everyday clothes with a more informed eye: knowing that the first bikini was deemed so outrageous that only a stripper would model it, that T-shirts were initially men's underwear and that the rivets on jeans were developed to strengthen workmen's trousers during the gold-rush era.

The book's objective, at its inception, rested on what would constitute an 'idea', about which there was much debate. We concluded that each idea had to be something that rerouted the course of fashion and without which womenswear would not be what it is today.

The most obvious ideas were the new inventions. These ranged from relatively small fashion-specific entities such as the zip or nylon to more far-reaching inventions such as the computer and air travel. Such inventions could not be ignored, but the book's focus is squarely on how fashion changed as a result of these brilliant leaps forward, rather than on the inventions themselves.

Fashion's reaction to major political or economic world events also had to be included, for the effect they had on the course of fashion was irrefutable. The Great Depression of the 1930s led women to copy costume trends from Hollywood movies as a means of escapism from those dark days, while the restriction of materials during World War II led to the evolution of new fashion ideas such as streamlined suits and wooden- and cork-soled shoes.

The emancipation of women was one of the greatest changes of the twentieth century, and its effect on fashion was immense and far-reaching. As society allowed women to do more for themselves – to go out to work, to vote, and, in the case of society women, to ditch their chaperones – clothing had to adapt. An independent unaccompanied woman clearly needed a handbag to carry her valuables.

More importantly, war work could hardly be done efficiently in a rib-compressing whalebone corset. Later, in the 1920s, competing against men in the workplace did not call for frilled dresses but, rather, for a plain skirt suit. The bias cut, the influence of sportswear and the introduction of synthetics all allowed women to dress with more comfort and ease, and to enjoy clothes suited to their increasingly dynamic lifestyles. Interestingly, many of these key innovations appropriated elements from menswear; being traditionally more casual, comfortable and practical, it was an obvious shift. Chanel was a great pioneer in this respect, adapting men's yachting trousers, jumpers and pea coats for women, while Yves Saint Laurent gave women the trouser suit, making it a respectable option for formal occasions.

Just as emancipated woman changed the course of fashion, so the arrival of the 'teenager' in the 1950s – a new, dynamic social force with spending power – created a different target market for designers and spawned numerous trends that feature as ideas in this book. Aside from mainstream teenage fashion, many youth-driven subcultural groups, with their own sartorial codes, blossomed from the middle of the century, ranging from 1960s mods and hippies to the skaters and indie kids of the 1990s. These in turn began to feed the creativity of designers, starting with Yves Saint Laurent in the 1960s, to Tom Ford, Anna Sui and many more in the 2000s, who were all creating luxury collections, and looking for new inspiration and energy.

The twentieth century saw a breaking down of the notion that dress codes demarcate social status, and this also threw up some interesting ideas for the book. Coco Chanel introduced the wealthy to the black dress and the suntan (which had formerly only been seen on working-class women), and persuaded society women that costume jewellery could be as acceptable as wearing real jewels. Meanwhile, the advent of mass-manufacturing, and an increase in social mobility, means that today the same trends can be enjoyed and worn by all, as the high-street stores knock out smart, affordable copies of the catwalk looks.

Fashion went truly global during the twentieth century, and this introduced a number of ideas to the book such as fashion's increasing use of motifs and silhouettes influenced by cultures outside the West; the emergence of Japanese designers on Western catwalks and the eclipse of Paris as the only credible centre of fashion. Today, fashion media, design, manufacturing and business operate internationally rather than nationally. The Internet spreads the fashion gospel worldwide, with the live streaming of fashion shows, as well as blogs, magazines and shopping sites.

Fashion designers themselves are included in this book only in relation to their best innovations. The very greatest designers and business giants, the arbiters of change, all merit a mention for their contribution to fashion – Coco Chanel, Elsa Schiaparelli, Yves Saint Laurent, Vivienne Westwood, Calvin Klein, John Galliano, Tom Ford and more.

While working on this book I gave birth to my daughter, Jessie. At the time, newspaper reports were claiming that this new generation, hers, could easily live for 100 years. What changes will she see in her lifetime? If the developments in the last 110 years have been extreme, then imagine the year 2110. The final idea in this book hints at the futuristic surprises that are just beginning now – computers integrated into clothing, and prints that change on a skirt with the push of a button. But what's coming next? If the last century is anything to go by, it is certainly destined to be challenging, dramatic and unlike anything we can possibly imagine today.

Made to measure for the super-rich

IDEA № 1

COUTURE

Couture clothes are made to measure for a specific woman's body size, as opposed to ready-to-wear clothes that are made in standard sizes. We would not have haute couture without Charles Frederick Worth, its founding father.

Lady Curzon in the Peacock Dress of 1909 by Charles Frederick Worth, the first couturier. He designed show-stopping gowns for royalty, actresses and the nouveaux riches.

Until the 1960s, the Paris couturiers led European fashion trends, largely defining the way in which women dressed. While the relevance of haute couture today is debatable, owing to its vast expense and limited client-base, before the 1960s couture designers played an essential role as trend-makers and -breakers.

Worth was the first designer to make his name as a fashion star. Born in Lincolnshire, England, in 1825, he moved to Paris at the age of 20, where he set up his own fashion house in 1858. It was the first designer atelier. The fashionable Empress Eugénie, wife of Napoleon III, took him under her wing, and thereafter Worth quickly became the darling of society. He made his name designing ostentatious gowns for royalty and the nobility, actresses and the nouveaux riches, and his business flourished. Worth had no time for shawls, bonnets and other such frippery – he focused on flattering the female figure, swathing it in luxurious fabric. He was especially fêted for his white tulle evening dresses.

The haute couture industry of today is Worth's abiding legacy. He was a great innovator, becoming the first to show clothes on live models, and the first to present a new collection every year. His garments were customized to each client and patiently adapted to her whims. In the manner of an artist, Worth even signed his dresses by hand.

Worth's successors, the couturiers of the early twentieth century, united in 1910 to form the Chambre Syndicale de la Couture Parisienne. This group actively promoted its clothes to overseas markets, and paved the way for the biannual couture shows that are staged in Paris today.

Until the 1990s the Chambre Syndicale had very strict rules of admission, but these rules have been relaxed recently to allow younger designers in. With members having included John Galliano for Christian Dior, and such mavericks as Jean Paul Gaultier and Viktor & Rolf, couture today is anything but dull. It is a quirky mix of fantastical and wearable pieces, and showcases the meticulous work of some of fashion's most expert crafts-people. The relevance of haute couture in the modern world may still be a subject of heated debate, but its drama and creativity are undeniable. ∎

*A John Galliano design
for Christian Dior couture,
Spring/Summer 2007.*

The lure of the fame game

IDEA № 2
CELEBRITIES

We unquestionably live in a celebrity-obsessed society. Television cameras and paparazzi lenses ensure that the lives of the rich and famous are thrust upon us in almost every medium, whether it be television, newspapers, magazines or the World Wide Web.

And we can watch celebrities' fashion triumphs and disasters as they happen, the Internet enabling information to be streamed to our homes at lightning speed. Throughout history, prominent people have always exerted tremendous sway in fashion. Royalty, actresses and royal mistresses have all been trend-setters. The first couturier, Charles Frederick Worth, benefited from the high-profile patronage of fashion icon Empress Eugénie, the wife of Napoleon III of France. During the 1900s society beauties and actresses were pictured on postcards and cigarette cards in order to show off new fashions. From the beginning of the twentieth century, celebrities started to play a crucially important role in fashion – by patronizing designers and, in wearing their clothes, giving prominence to their designs. Rather than on television or the Internet, reports appeared in newspapers and magazines.

By the 1930s women were flocking to the movies and copying the influential looks of Hollywood stars – Greta Garbo's trench coats, Joan Crawford's full painted lips, Marlene Dietrich's smouldering glamour. And the film studios' costume designers, such as Travis Banton and Gilbert Adrian, ensured that the stars looked as impeccable off-screen as they did on it.

Prominent actresses and fashion designers have often formed highly successful mutually beneficial relation-

ships, with the success of each raising the other's profile. A perfect example was the long-standing pairing of actress Audrey Hepburn and designer Hubert de Givenchy, notably for her clothes for the 1954 movie *Sabrina*, but just as importantly for the neat black trousers and bateau-necked tops that Hepburn wore off-screen.

Giorgio Armani's designs for Richard Gere in *American Gigolo* (1980) raised his profile, and popularized the loose, wide-shouldered jacket. Today Keira Knightley has teamed up with Chanel, and Scarlett Johansson with Louis Vuitton, with the stars featuring in the brands' advertising campaigns and wearing their clothes off-screen.

More than ever, designers are clamouring to dress movie stars for red-carpet events such as the Oscars. And with an increasingly media-hungry public, and the currency of celebrity being somewhat cheapened, the fashion houses are busier than ever trying to seduce the major stars of the moment with their designs. ■

*...s film star Marlene Dietrich
...s with a cigarette. Her
...red suits and languid beauty
... legendary.*

'It is tidy, flattering and neat,
without looking provocative'

The essential uniform for the working woman

IDEA Nº 3

THE SKIRT SUIT

Fashionable women have been wearing suits since the seventeenth century – but only when on horseback. It was not until the end of the nineteenth century that suits were adopted for wear outside the equestrian world.

Skirt suits, or tailor-mades as they were known, comprising a jacket or coat worn over a blouse and a long sweeping skirt, were worn by ladies in the early twentieth century for social calls and shopping expeditions.

Queen Alexandra, wife of King Edward VII of Britain and a fashion icon of her generation, became renowned for her sleek travel suits by her favourite tailor, John Redfern. The style was modern for the time, and feminists wore them to make a political point, in rejecting the femininity of sweeping dresses. This was, of course, an early precursor to the trouser suit of the 1960s. By the outbreak of World War I, working women had started to wear the coat and skirt. It was durable and practical, and pretty dresses suddenly seemed inappropriate for the office.

By the end of the 1930s, women of all classes had taken up the tailored streamlined skirt suit. They married in them and worked in them. In 1942 prominent British designers, including Norman Hartnell and Hardy Amies, designed sharp-shouldered women's suits as part of the UK government's mass-produced Utility range, which conformed to the stringent fabric and design constraints of the war, such as restricted pleats and shorter skirts.

After the boxy skirt suits of the 1960s, which hung away from the body, the suit really came into its own again during the 1980s. Thierry Mugler and Claude Montana perfected the working woman's power suit, with its tight skirt and jacket with wide masculine shoulders. Donna Karan devised her own softer working woman's capsule wardrobe, with her all-in-one leotard-style 'body', and flattering interchangeable wrap-around skirts and blazers. Today the skirt suit is the standard working uniform for professional women. It is tidy, flattering and neat, without looking provocative. ∎

Liberation for women

THE DEATH OF THE CORSET

In the early years of the twentieth century, respectable women in Europe and the United States took great pride in squeezing their bodies into unnaturally curvaceous shapes. They had to suffer in order to look beautiful.

American actress Camille Clifford shows off her distorted corset-bound figure in the early 1900s.

Their torsos were squashed into corsets, which were stiffened with metal or whalebone and tightened brutally hard with laces. With pads added to the hips and under the arms to exaggerate a tiny waistline, a full-length skirt finished off the look.

In the United States, the ideally proportioned woman of the era was popularized by the illustrator Charles Dana Gibson, and his drawings were personified most famously by the curvy actress Camille Clifford. Today, her wasp-waisted figure looks almost grotesquely distorted. Yet not all women were prepared to suffer the discomfort of a corset. The suffragettes of England began a campaign against these restrictive garments in 1904, and soon afterwards the French followed suit.

Salvation was at hand. In 1906 the French fashion designer Paul Poiret introduced a ground-breaking softer silhouette, inspired by the eighteenth-century empire-line style, which rendered extreme corsetry redundant. A Poiret skirt fell straight to the floor from a high empire-line band, which sat just under the bust. With no need of a tiny waist any more, women could breathe freely again. Poiret himself was keenly aware of the social implications of his innovation: 'It was equally in the name of Liberty that I proclaimed the downfall of the corset and the adoption of the brassiere,' he wrote. Poiret's fluid gowns were startlingly different from the rustling silks and bustles of the Victorian era. Other designers, including Madeleine Vionnet and the House of Paquin, also promoted the new look.

Nonetheless, women did not do away with control underwear completely. While whalebone stays were no longer desirable, tube corsets were still favoured: woven elastic, which pulled in the hips, flattened the stomach and liberated the bust. These were far from perfect, as they restricted movement in the legs. With the advent of World War I, women started to work in jobs that had traditionally been the preserve of men, and stretch corsets became correspondingly shorter in order to allow more mobility. Eventually, the modern choice became the stretch girdle, which just held in the hips, worn with a bra. ■

‘With no need of a tiny waist any more, women could breathe freely again’

This 1911 engraving from Les Robes de Paul Poiret *by Georges Lepape depicts Poiret's new languid, empire-line silhouette.*

'Fortuny devised, and patented, a secret method of creating permanent pleats'

The female form unfolds

IDEA Nº 5
THE DELPHOS GOWN

The Spanish designer Mariano Fortuny revolutionized fashion with his legendary Delphos gown of 1907 by offering women an alternative to structured dressing. Although he worked as a fashion designer, he regarded himself primarily as a painter, artist and inventor.

Actress and singer Régine Flory wears a Delphos gown by Mariano Fortuny in 1910.

His aim was to celebrate the female form through dress. He clothed both the unorthodox Russian ballet dancer Anna Pavlova and the modern dancer Isadora Duncan, who caused scandal with her unconventional views and her semi-nudity on-stage.

The pleated silk-satin Delphos gown could be rolled or twisted to fit into a tiny box. Once removed, it would stretch out again into a full-length dress, with its pleats intact. Fortuny devised, and patented, a secret method of creating permanent pleats, which involved laying wet, folded silk on heated porcelain tubes. His dresses hung from the shoulders while moulding to the body, without using conventional seams. The bright dye used to colour the dresses was sometimes graded, so that the colours seemed to melt into each other, and a tied silk cord drew in the fabric at the waist or neckline. Delicate Murano glass beads from Venice acted both as decorative devices and to weight veils and hems.

Fortuny's Delphos gown stemmed from his passionate interest in Greek antiquity and the English Aesthetic Movement. He named the dress after his inspiration, a famous ancient Greek sculpture, the life-sized bronze *Charioteer of Delphi*.

The Delphos gown appealed to newly liberated women, who wanted to express themselves and move freely, without the restrictions of corsets or stiff dresses. The dresses were modern, flattering, and elongated the figure. They were initially worn only for entertaining at home, and women didn't dare to wear them in public until the 1920s. The Parisian designer Madeleine Vionnet also shared a passion for ancient Greece, and introduced bias-cut draped dresses for high-society ladies. Later, American designer Mary McFadden experimented with pleated fabrics in the style of Fortuny, and later still, the Japanese designer Issey Miyake took up the Fortuny mantle with his Pleats Please collections, first launched in 1993. The Fortuny legacy lives on. ■

Push-up and plunge

IDEA № 6

THE BRA

While rudimentary bras, known as bust supporters, started to be worn as early as the 1880s, it was not until 30 years later that they began to make true fashion sense. This was due to the new empire-line silhouette of the 1910s.

This ground-breaking style looked best when worn over a girdle or a shortened corset that stopped above the waist, together with a separate brassière. Between 1890 and 1917 Samuel Gossard, Rose Kleinert, Gabrielle Poix and a handful more secured successful patents for their own versions of the brassiere. The best-known patent was by American Mary Phelps Jacob (later known by her more seductive married name, Caresse Crosby) who put forward a simple design in 1914 – two handkerchiefs held together by strips of ribbon. Her brassiere looked pretty, but was by no means supportive for the well-endowed.

By the 1920s most women had adopted the brassiere in bandeau form – a flattening, bandage-style bra that squashed down the breasts to help create the desired boyish silhouette of the era. New companies such as Lovable and Maiden Form catered for the demand for bras. The new cup sizes, padding and boning of the 1930s gave increased support; nylon, the durable and lightweight wonder-fibre, proved ideal for 1940s designs.

The curvaceous starlets of 1950s America such as Jayne Mansfield took full advantage of increasing support in bra design. The latest versions pushed the breasts up and out to a near point. These busty beauties inspired a generation of teenage girls to adopt the 'sweater girl' look – a tight jumper worn over an arrestingly protruding bust. While some 1960s women really did go braless, Rudi Gernreich offered them an alternative with his No-Bra

Bra of 1964, which gave transparent coverage but little breast support. Other designers followed in the 1970s with light bras made from sheer fabric.

By the 1990s full support was back, and the Wonderbra, which pushed the breasts up into firm globes, became a best-seller, aided by the notorious advertising campaign that featured model Eva Herzigová and the strapline 'Hello Boys'. The lingerie company Agent Provocateur, co-founded by Vivienne Westwood's son Joseph Corré in 1994, helped to put sex back into smalls in the UK, with luxury collections of underwear sold from shops with strikingly raunchy window displays, more often associated with the red light district than with respectable shopping areas of the time. The bust supporter had come a long way. ■

TOP: *An early bra, Paris 1930s.*

ABOVE: *American movie star Jayne Mansfield flashes her well-supported breasts during a night out in Hollywood in 1951.*

Sharon Tate marries Roman
Polanski in 1968 in a white
minidress. After the 1920s a
wedding dress was expected to
be white, but the cut could be
dictated by fashion.

The only colour for a bride

IDEA № 7

THE WHITE WEDDING DRESS

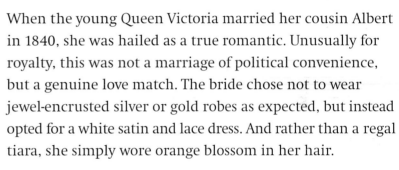

Queen Victoria's controversial white wedding dress caught the imagination of romantic 19th-century brides and was to influence wedding dress fashion throughout the 20th century.

When the young Queen Victoria married her cousin Albert in 1840, she was hailed as a true romantic. Unusually for royalty, this was not a marriage of political convenience, but a genuine love match. The bride chose not to wear jewel-encrusted silver or gold robes as expected, but instead opted for a white satin and lace dress. And rather than a regal tiara, she simply wore orange blossom in her hair.

Traditionally, women had married in blue or pink or their favourite colour, making a wedding dress a garment that they could then wear again. Working-class women frequently opted for practical black. But the young Queen Victoria's example was truly modern and attention-grabbing, and swiftly caught the public imagination. Quite soon, all new brides wanted to wear white for their big day. Initially, this was only possible for the rich, for who else could afford the luxury of a white dress that could only be worn a handful of times before showing its age?

By the 1920s, however, white was established as the only colour for a respectable Western bride. As class divisions gradually melted, it became harder to read a woman's position in society by her clothes. And if a lady could marry in white, why shouldn't her maid?

Thus the colour white quickly became the universal choice for bride's dresses, bringing with it associations of bridal purity and virginity. The colour blue, which had traditionally signified purity, came to be considered risqué for a bride. However, marrying in white would not always mean a long white dress. Bianca Jagger chose a tailored white skirt suit in the 1970s, while actress Sharon Tate married in a very short white minidress in 1968. More extreme was the actress Pamela Anderson, who tied the knot in a white bikini and high heels in Saint-Tropez in 2006.

Where previously a wedding dress might have been worn again, the modern bride will spend a huge sum on a dress designed to be used just once. It will probably be the most expensive gown she ever wears. Impractical, extravagant and to be worn a single time: for the modern bride, nothing but white will do. ∎

Movie star, princess and fashion icon Grace Kelly on her wedding day.

Style icons from parliament and palaces

IDEA Nº 8

ROYALS AND POLITICIANS

Royalty, senior politicians and politicians' high-profile wives exert a huge fashion influence on the public, helping to raise the profile of fashion designers, as well as spawning copy-cat looks on the street.

As wife to the French President, ex-model Carla Bruni-Sarkozy proves a stylish figure in public life.

Icons such as Jacqueline Kennedy and Diana, Princess of Wales, have always had to strike a difficult balance, having to look at the same time respectable, classy and fashionable, while being prepared for the media to scrutinize – and judge – everything they wear.

Queen Alexandra, wife of Prince Edward (later Edward VII), was a regal style icon of the late nineteenth and early twentieth century, with her striking poodle haircut, jewelled dog-collar chokers and high-necked blouses and dresses. More influential still was Wallis Simpson, the American divorcée for whom King Edward VIII renounced his throne in 1936. Rather than ostracize this interloper, society women copied her classy, elegant style, notably her Mainbocher wedding dress and its blue colour (known as Wallis Blue). And they paid close attention when she famously quipped that a woman could never be too rich or too thin. 'I'm nothing to look at, so the only thing I can do is dress better than anyone else,' was how she summed up her passion for clothes.

The fairytale life of Grace Kelly, who became first a Hollywood star and then royalty, upon marrying Prince Rainier of Monaco, provided inspiration to an entire generation of women. They slavishly imitated Princess Grace's coolly elegant style and could emulate her look with a Kelly bag, which

Hermès named after her. In 1949 the screen goddess Rita Hayworth married Prince Aly Khan wearing a striking blue dress by Jacques Fath, a fashion that many copied. And perhaps most famously of all, there was Diana, Princess of Wales, who lived constantly under the media spotlight. The public first copied her spectacular wedding dress, then adopted her hairstyle, and later subjected her ever-changing wardrobe to constant critical scrutiny.

Few female politicians make it on to the style pages, but the wives of politicians certainly do. First Lady Jacqueline Kennedy single-handedly brought pillbox hats back into fashion, and women copied her signature boxy trapeze-style suits, gilt-chained handbags and minimalist shift dresses. Her husband, John F. Kennedy, jokingly introduced himself to the British Parliament as her husband. More recently Michelle Obama, the only black First Lady to grace the White House, caused a stir with her vibrant and brightly coloured wardrobe, and her swanlike white chiffon inauguration dress by Jason Wu. The model, singer and ex-girlfriend of Mick Jagger, Carla Bruni, who married the French President Nicolas Sarkozy in 2008, also brought an injection of style to politics, raising the fashion bar with her demure Dior coats, neat ballet pumps and, of course, perfect good looks. ∎

LEFT: *First Lady Jacqueline Kennedy looks demure but effortlessly stylish in 1963.*

ABOVE: *The Duke and Duchess of Windsor in 1937. Wallis Simpson may have been blamed for the abdication of a king, but she was still revered as a style icon.*

This striking photograph was taken by Cecil Beaton for the October 1950 edition of UK Vogue.

The first fashion shoots

ABOVE: *Pages from a fashion shoot entitled 'The Birds' for* The Face, *February 1995.*

BELOW: *Writer and society beauty Nancy Mitford makes the cover of* The Bystander *in 1932.*

IDEA № 9

PHOTOGRAPHS IN MAGAZINES

Fashion magazines have always been illustrated – but until the latter part of the nineteenth century these illustrations were drawings. It took the introduction of photographs to bring the pages to life.

British photographic pioneer William Henry Fox Talbot introduced halftone printing in the 1850s and as the method was refined and commercialized over the next few decades, the impact on magazines was enormous. Fashionable ladies were now able to peruse the latest trends by means of excitingly realistic, full-colour, glossy photographs.

The *New York Daily Graphic* was the first newspaper to print a photograph, in 1873. The superiority of halftone printing over previous technology was obvious, and by the 1890s the process had spread to hundreds of publications. Halftone printing enables an image to be reproduced by breaking it down into a pattern of tiny dots, like a pointillist painting, using a series of fine mesh screens. The dots are of different sizes, which when seen from a distance are joined together by the human eye so that it appears to see a continuous-tone image – a photograph.

The ambitious launch of *Vogue* by American publishing company Condé Nast in 1909, and of the magazines that followed, such as *Harper's Bazaar*, spawned a new breed: the fashion photographer. The magazines' pages served as disposable galleries for their photographs, and the editors of these magazines were their new patrons. Condé Nast appointed Baron Adolphe de Meyer as the first salaried staff photographer in 1914. His job was to photograph not models but society ladies, whose fashionable clothing was displayed for *Vogue* readers to admire and emulate. De Meyer's style was flattering, with a strong emphasis on soft focus. He moved to *Harper's Bazaar* in 1923.

Fashion photography flourished with the experimental work of the early in-house photographers at *Vogue* and *Harper's Bazaar*, most notably Edward Steichen, George Hoyningen-Huene, Horst P. Horst and Cecil Beaton. They experimented with new techniques and composition, and set the tone for twentieth-century fashion photography, making it an integral part of the fashion industry we know today. ■

The Bystander, April 20, 1932.   NO. 1479. VOL. CXIV.

The BYSTANDER

THE HON. NANCY MITFORD
The eldest daughter of Lord and Lady Redesdale, who is at work on a new novel.

From Bunny Hug to breakdance

DANCE DRESS

Fashion designers love their clothes to be worn and promoted by youthful beauties; and youthful beauties like nothing more than to party and – almost always – to dance. As dance fads evolve with the cultural developments of each decade, so canny designers create clothes to reflect the new spirit and to complement the new moves.

A tango craze swept Europe and North America in the 1910s, and women stalked the dancefloor in dresses with slit hems and draped armholes, and shoes with ribbon ankle straps or Cleopatra sandals trimmed with a cameo. With the Roaring Twenties came an obsession for frenetic jazz beats. Dances such as the Bunny Hug and Kickaboo were best performed in short straight-up-and-down dropped-waist dresses in bold colours (the daring showed their knees) – the beads and fringes shook and sparkled with the dancer, while the obligatory diamanté 'slave' bracelets remained tightly secured, high up on the biceps.

The wide skirts and neat bodices of the 1950s complemented rock-and-roll moves, the skirts swirling as the girls were twirled, with the petticoats providing for modesty if they were swung up into the air. When the disco craze exploded in the 1970s, girls wanted to shimmer and shine like exotic fish under the flashing lights and spinning mirror balls. They chose stretch boob tubes, halter-neck jumpsuits and skin-tight shiny trousers, all worn with strappy sandals in gold or silver.

Brightly coloured loose unisex clothing was the look for the acid house parties and raves of the 1980s and early 1990s, with comfortable T-shirts, wide jeans and Day-Glo accessories for 24-hour ecstasy-fuelled dance marathons. Hip hop culture and breakdancing introduced a street-smart combination of bright, branded tracksuits, trainers with large laces, and loose stretch sportswear, with breakdancers often wearing nylon tracksuits, trainers and hooded tops. The energetic, athletic nature of the dancing meant that sportswear was ideal. Tracksuits were good for sliding on floors, and a bandana worn under a baseball cap was perfectly suited for head spins. As dance moves progress from the formal to the athletic, so the clothing adapts to suit the dancers and their changing moves. ∎

TOP: *1920s flappers danced furiously in beaded and fringed dresses that shook and sparkled as they moved.*

ABOVE: *London breakdancers in 1983 wearing denim, sportswear and trainers.*

Women dancing at the disco club Studio 54 in New York, November 1977.

'Girls wanted to shimmer and shine like exotic fish under the flashing lights and spinning mirror balls'

IDEA №11

MODERN TRAVEL

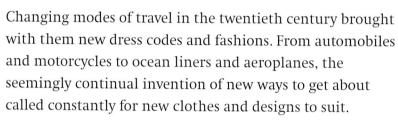

Changing modes of travel in the twentieth century brought with them new dress codes and fashions. From automobiles and motorcycles to ocean liners and aeroplanes, the seemingly continual invention of new ways to get about called constantly for new clothes and designs to suit.

Dunhill's Motorities advertisement, 1904. The invention of the car prompted radical developments in women's outerwear in order to protect their eyes, hairstyles and clothes.

From 1905, the rich started to buy motor cars to use for travel. Previously, cars had been purchased for their novelty value. Those who could afford an early open-topped car needed to dress appropriately, in order to protect the hair, eyes and clothes. Vast dustcoats, bonnets trimmed with veils, gauntlet gloves and goggles helped to keep at bay the dirt thrown up from the road. Dunhill made leather travel clothing for women from 1901 and Louis Vuitton crafted its own luxury leather luggage, designed to fit into the new motor cars. In 1959 the company developed a protective coating for its cotton canvas bags and trunks, to repel the grime of airports and the road.

The first woman to fly across the Atlantic was Amelia Earhart, in 1928. Female pilots were the epitome of glamour, and none more so than Earhart, resplendent in her leather jackets, silk scarves and slim-fitting trousers. She had a complete collection of flying clothes made for her by Elsa Schiaparelli. Earhart launched a fashion line endorsed with her name, and achieved some renown for her simple, stylish, hard-wearing clothes. In 2008 Jean Paul Gaultier at Hermès paid homage to her with his Earhart-styled catwalk models. In the 1930s Schiaparelli introduced a lightweight travel bag for women to take with them on flights, complete with an easy-to-pack capsule wardrobe. It included dresses, hats and a reversible coat for day and evening.

As commercial flying became common, the air hostess – as she was then called – also made her mark on fashion. Now viewed as overtly sexist, their prescribed uniforms often included miniskirts, catsuits and even hot pants.

Motorcycle and scooter owners created their own new subcultures and styles. The 1950s bikers, the disaffected youth who raced bikes and toured the States, wore leather jackets, blue jeans and dashing white scarves, as made famous by Marlon Brando's outlaw biker in *The Wild One* (1953). A decade on, rockers took up black leathers as their bike uniform. Their rivals, the mods, preferred green military-style parkas, to protect their slick Italian-style suits from dust kicked up by their scooters.

Space travel is not yet available to all, but this too may one day generate its own distinctive fashion style. ∎

1970s air hostesses working for Southwest Airlines wear hot pants as their uniform. The Texan airline's motto was 'sex sells seats' and in-flight drinks had names such as Passion Punch and Love Potion.

IDEA № 12

PROTEST DRESS

Why shout when you can wear your message on your sleeve and make just as great an impact? As an alternative to throwing yourself under a racehorse or going on hunger strike as the early twentieth-century suffragettes did, you could simply march wearing the movement's protest colours of white for purity, green for hope and purple for dignity.

Dressing for protest frequently influences mainstream fashion. The Afro hairstyle, used at first as a badge of black pride, was famously flaunted by activists Stokely Carmichael and Angela Davis, and made fashionable by singer James Brown. It caught on from 1968, the year that the Black Panthers made their mark as activists, taking as their uniform Afros, Cuban heels and black leathers. Similarly, when in the 1960s Germaine Greer stated that 'bras are a ludicrous invention', it became a feminist statement to go braless – a gesture that quickly lost its political value, however, as it became generally acceptable for women to go without a bra in the 1960s and 1970s. And while the hippie movement started as an anti-Vietnam War movement, others soon adopted their loose, layered clothes simply to look fashionable.

Katharine Hamnett boosted sartorial protest with her 1984 Choose Life collection of bold message T-shirts advocating world peace and environmental issues. That was also the year in which, famously, she met Prime Minister Margaret Thatcher while wearing a T-shirt printed with the words '58% Don't Want Pershing' – a reference to the public opposition to American Pershing missiles being based in the UK. The photographers immortalized her protest on camera, and it was featured in the press the following day. Hamnett set a trend for protest and slogan T-shirts, and in 2003 sent T-shirts on to the catwalk bearing the words 'Stop War, Blair Out', as a reaction to the war in Iraq.

Dressing for protest is not just the domain of single-issue campaigners. The punk movement rejected many of society's norms for anarchy and anti-authoritarianism. Their safety-pin accessories and outlandish clothing spoke eloquently of their rebellious nature. Conversely, sometimes it's what you do not wear that can make the greatest impact. The animal-rights group PETA made waves with its notorious advertising campaigns in the early 1990s featuring attractive undressed celebrities coupled with the slogan 'I'd rather go naked than wear fur'. And to reinforce the message, PETA protesters carrying banners with the same slogan stripped naked at Paris Fashion Week in 2007 and stormed the catwalk. Be it through overdressing or nudity, fashion became an acceptable vehicle for protest. Clothes could be used to shock, not merely to flatter the female form. ∎

ABOVE: *African American activist Angela Davis in 1971. Her Afro signals her support for the struggle for racial equality.*

BELOW: *Suffragette songsheet, 1911, in the movement's colours of purple, green and white.*

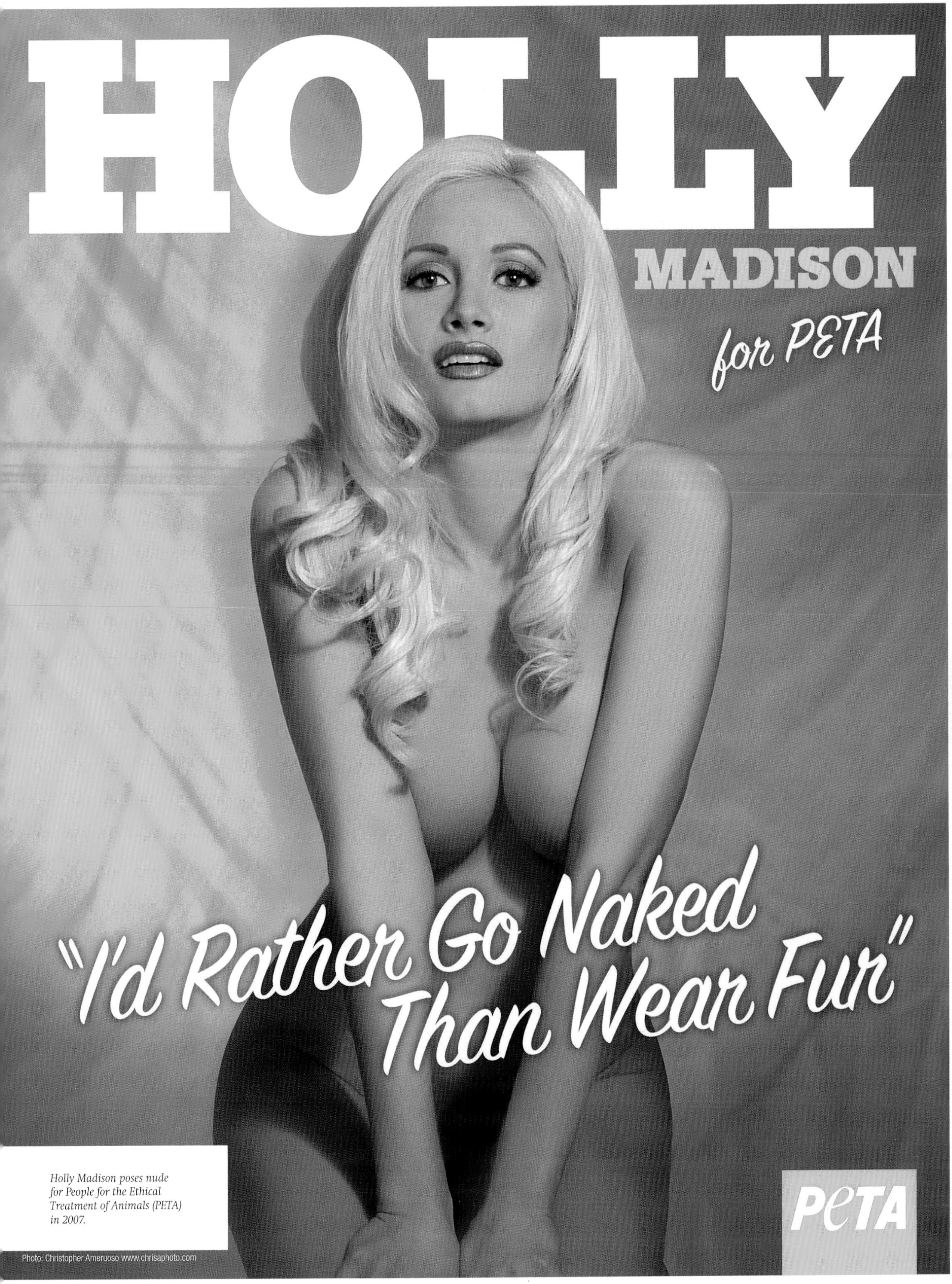

Holly Madison poses nude for People for the Ethical Treatment of Animals (PETA) in 2007.

Photo: Christopher Ameruoso www.chrisaphoto.com

Model Agyness Deyn attends
the tribute to Stephen Sprouse
after-party hosted by Louis
Vuitton in 2009. She wears a
bold tailored jacket and carries
a lime-green Stephen Sprouse
Graffiti Louis Vuitton bag.

From Poiret to Pucci

BOLD PRINTS

At the end of the nineteenth century, soft and delicate pastel shades were considered a sure sign of affluence, taste and gentility. But this demure approach to colour and design was not to last.

ABOVE: *German countess and model Veruschka shows off her flamboyantly printed trousers and shirt by Emilio Pucci in 1966.*

BELOW: *1911 illustration for Les Ballets Russes by Léon Bakst. The dance company inspired fashion designers such as Paul Poiret to introduce bold patterns and oriental references.*

As the twentieth century wore on, women were no longer expected to look delicately self-effacing, and they gradually came to welcome bold colours and patterns as a form of self-expression. Paul Poiret gave fashion a jolt, introducing bright oriental colour, bold patterns and prints inspired by the Ballets Russes' appearance in Paris in 1909. Women wanted to embrace this new-found opulence and its youthful sense of fun.

Screen-printing was to revolutionize the textile-printing industry, as fashion fabrics could be printed quickly and efficiently using this technique. Although some prints were worn through World War II, it was during the 1950s that bright, breezy and optimistic prints took off, with stripes, florals and gingham printed on wide skirts and dresses. Even bolder were the bright swirling patterned silks of Italian aristocrat Emilio Pucci, who cornered the market for luxury casualwear and printed lightweight silk jersey dresses. He said: 'My prints are ornamental designs worked in continuous motion; however they are placed there is rhythm.'

Young people in the 1960s were drawn to bold prints, including Pop and Op art designs, the Mondrian-inspired work of Yves Saint Laurent, and loud florals and coloured stripes. Sonja Knapp went for a gentler approach with her soft prints in loud colours for the house of Ungaro. By the end of the decade, the hippie movement had inspired a move away from graphic patterns with patchwork, tie-dye, paisley prints, and influences from the Far East. Ossie Clark covered his light silk and satin dresses with organic flowing prints by his wife Celia Birtwell. British designer Zandra Rhodes made her name with voluminous silk dresses using Art Deco zigzag motifs.

Christian Lacroix opened his couture house in 1987, and shot to fame with his signature fabric embellished with bold prints, bright colour, beading and embroidery. Gianni Versace's baroque and Byzantine-inspired black and gold prints became highly desirable.

The graffiti print influenced a number of designers who wished to inject their work with an urban street feel, such as Viktor & Rolf, Moschino and Martin Margiela. Vivienne Westwood used prints by Keith Haring in 1983, while Stephen Sprouse collaborated with Marc Jacobs in the early 2000s and covered Louis Vuitton luggage and bags with his trademark graffiti motif. Once more, a luxury design house had borrowed from the street. ∎

LES BALLETS RUSSES
PROGRAMME ÉDITÉ PAR
COMŒDIA ILLUSTRÉ

Prix : 2 francs

NIJINSKY
dans "La Péri"
Aquarelle de Léon BAKST

The original style bible

IDEA Nº 14

VOGUE

By the end of the twentieth century, fashion magazines, their editors, and their staff had grown powerful, able to make or break a designer or a trend with a few careful words. The most powerful of all, *Vogue*, is renowned not only as the most influential fashion magazine but also as one of the most long-standing. It set a precedent in quality and style for the numerous fashion titles that have come after it, and is now published in 19 countries.

Arthur Baldwin Turnure founded *Vogue* as a small New York society weekly in 1892. But it was a young lawyer and publisher Condé Nast who turned the magazine around when he bought it on Turnure's death in 1909, adding more colour, advertisements and articles on society and fashion. He produced it fortnightly instead of weekly, started successful British and French editions (and also launched an unsuccessful version in Spain) and transformed *Vogue* into an exciting and glamorous fashion magazine aimed at affluent society women. Crucially, Nast also persuaded advertisers to pay big bucks to reach this discerning readership, making the magazine as lucrative as it was appealing.

In 1913 Nast hired the celebrated portrait photographer Baron Adolphe de Meyer as his staff fashion photographer, stepping up the glamour and style sections of the magazine. Photographs of society ladies in the latest frocks were always a staple feature of *Vogue*, but he now introduced fashion photographs of actresses and lively society beauties prepared to play to the camera.

When *Vogue* reached Britain in 1916, World War I was raging and public morale was low. Wartime was, however, good for magazine publishing. Women left behind while their menfolk were at the front could indulge in the escapism of *Vogue's* world of fashion and high society, and they were also keen to work on magazines as editorial staff. After the war ended, it was the new middle classes who lapped up fashion magazines.

Subscriptions boomed during the Great Depression and World War II. When the chips were down, it seemed, women bought *Vogue*. As the journalist Penelope Rowlands wrote in a biography of Carmel Snow, fashion editor of *Vogue* in the 1920s, '*Vogue* was the summit, the apex, the *ne plus ultra* of the fashion world. It was, quite simply, It'. It was the biggest-selling American fashion magazine of all, she said: 'No other one could compete.' ∎

UK Vogue *cover, July 1928.*

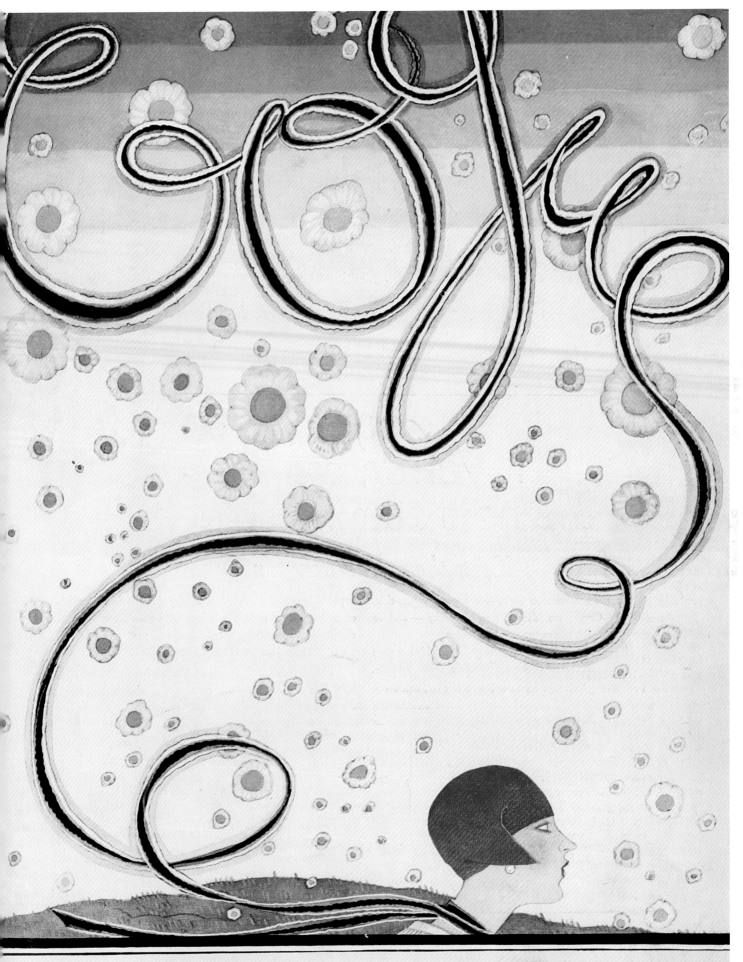

Vogue

Paris Forecast & Clothes for Scotland

Broadening horizons

IDEA № 15

GLOBAL INFLUENCES

Fashion designers working in the West use inspiration from other cultures and countries around the globe to enrich their collections. Whether gleaned from foreign travel, books or artefacts, the colours, prints, silhouettes or overall global themes help to inject new energy into fashion.

The dynamic nomadic style of designer John Galliano for his Autumn/Winter 2010 show.

When the Ballets Russes first came dancing into Paris in 1909 they caused a sensation with their exotic and opulent costumes – not least the dancer Nijinsky, who was painted blue and wearing an eye-catching pair of Turkish trousers. The fashion designer Paul Poiret responded by injecting his work with exotic colour and oriental detailing, including turbans, plumes, kimonos and harem pants. They became the height of fashion, for those who dared to dabble in this extravagant world.

Thus inspired, designers went on to use Slavic folk prints in 1917 and, later, Egyptian and Chinese motifs. Between the wars, Chinese and Japanese details became fashionable. And after World War II, South American colours and prints influenced North American casualwear – they looked sunny and bold, perfect for the beach or the weekend.

With the arrival of affordable airline flights in the 1970s, world travel became easier and fashion influences from abroad flourished. Hippies came back from their Asian wanderings with embroidered waistcoats, Afghan coats, kaftans and gypsy tops. They roamed around in flowing skirts in bright colours and the loose, layered clothing worn in hot climates. Designers took note and, incorporating global styles from other cultures, they developed a luxury hippie aesthetic. One of Yves Saint Laurent's most memorable shows was the Russian collection of 1976, boasting exotic peasant boots, shawls and full swinging skirts. As Cecil Beaton observed of Saint Laurent in his diaries: 'His life in Marrakesh has influenced him in cloth and thread embroidery. There are dull soft brocades with old thread in them that have all the restraint of early Persian art, and there are Chinese influences worked in garish colours ... It is unobtrusively elegant, different, new, uncompromising.'

Japanese designers including Issey Miyake and Yohji Yamamoto made an impact in the 1980s by employing wrapped and layered Eastern clothing. Versace concocted an Indian-inspired draped clothing collection while Rifat Ozbek included North American Indian feathers and beads – and prints inspired by Turkish Iznik tiles.

Romeo Gigli, Jean Paul Gaultier and John Galliano continued to absorb influences from around the globe. The latter's designs for Dior and his own label included fantastic concoctions, such as bright beaded collars inspired by the Masai people and dresses and vast kimono sleeves inspired by Japan. A collection from Galliano ensured a round-the-world tour, bringing beauty, rich ornament and spectacle to the catwalk. ∎

The decline of domestic service

IDEA Nº 16

D.I.Y. DRESSING

High society of the nineteenth and early twentieth century required complicated dress changes throughout the day: the day dress, the visiting dress, the tea gown, the evening dress. Waist-length hair had to be brushed out every night and artfully pinned up each morning, and corsets had to be laced up. None of this was possible without the help of a maid.

Upper- and middle-class households of the period took domestic service for granted, but World War I would change everything. In Britain, many working-class women left domestic service in order to fill what were traditionally male jobs. After the war, the middle classes tried to reclaim their servants, but without success. Former staff now wanted to remain in their civil-service, transport, factory or clerking jobs. They had enjoyed a taste of independence and the higher wages offered, and wished to better themselves in society.

In the 1920s, relaxed sporty clothes in dark colours (previously associated with the working classes) started to be worn by everyone. This meant less ironing, mending and washing; and dressing could be achieved at speed. Simple chignons or practical bobbed hair meant no more hours of fussing at the dressing table – shorter bobs, the Eton crop and the shingle were the fashionable styles, and boyishly simple to maintain.

While working-class women had a new taste of freedom in the workplace, middle- and upper-class women were freed from the fetters of elaborate, uncomfortable, time-consuming dress. 'The problems of quick dressing and the beginning of the lack of servants now became acute. Schiap made aprons and kitchen clothes so that American women could do their own cooking and still look attractive,' wrote Elsa Schiaparelli in her 1954 autobiography, *Shocking Life*.

Coco Chanel and Jean Patou inspired a modern and streamlined boyish silhouette for the Roaring Twenties. It was a world away from the bustles, corsets and sweeping dresses worn just 20 years before.

After World War II, the advent of refrigerators, vacuum cleaners and other labour-saving appliances meant less need for servants; and, moreover, not all the rich still enjoyed their prewar wealth and were able to afford domestic staff. A way of life had passed. ∎

FAR LEFT: *Advertisement, 1911. Society women of the Belle Époque would not have been able to get dressed without the help of a maid.*

LEFT: *This 1928 black beaded evening dress, fur-trimmed coat and short slick hairstyle epitomize the new simplicity of the Roaring Twenties.*

'Middle- and upper-class women were freed
from the fetters of elaborate, uncomfortable,
time-consuming dress'

*A 1920s flapper. Illustration
by Russell Patterson.*

Bronzed and beautiful

IDEA № 17

SUNBATHING

Until the end of the Victorian era, no self-respecting lady tolerated a suntan: a brown face and hands were indicative of the working classes, implying time spent at manual labour and physical work in the fields. Upper-class women took care to protect their fashionably pale complexions from the sun's rays with bonnets and parasols.

Brigitte Bardot in 1960, when she created a scandal by sunbathing topless in Saint-Tropez.

With the explosion of the craze for sunbathing in the 1920s came new fashions both on and off the beach, including revealing clothes that would show off a golden tan. In the early 1900s, doctors and scientists had begun actively to promote sun therapy for the benefits of vitamin D, which is produced by the skin when exposed to sunlight. The tide was already turning. Then, when the fashion designer Coco Chanel was spotted sporting a rich tan in the 1920s, her acolytes took note, and decided that they wanted a golden sun-kissed body too, ideally acquired on the French Riviera. By 1923, a December tan had become a status symbol, synonymous with the luxury of winter travel.

Fashion designers swiftly responded to the new craze. Jean Patou, Sonia Delaunay and Elsa Schiaparelli conjured up loud, attention-seeking swimming costumes whose bright colours emphasized a tan. The 1930s trend for halter-neck swimsuits allowed for a seamlessly golden-tanned back, which could then be displayed in a low-backed white slinky dress in the evening. The next decade brought with it informal beachwear that revealed the flesh – blouses showing the midriff, shorts and thong sandals.

The launch of the bikini in 1946 gave women an excuse to flaunt even more bare flesh. But in the 1960s Brigitte Bardot did the unthinkable and scandalously started sunbathing topless, at Saint-Tropez in the South of France. The designer Rudi Gernreich backed this celebration of semi-nudity by launching his monokini of 1964 – a pair of high-waisted bikini bottoms, held up only by long halter straps and completely revealing the breasts.

Today, topless or nude sunbathing is common (although nudist activities are not actively promoted by fashion houses). Bikinis are often tiny triangles of fabric, and swimsuits are sometimes slashed or pierced with large holes to reveal the flesh. Sunbathing, however, is hardly a health cure today, with excessive exposure to the sun known to cause premature ageing and, potentially, skin cancer. There is no going back to bonnets, parasols and darkened parlours at midday, but rather than baking in the sun, women are increasingly faking it with all-over spray-tans instead. ∎

_au Li do._

At the Lido _by Georges Barbier,_
1924, an illustration of sunbathers
on the beach in Venice.

Girls take on the boys

IDEA № 18

TROUSERS FOR WOMEN

Walk down any city street in the West today, and you will see more women wearing trousers than skirts. Yet trousers for women did not become even remotely acceptable until as recently as the 1920s.

Coco Chanel borrows from the boys and wears yachting pants in 1910.

The legendary French actress Sarah Bernhardt daringly wore trousers on stage in the late nineteenth century, while early enthusiasts of bicycling favoured divided skirts for practical reasons.

Designer Paul Poiret took inspiration from the costumes of the Ballets Russes for his harem pants of 1909 – wide trousers gathered with a band at the ankle. And at the society beach resort of Deauville, Coco Chanel introduced elegant yachting pants, at first for herself and then for other women who admired her style. She explained: 'It was Deauville and I never liked to stay on the beach in my bathing costume, so I bought myself a pair of white sailor pants, and added a turban and ropes of jewels, and I must say, I looked like a maharani.' Women in the 1920s started to choose trousers as beachwear and loungewear, but only the very outrageous dared to wear them on the street.

The bisexual film star Marlene Dietrich, sometimes referred to as 'the best-dressed man in Hollywood', caused a scandal during the 1930s and '40s by wearing trouser suits as daywear. The Parisian chief of police considered her attire so shocking that he ordered her to leave the city.

During World War II it became acceptable for women to wear trousers for wartime work in the fields and the factories, but when peace resumed in 1945 they went back to their skirts and dresses. Trousers on women were still generally viewed as unnatural and unattractive. However, capri pants,

bermuda shorts and tight trousers that laced up at the knee were still worn as leisurewear.

It was in the Swinging Sixties that women really started to embrace the comfort and practicality of menswear, wearing trousers for work and to parties. The practice still retained its shock value for some, and women wearing trousers were often refused entry to formal establishments, even restaurants. Yves Saint Laurent's 1966 sleek tailored trouser suit, known as Le Smoking, was controversial at first, but this would be the garment that eventually sealed the acceptability of trousers as an alternative to the skirt suit or dress. Here was a formal, elegant suit for the girls, acceptable to all. Women could finally wear the trousers and get the respect they deserved. ■

'Women wearing trousers were often refused entry to formal establishments'

LEFT: *Marlene Dietrich, 1940s. Dietrich scandalized the public by blatantly flaunting her bisexuality and wearing*

RIGHT: *Bianca Jagger looks sleek and elegant in a mannish three-piece trouser suit in 1972.*

The new artificial silk

IDEA № 19

RAYON

Rayon was one of the first man-made fibres to be used for clothing. 'Art silk', 'gloss' or 'fibre silk', as the fabric was first known, was soft and shiny, and was used as an alternative to silk, velvet, crêpe and linen. In 1924 the name was changed to rayon. It revolutionized the clothing market, as it was comfortable, economical to make and dyed well.

During the 1880s a Frenchman, Count Hilaire de Chardonnet, developed fabric made of cellulose after studying the silkworm, with a view to making a version of silk using chemicals. But the method for actually processing viscose rayon was invented by three British chemists, Charles Frederick Cross, Edward John Bevan and Clayton Beadle, and patented in 1892. The material is in fact produced from wood pulp, and so cannot be truly called a synthetic. The first reliable fabrics woven from viscose rayon filaments appeared between 1910 and 1914.

During the 1920s, manufacturers used rayon to make cheap dresses, linings, slips, knickers and stockings. With technological advances they could eliminate its artificial sheen, making it suitable for knitted fabric and more expensive daywear and evening wear. Thirties women on a budget bought slips and camiknickers made from lace-trimmed rayon instead of silk – perfect for the dark days of the Depression when money was tight. At the other end of the scale, high-end designers such as Elsa Schiaparelli experimented by blending rayon with natural fibres. Rayon was not resilient, but when combined with acetate it produced a stronger, more convenient fabric that retained its shape and was wrinkle-free, so eliminating the need for time-consuming ironing.

One of the benefits of rayon is that it can be controlled at the production stage, so that it can be made to imitate wool, silk, cotton or linen. It is still used for dresses, sportswear, skirts and suits, and is often found blended with other fibres. ■

A 1920s advertising poster promotes the benefits of rayon stockings.

'Thirties women on a budget bought slips and camiknickers made from lace-trimmed rayon instead of silk'

Coco Chanel astounded society by designing strings of pearls and ornate bejewelled crosses that were unashamedly fake, and by wearing them during the day rather than with evening clothes.

Flaunting great fakes

COSTUME JEWELLERY

The ancient Egyptians made beads of glass, and imitation pearls were worn in Europe as early as the fifteenth century. But the world of high fashion always shunned imitation jewellery as mediocre. This was all to change in the early twentieth century.

Paul Poiret first challenged the notion that 'faux' jewellery was unacceptable as an accompaniment to couture, and Coco Chanel and Elsa Schiaparelli were to make history with it.

Poiret was the first couturier boldly to use costume jewellery in his collections, and by 1913 his clients were happy to be seen flaunting his tassel pieces and his amber heart or stone Buddha pendants. Chanel then rocked the boat, coming up with imitation pearls the size of gulls' eggs, and gems in unnatural colours. Her attitude was, simply: Why not mix fake with real and keep everyone guessing? In her eyes jewels should be worn as fashion accessories, rather than as a demonstration of wealth or ancestry. French *Vogue* commented in 1927: 'This synthetic fashion, which is one of the typical symptoms of our time, is not without finesse, and that so many things are artificial – silk, pearls, fur – does not cease to make them chic.'

Chanel had opened her jewellery workshops in 1924 and began to use handfuls of paste jewels and fake pearls, combined with real gems in bold settings. They proved irresistible. Chanel herself flouted convention by wearing strings of fake pearls, long ropes of gilt chains and glittering Maltese crosses, even during the day. Her 1930s chains, pearls and glass-gemstone jewellery were designed to accessorize the clean lines of her sporty daywear collections. Chanel had brought the little black dress into fashion, and it now made the perfect backdrop for showing off large pieces of diamanté jewellery. Referring to her Fine Jewellery collection of 1932, she said: 'I wanted to cover women with constellations.'

Elsa Schiaparelli also had great fun with her jewellery collections during the 1930s, using wit and humour to attract her clients. They could not wait to get their hands on her snake hatpins, roller-skate brooches, charm bracelets, pins of can-can legs, lantern brooches that lit up and even facial jewellery, such as spectacles without the glass. At last fashion jewellery could be truly playful. ∎

Macaw feather fan earrings by Shaun Leane for Alexander McQueen, Spring/Summer 2003.

The success of the hidden fastening

Vivienne Westwood's iconic bondage trousers of 1977 used the zip as detailing.

IDEA Nº 21

THE ZIP

The humble zipper, that neat little fastener that women around the globe use to do up their clothes quickly each morning, is something that we take for granted. Imagine the fuss, and the time wasted, if there were no alternative to fiddly hooks and eyes, ties, buttons and poppers.

The modern zip as we know it, with its moveable clasp and interlinking teeth, was developed in 1913 by a Swedish–American engineer named Gideon Sundback. However, zips only started to be incorporated into womenswear fashion as late as the 1930s. Prior to that they were principally used as fasteners on money belts, US Navy jackets, underwear and luggage.

It was Elsa Schiaparelli who broke with convention in the early 1930s and ostentatiously used a zip as a fashion statement on the pockets of a beach jacket. A few years later, in 1935, she went a step further, dyeing zips to match the fabric of her collection and using them as decorative elements on evening dresses and jackets. Schiaparelli wrote in her 1954 autobiography, *Shocking Life:* 'What upset the poor, breathless reporters most were the zips. Not only did they appear for the first time but in the most unexpected places, even on evening clothes. The whole collection was full of them. Astounded buyers bought and bought. They had come prepared for every kind of strange button. Indeed these had been the signature of the house. But they were not prepared for zips.'

Designer Charles James followed Schiaparelli's lead and took the zip to another level when he created his bias-cut spiral Taxi dresses in the 1930s. For these he used panels of fabric wrapped round and round the body, fastening together with long zips instead of seams. Similarly, 1960s designer Rudi Gernreich used zips with large O-ring sliders as decorative devices snaking round the body, as if the garment could be unzipped into narrow bands of fabric. Ossie Clark even designed raunchy jumpsuits for Mick Jagger's performances, which would unzip themselves on-stage. Vivienne Westwood played with zips for her notorious 1970s punk bondage trousers – drainpipes with zips, buckles, straps and a bum-flap of hanging fabric.

The zip's role today largely tends towards the mundane. It is used mainly as a convenient hidden fastening for dresses, tops, skirts, trousers, coats and boots – and, just sometimes, for the odd fashion statement. ∎

The zip revolutionized the speed at which women could dress and undress. Farrah Fawcett in 1979.

'Subcultural movements have long been drawn to military clothes for their confrontational appearance'

Fashion enters the combat zone

IDEA № 22
MILITARY CLOTHING

When nations go to war, their citizens are exposed to more images of the military. And these influences inevitably creep into catwalk collections. Military clothing had a major impact on twentieth-century fashion, giving us such recognizable classics as pea jackets, aviator glasses and combat pants.

After World War I, womenswear adopted large patch pockets, braiding and frogging, and indeed the colour khaki. Thomas Burberry produced a civilian version of the raincoats worn by British Army officers, known as trench coats. The public also eagerly snapped up Ray-Ban aviator shades, which were launched to civilians in 1937, having been in use by US Army Air Corps pilots from the late 1920s.

World War II inspired designers to add practical detailing to their clothes, such as numerous pockets and thick leather belts. In the UK, all-in-one zip-up jumpsuits were designed for swiftly pulling over nightclothes in air raids; Winston Churchill famously wore his instead of a suit. Turbans and snoods, which were initially favoured for keeping workers' hair out of factory machines, became fashionable alternatives to hats.

Subcultural movements have long been drawn to military clothes, for their confrontational appearance as much as their practical qualities. The 1960s mods wore voluminous parkas, once worn by the US military, to protect their immaculate suits. Hippies also adopted the large coats, and adorned them with peace symbols. At the height of the Vietnam War, militant Black Power supporters and members of the anti-war movement wore multi-pocketed fatigue jackets as a form of protest. And punks paraded the streets in Dr. Martens boots with combat trousers, often combined with long leather army coats.

More recently, the Gulf wars also freshly inspired designers to adopt military influences in the 1990s and 2000s. Combat-style clothing and camouflage prints in bright colours became a new street uniform, and combat trousers worked as an easy alternative to jeans.

In the world of fashion it seems that military styling, rather like war itself, just will not go away. ■

TOP: *Suits from 1945. The suit on the right has strong military detailing.*

ABOVE: *Sarah Jessica Parker wears combat pants in 2006.*

The celebration of simplicity

IDEA № 23

THE JUMPER

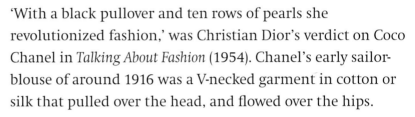

'With a black pullover and ten rows of pearls she revolutionized fashion,' was Christian Dior's verdict on Coco Chanel in *Talking About Fashion* (1954). Chanel's early sailor-blouse of around 1916 was a V-necked garment in cotton or silk that pulled over the head, and flowed over the hips.

Coco Chanel wears an elegant jumper with trousers, c. 1930.

Unusually for the time, it had no buttons or fastenings. She sold masculine-style jumpers for women, and adapted sweaters by slashing them down the front and trimming them with ribbons: they became best-sellers.

Before World War I broke out Chanel had opened her shop in Deauville, northern France, and introduced elegant clothing, much of it adapted from male dress, often customizing clothes from her lovers' wardrobes. She gave women comfort, elegance and the joy of dressing in clean lines and simple clothing. After the war, the jumper, or sweater, went on to form one of the keystones of the looks of the 1920s – it became a comfortable alternative to tailoring, often worn under a knitted cardigan with a simple skirt. By the 1930s knitted jumpers were starting to be worn as evening wear, glammed up with trimmings of chiffon, crêpe or sparkling jewel-encrusted embroidery.

The notorious sweater girls of the 1950s got pulses racing, as tight jumpers became popular with film actresses such as Lana Turner and Jane Russell. These sweaters emphasized the breasts, particularly when worn with a push-up-and-point bra, leaving little to the imagination. Teenagers of the 1950s swiftly adopted the look to their parents' horror and their boyfriends' delight. In the 1960s, the slimline skinny-rib jumper came into fashion. Mary Quant wrote in her autobiography:

'One day I pulled on an eight-year-old boy's sweater for fun. I was enchanted with the result. And, in six months, all the birds were wearing the skinny-ribs that resulted.'

Retailer and designer Joseph Ettedgui revolutionized the knitwear industry in the 1980s with his Joseph Tricot range, selling luxurious ribbed sloppy joe jumpers, and fine tightly knitted tops. With the demise of the tailored jacket during the 1990s, an elegant jumper became acceptable for evening wear. The best came in cashmere. A cashmere jumper is now viewed, like a well-cut pair of jeans or a little black dress, as a wardrobe essential. To fulfill the demand for simple luxury, affordable cashmere became available on the high street for the first time, with such stores as Primark and Marks & Spencer producing their own versions of the cashmere jumper.

Chanel had said: 'Simplicity is a very delicate thing, not to be confused with poverty. My luck was to have understood that luxury is inseparable from simplicity.' Once again she had helped to pioneer what would become one of the most basic fashion staples in any woman's wardrobe. ∎

Sweater girls Marilyn Monroe (left, in 1952) and Sophia Loren (right, in 1955) wear tight jumpers worn over conical bras to flaunt their assets. Teenage girls rushed to copy the look.

'The focus of the face
had to be a pair of childlike
wide eyes'

*Glass Tears photographed
by Man Ray in 1932.*

Maximizing feminine allure

IDEA № 24
FALSE EYELASHES

Where would flirtatious brides and red-carpet beauties be today without their false eyelashes? Some of the first falsies were created in 1916 by the American film director D. W. Griffith for his leading lady, Seena Owen.

He wanted her lashes to be so long that they brushed her cheeks when she blinked. Griffith asked a wig-maker to attach some interwoven human hair to a fine piece of gauze, which was glued to her eyelids. The effect was extraordinary.

However, it was not until several decades later that false eyelashes really took off for the woman on the street. They became popular in the 1950s, and by the 1960s were a fashion essential. Lipstick was worn pale, meaning that the focus of the face had to be a pair of childlike wide eyes. The waiflike supermodel Twiggy often wore false eyelashes above and below her eyes, or sometimes attached to her bottom lashes alone. The model Jean Shrimpton and actresses Marianne Faithfull, Sophia Loren and Elizabeth Taylor were all renowned for their luscious lashes, and the singer Dusty Springfield became known for her 'panda-eyed' look.

The 1960s versions were made of bristle-like plastic: their staying power was limited, and they tended to fall off. Salvation came in the 2000s when the Japanese invented individual fake lashes that could be glued on to real eyelashes, one by one. These were like hair extensions for the eyes, lasting up to two months. Today false lashes are as popular as earrings and lipstick. Shu Uemura created a set of paper-clip style lashes with Dutch fashion designers Viktor & Rolf, and in 2009 the UK band Girls Aloud launched their own range of false lashes in collaboration with Eylure. Flirting has never looked so good. ∎

Long lashes backstage before the John Galliano Autumn/Winter 2008 show.

ABOVE: *John Galliano poses with Princess Diana in 1996. She wears one of his slip dresses.*

BELOW: *John Galliano shows a seductive petticoat-inspired dress for Christian Dior in 1997.*

Why Coco Chanel was the original material girl

IDEA № 25

UNDERWEAR AS OUTERWEAR

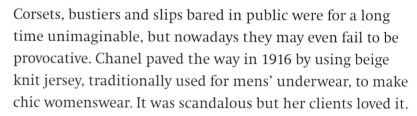

Corsets, bustiers and slips bared in public were for a long time unimaginable, but nowadays they may even fail to be provocative. Chanel paved the way in 1916 by using beige knit jersey, traditionally used for mens' underwear, to make chic womenswear. It was scandalous but her clients loved it.

Far from minding, the fashionable ladies of Deauville and Biarritz positively snapped up Chanel's new designs. Couturier Jacques Fath made waves with his risqué evening dresses with corset lacing in the 1940s, but it was the ever-provocative designer Vivienne Westwood who really changed fashion by offering underwear as outerwear. In the late 1970s, punks strutted the streets of London in rubber negligées and stockings, bought from Westwood and Malcolm McLaren's shop SEX. This was underwear worn as outerwear largely for its shock value.

The 1980s was the decade when underwear as outerwear made it to the mainstream. The image of Madonna dancing on-stage during her 1990 Blond Ambition tour wearing a Jean Paul Gaultier corset with a sharply pointed bra is unforgettable – but not scandalous. Madonna regularly performed in bras, slips and corsets. Jean Paul Gaultier offered corsets to wear with evening suits, and Westwood introduced satin bras layered over sweatshirts and dresses in 1982. When Westwood produced neo-Victorian short crinolines in 1985, she was ridiculed at first – and then, inevitably, other designers started copying the look. A Westwood corset top became highly desirable as evening wear, not least because it enhanced the cleavage magnificently.

During the 1990s, bejewelled thongs were worn to ride up above low-slung jeans. Women danced, partied and even got married in tiny slips of bias-cut silk, and camisoles with slim spaghetti straps or lace detailing. The master of these petticoat evening dresses or slip dresses, as they became known, was John Galliano. He famously managed to coax Princess Diana into one, and images of the People's Princess in her risqué petticoat made headlines around the world.

More recently, in 2009 Dolce & Gabbana produced a show-stopping tulle corset dress with sexy criss-cross lacing snaking up the sides of the body, demonstrating that underwear details that just hint at provocation are perhaps the most enticing of all. ■

'Madonna performed in bras, slips and corsets'

Madonna struts her stuff in Jean Paul Gaultier corsetry for her Blond Ambition tour, 1990.

IDEA № 26

THE CLUTCH BAG

At the turn of the twentieth century, a society lady would never be seen carrying her own handbag. Anything except the tiniest purse was given to a man or a maid to hold. All this was to alter as women grew more independent and their changing lifestyles required that keys, money and make-up be instantly available at their fingertips.

Embroidered clutch by Hilde Wagner-Ascher, 1925.

The clutch bag, or 'pochette', evolved between 1916 and 1920. With its streamlined shape and snap-jaw fastenings, it mirrored the modern, no-frills aesthetic of the 1920s. The architect and designer Le Corbusier enthused: 'The luxury item is well made, clean of line, pure and strong, revealing its quality in its very spareness.' In the early 1920s the style leader Coco Chanel produced clutch bags in leather or Bakelite or in fabrics matching her garments. Other designers, including Edward Molyneux, launched their own versions of the slimline bag. Sonia Delaunay and the jeweller Jean Fouquet introduced graphically ornate clutches in bold colours.

During the 1920s and 1930s, few fashionable women were seen without a clutch. It was the most popular bag of the era. As the shape was so simple, designers experimented with the bag's colour, texture and embellishment – snakeskin, lizardskin, shagreen and patent leather, with dramatic rhinestones and gold braid for evening. Designers used Bakelite and Perspex, the new modern materials, and simpler bags were embossed or embroidered. While sun-ray designs and Art Deco and Egyptian motifs were fashionable during the 1920s, designs of the 1930s focused more on exotic reptile skins and sparkling diamanté fastenings.

During World War II, women in Europe shunned the clutch for larger, more practical bags that would hold essentials while they were bicycling, doing war work or during air raids. However, clutch bags have remained popular since then in their different guises: long and slim in the 1960s, soft and pliable in the 1970s and quilted in the 1980s. In the 2000s they were ludicrously large, so that by 2008 the offerings from Céline, Louis Vuitton and Fendi looked more like embellished art portfolios than bags, owing to their size. Perhaps it was time again for the men to carry a woman's bag of tricks and prove that chivalry was not quite dead. ∎

Gold clutch by Halston, from the Spring/Summer 2009 collection. Small decorative clutches work well for evening. This one, due to its size and colour, works like a piece of jewellery against the orange dress.

'With its streamlined shape and snap-jaw fastenings, it mirrored the modern, no-frills aesthetic of the 1920s'

The timekeeping essential

IDEA № 27

THE WRISTWATCH

The first wristwatches were small clock faces attached to ladies' bracelets as ornaments, and were worn at the end of the nineteenth century. It was not until after World War I that wristwatches were in demand for both sexes.

When Rolex entrepreneur Hans Wilsdorf started to promote the wristwatch as the essential timepiece, male critics said that they would rather wear a skirt than a wristwatch, and stuck to their gold pocket watches on chains. However, for pilots and artillery officers fighting in World War I, the wristwatch was the only sensible solution to timekeeping. Expandable bracelets attached the clockface to the wrist, and pierced metal 'shrapnel guards' covered the glass. The soldiers brought home these 'trench watches' as souvenirs, and wristwatches finally became acceptable for men too. In 1914 Rolex was awarded a precision certificate by Britain's Kew Observatory (an endorsement previously bestowed only on marine chronometers), proving wrong those who criticized the accuracy of wristwatches. By the 1930s, the wristwatch had overtaken the pocket watch as the most desirable mobile timekeeping device.

New innovations started to drive watch design. The compact quartz time-keeping mechanisms first launched in 1969 meant that absolute accuracy could be achieved and marketed economically, while the digital displays of the 1970s inspired more

functional design. In 1983 the Swatch watch company launched inexpensive, fashion-led designs in brightly coloured plastic, with highly efficient and compact inner workings. They were an instant hit.

Just as they did with sunglasses and handbags, designer brands such as Gucci, Chanel and Louis Vuitton started to include luxury branded wristwatches in their ranges. However, by 2000, the mobile phone was beginning to replace the watch as the most popular method of telling the time. For the younger generation, wristwatches became less popular as functional items. This meant that a watch had to do something else as well as tell the time – such as double up as an elegant piece of jewellery. Marc Jacobs launched a series of watches on necklace chains using cherry or zipper motifs, brands such as Calvin Klein and DKNY produced pretty watches strung on charm bracelets, while other designers set watches into rings. Fashion had gone full circle in 100 years, with women desiring watches as jewellery once more. ■

ABOVE: *Marc by Marc Jacobs pendant watch, 2009.*

BELOW: *A striking alternative to a wristwatch, this 'Nougat' ring by Dior, 2004, is made from white gold with pink mother of pearl.*

Buccellati watch with engraved
silver face and gold leaf motif
bracelet strap, 1930s.

'They were perfect for showing off the nubile figures of film starlets'

Fluid bias-cut dress, 1944. Bias-cut dresses allowed the fabric to move and flow with the body.

Cutting at an angle to create curves

IDEA Nº 28

THE BIAS CUT

When fabric is cut on the bias, it is cut diagonally across the direction of the weave, so that the warp and weft (the 'grain' of the fabric) fall diagonally over the figure rather than horizontally and vertically.

Material cut in this way is naturally elastic, a property that can be used to make dresses cling and stretch on contact with the body's curves, producing an elegant effect and flattering the figure.

The French dressmaker Madeleine Vionnet, who opened her Paris fashion house in 1912, is known as the mistress of the bias cut. Until her ingenious ideas began to influence fashion in the 1920s, the bias cut had been used in the twentieth century principally for collars. Unusually, Vionnet designed her dresses by draping, gathering and twisting fabric on a small wooden dummy rather than using traditional pattern-cutting techniques. Many of her dresses had no fastenings, and pulled straight over the head – it was only when a body filled them that they magically came to life. Vionnet was one of the pioneers in rejecting the corset. She focused on achieving a figure-hugging fit with dresses that flowed smoothly over the body in one layer of fabric – they incorporated no under-dress. They were often long with halter or cowl necks, and sweeping low backs. She favoured lightweight crêpe, gabardine and satin, which were pliable and draped easily.

Bias-cut dresses reached the height of their popularity in the late 1920s and the 1930s. They were perfect for showing off the nubile figures of film starlets, and many of the slinky Hollywood gowns typical of the period were cut on the bias. Madame Grès, who opened her Paris house in 1934, also became famed for her bias-cut dresses and classical drapery inspired by ancient Greece. She took wool, silk and jersey and draped them into clever dresses, which looked simple on the body but had a masterly intricacy of design.

Vionnet's innovation has continued to provide inspiration for later designers. During the 1980s Azzedine Alaïa employed this cutting method for his skin-skimming dresses, and today's John Galliano and Zac Posen are both celebrated for reworking the bias cut into their own designs. 'The whole idea of cutting on the bias was brilliant,' said Galliano on the subject. 'It was elastic before there was elastic.' ∎

TOP: *John Galliano for Christian Dior combines a structured bodice with a figure-skimming bias-cut skirt for this white dress for Autumn/Winter 2007.*

ABOVE: *Dress by Madeleine Vionnet, 1938. The mistress of the bias cut, Vionnet revolutionized fashion with her draped and fluid dress designs.*

Fashion gets fit and fabulous

Jane Fonda works out in the studio in 1982.

IDEA Nº 29

SPORT

Sportswear played a central role in twentieth-century fashion, changing and driving clothing in a way no one could have anticipated. It altered the way women dress, move and feel in their clothes. Fashion and sportswear are irreversibly intertwined, and designers working in each field borrow ideas from the other.

Sports dress has crossed over to become acceptable daywear, inspiring women to dress more casually and comfortably. Today fashion designers draw on elements initially developed for sport; while sportswear itself is stylish as well as functional.

In post-World War I Europe the demise of the lace-up corset meant that women had to work hard to achieve the new lithe silhouette that fashion demanded. To be slim in the 1920s was essential. For their sporting activities women needed the appropriate skiwear, swimming costumes, skating clothes and tennis whites, and the sporting look became fashionable in itself.

Jean Patou and Coco Chanel were already designing daywear that was sportier and more boyish than ever before – simple, pared-down clothes, more practical and suitable for the increasingly independent woman. Patou adapted some elements of sportswear for his fashion lines. In 1925 he opened a sportswear store, Coin des Sports, and he designed the match outfits for the French tennis star Suzanne Lenglen – short dresses and headbands. They became instantly

fashionable. Chanel produced sleek sporty womenswear in cotton jersey, and introduced men's yachting trousers to her clients.

But the roots of modern sportswear, or casualwear, really lie in the United States. With the boom in mass-manufacturing after 1939, American women adopted a more casual style. They took to wearing comfortable and practical separates. And rather than following the latest fashion fads laid down by Paris couture, they looked to their own ready-to-wear designers, such as Claire McCardell. This tendency was to influence the way women dressed around the world. By the 1950s, American teenagers were wearing easy separates and trainers as casualwear.

From the 1970s onwards, there was a constant crossover from the gym and the court to the street. Aerobics brought disco-style Lycra leggings and leotards, while jogging and skating introduced shorts, legwarmers and headbands. American designer Norma Kamali raised the humble tracksuit to high fashion, with ra-ra skirts, leggings and cotton fleece tops. And in the cities, kids dressed like their favourite sports

stars, from basketball heroes in the 1970s to skateboarders in the 1990s.

Powerful sports brands were keenly aware of the influence of sports stars, and called in big-name players to endorse their products and boost sales, notably Michael Jordan for Nike and David Beckham for Adidas.

Fashion designers looked at new sports fabric technology to gain inspiration for their designs. They launched their own sports label spin-offs in the 1990s – among them Prada Sport, DKNY Active and Polo Sport. Meanwhile, other partnerships with sports brands were struck up for specific ranges of clothing or trainers – Yohji Yamamoto worked with Adidas, Alexander McQueen with Puma and Commes des Garçons with Speedo. High fashion had never looked so fit and fabulous. ∎

BELOW: *Collection for Adidas by Stella McCartney for Spring/Summer 2009.*

RIGHT: *Tennis star Suzanne Lenglen wears whites by Jean Patou in 1926. She started a trend for headbands and sleek, sporty dresses.*

N°5

N°5
CHANEL
PARIS

PARFUM

The world's most famous fragrance

IDEA Nº 30

CHANEL NO. 5

When Marilyn Monroe was asked what she wore in bed, she famously quipped: 'Why, Chanel No. 5, of course.' This distinguished scent, in its iconic bottle, is one of the most successful in history, worn by millions of women since it was launched in the 1920s. Still in production today, it changed fashion-house fragrances forever.

Chemical advances in the nineteenth century meant that perfumiers started to incorporate synthetic ingredients into scent, particularly in place of an expensive or rare natural ingredient. Synthetic components also made a fragrance last longer on the skin. But Coco Chanel turned the perfume industry on its head when in 1921, with her perfumier Ernest Beaux, she launched a perfume that *deliberately* smelt artificial – Chanel No. 5.

Until then, perfume was made to smell like flowers – jasmine, rose, lily of the valley – and came trussed in feminine bottles. Chanel had wanted a scent that reminded her of the soap she used as a child. The resulting fragrance had no recognizable floral scent, came in a bold medicinal-style bottle and looked clean and modern. Just as she celebrated costume jewellery, Chanel revelled in the scent's artificiality. Chanel No. 5 contained more than 80 different ingredients, and mixed numerous natural floral scents with synthetic ingredients. Radically for the time, its top note – what you first smell when the scent hits the skin – was created using floral aldehydes (powerful synthetic molecules that intensify aromatic scents).

In 1911, Paul Poiret had launched his own perfume range, Les Parfums de Rosine, named after his oldest daughter. He linked each fragrance to a gown he had designed, and used both chemical and natural ingredients. But he missed a marketing opportunity to brand it with the name of his fashion house. Chanel did not. Her scent bore her name. The House of Worth, Edward Molyneux and Elsa Schiaparelli quickly followed suit with their own branded fragrances, and Christian Dior had a 1947 hit with the successful Miss Dior.

Cheap international travel and duty-free shopping meant that women of all classes were able to buy fashion-house fragrances during the 1960s. Twenty years later the fashion brands were aggressively marketing their house scents with moving-image and still advertising campaigns, all clamouring to corner a segment of this lucrative market. Erotic imagery boosted sales, led by Calvin Klein's raunchy ads for Obsession. By the 1990s, Klein had made history again by setting a trend for unisex scent with his fragrance CK One. New perfume trends come and go but without the innovation of Chanel No. 5, we might all still have been smelling of roses or lavender. ∎

ABOVE: *Silkscreen prints by Andy Warhol of Chanel No. 5 (1985), used for the advertising campaign in 1997.*

OPPOSITE PAGE: *Actress Audrey Tatou features in an advertisement for Chanel No. 5 in 2009.*

Bow lips and smoky eyes

IDEA № 31

PAINTED LADIES

Cosmetics have been used for centuries, even millennia – the ancient Egyptians used kohl to emphasize their eyes as long as 6,000 years ago. But at the start of the twentieth century, the look for high-class ladies was pale, natural and demure. Their hair might be lavishly rolled and pinned up, but obvious make-up, painted nails and dyed hair were eschewed as vulgar.

By the 1920s the natural look was no longer fashionable. Artifice was all, as demonstrated by the 'Sisters G' in Berlin in 1925.

The 1920s were to introduce a new notion of beauty that could be achieved by artifice – short hair and a painted face. Quite suddenly, a woman would not be seen dead on the street without her lips painted into a cupid bow, her eyes defined with kohl and mascara and her complexion smoothed out with make-up. Flappers plucked and pencilled in their eyebrows, and coloured their nails. Elaborate hair was transformed with scissors into a boyish bob or Eton crop, and a high level of obvious grooming became fashionable and smart for the bright young things.

Virginia Woolf wrote in her 1925 novel *Mrs Dalloway*: 'To his eye the fashions had never been so becoming; the long black cloaks; the slimness; the elegance; and then the delicious and apparently universal habit of paint. Every woman, even the most respectable, had roses blooming under glass; lips cut with a knife; curls of Indian ink.'

Both the cool cats of Swinging London in the 1960s and the punks of the following decade would appropriate this appreciation of artifice. During the 1960s, the popular look was childlike and boyish – a pale made-up face framed by short hair snipped into a Vidal Sassoon crop – and was famously promoted by Mary Quant and the model Twiggy. Teamed with heavy black eyeliner, elaborately curled lashes and pale lipstick, the emphasis was on making women look like large-eyed dolls.

The punks particularly enjoyed playing with hair and make-up, and accentuated the shock factor, cutting off their hair or teasing it up into dramatic spikes of lurid colours. Faces were covered with white make-up, and black-rimmed eyes and dark lipstick were complemented by shiny black nails. Artifice was all: these girls were never going to wear flowers in their hair as the hippies once did. ∎

BELOW: *Twiggy, 1967. In the 1960s make-up focused on the eyes, and women emulated Twiggy's wide-eyed doll-like style.*

RIGHT: *A London punk, 1977. Punk make-up was shockingly bold, with black lips and nails.*

TOP LEFT: *Red sandals by Yves Saint Laurent, 2010.*

TOP RIGHT: *Black wedges by Salvatore Ferragamo, 1940.*

MIDDLE LEFT: *Black flat sandals by Valentino, 2010.*

MIDDLE CENTRE: *Pink flip-flops.*

MIDDLE RIGHT: *Black stilettos by Pucci, Spring/Summer 2010.*

BOTTOM LEFT: *Blue cutaway ankle boots by Sergio Rossi, Spring/Summer 2011.*

BOTTOM CENTRE: *Black heels with a flesh-tone trim by Yves Saint Laurent, Spring/Summer 2010.*

BOTTOM RIGHT: *Platform sandal by Salvatore Ferragamo, 1938.*

Daring to flaunt the feet

IDEA № 32
THE OPEN SHOE

Sandals are the most primitive shoes in human history. The ancient Egyptians, Greeks and Romans found them ideal for protecting the soles of their feet, and the simple yet practical design was standard for many centuries before more sophisticated shoes were developed.

A model steps out in cutaway boots at the Alexander McQueen Autumn/Winter 2003 show.

Their acceptance in twentieth-century fashion was, however, gradual. Sandals first came into fashion during the 1920s. As the French Riviera became the favoured summer destination for the upper classes, women started to feel more confident about showing naked skin in public. André Perugia made opulent high-heeled sandals in suede and snakeskin for the evening, while the Italian Salvatore Ferragamo introduced the sandal to America. Although peep-toes, slingbacks and sandals were available for day and evening by the end of the 1930s, some women still regarded them as taboo away from the beach. Respectable women had covered their feet in the past and, even in 1939, the style arbiters at *Vogue* deemed that sandals were too revealing to be worn on the street. The slingback, the design of which suggested the exposure of the rear, was seen as risqué. It was not until after World War II that it became fully acceptable to expose the insteps, heels and toes in public.

Pretty, opulent Italian sandals complemented the New Look fashions of the 1950s, while American designer Beth Levine pioneered flat-heeled sandals in clear acrylic. The 1970s brought a renewed enthusiasm for peep-toes reminiscent of the 1940s, as well as larger-than-life platform sandals. By the 1990s and 2000s, elegant strappy sandals had come back into fashion, with designers such as Manolo Blahnik and Jimmy Choo catering for stars and starlets, who loved the height and the delicacy – and probably the sexual connotations – of walking high above the ground on nearly-naked feet. On the street, sophisticated and ornamented versions of the flip-flop (particularly Brazilian Havaianas) and chunky Birkenstock sandals became *de rigueur* for summer casualwear.

In 2007 and 2008 gladiator sandals hit the catwalk and the streets. Some had lacing that snaked up the ankle to the knee, while others sported vertiginous heels. Two thousand years after its origins, Roman fashion was once more back in town. ∎

Every woman should own one

IDEA № 33

THE LITTLE BLACK DRESS

Sleek, black and simple, the little black dress is an essential fashion staple. The hemline hovers around the knee (it is never long), but the sleeve and neck detailing, as well as the fabric, change with the ebb and flow of fashion. However, its essence is in its versatility.

The LBD can be worn for the office, for cocktail parties and for dinners, and, like a white shirt or a pair of jeans, it is a true fashion classic whose popularity spans the decades. Yet this simple, understated wardrobe essential was once deemed unfit for a lady. Pale colours were more difficult to clean, and therefore were associated with status and wealth. Black was the opposite, and black dresses were worn by women in service. No rich woman wanted to dress like her maid.

When a black dress was worn by a lady, it signified mourning, and black would never have been chosen as a fashion colour. The fallen soldiers of World War I left behind them vast armies of mourning widows, sisters and mothers. Society became very used to seeing women of all classes clad in black outside the house, including many young widows.

Then Coco Chanel came along and changed the rules. To great fanfare, American *Vogue* first featured her sleek black dress in 1926. With its short skirt, long sleeves and diagonal detailing it looked new, streamlined and modern – perfect for the 1920s forward-thinking woman. *Vogue* even likened its simplicity of form to the model-T Ford. Once again Chanel had neatly taken the class values out of clothing. The little black dress could make any woman look elegant, and without great expense. It became a uniform, often made of velvet and lace for the evening, and wool for the day.

'You can wear black at any hour of the day or night, at any age and for any occasion,' said Christian Dior. 'A little black dress is the most essential thing in any woman's wardrobe.'

Fashion doyenne Wallis Simpson, later the Duchess of Windsor, agreed: 'When a little black dress is right, there is nothing else to wear in its place.'

And which woman today does not have a black dress in her wardrobe? From Prada to Preen to Calvin Klein, almost all designers offer some version of this fashion classic. It slims the figure; it is a fine backdrop for jewellery; it flatters blond hair. It can be worn for party after party and thanks to its anonymous colouring, does not run the risk of being remembered on future occasions. It is hard to imagine a time when an LBD will not still look modern and elegant. ■

Black crêpe dress with embroidered skirt by Chanel, 1926.

Little black dress by Christian Dior, 1959.

'It looked new, streamlined and modern – perfect for the 1920s forward-thinking woman'

A naked Sophie Dahl strikes a provocative pose in this advertisement for the Yves Saint Laurent fragrance Opium, 2000. Photograph by Steven Meisel.

OPIUM
le parfum par
Yves Saint Laurent

Letting it all hang out

IDEA № 34
PUBLIC NUDITY

Daringly low-cut dresses from the latter 1920s reveal the skin, a leap forward from the 1900s, when it was shocking to show an ankle in public.

In 1900 it was considered risqué for a respectable woman even to show her ankles in public. Yet that same woman's grandchildren, once grown-up, would be able to sunbathe topless or even naked on a public beach.

In the West, the twentieth century saw an extraordinary revolution in public attitudes to nudity, which swung from one extreme to the other. In fashion, as revealing more flesh became acceptable, so designers were able to experiment with ever-skimpier styles.

During World War I, skirts crept above a woman's ankle for practical reasons – bomb shelters and munitions factories were no places for sweeping dresses. The bright young things of the 1920s dared to reveal their knees and even a flash of stocking top, in their new short flapper dresses. During the 1930s, armless body-skimming dresses with daringly low backs showed even more flesh, and designer Madeleine Vionnet produced a bold evening dress that exposed the midriff.

Interestingly, sandals were still seen only as beachwear, as even adventurous women would still not reveal their naked feet. When Louis Réard launched his prototype bikini in 1946, he encountered a major problem: his models refused to wear it. He had to hire a stripper to model his new design to the public. But times were changing fast. By the 1960s Brigitte Bardot was sunbathing topless in Saint-Tropez; and other sun worshippers soon followed her lead, though perhaps delighting the onlookers less.

With the contraceptive pill available in the United States and Europe by the early 1960s, a new era of sexual permissiveness and liberation was born. The hippies gleefully embraced nudity and indulged in far greater sexual liberty than previous generations. Fashion reflected this in miniskirts reaching buttock-skimming heights, and these in turn gave way to the craze for hot pants in the 1970s. The desire to show naked flesh continued unabated, with G-strings and low-cut, pubic-hair-skimming hipster jeans becoming popular in the 1990s.

After the turn of the century the label Imitation of Christ launched a collection with topless models in microshorts pushing vacuum cleaners. When Sophie Dahl modelled naked in a sexually provocative manner for the Yves Saint Laurent Opium campaign in 2000, shot by Steven Meisel, the posters were banned by the British Advertising Standards Agency after more than 700 complaints. But this was tame compared with the soft porn images used for the Tom Ford men's fragrance ad in 2007, in which a bottle of perfume was photo-graphed between the spread legs of a nude model, her fingers resting gently on the bottle top. To previous generations it would have been unthinkably obscene. Today, it is just advertising. ∎

Borrowing from the boys

ANDROGYNY

BELOW: *Singer Ciara shows the strikingly androgynous effect of the trouser suit for women in 2004.*

BOTTOM: *Bianca Jagger cuts a dash at New York club Studio 54 in 1978 in sharply tailored black jacket, black trousers and white shirt.*

Fashion regularly swings between celebrating voluptuous, womanly curves and favouring a more boyish silhouette. The flappers of the 1920s epitomized the lithe, androgynous look, as did the more recent skinny waif models of the 1990s, whose style was condemned by critics as 'heroin chic'.

The first time that this boyish look came into fashion in the twentieth century was during the 1920s. It was a decadent time for survivors of both the war and the great flu pandemic of 1918. The ratio of young women to men left was about three to one. Some girls were simply never going to find a man, so why should they not enjoy life with a male kind of freedom – easy-to-wear clothes and hairstyles, a job, cigarettes, cocktails, sex and dancing all night? That is, if you were rich enough.

Coco Chanel and Jean Patou both pioneered the androgynous look. Borrowing from the boys, Chanel produced blazers, pyjamas, reefer jackets, open-necked shirts worn with cufflinks, and jumpers for women. The bachelor girls, as these 1920s liberated women became known, strapped down their breasts, cut their hair short into shingles or Eton crops, masked their hips with dropped waistlines and revealed their legs with daringly short dresses. They were nicknamed *garçonnes* after Victor Margueritte's censored 1922 novel *La Garçonne* – a romp of career girls cutting off their hair and sleeping around. Yet in real life they were not the majority. The look made no real impact until 1926, and even then it was for the glamorous and elite. But its effect slowly filtered down, and for a while modern women took up a masculine style and smoked, drank and ditched their chaperones.

The 1960s ushered in another era that celebrated and almost worshipped youth. The Twiggy silhouette was sexless and childlike – skinny, with a big head and oversized eyes, and a tiny frame on which to hang wide clothes that hardly touched the body.

In the 1970s, as second-wave feminism gathered momentum, the gender distinction between fashions for young people grew increasingly blurred. Both sexes grew their hair and wore T-shirts, jeans and beads – while glam-rock stars David Bowie and Marc Bolan dressed up like showgirls, as did their fans. At last Yves Saint Laurent's Le Smoking trouser suit for women became acceptable.

Streetwear and workwear of the mid-1980s allowed men and women to adopt a similar unisex style, and today women have a choice. They can dress up in heels and dresses and flaunt their womanhood one day, and go for androgynous casualwear or a sleek trouser suit the next, and no one will think to comment. ∎

Coco Chanel models her own designs in the 1930s. Her success as an innovator was built upon adapting traditional masculine clothing for the 20th-century woman.

'Modern women took up a masculine style and smoked, drank and ditched their chaperones'

IDEA № 36
THE SHOULDER BAG

An independent urban woman, who needs to keep both hands free and her valuables safe, would be lost without her shoulder bag. A handbag with a strap that either hooks over one shoulder or is slung diagonally across the chest is far more practical than the strapless clutch bag, which is easy to lose and perfect for prowling muggers to snatch.

ABOVE: *Wartime belles make full use of the practical straps on the new handbags in Paris in 1942, leaving their hands free for bicycling.*

BELOW: *Big and bold bag by Versace for Autumn/Winter 2008.*

Elsa Schiaparelli had designed functional bags with shoulder straps as early as the 1930s. The benefits of the shoulder bag became obvious during World War II, when practicality was paramount. Hands could be kept unencumbered for more important tasks, while the bags could hold a gas mask as well as match an outfit.

After the war, European women wanted to leave the memories of practical austerity behind, and enjoyed the decadence of prettier, short-handled bags. But they still used the shoulder bag for country pursuits, in the summer and as a casualwear accessory. In the United States the shoulder bag stayed in fashion.

In 1955 Chanel introduced the much-copied quilted leather 2.55 shoulder bag, with its long gold chain strap (she used similar chains to weight the inside hems of her jackets). Other designers copied it, creating their own small bags strung on long straps.

During the 1960s the shoulder bag enjoyed a resurgence, accessorizing the new get-up-and-go youthful fashions of Swinging London; later the hippies carried large patchwork or embroidered carpet shoulder bags. As they in turn grew up and moved on, less flamboyant bags were in demand – either in soft leather and fitted with zips and integral straps, or practical satchel styles.

Prada's nylon rucksack of 1985 paved the way for light, sporty carryall bags for the girl about town, but by the turn of the century the rucksack had fallen from favour and sleeker bags were once again in demand. Fendi came up with one solution, designing a sleek compact bag with a short removable strap. It could be strung up over the shoulder and tucked under the arm, or carried strapless as a clutch. It was christened La Baguette.

Whether long or short, detachable or permanent, the shoulder strap had become a truly integral part of a woman's handbag. ■

Paris Hilton keeps her Fendi bag strapped close to her in 2006.

Shady ladies

IDEA № 37
SUNGLASSES

The Roman emperor Nero allegedly used polished emeralds to shade his eyes from the sun when watching the gladiatorial games. And although modern celebrity decadence might not go quite so far, where would today's paparazzi-shy celebrity be without her ubiquitous pair of shades?

Jackie Kennedy Onassis wears her signature large shades in 1968.

Lightly tinted corrective glasses were available during the nineteenth century for those with poor eyesight. But when in 1929 Sam Foster started to sell his Foster Grant sunglasses on the boardwalk in Atlantic City to the public, he started a revolution in eyewear. Not long afterwards, Bausch & Lomb launched their Ray-Ban aviator shades with anti-glare lenses, based on the green goggles the company supplied to the US Army Air Corps. They were the perfect solution for Hollywood starlets, who revelled in flash-bulb publicity, but wished to hide their eyes behind a layer of tinted glass. Women who in a previous age would have hidden behind a fan, could now smoulder mysteriously behind dark glasses.

The market grew rapidly during the 1930s, and sunglasses quickly became an essential fashion accessory, spurred on by images of movie stars in dark glasses in magazines and on the screen. Branded shades started to become more commonplace during the 1960s, and today a multinational fashion brand is incomplete without its own range of shades, alongside fragrances, jewellery and handbags.

Trends in sunglasses continually evolve. In the 1950s cat-eye sunglasses often had an upward flick. Small round glasses, as famously worn by John Lennon, were popular with hippies during the 1960s, but more stylish were Space Age white plastic opaque glasses by André Courrèges, perforated with a single horizontal slit for viewing the outside world. Frames grew to outsize proportions in the 1970s, as frequently seen on former First Lady Jacqueline Kennedy Onassis and singer Elton John. But by the 1980s and early 1990s the large rounded shades had been replaced by dramatically angular frames and dark lenses epitomized by the Ray-Ban Wayfarer. In 2000 designer Stella McCartney revived aviator-style shades. She decorated them with a small rhinestone heart, and they became one of the most sought-after accessories of the year. ■

'Women who in a previous age would have hidden behind a fan, could now smoulder mysteriously behind dark glasses'

Hollywood icon Joan Crawford leaves her dressing room in 1935.

Jacket, shirt and trousers by Balmain, shot for American Vogue, 2009. Designer Christophe Decarnin for Balmain revitalized the shoulder pad with this show-stopping collection.

'Power-dressing became popular with ambitious working women seeking to make an impact in a man's world'

Wearing it like a man

IDEA № 38
THE SHOULDER PAD

Before the 1930s wide shoulder pads were exclusively for the use of men. But in 1931 the radical designer Elsa Schiaparelli designed the first wide-shouldered suit for women and everything changed.

The suit caused quite a stir. Hollywood studios took note, speedily appropriating it for such stars as Marlene Dietrich. With Joan Crawford's costumes for the 1932 film *Letty Lynton* helping to popularize the look, the trend for wide shoulders was sealed.

Elsa Schiaparelli wrote in her 1954 autobiography, *Shocking Life*: 'In Hollywood, one special item of popularity had preceded me – that of the padded shoulders. I had started them to give women a slimmer waist. They proved the Mecca of the manufacturers. Joan Crawford had adopted them and moulded her silhouette on them for years to come.' Sharp suits with squared-off padded shoulders were to take women through the 1930s and into the war years, until Dior revolutionized fashion with his New Look in 1947.

Shoulder pads came back into favour again, later in the century, with heavy-shouldered powersuits for women in the 1980s. Thierry Mugler and Claude Montana made some of the most extreme designs of this period. Power-dressing became popular with ambitious working women seeking to make an impact in a man's world, their top-heavy suits either imitating or challenging the broad-shouldered outline of the male torso.

By 2009, thanks to a legendary collection by Christophe Decarnin for Balmain, the neat little shoulder pad returned. This time round it was not wide, strong and manly, but feminine, with upturned pagoda shoulders and slim sleeves. 'They reflect a need for protection in this time of financial turmoil and, I must say, I personally find nothing gives a greater sense of security against encroaching bankruptcy than sinking my head between some giant boulders on my shoulders,' wrote *The Guardian*'s fashion columnist Hadley Freeman in March 2009, with perhaps a pinch of satire, on the new revival. ∎

TOP: *Giorgio Armani advertising campaign for Autumn/Winter 1984, photographed by Aldo Fallai, featuring a powersuit with tailored masculine cut and wide shoulders.*

ABOVE: *Aviator Amy Johnson wears a suit in 1936 from the collection of flight clothes designed for her by Elsa Schiaparelli for her solo flight from London to Cape Town.*

'Cecil Beaton said of Garbo, "She has no friends, but a million fans are ready to die for her"'

A groomed Greta Garbo in furs, 1929.

Glitz, glamour and superstars

IDEA № 39

HOLLYWOOD AND THE TALKIES

Until the 1930s, the Paris couturiers had the last word in setting the high-fashion trends. But with the advent of the 'talkies', everything changed. Suddenly it was Hollywood costume designers who were generating new looks and trends – and communicating them to millions of viewers via the silver screen.

On 24 October 1929, Wall Street suffered its notorious crash, known as Black Thursday. It threw America into the Great Depression and sent the world economy spinning into chaos. The recession of the 1930s was a time of poverty and hardship for millions. Economic crisis meant that clothes shopping became a luxury; but women still wanted escapism.

The lives of the Hollywood stars, both on-screen and off, gave women a window into a highly desirable world of riches and glamour. Recorded sound was introduced to cinema in 1927, and cinema-goers flocked to the movies. The women dreamed of wearing Greta Garbo's hats, having Marlene Dietrich's legs, being as bottle-blond as Jean Harlow or owning Joan Crawford's *Letty Lynton* dresses. Cecil Beaton said of Garbo in *Vogue* in 1930: 'She has no friends, but a million fans are ready to die for her.'

The cinema-going public slavishly copied the on-screen trends, when they could afford it, with long bias-cut low-backed dresses in white for evening, and sharply cut wide-shouldered suits for day. Fur trims, wraps and the glitter of diamanté spread like fairy dust, adding more glamorous touches.

The Hollywood leading ladies were styled to within an inch of their lives. Presenting the perfect image was all, and cosmetic surgery was rife. The 1930s Hollywood studios spent vast sums on the wardrobes of their stars, employing costume designers such as Gilbert Adrian, Edith Head and Travis Banton to transform the girls into screen goddesses. The impact that such designers made on fashion has been as significant as any major designer working today, and they are remembered as fashion designers in their own right.

Hollywood stars continued to influence fashion with their on- and off-screen wardrobes – with Marilyn Monroe, Doris Day, Brigitte Bardot, Audrey Hepburn, Grace Kelly and Jane Fonda leading the way in the 1950s and beyond.

When, during the 1980s, designer Giorgio Armani designed costumes for the film *American Gigolo* and dressed the Hollywood stars for awards ceremonies, other designers followed suit, spotting the lucrative financial possibilities. Mutually beneficial relationships between leading designers and Hollywood stars began to blossom once more, the publicity helping both sides. And today no major fashion show is complete without its carefully dressed stars lined up in the front row for the cameras. ∎

TOP: *Marlene Dietrich stars in* Angel, *1937, in a costume by Travis Banton, with fashionably wide shoulders.*

ABOVE: *Gloria Swanson poses in a long white dress, a Hollywood favourite.*

'Disposable fashion was now decidedly hip; off-the-peg clothing was more popular than couture'

An advertisement for Monsoon in 2010. High-street retailers sell mass-produced clothing at reasonable prices.

Fashion for all

MASS-MANUFACTURING

Postwar America led the boom in mass-manufacturing ready-to-wear clothes. Off-the-peg clothes that were both fashionable and affordable were to become widely available in the latter half of the twentieth century. Fashion and style would no longer be the sole preserve of the wealthy.

The United States had suffered less from the war than had Europe. In fact, between the wars it had experienced a manufacturing boom. In the clothing market America boasted the most advanced research, development, production and retailing systems. The combination during the 1920s of simple clothing silhouettes, better communication to spread the trends around the world, less expensive man-made fabrics and easy fastenings such as the zip, all served to benefit mass-produced clothing. The depression of the 1930s also fuelled a demand for cheaper clothes, and these could be made using the new mass-production methods in factories, using specialized sewing-machines, overlockers and power-driven cutting equipment. After 1945, Europe began to copy America's efficient production methods.

American women started to look to their domestic designers for fashion ideas, rather than merely buying copies of Parisian clothes. A new American style emerged, its emphasis on casual, interchangeable separates. These could be easily produced with the new manufacturing methods. This casual style of dress began to influence European fashion, particularly the teenage, beach- and leisurewear markets. The new clothes were sold in high-street and department stores and, crucially, were affordable.

By the 1960s, designer fashion trends could be copied fast and efficiently. Throwaway youth fashions that had been mass-manufactured were in demand. Disposable fashion was now decidedly hip; off-the-peg clothing was more popular than couture. In order not to lose out, couture houses began to launch their own ready-to-wear lines offering mass-produced clothes in set sizes – with a designer label. 'What ready-to-wear does today ... even the Paris couturiers confirm tomorrow,' said Mary Quant. 'It has happened several times already. I think it will go on happening.' ∎

Seidenleichte Tergal-Kleider verlocken unwiderstehlich...

TOP: *Mass-manufacturing meant that the newly emerging phenomenon of 1950s teenagers could dress in new, smart fashions and all look the same.*

ABOVE: *This 1967 advertisement is for the polyester fibre Tergal. Mass-manufacturing and new synthetic fibres meant cheap clothes for all.*

Salvador Dalí inspired this extravagant coat with eight bureau-drawer pockets by Schiaparelli, and photographed here by Cecil Beaton.

Fashion enters a dream world

SURREALISM

A jacket bearing an image of a smashed mirror. Buttons that look like beetles. A black velvet handbag in the shape of a telephone. These quirky fashion ideas were inspired by Surrealism, one of the most significant art movements to make an impact on twentieth-century fashion.

Pearl, ruby and gold brooch by Salvador Dalí, 1949. © Salvador Dalí, Fundació Gala-Salvador Dalí, DACS, 2010.

The avant-garde Surrealists shunned rational and formal thought in favour of fantasy and the creation of a dream world. In fashion, some of the most original Surrealist ideas can be seen in the 1930s work of designer Elsa Schiaparelli, whose circle of friends included the Dada and Surrealist artists Man Ray and Marcel Duchamp.

She collaborated with one of the leading lights of Surrealism, Salvador Dalí, to make a daring dress with *trompe l'oeil* rips and tears, and a hat in the shape of an upturned shoe. Controversial American socialite Wallis Simpson was bold enough to wear Schiaparelli's 1937 white silk dress printed with a vast lobster, a motif that was taken directly from a Dalí painting. With Jean Cocteau, Schiaparelli produced a coat decorated with two faces in profile, the noses nearly touching: the negative space between them formed the optical illusion of a vase of roses.

Schiaparelli found it intensely exciting to work with such original thinkers. 'Working with artists like Bébé Bérard, Jean Cocteau, Salvador Dalí, Vertès, Van Dongen, and with photographers like Hoyningen-Huene, Horst, Cecil Beaton and Man Ray, gave one a sense of exhilaration,' she wrote in her 1954 autobiography, *Shocking Life*. 'One felt supported and understood beyond the crude and boring reality of merely making a dress to sell.' In the Paris of the 1930s great Surrealist balls took place, which formed the perfect showcase for Schiaparelli's fantastical clothing.

The photographers Horst P. Horst and Man Ray both experimented with Surrealist fashion imagery for their editorial work, as well as in their advertising images and fine-art photographs. The editors of *Vogue* and *Harper's Bazaar* took note of their arresting images, and commissioned Surrealist-inspired graphics for their covers during the late 1930s.

Surrealism continues to influence fashion design, advertising and graphics. Yves Saint Laurent used Surrealist sequin lip motifs for his 1971 collection, Marc Jacobs made a dress using hand-prints at the waist in 1986, and in 1997 British department store Selfridges commissioned John Galliano and Moschino to create Surrealist window displays. For their 2009 collections, both Moschino and Viktor & Rolf incorporated pipe, cloud and bowler-hat motifs, a nod to the paintings of Surrealist artist René Magritte. A playful Surrealist legacy lives on. ∎

Dress and headscarf by Elsa Schiaparelli in collaboration with Salvador Dalí, using a tear-print fabric, 1937.

Walking tall

IDEA № 42
PLATFORMS AND WEDGES

Wearing heels does not have to mean tottering along on stilettos. Platform and wedge heels give height and, sometimes, more stability, and can be hidden by long trousers or flowing skirts.

In 1937 the legendary Italian shoe designer Salvatore Ferragamo introduced a revolutionary new shoe with a wedge heel – a built-up heel that slopes down in a solid triangle to meet the sole at ground level. The design was born as much from necessity as anything else. Ferragamo had been forced to hunt around to find new materials, and owing to wartime steel shortages, he decided on cork glued together in layers. As with many fashion innovations, at first the wedge heel was scorned. But then it was copied, and subsequently became the height of fashion, with new styles developing to keep the trend alive. Designers started to cut wedge heels into sculptural shapes and added ankle straps to hold the shoes to the feet.

Shoe designer Roger Vivier is credited with inventing the modern platform shoe – with built-up heels and soles – in the mid-1930s. His first platform heel was in a chinoiserie style, and the influential fashion designer Elsa Schiaparelli showed it as part of her collection in 1939. The fashionable women of the 1940s swiftly adopted the look; heavy shoes neatly balanced the high millinery, another popular wartime trend. However, the idea was not entirely new. Vivier had been doubtless influenced by the towering chopines of sixteenth-century Venice – platform shoes soaring up to 22 centimetres (10 inches), worn by courtesans to save their dress hems from dragging in the mud.

Salvatore Ferragamo designed some of the most flamboyant and beautiful pre-war platform sandals. He embellished wooden soles with bright colours and bold patterns, and constantly experimented with new materials, from cork soles studded with brass and jewels to shoes made with snail shells, lace and nylon. More luxurious were his platforms covered in softly padded red suede. His 'invisible' sandal had a curved, sculptural wedge heel and an upper of nylon fishing line.

The 1970s put platforms firmly back on to the fashion stage, with wedge shoes for summer and platform boots for winter. They were the ideal footwear for the fashionable flares that kicked out at the hem. For daywear, moderate platforms and wedges were a less precarious option than traditional high heels, as they helped to elongate the figure but were easier to walk in. Platform sandals were a favourite for the evening, the delicacy of the cutaway uppers helping to soften the bulky look of the shoes with their large soles.

Vivienne Westwood revived platforms for the 1990s. Her creations included towering black patent versions punched with metal studs, and rocking-horse ballerina shoes with high curved wooden soles and ribbon straps wound around the ankles. It was time to walk tall again. ∎

ABOVE: *Carmen Miranda poses in vertiginous sandals in 1948. She was famed for her collection of platform shoes.*

BELOW: *Marilyn Monroe models wedge sandals in 1950.*

*Black patent platform shoe
with metal studs by Vivienne
Westwood.*

LEFT: *The runway circus – a Valentino couture show in Paris, 2006.*

ABOVE: *Elsa Schiaparelli's Circus show set a new standard, with its jugglers, clowns and ice-cream cone hats. Illustrations by Christian Bérard.*

IDEA № 43

THE FASHION SHOW AS THEATRICAL SPECTACLE

When Elsa Schiaparelli presented her 1938 Circus collection she included jugglers, tightrope walkers and clowns. The models wore outlandish hats resembling ice-cream cones and carried handbags shaped like balloons.

Live monkeys and trained dogs stalked the catwalk, helping to sell clothes printed with clowns, elephants and horses. The detail was fun and flamboyant – necklaces featuring a series of swinging trapeze artists and buttons in the shape of cavorting acrobats. Entertainment and fashion were dazzlingly combined to produce a spectacle that was more like theatre than a traditional catwalk show.

The 1930s and 1940s had seen stage sets, music and lighting added to the whole fashion show experience, but Schiaparelli was the first to theme her fashion shows, and turn them into extravagant spectacles. Her themes included musical iconography, astrology and even paganism. The press loved her for it, and she gained high-profile

clients, including Marlene Dietrich and Claudette Colbert, who were both drawn to Schiaparelli's sense of fun.

Thanks to Schiaparelli, themes, choreography, styling and music would become as central to the fashion show as the clothes. Mary Quant exemplified the mood of the 1960s by sending her models dancing down the runway. Kenzo caused a scene when he asked his models to improvise for his Jungle Jap shows in the 1970s – they frolicked, danced the can-can and even bared their breasts to the audience. But it was in the indulgent 1980s that fashion shows were at their most extravagant. With film and rock royalty in the front row, supermodels on the catwalk and the paparazzi documenting every moment and every detail, they were

epic theatrical experiences. The flamboyant Gianni Versace directed some of the most notable spectacles.

The theatrical show experience continues, with celebrities at the shows and the world's media at the ready. Alexander McQueen asked dance choreographer Michael Clark to put together his 2004 show, so that it was more akin to performance art than fashion. McQueen also wrapped his models' heads in nets containing live butterflies, and once used a pair of robotic spray guns to colour a white dress on the catwalk. The exuberant ideas instigated by Schiaparelli continue to bring drama and magic to the fashion show. ■

The runway for the Alexander McQueen Spring/Summer 2001 show was a mirrored cube lit from the inside, designed to represent a psychiatric ward. The finale revealed a reclining semi-naked masked woman surrounded by live moths.

'Entertainment and fashion were dazzlingly combined'

'Nylons were cheaper than silk, did not wrinkle around the ankles and added a smooth, flattering sheen to the legs'

Southend, 1938. Every fashion-conscious woman in Europe craved a pair of luxurious nylon stockings during World War II.

The revolutionary wonder-fibre

IDEA № 44

NYLON

The fibre nylon started with humble origins: it was first used to make toothbrush filaments in 1938. But within a decade its name had come to stand for the ultimate in fashion, every woman's wartime dream – a precious pair of nylon stockings. These became, owing to their scarcity in the wartime years, a symbol of almost unattainable luxury.

1956 magazine advertisement for Nylon by DuPont.

With a shortage of silk supplies from the Far East in the 1920s, the Americans started looking into developing possible alternatives. The chemical company DuPont established its own research division, one that was to make great strides in the world of synthetic fibres. There a team of scientists led by Wallace Carothers created a new fibre made from immensely long chains of synthetic molecules called polymers. They patented it and named it nylon, and a legend was born.

Nylon was the first synthetic fibre, and combined extraordinary strength with elasticity. After its early use in toothbrushes, this wonder-fibre was turned to knitted hosiery in 1939, and stockings in 1940. 'Nylons', as the stockings became known, were cheaper than silk, did not wrinkle around the ankles and added a smooth, flattering sheen to the legs. Supplies were cruelly interrupted when in 1941 DuPont shifted its manufacturing of nylon to more urgent matters: parachute fabric, tents and ropes for the war effort. Women either had to wait until the war ended for their precious nylons, or buy them on the black market at exorbitant cost.

At the end of the war, Macy's department store in New York sold out of their stockings almost immediately – selling a reputed 50,000 pairs in just six hours. The press reported nylon riots on the streets of Manhattan.

In postwar years, the women's fashion industry used nylon as a substitute for silk for dresses and underwear – it felt soft and had an attractive sheen, and most importantly it was easy to launder and iron. Nylon was seen as chic and modern rather than down-market. *Harper's Bazaar* featured a fashion shoot entitled 'Nylon Tricot, Dream Fabric for Lingerie', accompanied by soft-focus shots of nylon peignoirs and gowns. Designers such as Madame Grès experimented with the fibre to make dramatic evening gowns and soft lingerie.

Today clothing in pure nylon may not be promoted as the height of high-end fashion, but nylon and the hundreds of other synthetics that have flooded the market have revolutionized fashion, making garments easier to wash, cheaper to buy and often more comfortable to wear. ∎

A jumpsuit inspired by 1920s pilot Amelia Earhart from the Hermès Autumn/Winter 2009 collection, designed by Jean Paul Gaultier.

TOP: *An American mechanic in 1943. Women working in the wartime factories wore practical all-in-one boiler suits.*

ABOVE: *Peter Brown and Pam Grier star in blaxploitation film* Foxy Brown, *1974. She sports a low-cut, figure-hugging jumpsuit.*

The success of the all-in-one

IDEA № 45
THE JUMPSUIT

The first jumpsuits of the twentieth century were worlds away from today's alluring catwalk versions. They were worn purely for functional convenience. During World War II, American and European women donned all-in-one boiler suits in cotton or denim to work in the factories.

Elsa Schiaparelli designed stylish versions of the siren suit – jumpsuits with pockets and a large hood, perfect for impromptu moonlight trips to the bomb shelter – as famously worn by British Prime Minister Winston Churchill at the office.

By the late 1960s and early 1970s, the jumpsuit had completely crossed the line from being a practical and protective piece of clothing to being a desirable fashion item. Rather than covering up a woman's body to shield it, when executed in sexy stretch fabric a jumpsuit became slinky and provocative, perfect for some serious moves on the dancefloor. The sight of the astronauts in their NASA space suits during the much-publicized 1969 moon landings had inspired the fashion designers to rethink the all-in-one. Rudi Gernreich, Yves Saint Laurent and Donald Brooks all launched their own versions. Norma Kamali made hers in parachute nylon. But while the fashion industry made jumpsuits sexy enough to wear with high heels, feminists of the 1970s wore sturdier

versions of the boiler suit to make a political statement and cover their curves.

Variations on the theme include the catsuit, a skin-tight version; and the playsuit, a jumpsuit with its legs cropped into shorts. In 2008 and 2009 designers such as Alexander McQueen, Preen and Stella McCartney sent a set of flattering, narrow-legged jumpsuits sashaying down the catwalk. The all-in-one may swing in and out of fashion, but it is rarely taken up as daywear, except for manual labour. It comes into its own as night falls, as a sexier, more modern alternative to a long, fluid dress. ∎

Wartime restrictions impose a new silhouette

IDEA Nº 46

RATIONING

Shortages of fabric during World War II did not completely curtail fashion; rather, the restrictions forced designers and women to think creatively about their wardrobes. In Europe, the trend for wide fabric-rich skirts was put on hold, and a more frugal, streamlined silhouette with defined shoulders and knee-length skirts took centre stage.

As the war effort required essential fabric and materials, fashion designers became increasingly inventive with what remained. In Paris, the couturiers Coco Chanel and Madeleine Vionnet shut up shop, and many, including Mainbocher, Charles James and Edward Molyneux, fled abroad. Times were hard and raw materials scarce, so couture evening-wear hemlines became shorter, and less fabric was used for daywear. Nazi restrictions dictated that leather belts could be only 4 centimetres (1.6 inches) wide, and coats could use no more than 4 metres (157 inches) of fabric. White collars and cuffs helped to economize on the harder-to-find coloured or patterned fabric, and ribbons, unrationed as they were, proved vital for decorative detail. French women took to wearing wooden-soled shoes and were also enthusiastic recyclers of old clothes.

In Britain, the Board of Trade called on a group of designers to design stylish clothes in line with the official fabric restrictions of 1941. Hardy Amies, Edward Molyneux and Norman Hartnell were among those who rose to the challenge, and 32 designs went into mass production. They became known as Utility garments.

As the bodily silhouette grew slimmer, European hats and shoes became outsized, as if to compensate.

Then when straw ran out for making straw hats, women turned to turbans, berets, veils and snoods, and began to decorate their own hats at home with scraps of fabric. And as leather became scarce, cork and wood were used for shoes with platform soles. Elsa Schiaparelli wrote in her 1954 autobiography *Shocking Life*: 'Because of the lack of buttons and safety-pins there were dog chains to close suits and to hold skirts.'

The Americans also faced rationing from 1942, and restrictions on clothing included no full evening dresses or wraps in wool, and no bias-cut sleeves or wide leather belts. The American designers, such as Claire McCardell, were innovative, creating, for example, the 'capsule wardrobe' of coordinates, so that the same tops and bottoms could be mixed and matched in different combinations to suit the varying sartorial demands of each occasion. ■

Innovative US designer Claire McCardell designed this modern wrap skirt and bathing suit as early as 1946.

British designer Hardy Amies prepares his Spring collection in 1940. Rationing imposed strict restrictions on wartime fashion.

A British punk in 2003 with customized trousers and leather jacket.

Knitting for victory

IDEA № 47

MAKE DO AND MEND

When World War II broke out in 1939, women had little idea of the impact it would have – not only in terms of fatalities, but also the way in which everyday life would be transformed. Wartime restrictions forced designers and ordinary women to be resourceful when it came to fashion, and this led to new ideas, materials and trends.

Domestic rationing and the German occupation of Europe both took their toll on fashion. Voluminous designs and needless embellishments were out of the question. Silk was used for making parachutes and not for elegant ladies' dresses. The British government advised: 'When you feel tired of your old clothes, remember that by making them do, you are contributing to some part of an aeroplane, a gun or a tank.'

The era of Make Do and Mend was therefore a time of enforced creativity. Women started knitting and recycling old clothes – sewing ribbons onto old dresses, and using domestic furnishing fabrics to make coats and other clothing. It was not unknown for dressing gowns to be fashioned from captured German flags. The Italian shoe designer Salvatore Ferragamo used cork, Bakelite and raffia to make wedge heels. Vaseline, cocoa powder and charcoal made for alternative cosmetics, and women pencilled seams up the back of their legs with liquid gravy browning to create the illusion of stockings. Rather than wearing conventional matching suits, the astute mixed separates to suggest the impression of a larger wardrobe.

The end of the war did not mark the end of such creativity. The hippies in the late 1960s and early 1970s also embraced the idea of craft and homespun clothing, embellishing their jeans and jackets with patches and beads. Similarly, punks customized leather jackets with chains, made jewellery from safety pins and creatively ripped their T-shirts.

During the 1990s recycling became fashionable. Expensive vintage boutiques sprang up alongside traditional charity shops, and thrift was no longer viewed with disdain. Designer Helen Storey launched a collection called Second Life, consisting of altered and customized vintage clothes. By the turn of the century, craft, homespun and handmade clothes had become hip again, and young craft-inspired designers could now sell directly to the consumer on the Internet, bypassing traditional retail outlets such as shops. The Make Do and Mend aesthetic was still alive and kicking. ∎

Punks and policemen walk on air

LEFT: *1980s British skinheads wear DM boots as part of their street-style uniform.*

ABOVE: *The men who invented the DM boot, Dr Klaus Maertens (left) and Herbert Funck, photographed in the 1960s.*

IDEA № 48

DR. MARTENS BOOTS

Walking on air is not just the stuff of dreams. When a 25-year-old doctor in the German Army, Dr Klaus Maertens, thought up the air-cushioned sole after breaking his foot skiing in the Bavarian Alps during World War II, he can have had no idea that his boot would go on to become the favourite footwear of skinheads, punks and football fans.

At the end of the war, Maertens joined forces with a mechanical engineer, Herbert Funck, to go into business manufacturing the new boots. At first they used scavenged materials. The rubber for the soles was bought from former Luftwaffe airfields, metal regimental numbers from old army jackets were reused as eyelets, and the leather was garnered from army officers' trousers.

The new air-cushioned boots first sold for their comfort and sturdiness, with factory and construction workers soon recognizing their practical advantages. In 1960 Maertens sold the UK patent rights to the British firm Griggs, which began making the boots in England in 1960 in black and cherry-red versions, adding the distinctive yellow outer stitching. The unique air-cushioned soles were trademarked under the name AirWair.

British skinheads adopted the boots in the 1960s, wearing them with skinny trousers; in the 1970s punks customized them with paint and chains, while football fans adorned them with their team colours. Even as the boots' popularity spread through the sub-cultures, Dr. Martens also became part of the official British police uniform in the 1970s.

But it took two Japanese designers to help the boots find a place in mainstream fashion. Yohji Yamamoto and Rei Kawakubo of Comme des Garçons put them on the catwalk. Ideally coupled with 501 jeans, and black leather or bomber jackets, DMs, as they had become commonly known, were part of the unisex urban uniform of the 1980s.

Nike introduced air-cushioned soles for running shoes in 1979, releasing the iconic Air Max trainer in 1987, while DMs remained favourites with students, goths, grunge fans and indie kids. And so the new technology stemming from Dr Klaus Maertens' accident in the mountains continues to be felt under the feet of millions. ∎

Jean Paul Gaultier raises the humble DM boot to high fashion at his Autumn/Winter 2009 show.

'Punks customized them with paint and chains, football fans adorned them with their team colours'

'Paris is now just one fashion player'

ABOVE: *French actress Catherine Deneuve and her husband British photographer David Bailey (centre, back) watch the Annacat Fashion Show in London in 1965.*

LEFT: *Spectators at a Dior fashion show in Paris, 1955. Centre front: Marie-Louise Bousquet, Paris Editor of* Harper's Bazaar *and Carmel Snow, Editor in Chief of* Harper's Bazaar. *Second row: Alexander Liberman, Art Director of American* Vogue.

Fashion's favourite city loses her crown

IDEA N° 49

PARIS CHALLENGED

In the first half of the twentieth century, Paris was still the undisputed queen of fashion, its haute couture collections setting the international trends. Fifty years later, at the turn of the new millennium, New York, London and Milan had all become serious contenders for the crown.

Over the next ten years Sydney, Mumbai and Tokyo all began to host major fashion events, and by the early 2000s even more cities opened their arms to the international markets.

After World War II, the United States was a world leader in manufacturing, and was offering cheaper and better-quality fashion. For sartorial ideas, affluent Americans in the 1950s looked to their home-grown designers, including Mainbocher and Norman Norell, rather than solely to Paris. America became known for its sporty leisurewear, and New York Fashion Week started in 1943, under the title Press Week, because the war made it impossible to travel to the Paris shows. It became a crucial fixture on the international fashion circuit.

Milan Fashion Week also became a regular feature on the calendar of buyers and the fashion press, evolving after the war, when new Italian designers such as Simonetta and Alberto Fabiani began to make waves with their brightly patterned clothes. A group of ten designers from Rome and Milan put on a show in Florence in 1951 called the Alta Moda Pronta, which grew into a biannual event at the Pitti Palace. It put designers such as Emilio Pucci and Roberto Capucci on the international fashion map. From the late 1970s, Milan rather than Florence hosted the Italian ready-to-wear shows.

During the 1960s the fashion industry turned its gaze on London, whose youthful and often irreverent trends were exerting a big influence on international fashion. The British Fashion Council formed in 1983 and raised the profile of the London fashion shows with its organization of London Fashion Week for press and buyers.

Paris unquestionably remains the centre of haute couture and still stages highly influential shows of ready-to-wear womenswear twice a year. But the French capital cannot afford to rest on its laurels and rely on past reputation alone – the buyers and press who flock there are well aware of what other global cities have to offer. And with live streaming, shows can be watched on computers around the world as they happen. Paris is now just one player among many on a busy international fashion stage. ■

Fashion press and buyers flock to the biannual Milan ready-to-wear shows.

Models make the A-list

THE SUPERMODEL

Jean Shrimpton, Twiggy, Lauren Hutton, Jerry Hall and Kate Moss are some of the beauties who have acquired supermodel status. When the girls became household names outside the fashion industry, the public began to view them as fashion icons and personalities. Often they outshone the clothes on their backs.

Originally, models were pretty girls used to show clothes, and not generally known or promoted by name. The Swedish model Lisa Fonssagrives, who rose to fame in the 1940s, changed all this. She is acclaimed by some as the first supermodel, not least for appearing on more than 200 covers of *Vogue*. A modest girl (for the highest-paid model of her era) she told *Time* magazine: 'It is always the dress, it is never, never the girl. I'm just a good clothes hanger.' Others regard 1960s model Lesley Hornby – better known as Twiggy on account of her diminutive stature – as the first supermodel.

During the 1970s, the American models were the big stars, and their modelling careers often led them into acting roles. Lauren Hutton negotiated a vast contract with the cosmetics company Revlon – the most lucrative secured by a model at the time – paving the way for future contracts in the industry. In the 1980s, with the increase of fashion and fragrance advertising on television and large billboards, the public simply could not miss the airbrushed faces of the supermodels. And astute models such as Christie Brinkley realized that endorsing products not only brought higher fees, but also raised their public profile and celebrity status – which could only lead to more work.

However, the true decade of the supermodel was the 1990s. Linda Evangelista, Naomi Campbell, Christy Turlington, Cindy Crawford, Claudia Schiffer and Kate Moss, among others, became household names. They commanded vast fees, signed contracts with cosmetics giants, frequented chat shows and were routinely mentioned in gossip columns – just like the movie stars. Nor did the passage of years dent their earnings potential. Elle Macpherson launched a successful underwear company and Christy Turlington brought out a clothing collection. Kate Moss followed in 2007 with a collection for Topshop. Linda Evangelista was not quite as unassuming as Fonssagrives before her, famously declaring in 1990: 'We have this expression, Christy and I: We don't wake up for less than $10,000 a day.'

Now, however, the true age of the supermodel has passed. Actresses are likely to be used for brand endorsement, especially for cosmetics companies, and few models today are household names. ■

TOP: *Lisa Fonssagrives, arguably the first supermodel, poses for photographer Horst P. Horst in 1949.*

ABOVE: *Kate Moss as a young supermodel, 1997.*

'They commanded vast fees and were routinely mentioned in gossip columns – just like the movie stars'

Photographer Peter Lindbergh enjoys the attentions of some of the leading 1990s supermodels: Christy Turlington, Tatjana Patitz, Naomi Campbell, Cindy Crawford and Linda Evangelista.

Sex-bomb Ursula Andress wears her famous white bikini in the Bond film Dr. No in 1962.

More powerful than
an atomic explosion

THE BIKINI

The bikini has been likened to 'a picture frame that highlights all the erogenous zones', and there is no doubting its erotic appeal. When it was first shown at a 1946 fashion event in Paris, its inventor, Louis Réard, found that no model would agree to wear it.

Louis Réard's risqué bikini of 1946 caused a sensation. Unable to find a respectable model to wear his new creation, the job went to this stripper from the Casino de Paris.

In fact, two men are accredited with the invention of the bikini in 1946, independently of each other – Réard, and Jacques Heim. Heim first called the garment the Atome, but Réard named it the bikini after the Pacific atoll on which the Americans performed a nuclear test in July 1946, and this was the name that caught on. Réard hired a stripper called Micheline Bernardini to show off this novel creation, so daringly revealing for the times – just a bra top worn with two lower triangles of fabric held together by strings.

Within a decade, French girls were parading their summer tans in bikinis trimmed with pretty artificial flowers or animal motifs. The Americans were less adventurous, and did not fully accept the bikini until as late as the mid-1960s. Similarly, in other European countries the bikini was slow to be accepted and in Italy, Spain and Portugal it was even banned.

The bikini was the perfect vehicle for up-and-coming starlets to advertise their pert figures. It could only help their careers. Rita Hayworth was famously photographed for the cover of *Life* magazine in a white bikini. Jayne Mansfield attended a ball in 1956 wearing nothing but a leopard-print bikini. The images of Raquel Welch in her animal-skin bikini in *One Million Years B.C.* (1966) and of Bond girl Ursula Andress in *Dr. No* (1962), emerging from the surf, have become icons of the age.

Réard had advertised his creation as 'smaller than the smallest swimsuit', but it was to get smaller still. Those who had thought Réard's early version risqué would have been outraged by the string bikini of the 1970s – it comprised four minuscule triangles of fabric fastened with strings around the body. It was almost nonexistent, and allowed for a nearly seamless tan.

Public attitudes to nudity were changing fast. Today the bikini is accepted on every beach in the West, and is worn by women of all generations, from small children to grandmothers. ∎

Decadent dresses in an impoverished world

IDEA № 52

THE NEW LOOK

Scandal was in the air when Christian Dior launched his 1947 couture collection. He called it the Corolle line because his voluptuous skirts exploded outwards from the tiniest of waists like a corolla of flower petals, but it was quickly dubbed the New Look by *Harper's Bazaar* editor Carmel Snow, and this was the name that stuck.

Dior used many metres of fabric for these huge dresses. As there were still severe shortages of materials all over Europe, the designer seemed to be mocking the rationing of World War II, deliberately flaunting the strict rules of Make Do and Mend.

Women were both mesmerized and horrified by the extravagance of the collection, and indeed it represented a startling contrast to the workaday overalls and utility clothing of wartime Europe. These new designs suggested abundance and a time of plenty. Under the dresses, waists had to be nipped in with waspie corsets, and hip pads made a woman's figure under her skirts look even more voluptuous. *Vogue* reported: 'Dior is the new name in Paris. With his first collection he not only shot to fame, but retrieved the general situation by reviving interest in a somewhat uninspiring season.'

By referring back to the hourglass silhouette of the nineteenth century, a time when middle- and upper-class women led highly pampered lives, Dior and his dresses offered women a dream of optimism and affluence after the dark years of the war. It is fair to point out that the trend had been inching this way even before the outbreak of war in 1939, with the designers Cristobal Balenciaga, Jacques Fath and Pierre Balmain all beginning to introduce wider skirts – but Dior's timing was impeccable with his postwar launch.

Scandalized by the extravagance – as much as 15 metres (49 feet) of fabric could go into a day dress and 25 metres (82 feet) into an evening dress – angry mobs picketed the house of Dior. A model in Paris was stripped of her dress in public, and politicians fulminated against the needless waste of fabric. But the controversy only lent further publicity to the trend, and as postwar shortages gradually came to an end, opposition soon ceased. And women loved what they saw. The New Look remained firmly established as the dominant fashionable silhouette until the mid-1950s. ∎

Christian Dior's Bar Suit, from his revolutionary 1947 couture collection, was a tempting proposal for women who had suffered fabric restrictions and rationing during World War II.

This dress by Christian Dior from c. 1949 epitomizes the voluptuous New Look silhouette and decadent use of fabric.

Drip-dry and wrinkle-free

IDEA № 53
SYNTHETICS

From nylon to polyester, the gradual development of synthetics over the course of the twentieth century has changed the way we dress today. Synthetics have several advantages over natural fibres, among them allowing clothes to dry faster, to wear better, to stretch more and to wrinkle less.

A model wears a dress made from Dracon polyester fibre and cotton in 1969.

Nylon was introduced in 1938 by DuPont, becoming the first truly synthetic fibre on the market for domestic use. It initially allowed women during and after World War II to wear stockings that did not run or wrinkle, and was later used for underwear and womenswear. Nylon combined strength and elasticity.

Since then synthetic fibres have become an essential component in clothing manufacture and design; prominent fibres include acrylic, nylon, polyester and Spandex (also known as Lycra and elastane). Designer Elsa Schiaparelli was excited by the new fibres and worked with textile manufacturers, using fabrics such as cellophane for her couture garments.

Drip-dry fabric was to save millions of housewives from the drudgery of drying and ironing and coincided usefully with the demise of domestic service and the advent of domestic appliances such as washing machines. Cotton–acrylic mixes of the 1950s made up some of the very first drip-dry fabric, and the polyester fibre that followed was snapped up by clothing firms and used to make even more efficient drip-dry clothing. Synthetics also ensured that colours did not run in the wash.

By the 1960s a host of new synthetics had flooded the market and were driving fashion trends. Dynel and Teklan were used to make fake furs and fake hair for wigs. Designers experimented with plastic and heat-fusing techniques – the hip cats of Swinging London wore wipe-clean clothing in PVC and vinyl. Dacron, a type of polyester, was used in arrestingly bright colours. Textile companies worked with designers such as Mary Quant to raise the profile of the new fabrics and fibres.

Synthetics continued to be associated with disposable and cheaper lines, but by the end of the millennium it had become acceptable, and even expected, that synthetics would be added to natural fibres. This combination retained the natural look of a fabric such as silk or cotton but added strength, stretch or anti-wrinkle qualities. The introduction of micro-fibres revolutionized sportswear and underwear, with lightweight second-skin fabrics that were tough and strong.

The benefits of synthetics have been widespread, particularly for sportswear, underwear and accessories. The extra stretch and durability, together with the easy-care qualities and cost-effectiveness, have undoubtedly revolutionized fashion. ∎

A 1960s magazine advertisement for the acrylic fibre Orlon by DuPont.

Great Fashion Stories from Du Pont

DUPONT

The power of youth

TEENAGE FASHION

There has never been a world without teenagers – yet only relatively recently have they been considered on their own terms, and not as slightly older children or slightly younger adults. Between the wars young people began to have their own fashions and trends, but it was in the 1950s that teenagers gained power and prominence as a distinct group.

1950s teenagers hang out at The Two I's Coffee Bar in London's Soho.

The postwar period was one of prosperity for Britain and, particularly, the United States. Affluence brought a new freedom to ordinary families, and teenagers were not exempt. They had both spending power and leisure time – a heady combination that advertisers were quick to target. They became a distinct group with their own looks, attitudes and styles. Teenagers were eager to spend their cash on clothes, records and desirable consumer goods. In rock and roll – Satan's music, as their parents called it – they had their own defining music. They hung out in soda shops (in America) and milk bars (in Britain), they rode scooters or drove convertibles, they went to hops, proms and dances, and they dressed in a completely different way from their parents.

American styles via television, cinema and music were influential on European teenagers. James Dean was the ultimate teen rebel, along with Paul Newman and Marlon Brando; Marilyn Monroe, Doris Day and Elizabeth Taylor were models for the girls; and Elvis Presley, Bill Haley and Jerry Lee Lewis provided the rock-and-roll soundtrack.

Girls no longer wanted to dress exactly like their mothers, in neat suits. They wanted looser, less formal clothes that emphasized their youth and independence. They wore circle skirts with wide belts, topped with white shirts, sweaters or cardigans; or floral-print dresses with full skirts and a scarf tied at the neck. Polo necks, jeans and pedal-pushers offered a more casual look. Hollywood movie stars inspired the teen sweater-girl style, in which provocatively tight jumpers were stretched over thrusting breasts.

By the 1960s, the teen and youth market was leading mainstream fashion. The young wanted disposable clothes that they could change regularly as trends ebbed and flowed; and the record companies, fashion labels and shops increasingly began to employ, or be run by, young people themselves. Within a decade, the generation gap had widened dramatically.

Teenagers were now a sociological group of their own, with an influence and spending power that would only increase as the decades wore on. ■

Tokyo 16-year-olds create their own
carefully styled street look wearing
labels including Fila, Converse
and Chanel, 2006.

'An emblem of toughness'

A leather jacket by John Richmond
for Spring/Summer 2006.

For punks, rockers and rebels

IDEA № 55
THE BLACK LEATHER JACKET

The anti-establishment sartorial statement of punks and bikers, the black leather jacket used to signify rebellion. Today it is a classic fashion staple, almost as common as jeans or trainers. Yet, although its associations with dissatisfied youth may have been diluted, the black leather jacket is unlikely ever to lose its aura of cool.

As with many pieces of clothing popularized as street fashion, the origins of the black leather jacket lie with the military. They were issued to German pilots in World War I, while German submarine crews, bomber pilots and members of the SS wore them in World War II. A seductive Marlene Dietrich immortalized the look for women in the film *Dishonored* (1931), starring as a Viennese prostitute turned secret agent – clad in black leather.

After the wars, the black leather jacket became the uniform of American policemen, selected for its resilience. As an emblem of toughness as well as for its protective qualities, it was taken up in the 1950s by bikers – often dissatisfied ex-servicemen – who congregated in gangs or at motorbike rallies and gained a reputation for violence and hard drinking. Their black leather Perfecto or Bronx jackets, worn with jeans and white scarves, looked tough and proudly working class, in an era where respectable men wore suits. The few girls who dared to join the biker boys went for unisex leathers too. László Benedek's film *The Wild One* (1953) chronicled this hedonistic yet intimidating group, casting the brooding Marlon Brando as the black-leather-clad lead.

Though Yves Saint Laurent dared to put a black leather jacket on the catwalk in 1960, it was Britain's rockers who at that time made the black leather jacket their own. Greasers, punks and heavy-metal fans all wore versions of the black leather jacket, while in the United States it was taken up by members of the Black Power movement, the Black Panthers. Gay men wore leather clothing, including leather jackets, as a symbol of their sexual status – they were sometimes referred to as leathermen. Both Chanel and Versace later put the leather jacket on the catwalk and soon enough it became part of the respectable unisex street uniform of the 1980s, especially when combined with Levi's jeans and Dr. Martens boots.

And the leather jacket, post 1960s, was not restricted to the original Perfecto biker style. A leather jacket could be tailored or bomber-style, long and sleek or short and cropped. Designers reinterpreted both classic and new shapes in leather, and did not restrict the colour to black. Textured skins such as suede, or leather with an ostrich or alligator finish, added a new exotic interest to classic styles. Leather was no longer a symbol of rebellion. ∎

TOP: *Marlon Brando in cult biker movie* The Wild One *in 1953.*

ABOVE: *Marlene Dietrich stars as a prostitute turned secret agent in* Dishonored, *1931.*

From underwear to outerwear

THE T-SHIRT

When Marlon Brando dramatically appeared on cinema screens in *A Streetcar Named Desire*, his clothing came as a profound shock to most viewers. His character – the sensual, violent Stanley Kowalski – wore a ripped, sweat-soaked T-shirt. This was 1951, and T-shirts at this time were known only as men's underwear.

But what Brando wore to such shocking effect in 1951 was – ironically – to become one of the most popular garments of the latter half of the twentieth century. T-shirts were worn as undershirts by the American military, and during World War II troops had begun to strip down to their T-shirts in order to keep cool while working. But such a thing was never done in a civilian environment. It took Brando's iconic screen presence – along with that of James Dean in *Rebel Without a Cause* (1955) – to sell this novel idea to 1950s youth. They enthusiastically took to white T-shirts, and wore them as symbols of rebellion and individuality.

In the 1960s women took up the T-shirt. Tie-dyed and screen-printed motifs added pattern and colour, and teamed with long hair, jeans and a string of beads, the T-shirt became a unisex uniform of the 1970s. T-shirts provided a classic means for promoting bands, activists, politicians and almost anyone else with a message, and it was not long before advertisers, too, discovered their lucrative power.

Katharine Hamnett was more thoughtful than most with her use of slogan T-shirts for her Choose Life collection in 1984. Hamnett devotees wore T-shirts emblazoned with bold messages in capital letters: Ban Pollution, Heroin Free Zone, Worldwide Nuclear Ban Now. Her garments gave their wearers the chance to make potent political statements without opening their mouths.

Hamnett herself was amazed by the initial reaction to her slogan T-shirts. 'Hard to believe it now, but they used to be considered offensive,' she said. 'In the early 1980s American *Vogue* finally deigned to visit my showroom, which was at the time a very chic faux cave, and when they saw T-shirts saying "Love" and "Peace" they spun, literally spun, on their kitten heels and walked straight out.' ∎

ABOVE: *Marlon Brando shocks audiences in cult movie* A Streetcar Named Desire *(1951).*

RIGHT: *Johnny Rotten of the Sex Pistols poses in a confrontational punk T-shirt.*

'They were worn as symbols of rebellion and individuality'

Save the Sea T-shirt by Katharine Hamnett for YOOXYGEN, 2010.

A pair of killer heels

IDEA № 57

THE STILETTO

In Italian, a stiletto is a type of small dagger. The shoe that bears its name was launched in Italy in the early 1950s, and changed the female fashion silhouette irrevocably, as well as the way a woman walked and moved in her clothes. A fetish object as much as a fashion item, the stiletto heel has an eternal, defiantly sexual, allure.

Senso boot for Autumn/Winter 1998. Design and drawing by Manolo Blahnik.

It is still not entirely clear who first came up with the idea. Shoe designers Salvatore Ferragamo and Roger Vivier both lay claim to the invention of the thin steel reinforcing bar that provides the core support to a stiletto heel. High heels were not a new phenomenon, but before the 1950s they had to be thick and sturdy if they were to be very tall, their cores being made of a relatively weak material such as wood.

When Christian Dior added shoes to his stable in 1953, he asked Roger Vivier to be his designer. Vivier introduced the stiletto heel to the Dior clients the following year, while in Italy Salvatore Ferragamo designed his own version. Whoever was first, this was clearly an idea whose moment had come. Now women could weave high above the pavements with confidence, on just a skinny support. The movie stars and pin-up girls loved them, including Jayne Mansfield, Bettie Page and Marilyn Monroe.

The high stiletto goes in and out of fashion, but many women (and the men who watch them) have a never-ending love affair with these often-punishing inventions. They straighten the ankle, arch the foot into a point, tilt the pelvis, lift the buttocks and raise the bust, tilting the posture into a sexy stance. Stiletto heels force a woman to slow down and encourage her hips to swing as she walks. They flatter the figure by elongating and slimming the leg, making a woman taller, and finishing everything off with a pretty pointed foot. No wonder so many women put up with the undeniable discomfort: they feel transformed into *femmes fatales* when they put on their shoes.

Both the French designer Christian Louboutin and the London-based Spanish designer Manolo Blahnik continue to dress their clients in gravity-defying stilettos, as do Jimmy Choo, Rupert Sanderson and Givenchy. But the Italian houses still lead the way, with Prada, Miu Miu, Gucci and Dolce & Gabbana keeping hold of the stiletto crown. ∎

'Stiletto heels force a woman to slow down
and encourage her hips to swing as she walks'

*An image from the famous shoot
for Charles Jourdan's Autumn
1979 campaign by legendary
photographer Guy Bourdin.*

Calvin Klein Jeans

The denim revolution

IDEA № 58

JEANS

Whether they be bootleg, skinny, baggy or low-slung, denim jeans are a unisex mainstay of Western fashion for both young and old. Almost everyone owns a pair of jeans. The trousers that started as masculine workwear can today be respectably smartened up with heels and a jacket and regarded as feminine and chic.

They are not quite yet acceptable in financial, trading or legal offices where a suit is *de rigueur*, but they have certainly come a long way from their humble beginnings.

Hardwearing denim trousers were worn in nineteenth-century Europe, but jeans as we know them today were launched in 1873 by Jacob Davis and Levi Strauss in the small gold rush town of San Francisco. They wanted a robust product for the tough outdoor world of the Far West, and their breakthrough was to use robust copper rivets to strengthen the pockets and points of strain. A numbering system helped retailers to identify the different styles of the so-called 'waist overalls', and the best quality were given the number 501. Blue denim jeans soon became the workwear of cowboys, lumberjacks, farmers and ranchers.

American teenage rebels in the 1950s started to wear jeans, encouraged by the silver-screen appearances of denim-clad idols, such as Marilyn Monroe in *Clash by Night* (1952) and James Dean in *Rebel Without a Cause* (1955). Jeans were imported to Europe, and Lee, Wrangler and Levi's gave the teenagers on both sides of the pond a taste of postwar prosperity and youthful identity.

By the 1970s blue jeans were the uniform of youth. Girls and boys wore matching flared versions, along with their long hair and beads. This was also the era of the first branded designer jeans, with Fiorucci, Ralph Lauren, Gloria Vanderbilt and Calvin Klein all cashing in. Bianca Jagger and Jacqueline Kennedy Onassis became fans of the new designer denim. Klein controversially hired the teenage Brooke Shields for a series of provocative jeans ads, shot and directed by Richard Avedon. In one dynamic stills photograph she looks like she is about to whip off her shirt. In another commercial she coos: 'You wanna know what comes between me and my Calvins? Nothing.' *The Sunday Times* reported that sales of blue jeans turned Klein's company from a $25 million into a $180-million business in just a year.

Levi's 501s themselves swung back into fashion for men and women during the 1980s, with a stream of cult TV and cinema ads, the most notorious featuring the model Nick Kamen

TOP: *High-waisted jeans on a Los Angeles street in 1979.*

ABOVE: *1950s magazine advertisement for Levi's. This was the decade that jeans, used as working men's overalls, become fashionable unisex casualwear for teenagers.*

OPPOSITE PAGE: *The controversial Calvin Klein Jeans advertisement photographed by Richard Avedon, featuring a teenage Brooke Shields, 1980.*

stripping to his boxer shorts in a launderette. During the following decade the bootleg jean and low-slung hipster trousers were the dominant trends in denim. New brands started to appear on the market, such as Earl Jean, 7 for All Mankind and True Religion Brand Jeans. Some, catering specifically for women, focused on flattering cuts and added stretch – and bore a high price tag to match. Jeans had made the dramatic leap from men's workwear to women's designer wear in just 100 years. ■

French university students
dance the jitterbug in sneakers,
Paris, 1949.

Run-DMC helped to make Adidas
trainers hip, with their single
'My Adidas' of 1986.

The street's favourite footwear

IDEA № 59
TRAINERS

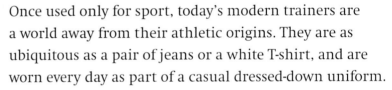

Once used only for sport, today's modern trainers are
a world away from their athletic origins. They are as
ubiquitous as a pair of jeans or a white T-shirt, and are
worn every day as part of a casual dressed-down uniform.

Their forerunners, rubber-soled canvas plimsolls, had been worn on the beach and for sport since the late 1800s. Keds, one of the early successful plimsoll brands, was introduced to the United States in 1916. The shoes became known as sneakers owing to their quiet rubber soles, which allowed the wearer to sneak around noiselessly. Next came the popular Converse All Star shoe in 1917. Converse was canny enough to see, early on, the business benefits of celebrity endorsement, persuading basketball legend Chuck Taylor to add his signature to the All Star motif in the 1920s, and badminton star Jack Purcell to endorse the Converse Jack Purcell sneaker in the 1930s.

American teenagers started to wear trainers or sneakers as casualwear off the sportsfield during the 1950s, inspired by movie stars such as James Dean seen in his Levi's and white sneakers in *Rebel Without a Cause*.

Meanwhile in Germany, the two Dassler brothers were developing running shoes with leather uppers. In 1948, the brothers argued, split and never spoke to each other again, but each went on to form a brand that would be a market leader in sports clothes and trainers – Puma and Adidas. Nike, named after the ancient Greek winged goddess of victory, launched in 1971 in Oregon.

The crossover from sport to fashion continued after athlete Tommie Smith wore Puma Suede trainers (known as Clydes) to win the 200 metres at the Mexican Olympics in 1968. He raised his fist in the Black Power salute when he received his gold medal and the shoes became a cult item on the street, associated with Black Pride. Soon football fans started to wear trainers, and a surge in the popularity of jogging took sports shoes onto the street. By the 1980s trainers had become universally popular, and the sports brands put

aside large marketing budgets for advertising and celebrity endorsement.

By the turn of the millennium, high-fashion designers were teaming up with leading trainer brands to get their cut of the lucrative market. Yohji Yamamoto's collaboration with Adidas brought the consumer sleek black-and-white three-stripe trainers for the cult Y-3 range. Stella McCartney took a more practical approach with Adidas for a range that aimed to make outdoor sports hip, with tennis and running shoes. Paul Smith designed a limited-edition Reebok running shoe in a series of bright colour combinations, while Mihara Yasuhiro's trainers for Puma focused on quirky fun with studs, fur, stripes and metallics. These are certainly shoes for the street – their impact would be wasted on the gym. ∎

MAIN PIC: *The oldest known Converse All Star basketball shoe in existence, c. 1918.*

TOP LEFT: *Lunar trainer by Nike, created for the Beijing Olympics in 2008.*

BOTTOM LEFT: *Trainer by Adidas for Spring/Summer 2010.*

TOP RIGHT: *Gola Go Future White high top. With a fondness for punchy block colour and cartoon capers, Jean-Charles de Castelbajac has injected his creative genius and love for quirky Pop-art styling into an exclusive collection for British sportswear brand Gola for Autumn/Winter 2010.*

BOTTOM RIGHT: *Archive 1980s-style Suede trainer by Puma.*

Grace Jones models a dress by Azzedine Alaïa, the 'King of Cling', in 1987.

The next wonder-fibre

IDEA № 60
LYCRA

Not long after they invented nylon, the scientists at the chemical company DuPont gave us a new wonder-fibre: Lycra. This super-stretchy invention was a complete revolution; no previous textile had ever behaved like it.

Garments incorporating Lycra fibres would stretch and bounce without losing their shape, and dry out quickly. They could be dyed and machine-washed, and unlike rubber, contact with perspiration and cosmetics would not cause them to deteriorate.

DuPont invented Lycra, also known as Spandex or elastane, in the late 1950s as a replacement for rubber in corsetry. By the 1960s Lycra had become a crucial component of swimsuits, ski-suits and the new virtually seamless underwear. Tight shiny clothes were essential for any girl who wanted to rock it on the dancefloor or in the aerobics studio in the 1970s. Lycra-mix leggings, leotards and second-skin jeans clung glossily and satisfyingly to the body without sagging.

Leading fashion designers noted the benefits that Lycra had brought to hosiery and underwear in the 1980s, and became interested in experimenting with stretch fabrics. The Tunisian designer Azzedine Alaïa became known as the 'King of Cling' because of his fondness for body-hugging stretch dresses. He produced skin-tight outfits of Lycra and wool, which he moulded to the body with the help of strategically placed zips. 'Magazine editors and the supermodels – Christy, Cindy, Naomi and Linda – knew better than anyone what an Alaïa dress could do for them: it has the pleasing effect of plastic surgery without the mess,' said fashion editor Susannah Frankel in 2003.

Hervé Léger designed his first signature bandage dresses in 1989. He used rainbow-coloured horizontal bands of wool or silk, often mixed with Lycra, to create frocks that encircled and contained the curves not unlike early twentieth-century control underwear. In the late 2000s Canadian designer Mark Fast introduced his sexy skin-revealing dresses, in a similar vein to Alaïa's and described by *Vogue* as 'gossamer thin but strong as a pair of Spanx' (control underwear). Clothes never needed to sag again – and nor did the flesh inside. ■

TOP: *Lycra gives swimwear and underwear the stretch that it needs to mould tightly to the body.*

ABOVE: *A signature bandage dress by Hervé Léger, 1997, emphasizing the curves while moulding the figure.*

Rock royalty makes fashion headlines

IDEA № 61
POP STARS

The first major pop stars were the crooners of the 1930s and 1940s such as Bing Crosby and Frank Sinatra, and then came the 1950s, rock and roll and Elvis Presley. But it was the Beatles that set the pop standard for the stars who would follow in their wake.

The Fab Four were pop and rock royalty, writing their own material, hugely influencing fashion, lifestyle and music in the UK and beyond, and providing teenagers and twenty-somethings with style icons to aspire to.

Teddy boys adopted the rock-and-roll elements of Elvis's dress in the 1950s, while in the following decade men emulated the Beatles' haircuts, skinny suits and Nehru collars. By the 1960s women had also started overtly to emulate their pop and fashion icons. Janis Joplin advanced the hippie look with tie-dye and velvet, and the French lithe-hipped beauty and singer Françoise Hardy endorsed Space Age style and was dressed by Paco Rabanne and André Courrèges.

With the 1970s came the flamboyant glam-rock style of David Bowie, with his heavily made-up alter egos Ziggy Stardust and Aladdin Sane. Both men and women imitated his androgynous style – the stardust could spread by association too. The glamorous wives of Mick Jagger attained influential star status: Bianca Jagger patronized Yves Saint Laurent and Ossie Clark and was famous for her regular appearances at nightclub Studio 54, while later the Texan model Jerry Hall also came to dominate newspaper headlines. Jagger himself was a flamboyant dresser, and performed in Hyde Park in an androgynous white-frilled top and leather choker. At the same time, the punk band the Sex Pistols were openly used as clothes horses by Vivienne Westwood to promote the punk designs she sold from her London shop.

Madonna was perhaps the most prominent icon of the 1980s, in her low-life corsets and short skirts worn with fishnet tights and strings of rosaries and beads. Jean Paul Gaultier often designed her stage clothes, and she went on to star as the face of Louis Vuitton's advertising campaigns as late as 2009. Streetwear style was brought to the masses when the Beastie Boys launched their album *Licensed To Ill*, and hip hop band Run-DMC made Adidas trainers desirable with their song 'My Adidas'.

The Seattle band Nirvana popularized the grunge look during the following decade, while singer Courtney Love, married to Nirvana's lead singer, Kurt Cobain, became something of a style icon, dressing in glamorous dresses by Versace. When the pop diva Mariah Carey cut the waistband off her jeans, millions of adoring fans followed – what better way to show off a trim midriff and bejewelled navel? Pop princess Gwen Stefani became known for her kookie image, and went further than most by launching her own high-fashion label L.A.M.B. in 2003.

Lisa Armstrong wrote in UK *Vogue* in 2003: 'Fashion and music are now so embedded in one another's cultures that some artists feel that designing clothes is the next logical outlet for their creative impulse.' Certainly the relationship between the two worlds has never been closer. Singer Rihanna starred in a Gucci advertising campaign in 2009, while fashionista Lady Gaga was happy to strut the streets in nothing more than a flesh-coloured body, jacket and heels – one of her frequently outrageous looks. Despite a public battle with drug addiction, Amy Winehouse also spawned a wave of copycat looks with her beehive hair.

Post-1990s hip hop stars such as Lil' Kim have popularized a high-glam look, and numerous hip hop performers have launched their own fashion brands, notably Kimora Lee Simmons with Baby Phat, Sean 'Puff Daddy' Combs with designer label Sean John, and Russell Simmons with Phat Farm. Left Eye of TLC initiated a trend for baseball caps worn with neon clothing, while rap duo Kris Kross encouraged their fans to wear their clothes backwards.

The fashion industry has now learned to surf the waves of the music machine as it rolls on. ∎

TOP: *David Bowie poses in 1974. He was revered for his glam rock style and his stage personas Aladdin Sane and Ziggy Stardust.*

MAIN PICTURE: *Fashion fanatic Lady Gaga performs in full stage get-up in 2008.*

INSET: *Madonna strikes a pose in New York, 1982.*

'The mods were minimalists at heart'

Mod style inspired Mary Quant, seen here in 1965, to chop off her hair and design neat little mini-dresses. Her look inspired 1960s style as we know it today.

The subculture that inspired 1960s style

IDEA № 62
MODS

The mods were a small subcultural group whose influence spread far beyond their humble beginnings. Although they were British in origin, their distinctive sartorial style – sharp Italian suits for the boys, miniskirts for the girls, short, neat hairstyles for both – soon became an unmistakable look of the early 1960s.

TOP: *Mods pose in Streatham, London, 1976.*

ABOVE: *Phil Daniels and Leslie Ash star in cult mod movie* Quadrophenia, *1979.*

At the end of the 1950s, groups of fashion-minded teens and 20-somethings in London and southern England coalesced, cutting their hair in sharp French styles, saving up their wages for neatly tailored Italian-style clothing, and riding Italian scooters. Their style was modernist, and from this their title 'mod' was derived. It was essential to look stylish and perfectly groomed. The boys favoured expensive suits, Fred Perry shirts and pointed shoes; the girls flaunted their figures in daringly short skirts and tight hipster trousers. The mods wanted to consume. They were earning money and wanted to show it off – this was the first postwar generation that had not only a disposable income but also the opportunity to spend it on nightclubs, music, scooters and clothes.

Although they became famed for peppering their clothing with badges and for customizing their scooters with multiple mirrors, the early mods were minimalists at heart. When they wore big green hooded parkas on their scooters, it was to protect their precious suits from the dirt of the open road.

By 1962 the media had started reporting on the mod look and lifestyle. Amphetamines kept the mods dancing all night, and new mod pop groups emerged. But by 1964 the newspaper headlines were more often about mod violence than mod style. Mods and rockers – their leather-clad rivals – clashed violently in brawls in Brighton and other southern English seaside towns, scenes that would later be depicted in the 1979 cult film *Quadrophenia*.

The mods inspired the designer Mary Quant to produce neat little mini-dresses and to sport a sharp Vidal Sassoon five-point haircut; mod suits started to be mass-produced. When they adopted their small-collared, tight-trousered suits, the Beatles at once immortalized the style, and it moved into mainstream fashion. But the look faded in popularity as swiftly as it had grown. Though there was a mod revival in the UK in the late 1970s, by 1966 most of the original mods had grown up, got married or become so disillusioned by the commercial hijacking of their style that they had simply moved on. But their influence remained – not least in the way they inspired the designs of Mary Quant, one of the driving forces behind 1960s style. ∎

Catherine Deneuve wears Rive
Gauche, Yves Saint Laurent's
ready-to-wear line, in 1966.

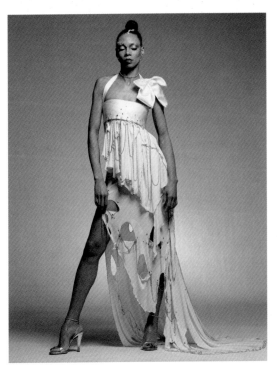

Punk-inspired wedding dress by designer Zandra Rhodes, 1979.

From sidewalk to catwalk

IDEA № 63

INFLUENTIAL STREET FASHION

The elegant ladies who shopped at Dior were appalled when Yves Saint Laurent introduced references from biker and beat subcultures for his 1960 Beat collection for Christian Dior. Why should they pay high prices for street fashion, even if it was reworked in luxurious crocodile and mink?

Yet Saint Laurent's finely crafted black leather jackets, turtleneck jumpers and helmet-style hats marked the start of what would be a long-standing symbiotic relationship between the street and the designer.

Previously it was mainstream fashion that had reworked the trends and silhouettes set by the designers, but this time it was the other way around – street fashion had influenced a leading couture house. American *Vogue* disapproved, commenting that the collection was designed for youthful women 'who expect to change the line with frequency and rapidity, and who are possessed of superb legs and slim, young, goddess figures'. But the world of couture was about to get a sharp wake-up call. Youth fashion and miniskirts were set to dominate the next decade, and many young designers were to reject couture as stuffy and old-fashioned.

After 1960, subcultural fashion and street style continued to have a major impact on the catwalk. When Saint Laurent opened his own fashion house in 1961, he offered his clients a new take on the existentialists of the Left Bank. Mary Quant borrowed from the mods; Bill Gibb drew references from the hippies in their kaftans; Zandra Rhodes took on punk, accessorizing expensive dresses with safety pins. During the 1980s, Commes des Garçons and Yohji Yamamoto took that punk and skinhead staple, the Dr. Martens boot, and raised it to high fashion, starting a mainstream craze for the shoes and boots. Fast-forward to the 1990s, and designers continued to regurgitate their different versions of subcultural movements: Marc Jacobs with grunge, Chanel with surfer style, Rifat Ozbek with the Rasta look.

International designers regularly send their scouts down to London markets such as Portobello and Brick Lane, in order to bring street fashion influences back to the drawing board. But unlike those early Dior-clad women, today's ready-to-wear and couture clients are thoroughly happy about it. ■

Dress by Givenchy for Spring/Summer 2010. The black-and-white graphic motifs of Op art continue to inspire designers.

Straight out of the gallery

IDEA № 64
OP AND POP ART

The term Op art was coined in the early 1960s to describe an art movement that focused on contrasting lines and patterns that played games with human perception. Pop art, which emerged in London and New York in 1960, celebrated consumerism and pop culture, and was led by artists such as Roy Lichtenstein, Jasper Johns and Andy Warhol.

The graphic modern look of Op art was exactly what young people wanted. Larry Aldrich, an art collector and dress manufacturer, printed dresses inspired by the graphic Op art style of the painter Bridget Riley, without her knowledge. Riley eventually sued Aldrich, but it was too late to stop the imagery from her paintings being imitated, and between 1963 and 1966 not only fashion but numerous upholstery and wallpaper designs were inspired by Riley. Even Mary Quant designed a black-and-white striped Op art suit in 1966.

Some Op artists decided to produce fashion goods themselves. The Italian painter Getulio Alviani worked with the designer Germana Marucelli to produce Op-printed sheath dresses and long pleated silk gowns. He went on to collaborate with the American designer Rudi Gernreich, to create a provocative swimsuit in 1966 made from strips of adhesive tape stretched in a V from the shoulders to the crotch.

Andy Warhol produced silk-screen printed dresses and shirts bearing images from his artworks such as Brillo boxes and S & H Green Stamps. Other fashion designers used Pop art as inspiration for their collections, such as Yves Saint Laurent with printed comic-strip dresses, Pierre Cardin with arresting red vinyl coats and Halston with dresses printed with Warhol-inspired flowers.

During the 1980s, artist Keith Haring, known for his bold graffiti-inspired Pop art paintings, opened a New York store called Pop Shop, where he sold, among other things, T-shirts and badges bearing his images. In 1983 he moved further into fashion and collaborated with Vivienne Westwood for her Witches collection, for which she reproduced his artwork on printed fabrics in fluorescent colours. In 2003, Japanese artist Takashi Murakami, known for his own Pop style called Superflat, began a collaboration with Marc Jacobs at Louis Vuitton, starting with a new multicoloured monogram for Vuitton followed by limited-edtion handbags in 2007. Murakami's bright colours and cartoon-style aesthetic breathed new life into the range of accessories. Jacobs explained in *Women's Wear Daily*: 'I wanted everything to be joyous.'

During the 1990s Versace created a dress covered in screen-printed heads of Marilyn Monroe, paying homage to Andy Warhol. The master of Pop and self-promotion may be long gone, but his legacy lives on. Warhol's fame, at least, has lasted for longer than the prescribed 15 minutes. ∎

TOP: *Yves Saint Laurent's striking dresses of 1966 act as a canvas for Pop art images by Andy Warhol.*

ABOVE: *Andy Warhol's legacy lives on with this dress designed by Gianni Versace, worn here by Naomi Campbell in 1991.*

A short, sharp shock

IDEA № 65

THE MINI

Daring short skirts exposing acres of leg were an exciting proposition for young women of the 1960s, and they could not get enough of them. Never had so much leg been revealed in public. By 1965 miniskirts had reached mid-thigh, and still they crept further up. Their shock value is hard to overestimate.

While designers such as André Courrèges and John Bates had introduced short skirts in the early 1960s, it is Mary Quant who should be remembered as the true progenitor of the miniskirt. Inspired by the mods with their neat, geometric tailoring and Italian-influenced dress, Quant produced minidresses to sell at her King's Road boutique, Bazaar. The pinafore dresses and short, brightly coloured skirts were, crucially for the fashionable 1960s girls who wore them, worlds apart from the voluptuous New Look style that had entranced their mothers.

Quant's ever-shorter designs were said to have made 'whole countries' gasp with outrage and reluctant admiration. 'Everybody knows how dramatically Mary skittled the staid old fuddy-duddy fashion industry,' said *Vanity Fair* in 1971. Many were outraged by what they saw as common indecency. Coco Chanel denounced miniskirts as disgusting. And Cecil Beaton opined: 'Never in the history of fashion has so little material been raised so high to reveal so much that needs to be covered up so badly.'

Short skirts resurfaced again during the 1980s, with designers such as Azzedine Alaïa producing tight curva-ceous minis; and a black miniskirt worn with opaque tights became the standard uniform for young working women.

And so the short skirt drifts in and out of fashion, without ever quite going away. Whether worn in flared, ruched, stretch or puffball form, the mini is here to stay. ■

TOP: *Jungle-print minidress, 1967.*

ABOVE: *Mary Quant, the Brit who ensured the popularity of the mini, poses here in 1967.*

Twiggy shows a bit of leg for British Vogue, *July 1967.*

'Quant's ever-shorter designs
were said to have made whole
countries gasp with outrage'

When legs became the new erogenous zones

IDEA № 66

TIGHTS

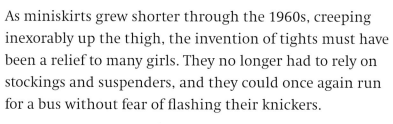

As miniskirts grew shorter through the 1960s, creeping inexorably up the thigh, the invention of tights must have been a relief to many girls. They no longer had to rely on stockings and suspenders, and they could once again run for a bus without fear of flashing their knickers.

The new opaque tights in bright colours were the perfect partners for the short skirts of the 1960s.

Indeed, it was probably only because of the thick tights that could be worn with them that skirts reached their shortest ever, in 1969, with the micro-mini. Tights revolutionized the way women moved in skirts or shorts, and allowed the long-limbed to show off their assets to the maximum – the legs were the new erogenous zones.

Ribbed woollen tights became available in the early 1960s in Europe, while sheer nylon stockings attached to a heavy denier pant (known as pantyhose) came into the shops in the USA. It was the freezing winter of 1963 that inspired some women to ditch their stockings and opt for tights or pantyhose instead.

In 1965 Pierre Cardin was one of the first fashion designers to offer women tights. They were thick, opaque and monochrome in bright colours for winter, and white or patterned for summer. In the same year Mary Quant launched her collection of tights in myriad colours, while Emilio Pucci offered versions covered with his signature swirl prints. Other late-1960s trends included hosiery with diamond patterns, fishnets, and tights in deep natural tan. Tights were initially slow to filter into the mainstream, but by the 1970s most women were choosing

tights or pantyhose for their convenience and comfort, and stockings accounted for only 5 percent of the market.

During the late 1970s the punks realized that ripped and torn fishnet tights would make a shocking impact, particularly when teamed with black stilettos. But by the 1980s women wanted more feminine, sexy tights, so they opted for lacy hosiery, fishnets and dark or black opaque tights worn with tight miniskirts. In the 1990s women enthusiastically embraced a new development: control tights, which – rather like stretch corsetry – were designed to mould the stomach and buttocks towards curvaceous perfection. Liberating, figure-enhancing and practical, what would the modern woman do without tights? ■

MAIN PICTURE: *Actress Daryl Hannah models sheer hosiery in 1999.*

INSET: *A provocative Pretty Polly advertisement, 1970s.*

For the first time, tough tights that don't look it.

'Tights revolutionized the way women moved in skirts or shorts, and allowed the long-limbed to show off their assets'

Pioneering designer André Courrèges, famed for his all-white collection, shows reversible pink and white gabardine outfits worn over shorts in 1965.

Fashion's futuristic pioneers

IDEA № 67
SPACE AGE

As the Space Race gathered pace in the mid-1960s, with the American and Soviet superpowers obsessively intent on chalking up firsts in space exploration, so the hip young things slung on their flat white boots, short tabard dresses, catsuits and helmets. The Space Race was in full flow, and everyone was going NASA-crazy.

French designer and ex-civil engineer André Courrèges launched his 1964 Space Age collection in an all-white chrome-trimmed showroom. His geometric-cut clothes were uncompromisingly heavy and hung away from the body, giving them a life of their own. The look may not have been universally loved, but a pair of Courrèges-style white boots became one of the iconic accessories of the decade. 'Can one show oneself in the street dressed in creations designed for the year 2000?' asked *Vogue*.

Pierre Cardin followed with his 1967 Cosmocorps collection of belted tabard dresses and zip jackets for men, and even went on to design spacesuits for NASA in 1970. And the innovative Paco Rabanne was not content with dresses of fabric or even leather – his were intergalactic chain-mail concoctions in plastic or metal. He called his first haute couture collection of 1966 'Twelve Unwearable Dresses'. Numerous other designers embraced the new Space Age look, celebrating their diverse visions of the future by experimenting with new materials: Mary Quant with PVC macs; Betsey Johnson with cheeky frocks in sheer plastic; and Pierre Cardin with his newly developed fabric Cardine, for taut dresses that hung away from the body as if they were moulded rather than stitched.

The Space Age aesthetic has continued long after the 1960s. Issey Miyake played with new textiles and silhouettes in the 1980s, developing bamboo, paper and plastic, and casting breastplates from laminated polyester. In the 1990s Helmut Lang decorated shift dresses with holograms and reflective stripes. Contemporary British designer Hussein Chalayan continued to test the boundaries of fashion and technology, in 2007 producing fabric combining Swarovski crystals and flickering LED lights – and for the ultimate party trick, dresses made of aircraft materials that changed shape by remote control. ∎

Hussein Chalayan's avant-garde Spring/Summer 2007 show included futuristic dresses that changed shape on the catwalk using computer technology. The skirt shown here (top and above) widens, and the hat has a shrinking brim.

The Terrible Trio break the mould

IDEA № 68

RAW PHOTOGRAPHY

In the 1960s fashion photography was redefined by a trio of London photographers: David Bailey, Brian Duffy and Terence Donovan. Until then fashion photography had presented aspirational images of a rarefied, high-class world. These three photographers broke the mould with their sexually charged, documentary-style photographs.

Their pictures were honest and raw, shot in high contrast on grainy film, and influenced by French New Wave cinema. Models were portrayed as attainable real women, rather than impossible mannequins on pedestals, untouchable and refined in their tight poses. And the backdrops for the pictures were no longer elegant drawing-rooms; these working-class rebels preferred to go back to their roots, shooting the girls in London's gritty East End, celebrating its dirty streets and industrial backdrops as if in a documentary photograph.

Society photographer Norman Parkinson dubbed them the Black Trinity and *The Sunday Times* called them the Terrible Trio for their defiant break with the accepted notions of glamour. Bailey, Duffy and Donovan were proudly working class, heterosexual and irreverent, cast in a different mould from their effete society predecessors such as Cecil Beaton. Despite their working-class roots, they moved with a fashionable, chic set of actors, artists, musicians and celebrities, gaining celebrity status themselves. Bailey, for example, photographed the wedding of East End gangster Reggie Kray, and was himself married to the actress Catherine Deneuve and then model Marie Helvin.

Rather than treating models as clothes-hangers for the latest trends, they tried to capture the girls' personalities, and the relationship between a woman and her clothes. *The Times* commented: 'Bailey quickly stirred up the fashion department at *Vogue*, where, in the early Sixties, the implicit sexuality of his photographs was at odds with the prevailing style of tight, well-behaved polish.'

Bailey, Duffy and Donovan's irreverent and lively photographs mirrored the energetic new fashion scene of Swinging London, with its focus on youth and consumerism. Their work was hugely in demand from *Vogue*, *Elle* and scores of other fashion magazines and newspapers throughout the decade and afterwards. Their legacy lives on, with informally posed photographs still appearing in magazines – although, in contrast, today's models are airbrushed to an almost robotic perfection. ■

TOP: *A model wearing a dress by Laura for Joan Arkin poses with British band Blossom Toes on a London street in 1968. The new fashion photography was gritty, urban and informal.*

ABOVE: *Brian Duffy photographs a* Vogue *shoot in action.*

'They were proudly working class, heterosexual and irreverent, cast in a different mould from their effete society predecessors'

Photographer David Bailey poses with model Penelope Tree in London, in 1967.

*Movie star Evan Rachel
Wood flaunts her tattoo
at the 2009 Oscars.*

Body art goes mainstream

IDEA № 69

TATTOOS

Traditionally, tattoos were the preserve of sailors and criminals, and definitely of men; it was not until the late twentieth century that the tattoo as a fashion statement for women became acceptable.

Human beings have always liked to decorate their bodies. The famous Ötzi the Iceman, whose perfectly preserved body, dating back to c. 3300 BCE, was discovered in 1991, had more than 50 tattoos. The future King Edward VII of Britain had a Jerusalem Cross tattooed on his arm, sparking a trend among the British aristocracy. Winston Churchill's mother, Lady Randolph Churchill, was said to have had a tattoo of a snake around her wrist, though this is no more than a rumour, and it certainly would not have been shown in public.

Tattoos bridged the gap between decorative clothing, jewellery and make-up, and added a new dimension to late twentieth-century women's dress. Rock stars of the 1960s such as Joan Baez were forerunners of the trend. Janis Joplin had a wrist tattoo and a small heart emblazoned on her breast. By degrees tattoos for women became more socially acceptable, and by the 1990s every supermodel, actress and 20-something fashionista worth her salt sported a tattoo. The Brazilian model Gisele had a small star on her wrist and the actress Winona Ryder acquired a delicate S-shaped tat on one forearm.

The new tattoos were frequently monochrome and usually discreet – on wrists, ankles or lower back – so that they could be hidden with clothing or jewellery when needed. For those unwilling to take the plunge, both adhesive tattoos and henna-painted designs provided a popular, pain-free and forgivingly temporary alternative.

On the catwalk, Jean Paul Gaultier put real and fake tattoos under tattoo-print chiffon clothing for his Spring/Summer 1994 collection, and revisited the tattoo print again for 2009. John Galliano designed tattoo-print body stockings for Christian Dior in 2004. Some people even used well-known brands as tattoos: 'Not only do dozens of Nike employees have a swoosh tattooed on their calves, but tattoo parlours all over North America report that the swoosh has become their most popular item. Human branding?' wrote Naomi Klein in *No Logo* (2000). Chanel launched sets of temporary transfer tattoos in 2010, based on interlinked chain motifs, and Louis Vuitton followed with tattoos of its signature monogram in 2011.

And for those who merely want to enhance their looks, tattoos can merge with cosmetics in the form of permanent make-up. Colour is carefully tattooed onto the face to give the impression of lip-liner, lipstick or eyeliner. A cosmetically tattooed woman need never be without her make-up again. ∎

TOP: *Temporary tattoos by Chanel for Spring/Summer 2010. These were a short-lived product.*

ABOVE: *Dramatic tattoo effects at the Jean Paul Gaultier couture show for Spring/Summer 2008.*

Light as air, fashion's new finery

IDEA № 70

THE DELICATE KNIT DRESS

The term knitwear no longer just conjures up chunky jumpers and frumpy twinsets. Thanks to a new breed of designers, fine yarn has been worked into show-stopping red-carpet dresses, ethereal kaftans and even sparkling bikinis.

When husband and wife team Ottavio Missoni and Rosita Jelmini joined forces to found the ready-to-wear knitwear firm Missoni in 1953, no one could have guessed they were to make such a major impact on the fashion industry. The breakthrough came in 1962, when they boldly took an obscure knitting-machine, previously used only to make shawls, and used it to manufacture fine knitted dresses from synthetic and natural yarn.

Missoni's delicate knitwear came coloured and patterned in rainbow stripes, geometric shapes and abstract florals. It was the bright, painterly colours that impressed buyers world-wide, and the press was instantly enthralled. The Missoni collections single-handedly revived an enthusiasm for knitwear. And the designers caused a scandal when they allowed their models to walk the catwalk braless. 'Missoni is in the lead with one of the most sinful dresses among those inspired by Art Deco,' was the judgement of *Women's Wear Daily*.

The designers Julien Macdonald and Lainey Keogh took the delicate knit dress a step further during the 1990s, with their luxury cobweb and feather-weight crochet knits. Karl Lagerfeld had spotted Macdonald at the Royal College of Art in London, scooped him up, and asked him to design the knitwear at Chanel while he was still a student. Macdonald went on to launch his own label, which included exquisite knitted evening dresses in bright colours. British *Vogue* commented: 'Cobwebby, intricate and light as air, Julien Macdonald's knitted dresses are irresistible.' When the buxom British model Kelly Brook arrived at a film premiere bursting out of a clinging pink knitted Macdonald dress (with matching pink knickers) the paparazzi went wild.

Between them, these designers helped to dramatically alter the fashion industry's attitude to knitwear as a lowly product, proving that it can be beautiful, dressy and delicate. As Julien Macdonald said in *Elle*: 'I wanted to show that being a knitwear designer is not just about jumpers.' ∎

ABOVE: *Fine-knit striped dress with pleat detailing by Missoni for Spring/Summer 2006.*

OPPOSITE: *A model clad in Missoni's cobweb-fine knitwear reclines on pillows in 1975.*

'Missoni's delicate knitwear came coloured
and patterned in rainbow stripes, geometric
shapes and abstract florals'

ABOVE LEFT TO RIGHT:
Beige, black and white bonded fibre paper dress by the Scott Paper Company, 1966.

Short sleeveless red paper dress, c. 1967.

Black and white spotted paper dress by the Waste Basket Boutique, 1967.

Printed orange, pink and purple paper dress made from bonded cellulose fibre by Dispo, 1967.

MAIN PICTURE: *Disposable blue and green printed paper dress, 1967.*

'Dresses and underwear made out of synthetic paper became the ultimate in 1960s chic'

Throwaway clothing for a new age

IDEA № 71

DISPOSABLE FASHION

One of the youth trends of the Swinging Sixties was the indulgent habit of quick-fix fashion – buying the latest hip garment, wearing it and throwing it away. Such behaviour was in complete contrast to the meticulous hoarding mentality of the war generation and brought with it a heady sense of freedom, progress and leaving the past behind.

Wonderland was the result of a collaboration between Helen Storey and Professor Tony Ryan, and was conceived as a series of disappearing dresses made from textiles that slowly dissolve in water.

The 1960s saw a boom in the production of cheap synthetic fabrics, and a short-lived, but major, trend for clothes made out of paper emerged. The Scott Paper Company had first produced paper clothing as a marketing gimmick in the United States in 1966. Dresses and underwear made out of the synthetic paper called Tyvek became the ultimate in 1960s chic, and paper-clothing boutiques sprang up. Dispo launched paper garments bearing swirling psychedelic prints, and fashion designers Betsey Johnson and Zandra Rhodes made paper dresses for their up-market clientele.

Even the artists and poets joined in – Andy Warhol with a paper dress printed with his trademark Campbell's soup cans, and Allen Ginsberg with a dress covered in poetry. A paper dress could be easily cut to any length and, amazingly, was tough enough to survive up to five nights on the dancefloor. Soon there were waterproofed paper bikinis and raincoats, paper suits, and even a paper wedding dress.

Several decades later, designer Hussein Chalayan experimented with paper clothing for his graduation collection in 1993, and during the 1990s Issey Miyake recycled pleated rice-paper to make a series of delicate dresses. For her Wonderland project of 2008, designer Helen Storey took disposable fashion even further, with plastic dresses of biodegradable polyvinyl alcohol that dissolved on contact with water. 'This is the ultimate in disposable fashion. A symbol of our throwaway society – not to mention the stuff of male fantasies. Here is the world's first dissolvable dress,' wrote Roger Highfield in *The Daily Telegraph* in 2007.

There is, of course, another less attractive side to the concept of fashion as disposable. With high-street retailers such as Primark, Zara, H&M and Topshop retailing clothes for extraordinarily low prices, almost everyone can now buy clothes, jettison them and replace them for a pittance. As a result, textile waste is on the rise, and countless tonnes of unwanted clothing end up as landfill each year. Our new love for super-cheap clothes may come at a terrible cost to the planet. ∎

'Hippies rejected consumerism and artifice and anything slick or urbane'

A young hippie chills out in Rome in 1970.

Flower power

IDEA № 72
HIPPIES

'Tune in and drop out.' 'Make love not war.' These were the mantras of the hippies who emerged in mid-1960s America, promoting sexual liberation, experimenting with psychedelic drugs and expressing their pacifist values by demonstrating against nuclear weapons and the Vietnam War.

With an interest in ecology and craft-based or multi-ethnic fashion, they instigated a new dress code for a generation.

Between 1965 and 1967, young beatniks gathered on the coast of California, and became known as hippies, derived from the word 'hip', or up to date. They were worried about getting drafted to Vietnam, sickened by the soulless consumerism that they saw surrounding them, and concerned about the environment. Ardently keen on getting back to nature, many dropped out of mainstream society in order to form communes. Haight-Ashbury in San Francisco became a centre of the movement, and the summer of 1967 saw a peak of as many as 100,000 people gathering there in what was known as the Summer of Love. After this, the hippie style and philosophy spread quickly across the rest of America, and would go on to expand its influence around the world.

The hippie look appealed to those who wanted something other than the mod-style miniskirts and slick short haircuts of the early 1960s.

Unlike their predecessors, hippies rejected consumerism and artifice and anything slick or urbane.

Instead they borrowed from foreign cultures. In their search for spiritual enlightenment, many travelled to spend time in the ashrams of India, or simply embraced Eastern value systems and therapies. Through this fascination with the East numerous oriental references found their way into hippie fashions. They wore loose, layered clothing in bright Indian silks, and teamed flared jeans with thick Afghan sheepskin coats and embroidered or fringed jackets. Long hair dressed with flowers, headbands and strings of beads finished off the look – for both women and men. And for the jetset who preferred expensive hotels to overland travel, but wanted the hippie look, designer Yves Saint Laurent was on hand to provide printed calico smocks and luxury patchwork with a high price tag, while Zandra Rhodes offered voluminous printed chiffon dresses.

With the end of the Vietnam War in 1975, the movement somewhat lost its focus. It was time to make way for the punks, who were as confrontational as the hippies were peaceful.

The impact that the hippie movement has had on late twentieth- and early twenty-first-century fashion is enormous. Designers repeatedly return to dip into the hippie archive for inspiration – from the long, flowing silhouettes, to the prints and homespun detailing. Dolce & Gabbana played with patchwork and beads in 1993. Tom Ford for Gucci offered feathered jeans and bold floral patterns in 1999. Anna Sui offered folksy floral prints in 2008 and an urban hippie look complete with suede tassels and patterned tights for 2010. In the world of fashion at least, the Summer of Love still lives on. ∎

A bejewelled pierced belly button was the height of chic during the 1990s.

Drew Barrymore arrives at a film premiere in 2009 and shows off her new pierced tongue.

IDEA № 73

BODY PIERCING

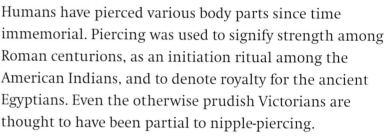

Humans have pierced various body parts since time immemorial. Piercing was used to signify strength among Roman centurions, as an initiation ritual among the American Indians, and to denote royalty for the ancient Egyptians. Even the otherwise prudish Victorians are thought to have been partial to nipple-piercing.

Of course, women had pierced their earlobes for centuries. But it was not until as recently as the 1990s that piercings elsewhere on the body became acceptable to mainstream society in the West.

When, in the 1960s, the American hippies returned home after travelling to India, some sported pierced noses inspired by the bejewelled nasal piercings of Indian women, for whom they were a mark of beauty and social standing. Gradually other Westerners started to copy the look, especially among the various subcultural youth 'tribes'. The punks used body piercing to shock, running studs and pins through eyebrows, cheeks and lips, while by the 1980s a pierced nose was part of a goth's essential uniform. But it was the 1990s when nipples, tongues, eyebrows and navels regularly became sacrificed to the piercing gun. Supermodel Christy Turlington began to flaunt a bejewelled belly button, and a navel piercing thus became the latest fashion look to complement a pair of low-slung hipster jeans.

At the end of the twentieth century, with fashion trends ebbing and flowing at whiplash speed, and consumerism at its height, for some people piercings provided a sense of permanence and authenticity. Piercings could still symbolize a rite of passage, or a sense of belonging to a certain group or style tribe. And for those who just wanted to get the look there were magnetic chin studs, clip-on nipple rings and stick-on nose studs all available at the click of a mouse over the Internet. ∎

'Piercings could still symbolize a rite of passage, or a sense of belonging to a certain group or style tribe'

*A young girl flaunts her
Amazon-style pierced mouth*

American singer Marsha Hunt works it for the crowd in raunchy hot pants, 1969.

'Big Afro hair, hot pants and bold make-up and jewellery completed the look'

Fashion gets into the groove

IDEA Nº 74

FUNK

The African-American slang word 'funk' originally meant something that smelled pungent, or more particularly of sexual intercourse. In the early twentieth century it was applied principally to black funk music, which had a mellow and syncopated rhythm suggestive of the sexual act. The distinctive dress styles of various funk artists were keenly followed by their fans.

ABOVE: *Singers The Three Degrees flaunt their funky style – crotch-hugging flares and big hair – in 1974.*

BELOW: *Dancers in the USA, 1974. The girl sports platform shoes and a glossy pair of blue trousers with matching shirt.*

James Brown was one of the first artists to become known for his distinct funk sound. The African-American funk music of the 1960s and 1970s with its driving bass lines, was a fusion of soul, jazz and R&B, played by Sly and the Family Stone, Bootsy Collins and George Clinton. Funk also came to be associated with radical black politics.

The roots of funk dressing lie in the black ghettoes of America, where the successful wore highly flamboyant clothes to advertise their riches in their own way – one that did not conform to white society's values. They combined flares with close-fitting shirts, hats with gold chain bands and big gold jewellery. The funk dress code was all about sex and money. Flared trousers drew the eye down to the flapping fabric, but also drew attention to the tight area around the crotch. Tom Wolfe wrote: 'They're into the James Brown look, they're into the ruffled shirts ... looking sharp.'

For the girls, the funk look was about showing off a body both beautiful and provocative in high platform shoes and slinky dresses or flares. Satin and lamé jumpsuits and glittery make-up made an impact on-stage. Big Afro hair, hot pants, bold make-up and jewellery completed the look. Blaxploitation films of the early 1970s, such as *Shaft* and *Super Fly*, immortalized the look and introduced funk style to a much wider audience.

The look was indisputably carried off by urban African-Americans better than their white counterparts. The 'funky chic' look spread from black to white culture in New York, Los Angeles and San Francisco, and on to Europe. But the white adaptation of the funk look was more toned down and less erotic and ostentatious. Funk, together with the psychedelic movement, went on to inspire the glam looks adopted by David Bowie and Gary Glitter at the end of the decade. ■

Wear them if you dare

IDEA № 75

HOT PANTS

Hot pants were immortalized in song by soul legend James Brown in 1971, but they were not new. Marlene Dietrich wore hot pants in *The Blue Angel* in 1930 in her role as a club singer, and these daringly brief shorts had been associated with cabaret and prostitutes until they appeared on European streets in the late 1960s.

By 1971, hot pants as mainstream fashion had spread to North America. Along with the micromini, they were the most revealing piece of clothing a woman could wear on the lower part of her body in public – away from the beach.

It was *Women's Wear Daily* that coined the name 'hot pants' for these briefest of brief shorts. They were a natural progression from the 1960s miniskirt, which had grown increasingly and indecently short. Mary Quant designed hot pants in the late 1960s, and minimal shorts appeared on the catwalk in Paris by André Courrèges and Christian Dior. The style soon filtered down to mainstream street fashion, in leather, denim and wool for day, and velvet and satin for night. Often worn over thick coloured tights,

they were teamed with mid-calf low-heeled go-go boots or platform wedges.

Southwest Airlines of Texas even adopted hot pants for its flight attendants, while during the 1970s the baseball team the Philadelphia Phillies employed a group of hot-pant-wearing usherettes, known as the Hot Pants Patrol, around their stadium. In 1971 those in hot pants were even allowed access to the Royal Enclosure at Ascot Racecourse, with its strict dress code, but only if the overall outfit was deemed satisfactory.

During the 1980s female hip-hop groups and rappers such as Salt-N-Pepa wore hot pants with bomber jackets, outsize earrings and long fake nails. In denim, hot pants became known as 'Daisy Dukes', thanks to the hot-pant-clad sex-bomb played by Catherine

Bach in the television series *The Dukes of Hazzard* (1979–85). A decade later they became popular again, partly influenced by the action-film and computer-game character Lara Croft.

But for many, hot pants will be best remembered for the pair in gold lamé that barely covered the perfect buttocks of Kylie Minogue in the video for her 2000 hit single 'Spinning Around'. Hot pants helped to relaunch her career. ∎

Bowie fans flaunt their hot pants in 1973.

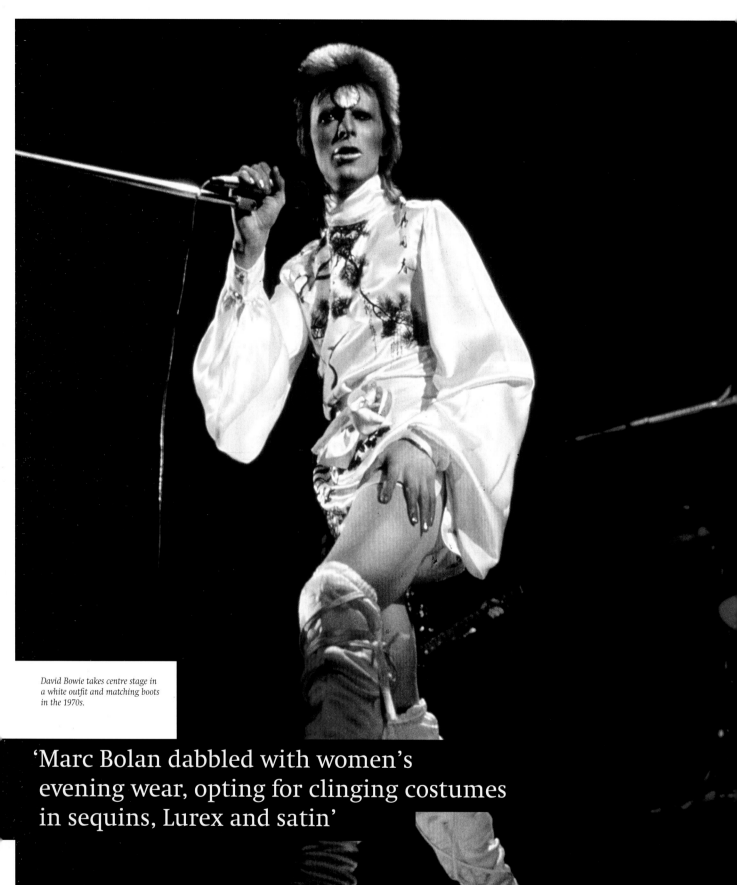

'Marc Bolan dabbled with women's evening wear, opting for clinging costumes in sequins, Lurex and satin'

Glitter, glitz and glamour for the boys

IDEA Nº 76
GLAM

In the 1970s glam rock gave men a chance to dress up like women and flaunt their finery and feathers. With its glitter suits, make-up and heels, this was one of the few times during the twentieth century that fashion challenged preconceived notions of masculinity.

TOP: *Marc Bolan struts his stuff in full glam getup, a gold jumpsuit and white jacket, in 1973.*

ABOVE: *Mick Jagger performs at Hyde Park, London, in 1969, wearing a studded leather choker, white flares and a white tunic top.*

While hippies had embraced unisex dressing, they looked downbeat and celebrated a return to nature. Glam fans rejected the homespun and delighted in outrageous style and artifice, taking inspiration from science fiction and 1930s Hollywood films.

The extraordinary stage costumes of David Bowie spearheaded this outbreak of camp drama, which found popularity mainly in Britain. Together with Marc Bolan, the extrovert lead singer of T. Rex, and members of such bands as Sweet, Roxy Music, Slade and The Glitter Band, Bowie adopted platform heels, flamboyant make-up and highly theatrical clothing. Gary Glitter always performed in high platform boots. When Mick Jagger took to the stage in London's Hyde Park in 1969, he dared to wear a leather choker festooned with studs, a frilled tunic top and white flares. Marc Bolan meanwhile dabbled with women's evening wear, opting for clinging costumes in sequined Lurex and satin, with an infamous feather boa for that final showgirl touch.

David Bowie as Ziggy Stardust dyed his hair in bright colours, and was celebrated for his extreme stage make-up. By 1973 he had spawned both male and female Ziggy clones, who flocked to his concerts in costume; some even flaunted their sparkling futuristic outfits on the street during the day. Bowie daringly claimed, in a 1972 interview in *Melody Maker*, that he was bisexual. 'For all his "fag" image, nowhere is he more loved than in traditionally "earthy" working class cities like Glasgow, Liverpool, Leeds … All across the country on his last tour, boys and girls, men and women were turning up in their Bowie make-up and garb,' reported *Music Scene* in 1973.

These gender-bender glam kids were paving the way for the punks and the New Romantics, who were to continue the party by celebrating artifice, make-up and dressing up for both sexes. ■

'Halston's kaftans, shift dresses, shirt dresses, tunics and wide-legged trousers embodied everything that the elegant modern woman craved'

Sleek, chic and feline: the new seventies simplicity

IDEA № 77

LOW-KEY LUXURY

By the 1970s, the independent woman required a simple, practical wardrobe – and the United States was the country to give it to her, with an elegant, no-frills approach to dressing incorporating fluid lines, simple cuts and lengths of durable fabric.

ABOVE: *The signature languid lines and soft elegance of this 2009 Halston dress look strong and modern while continuing the 1970s aesthetic.*

OPPOSITE: *This elegant 1972 dress by Halston combines glamour with comfort and, crucially, looks effortless.*

New York had developed into an exciting artistic centre, and America became known for its sophisticated ready-to-wear collections, which were neither Paris couture, nor mass-manufactured high-street styles. This was new, relaxed, luxurious off-the-peg clothing.

Roy Halston Frowick, or Halston as he was known, was a true all-American designer. After working as a milliner, he launched his own ready-to-wear line in 1966, combining comfort and glamour with a relaxed sporty style. His kaftans, shift dresses, shirt dresses, tunics and wide-legged trousers embodied everything that the elegant modern woman craved. 'Halston's proportions were perfect. His clothes followed the shape of a woman's body without being tight; they held the body while still retaining a certain languor,' explained Grace Mirabella in Steven Bluttal's book *Halston* (2001).

Fellow designer Geoffrey Beene continued this low-key approach– keeping clothes striking and elegant in black and white, while minimizing accessories. Beene made his name with simple suits in jersey, flannel and wool. He designed sequin dresses inspired by American football shirts, and used long zips in bright colours as decorative devices. Bill Blass was another master of American daywear, with his frilled dresses and careful tailoring, highlighted with discreet detail or trim in a flash of bright colour. Marketing geniuses and designers Ralph Lauren and Calvin Klein saw the way to producing luxury everyday clothing for men and women – the beginnings of the fashion empires they were to build in the next 40 years.

Over the water in London, Jean Muir was fulfilling a similar aesthetic, creating relaxed but sophisticated womenswear. She worked with jersey and suede to make carefully cut fluid suits, shawls, and dresses with drawstring waists.

The new designers had proved that fashion could be comfortable and practical, while remaining stylish and modern. ∎

TOP: *Model Alek Wek in 2008, promoting Speedo's swimwear line for the World Swim Against Malaria.*

ABOVE: *A black model appears on the cover of American* **Vogue** *for the first time in 1974. Her name was Beverly Johnson.*

IDEA Nº 78

BLACK IS BEAUTIFUL

It was not until 1974 that a black woman appeared on the cover of American *Vogue*, a fact that seems astonishing today. That cover, featuring the model Beverly Johnson, marked a key point in fashion for black women.

African–American model Donyale Luna had appeared on the cover of British *Vogue* in 1966, but it would be another decade before black women were truly accepted by the Western fashion industry.

'If the political protests of the 1960s forced America's eyes open to the undeniable presence and varied beauty of black people, the '70s consolidated that vision,' wrote Barbara Summers in *Black and Beautiful: How Women of Color Changed the Fashion Industry* (1988). The first women of colour to become influential fashion models included Mounia Orhozemane, Beverly Johnson and Princess Elizabeth of Toro. Iman, the daughter of a Somali diplomat, began her modelling career in *Vogue* in 1976 and went on to become one of the highest-paid models of her time.

Just as Western fashion opened up globally during the 1970s, with designers incorporating influences from different cultures into their collections, so it became more open to using non-Caucasian models. During the 1980s Gianni Versace and Yves Saint Laurent routinely used models of all races to promote their work. The retailer Benetton went much further, deliberately selecting young models of widely differing skin colours. By the 1990s Naomi Campbell had reached the elite ranks of the supermodels, becoming a household name all over the world.

In practice, however, for those working in the fashion industry, colour equality was far from evident. In 2008 Italian *Vogue* made a stand against this inequality by dedicating the complete July issue to black women, using black models for all its shoots. The surprise that this caused clearly demonstrated that the fashion industry is anything but colour-blind. The fashion photographer Steven Meisel told the *New York Times* in 2008: 'I have asked my advertising clients so many times, "Can we use a black girl?" They say no.' Naomi Campbell told *Glamour* magazine: 'The American president may be black, but as a black woman, I am still an exception in this business.' Speaking as recently as 2009, she said: 'In the past, there were more opportunities for black models but the trend towards blond women has again become extreme. In magazines, on the catwalk, I see blond, blue-eyed models everywhere.' ∎

British supermodel Naomi Campbell works it for the camera in 1990.

'In 2008 Italian *Vogue* made a stand against this inequality by dedicating a complete issue to black women, using black models for all its shoots'

Rudi Gernreich's unisex thong swimsuits, Los Angeles, USA, 1974.

Daring to bare it on the beach

On the beach, the thong looks its best on a perfect body and all-over tan.

IDEA № 79
THE THONG

The word 'thong' originates from the Old English 'thwong', meaning a flexible leather cord. These rudimentary loincloths for men were one of the earliest forms of clothing. The modern thong, however, is thought of mainly as a woman's garment, and was taken up during the twentieth century as beachwear and underwear.

Liberating and provocatively sexy, the thong as we know it was launched in the 1970s, when fashion designer Rudi Gernreich launched his unisex thong swimsuit. Gernreich's background as a dancer inspired him to combine the stretch of leotards and tights with a pared-down Bauhaus functionalism in his designs.

Brazilian women were some of the first to take up thong bikinis as swimwear – in Rio very thin versions were known as *fio dental*, or dental floss. By the 1990s thongs were *de rigueur* on American and European beaches.

In the underwear market, the 1980s thong brief, with its strip of fabric that sits between the buttocks, served a useful purpose by diminishing the visible panty line. As low-slung and hip-hugging jeans came into fashion in the following decade, the thong would inevitably ride up to be seen above the jeans. This soon became a deliberate effect, and thongs were designed with feathers, beads and diamanté detailing in order to be shown off.

With their minimal design, thongs reveal a large expanse of buttock. It was reputedly a glimpse of Monica Lewinsky's thong that got President Bill Clinton's pulse racing at the White House, leading him to risk his political career over the illicit affair. In 2010 *Cosmopolitan* magazine declared 'the thong is dead', but on the beaches of Rio this is destined to be ignored. ∎

Sex, studs and safety pins

IDEA № 80
PUNK

When punk first exploded onto the streets in the 1970s, many people were shocked by the appearance of these disaffected youths. Who were these kids with their heavy make-up, tattered clothes and offensive slogans?

Punk was a surprisingly short-lived cultural phenomenon but it had a major impact, particularly in Britain, and spread to New York, Sydney and around the world. In 1970s Britain the economy was in disarray, unemployment was running high, and many teenagers were bored and restless. British punk was a movement born principally out of angry youth protest. In the summer of 1976 London art students and the unemployed started hanging out on the King's Road in Chelsea, gathering around a shop run by Malcolm McLaren and his fashion designer girlfriend, Vivienne Westwood. The shop – named SEX – sold fetish clothing, bondage trousers, obscene earrings, and deliberately ripped T-shirts featuring in-your-face slogans.

McLaren and Westwood astutely tapped into the psyche of the angry teenager at precisely the right time. In 1976 McLaren founded a band, the Sex Pistols, whom Westwood then dressed in her own designs. With their shocking antics, offensive lyrics and outrageous clothing, the band shot to newspaper prominence, and achieved overnight notoriety as the leaders of noisy, discontented urban youth. McLaren and Westwood were thus a driving force in the creation of the punk movement in Britain, weaving together a winning combination of music and fashion.

Punks wore leather, rubber and PVC. Their clothes were frequently slashed, painted, studded and adorned with safety pins and chains, while hair was often dyed bright, unnatural colours and teased into spikes or a 'mohawk'. Facial piercings were common. Shock value was paramount.

Having emerged as a musical movement independently in the United States and Britain, punk spread throughout Europe. But the moment did not last. By 1979 the Sex Pistols had broken up, their lead singer, Sid Vicious, was dead of a heroin overdose and Westwood had moved on to design New Romantic collections. But despite its brevity, punk style left a palpable impact – it showed how fashion could challenge stereotypes of gender and beauty. Punk put London on the map once more as a centre of innovative fashion, and it paved the way for the numerous punk fashion revivals that were to follow. ∎

London punk, 1981. Bold make-up and customized leathers were all part of the look.

'Punk style showed how fashion could challenge stereotypes of gender and beauty'

Punk pioneers including Chrissi Hynde and Vivienne Westwood pose at the King's Road shop SEX in 1976.

IDEA № 81

COMPUTER TECHNOLOGY

Life today would be inconceivable without the computer, and it has had a major impact on fashion, from the textile design of a garment, through to its manufacture, marketing and sales. Computer-aided design (CAD) and computer-aided manufacturing (CAM) are now essential tools for the fashion industry.

However, the fashion business was slow to pick up on computer technology. CAD and CAM were not adopted commercially until the early 1970s, when they were used for automated pattern cutting and for grading clothes into sizes, which minimized fabric waste. Computers to control knitting and weaving machinery came next.

It was not until the 1980s that designers started to use computers as part of the creative process, mainly to modify textile prints, as the technology could recreate a print or pattern in a number of different colour schemes quickly and efficiently. Since then, the industry has embraced computer technology for the full design process and for mass-production, particularly for making cheaper clothes in large quantities. The technology improves lead time and overall quality, and as a result new garments can be injected into the high-street stores more quickly – every few weeks, rather than months.

Calvin Klein, Jasper Conran and Ghost started to experiment with CAD, though most high-end fashion designers preferred to use the technology for print rather than garment design. But things are changing with the new generation of designers, reared on computers, who no longer view designing with new technology as soulless or somehow inauthentic. 'We're really on the brink of dramatic change in everything,' predicted Tom Ford in *Women's Wear Daily* in 1999. 'It's all about technology, computers, video conferencing. We're going to live in a more graphic world. It's all about bullet points. Style in the future is going to be the graphics on a computer screen.'

In 1999 Levi's installed a 3D body scanner in its stores. These machines could take a 3D scan of the body and automatically convert it into a pattern for clothing to fit that figure. Was this the future of mass-market couture? Computers can also be used to display clothes. In 1998 a Thierry Mugler dress appeared on a 3D animated catwalk, using virtual models, to be watched on a screen. The future might seem a little dull with no shops and no live fashion shows, but new technology is offering exciting new alternatives to the status quo. ∎

A digital hologram model features in a 2007 virtual fashion show by retailer Target.

'New technology is offering exciting
new alternatives'

*Dramatic printed dress by Versace
for Spring/Summer 2001. High-end
designers initially used CAD only
for print design.*

Pirates and posers

NEW ROMANTICS

The New Romantics were a small group of London-based posers who originally formed an exciting subcultural tribe during the 1980s. With their extravagant dress and their carefully cultivated sense of style they rapidly influenced the fashion scene, designing clothes, running nightclubs and inspiring the fashion coverage in the hip new magazines _The Face_ and _i-D_.

When Steve Strange and Rusty Egan designated Tuesday nights as Bowie Nights at a club in London's Soho in 1978, it attracted a new fashion following. Consisting largely of former punks, these were young people who had enjoyed the sartorial aspect of punk but shied away from the movement's violent and anarchistic lifestyle. They formed a glamorous, colourfully dressed crowd, whom the press first dubbed the Blitz Kids (after the Blitz nightclub, a favourite haunt), and then the New Romantics. Other clubs sprang up to cater for the movement's growing popularity, playing music from the new electronic pop/synthesizer bands such as Duran Duran, Adam and the Ants and Spandau Ballet.

New Romantic fashion centred around luxurious fabrics such as velvet, silk and brocade, and a new taste for romantic and flamboyant dress. These self-proclaimed posers took inspiration from both the glamour of the 1930s and the opulence of David Bowie in his Ziggy Stardust phase, finishing off the look with white make-up and deep stripes of coloured blusher on the cheekbones. The boys dressed with the panache of buccaneers, and would happily dress in women's clothing if they felt the urge. The look, in fact, was androgynous: both girls and boys spiked their hair, painted their faces and wore frilled shirts, leggings or voluminous trousers nipped in at the ankle. Pop star Adam Ant popularized his own version of the New Romantic look, dressing as a swashbuckling highwayman, or as a pirate of the high seas. Designers such as Stevie Stewart and David Holah, who went on to form Body Map, offered New Romantic collections. Vivienne Westwood indulged her penchant for the theatrical to the full and toyed with the Regency dandy for her collections, and in 1981 introduced frilled shirts and hussar jackets trimmed with gold braid as part of her Pirates Collection. Romance was far from dead, and the New Romantics and their followers dressed up, went out, and flaunted their pretty new clothes. ∎

TOP: _New Romantics pose for the camera in London in the 1980s._

ABOVE: _The New Romantic style encouraged the boys as well as girls to dress up and flaunt their finery._

'Both girls and boys spiked their hair, painted their faces and wore frilled and ruffled shirts'

Adam Ant wears swashbuckling New Romantic clothes in 1983.

Jock straps and boxer shorts for girls

IDEA № 83

CALVIN KLEIN UNDERWEAR

In 1984 Klein launched boxer shorts for girls complete with a three-button fly, plus a version of the jockstrap with a wide waistband. *Time* magazine called them 'Calvin's New Gender Benders'. Locker-room underwear for women became a sign of the times, a reaction against the push-up Wonderbra and lacy lingerie of the 1980s.

Calvin Klein had first launched his men's shorts and briefs with a branded elastic waist in 1982. They were brilliantly marketed. Bruce Weber's stunning photographs of a well-endowed Olympic pole-vaulter, shot erotically from below, ensured good sales of these simple cotton shorts bearing a designer price tag.

The success of Klein's suggestive ads of girls wearing the underwear while pulling off their T-shirts to just skim the nipple, proved once again that sex sells. Sales rocketed. Klein said: 'I think there's something incredibly sexy about a woman wearing her boyfriend's T-shirt and underwear.' In 1992, Klein pushed the limits even further, by using a topless Kate Moss, and a half-naked rap musician, Marky Mark, to promote his underwear. Overnight, sales increased by a third, and many stores quickly sold out.

Klein had timed his underwear launch well, cleverly tapping into the 1980s obsession with designer labels, andthe enthusiasm for sport and the gym. Men allowed the branded elasticated waistband to be seen when wearing low-slung jeans, using their underwear as another way to flaunt a designer logo. For women the style was athletic, straightforward and strangely sexy in a new fresh way, with a unisex, androgynous style that also chimed in well with the pending 1990s minimalist aesthetic. Klein had successfully set the tone for the new decade. And of course other brands such as Fila and Sloggi soon followed with their own versions. ∎

Striking a pose in black Calvin Kleins.

Gisele Bündchen models Calvin Klein underwear.

Flygirls and B-boys take centre stage

IDEA № 84

HIP HOP

In the 1980s a vibrant new street culture emerged from the African–American, Caribbean–American and Latino youth of New York's South Bronx. It centred around breakdancing, rap music and graffiti art. Spreading swiftly from the States to Europe, hip hop was to dominate the 1980s as a leading subcultural movement.

To the flygirls and B-boys, as they were known, the sneaker was everything. Hip hop group Run-DMC paid homage to the trainer with their song 'My Adidas' in 1986. They wore their trainers unlaced, in the style of prisoners in jail, who had to hand their laces in to the authorities.

Initially the girls dressed like the boys, in loose tracksuits, trainers, caps and large gold jewellery. Later they cultivated their own look, embodied in the sartorial style of hip hop stars Salt-N-Pepa and Roxanne Shanté. They wore bomber jackets, tight leggings, oversized gold earrings and name belts – though tight bright jersey minidresses and hot pants were a sexier look for summer and stage. The trainers most in demand were by Adidas, Puma and Nike, with underwear by Calvin Klein. Some rappers, such as Queen Latifah, promoted Afrocentric clothing such as Africa-shaped pendants and clothes coloured the red, green and black of the Afro–American flag, and combined it with sportswear.

The designers were quick to catch on. In the late 1980s, Isaac Mizrahi designed a hip hop-inspired collection that included black catsuits and fur-trimmed black bomber jackets, with big gold chains and belts. Even Chanel gave a nod to hip hop style, dressing up black dresses with large padlocked silver chains, as worn by Treach of Naughty by Nature (the padlock jewellery was said to show respect for his friends in prison).

The hip hop fraternity coveted designer labels such as Gucci, Tommy Hilfiger and Chanel. When Snoop Doggy Dogg appeared on *Saturday Night Live* in 1994 wearing an oversized Hilfiger sweatshirt, sales rocketed in New York and the sweatshirt reputedly sold out. Female hip hop stars of the 1990s, such as Lil' Kim and Foxy Brown, promoted ultra-glamorous high fashion for the girls, and new labels including Baby Phat sprang up to meet the demand. After the 1990s a host of hip hop stars including Sean 'Puff Daddy' Combs, Nelly, Jay-Z, 50 Cent and others decided to cash in on their fashion following, and started up their own fashion labels to sell and promote their on-stage style. ■

Salt-N-Pepa epitomise flygirl style in 1987 with their heavy gold chains and tight catsuits.

Rapper Treach from Naughty by Nature performs on the Tommy Hilfiger catwalk in 1996.

'A garment price tag on show even became a status symbol'

You are what you wear

IDEA № 85

BRAND CULTURE AND LOGO WORSHIP

Flaunting shop labels became a status symbol.

The 1980s ushered in a yuppie culture of work hard, play hard and sweat it all off at the gym afterwards. It was the decade of making it big – big hair, big breasts, big expense accounts, big jewellery and big shoulders. And it was fashionable to be seen to be splashing the cash.

It was also a decade of fashion companies using big marketing budgets and expensive ad campaigns to raise the profiles of their brands. They were selling the image rather than the actual product, and cashing in. And the consumer was led by the nose.

With this ostentatious style of dressing, it became fashionable to wear your preferred label on your wrist, your belt or your chest – be it the relatively discreet polo player of Ralph Lauren, Chanel's linked Cs or the designer logos of Versace, Moschino and Dior. For sports and casualwear the essential logos were the Nike swoosh and the Adidas stripes. If you could not afford the head-to-toe look, you could say it with accessories – a Louis Vuitton bag, a Rolex watch, a Moschino belt or Chanel sunglasses. On the street, a price tag on show even became a status symbol.

Logos had been around for decades. Georges Vuitton branded early twentieth-century luggage with the Louis Vuitton initials and iconic flower. In the 1920s Jean Patou monogrammed knitwear, while Coco Chanel, Christian Dior, Pierre Cardin, Yves Saint Laurent and then Ralph Lauren and Calvin Klein were masters of brand-building. But in the 1980s it was vital to show your logo. Naomi Klein wrote in her book *No Logo* (2000): 'Gradually, the logo was transformed from an ostentatious affectation to an active fashion accessory. Most significantly, the logo itself was growing in size, ballooning from a three-quarter-inch emblem into a chest-sized marquee.'

By the 1990s the big-budget marketing campaigns had backfired for some of the luxury brands. The ordinary person on the street started to wear clothing and accessories bearing the logos or insignia of such brands as Burberry, but teaming them with casual and high-street clothing. This damaged the brands' luxury image. Loud logos went out, and the marketing machines had to work even harder to validate and sell the new designer clothes that looked minimalist and utilitarian rather than obviously expensive.

Today the consumer has become more demanding, more savvy and less prone to brand loyalty. He or she wants something individual and of real value if it bears a high price tag – a limited edition handbag, or a one-off vintage piece. Clothing and accessories by successful fashion brands (but with subtle logos) are still sought after, but it is much more chic to own something that is rare or unavailable to others, or that only those in the know can recognize as elite and special. ∎

Ex-soap star Daniella Westbrook overdoes the Burberry check on London's Bond Street, 2004.

From backpacks to bum bags

IDEA № 86

UTILITARIAN BAGS

When designer Miuccia Prada launched a black nylon rucksack with no logo in 1985, it provided a welcome antidote to the showy designer bags of that decade. Stark, minimal and fitted with plain leather straps, it was inspired by sportswear and military accessories. When Prada decided to add a logo, it was low-key – a simple flat triangular metal tag.

The idea of luxury goods made from industrial materials appealed, and the backpack was soon the bag of choice for many urban women. It was no-nonsense and stylish and kept the hands free for public transport and shopping. Other brands copied fast, and the clean lines and simple practicality of these utilitarian bags became essentials for the girl about town. Gucci's backpack was in terracotta suede, while Donna Karan went for the Eurotrash look in buckled white, and a Louis Vuitton version was executed in the signature Vuitton monogram canvas.

Nineties clothes and accessories lent considerable emphasis to hands-free storage, with bags or pockets that hung outside garments. The 'J' bag was designed to be slung across the chest, with its single strap and asymmetric lines. Chanel produced bum bags in quilted fabric that hung from belts. There were messenger bags, belt bags, arm packs and body pouches by companies such as Yak Pak.

Instead of leather, designers opted for modern fabrics such as nylon and polyester with sportswear-inspired waterproof coatings. Backpacks became flatter, sitting closer to the body like another layer of clothing. In line with the fashionable parkas and combat trousers, military-inspired bag design, such as holster bags, became popular on the street. A flat white Helmut Lang body bag was to be worn strapped around the waist and attached to the thigh like a large removable pocket. In pursuing pure practicality above all else, these bags openly rejected any notions of elegance. Strapped uncompromisingly to the back or the waist, they presented a silhouette that was anything but feminine. ■

Brown rucksack with a beige leather trim by Louis Vuitton for Spring/Summer 2010.

The bumbag, a 1980s favourite, comes back into fashion for 2010.

'The designers helped to redefine the preconceived ideals of the female silhouette'

Fabric drives fashion

JAPANESE DESIGN

When the Japanese designers came to Paris in the 1980s, they tossed all Western preconceptions and assumptions about fashion up into the air, introducing their own materials, ideas and cuts. They were to make waves that rocked the fashion world with their new aesthetic.

Issey Miyake shows a directional design in black in Paris for Spring/Summer 1994.

Kenzo Takada and Kansai Yamamoto were already showing in Paris by the 1980s. Yohji Yamamoto and Issey Miyake joined them, along with Rei Kawakubo and her label Comme des Garçons.

Miyake played with new fibres and garment construction in a way that had never been seen before in the West: tunics and stoles of pleated synthetic and metallic yarn; hats created from polyurethane foam sheeting; wind coats more reminiscent of parachutes than clothing; moulded body corsets of the female torso. His pieces often hung away from the body rather than following its natural curves.

Kawakubo of Comme des Garçons perfected the idea of conceptual fashion, deconstructing garments to remake them into something new and surprising. She introduced holes into knitwear and in 1996 produced a series of bizarre dresses swollen with padded fabric like unconstrained areas of bulging flesh. Together with Yohji Yamamoto, Kawakubo also helped to inspire the all-black urban uniform seen today on so many city streets.

Yamamoto was one of the founding fathers of minimalism, and a master of the cut. Rather than fitting a piece of clothing to the body with conventional seams, he used layering and volume to make garments that wrapped the figure loosely. This way of dressing was new to Western eyes, and explained by Issey Miyake: 'The cut of a Western garment is determined by the body, a Japanese one by the fabric.'

Between them, the designers helped to redefine the preconceived ideals of the female silhouette, with garments that would impose their own rules on the body. But it took a confident woman to sacrifice showing off her carefully honed curves for this subtler Japanese style of dress. ∎

The new urban uniform

STREETWEAR

In fashion, 'streetwear' means more than literally what people are wearing on the street. It refers to an urban youth movement and mode of dress, which started in 1980s New York. Street style involved elements of Californian skateboard and surf culture, hip hop, punk and Rastafarian clothing: the look was urban, sporty and practical.

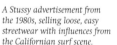

A Stussy advertisement from the 1980s, selling loose, easy streetwear with influences from the Californian surf scene.

Engle hooded shirt with a country check by Staple Design for Spring/ Summer 2010.

When the white New York band the Beastie Boys exploded onto the scene in 1986 with their punk-inspired hip hop album *Licensed to Ill*, they personified this urban street look with their trainers, hooded tops and branded T-shirts. They took Volkswagen insignia ripped from cars and hung them from chains around their necks: naturally their fans copied them, much to the fury of unsuspecting VW owners.

Streetwear could not be divided into daywear and evening wear – the same loose trousers, trainers, big T-shirts and casual jackets could be worn on the street during the day or in a club at night. Streetwear changed fashion. It created an urban uniform that spread beyond the United States to Japan and Europe, and spawned a host of new clothing brands during the 1980s and 1990s, such as SSUR, New York's Staple Design and ONETrueSaxon.

The timing was perfect. Designer fashion from Paris had started to be regarded as stuffy and overpriced by some urban youth, and this made way for the cooler street brands that offered dressed-down clothes. It looked hipper and more youthful, cost less and had a tantalizingly underground feel. It appealed to those who felt their life-styles were far removed from catwalk shows and luxury designer boutiques, but who could respect urban brands that were started as small businesses (often initially as T-shirt collections) by people like them – with similar interests in music, art or sport scenes such as punk, hip hop, graffiti, surfing and snowboarding.

Erik Brunetti started his label FUCT in the 1990s after working as a graffiti artist and designing skateboard artwork. Hiroshi Fujiwara, regarded as one of the most influential streetwear designers, worked as a DJ and music producer and was influenced by punk culture. The designers of US label X Large were architects. One of the most respected streetwear pioneers was Shawn Stussy, a surfer in California. He started to print T-shirts bearing his name, in the style of a graffiti tag, during the 1980s surf boom and sold them alongside surfboards. Today Stussy is a hugely successful urban street-style brand, mixing influences from skatewear, workwear and army surplus. The streetwear legacy lives on. ∎

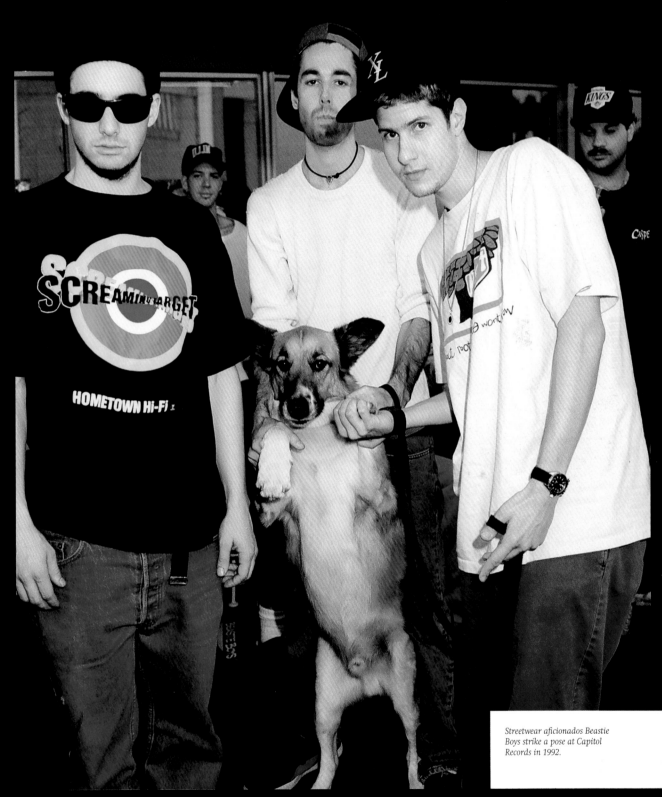

Streetwear aficionados Beastie Boys strike a pose at Capitol Records in 1992.

'It appealed to those who felt their lifestyles
were far removed from catwalk shows'

A London clubber on the new rave scene celebrates the origins of the movement with the Smiley face insignia and clashing bright coloured accessories, 2007.

'The energetic party animals who went to raves wore coloured loose jeans and hooded tops with trainers and bright hats'

The power of Smiley culture

IDEA № 89

RAVE

The rave scene emerged in Britain and America during the 1980s, centred around electronic dance music such as acid house and techno, and creating its own fashion and culture. Unusually, it brought together young people from very different backgrounds, united by an appetite for the music, parties and, often, drugs, particularly Ecstasy.

TOP: *Dancing in a field at the Glastonbury Festival in the UK, 1995, in a toned-down New Age take on rave clothing.*

ABOVE: *A smiling raver dances at the club Shoom in London, 1988.*

House and acid house music had developed as part of the 1980s Chicago club scene in America, when DJs began to make music using electronic synthesizer-sequencers. It spread to other cities such as New York and Detroit, and then to Australia and Europe, particularly the UK. There, the movement took off after a group of London DJs was influenced by the combination of early house music and the drug Ecstasy in the open-air clubs of Ibiza in the summer of 1985. On their return, they opened clubs such as Shoom and Project Club in London to continue the Ibiza vibe, while in Manchester, the Hacienda Club started to introduce nights playing acid house music.

As the movement spread in the UK, more clubs opened, and illegal parties started to be held in warehouses. During the late 1980s and early 1990s, illegal raves held in office blocks, aircraft hangars, clubs, car parks or simply open fields attracted thousands of young ravers, who took Ecstasy and danced to music with fast repetitive beats. Venues were often kept secret until the evening of the party, when ravers had to call a special phone number to discover the location. The huge raves, often lasting all weekend, were similar to the festivals of the 1960s, though with less free love and more dancing; 1988 was dubbed the Second Summer of Love.

The energetic party animals who went to raves wore coloured loose jeans and hooded tops, accessorized with trainers and bright hats – and an obligatory whistle for the dancefloor. T-shirts and tops were emblazoned with psychedelic prints and patterns. The emblem of the movement became the yellow Smiley face, which appeared on T-shirts, badges and pendants. As New Age travellers joined forces with the ravers to organize festivals and parties, dreadlocks, piercings and combat trousers worn with bright T-shirts became part of the traveller–raver uniform.

In 1994 the Criminal Justice and Public Order Bill clamped down on unlicensed outdoor music events, and the rave spirit and culture in the UK dwindled. But rave fashion re-emerged in 2006 as new rave, with bright, fluorescent, sports-inspired streetwear covered in Smiley face emblems, and catwalk versions of the look designed by Gareth Pugh, Christopher Kane and Karen Walker. ∎

Shock tactics to sell clothes

THE BENETTON ADVERTISING CAMPAIGNS

A nun kisses a priest. A white baby suckles at a black breast. A blood-streaked newborn baby takes its first breath, its umbilical cord still attached. These are some of the controversial and award-winning advertising images that creative director Oliviero Toscani masterminded for the clothing brand Benetton between 1982 and 2000.

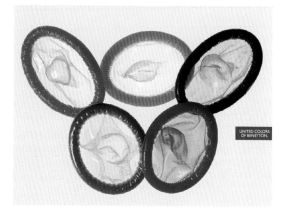

Toscani created this Benetton advertisement to coincide with the 1992 Olympic Games in Barcelona.

Toscani was a master of publicity, and he succeeded in selling clothes for Benetton through controversy. In 1984 he photographed groups of models of all races wearing Benetton clothing, for the 'All the Colors of the World' advertisements. It was daring for the time. After 1989, his more political and shocking images started to appear on billboards and in magazines, with no images of the clothes at all. His ads resembled pieces of fine art – a famous campaign included a photograph of a man dying of AIDS, which caused controversy mainly thanks to its resemblance to a *Pietà* painting – but the company used them very successfully to sell clothes.

Toscani changed the ideas behind fashion advertising, proving that images devoid of fashion references and imagery could still be used to sell. It was a clever move, as consumers of all races, worldwide, could interpret in their own way the photographs that drew on the big themes of human experience – life, death, war and religion.

In 2000 Toscani pushed the limits of taste too far with a Benetton campaign entitled 'We, on Death Row', which showed portraits of condemned men, convicted killers. There was a public outcry. 'Benetton is glamorizing killers,' said a member of the victims of crime group Justice for All. 'Benetton has built their campaign on the blood of victims.' When the retailer Sears, Roebuck and Co. axed its Benetton clothing franchise, Benetton and Toscani finally parted company. 'If the death sentence were handed out to those who are guilty of producing excruciatingly tasteless, ineffective advertising and inflicting it on the masses, Oliviero Toscani, the self-proclaimed genius behind Benetton advertising, would be appearing in his own anti-capital-punishment ads,' raged Jerry Della Femina in the *Wall Street Journal*.

Toscani's novel approach of excluding the very clothing that he was advertising, twinned with unforgettable images, meant that his work dramatically raised the profile of a brand that had been known until then principally for its brightly coloured jumpers. He not only built his career, he helped to rebuild the Benetton brand. ■

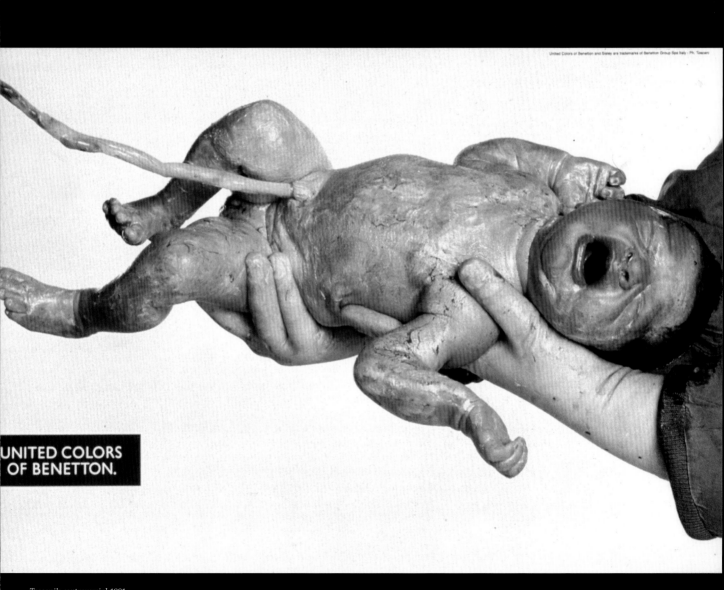

UNITED COLORS
OF BENETTON.

Toscani's controversial 1991
advertisement for Benetton
featuring a newborn baby is
arrestingly raw and dramatic.

IDEA № 91

DECONSTRUCTION AND ANTWERP

In the 1980s, six avant-garde designers who had trained at the Royal Academy of Fine Arts in Antwerp, Belgium, decided to launch their talents in London. They included Ann Demeulemeester, Dries Van Noten and Dirk Bikkembergs. With Martin Margiela, who launched his first Paris collection in 1989, they introduced a radical low-key style of dress for the 1990s.

Innovative Belgian designer Martin Margiela shows loose layered outsize garments, with hair to match, in 2000. The uneven raw cuffs are typical of his signature style.

Although each had his or her own individual style, they often worked with distressed clothes in monotone colours. Martin Margiela and Ann Demeulemeester enjoyed reassembling clothes, and introduced tailoring with unstitched seams, exposed lining and frayed edges. They steered away from colour, and focused on detail and contrasting fabrics. Margiela incorporated antique tulle and patchwork from flea markets into his work, and put seams and zips on the outside of garments. The press labelled it Deconstruction, although he disagreed with the term. 'I don't see the idea of "deconstruction",' he said. 'When I slash down old or new clothes to transform them I do not believe that I am destroying them, but bringing them back to life in a different way.' Margiela went on to design for Hermès in 1997.

Demeulemeester focused on layered, flowing clothes, without ostentatious colour, instead using texture as ornamentation. She became known for her long coats and dresses, as well as trousers cut radically low to show off the hip bone; she also put laddered stockings on the catwalk.

Dries Van Noten's work was more feminine. Referencing the East, he layered sarongs, jackets and trousers, using dark colours and minimal ornamentation.

Dirk Bikkembergs started out as a menswear designer, launching womenswear in 1993. He focussed on offering minimalist, strong shapes in muted tones that he then treated with his deconstructed aesthetic. He is well known for using, and often layering, wool and leather, and for his strong military influences.

Their timing was perfect, with a downbeat look that would not have worked during the showy 1980s, but instead fed the next decade's modest appetite for minimal ostentation and clothes that looked more authentic and unfinished. ∎

'They introduced tailoring with unstitched
seams, exposed lining and frayed edges'

*French actress Sophie Marceau
poses in a long white skirt, white
shirt and loosely tailored black
coat by Dries Van Noten.*

'Some designers choose to host their fashion shows on the Internet, streaming images directly into domestic computer screens'

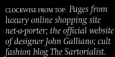

CLOCKWISE FROM TOP: *Pages from luxury online shopping site net-a-porter; the official website of designer John Galliano; cult fashion blog The Sartorialist.*

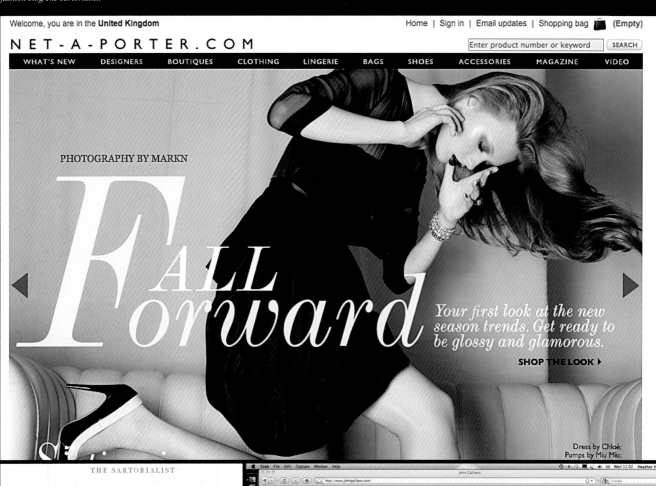

Fashion in cyberspace

IDEA № 92
THE INTERNET

Developed initially by the US military during the Cold War as a response to the Soviet launch of Sputnik in 1957, with the intention of regaining the technological upper hand, the Internet began life as ARPANET. It developed progressively throughout the 1960s, '70s and '80s to become a globe-encompassing network.

It was still mainly used by the military and academics, however, and it was not until Tim Berners-Lee invented the World Wide Web in the late 1980s that public use took off. Then there was no stopping it.

The Internet has had a dramatic impact on many aspects of modern life, including the fashion industry. In order to hold their own in the market, all leading brands today have their own promotional websites, showing the latest collections, press office information and links to their stores and stockists. Designers were quick to latch on to the marketing potential of websites, and the Internet has become a valuable research tool for members of the public seeking brand and stockist information.

Catwalk shows and new street trends are transmitted straight to consumers' homes as they happen, with a startling immediacy that has never before been possible. Websites such as style.com and firstview.com became some of the first to publish photographs and videos from the international fashion weeks. Some designers choose to host their fashion shows on the Internet rather than as live events, streaming images directly into domestic computer screens. Burberry launched a click-and-buy formula, through which customers can order selected items online while watching its catwalk show – and the pieces will be delivered just seven weeks later. 'The fast pace dictated by the Internet is rewriting the archaic rules of the fashion industry. Live streaming of catwalk shows and the rise of a generation of bloggers have formed a direct connection between catwalk and customer,' wrote Jess Cartner-Morley in the *Guardian* in 2010.

Retail has been revolutionized, with thousands of online 24-hour shopping sites selling everything from vintage designer-wear to new labels. Jackets and shoes can be ordered and delivered to the home with just a few clicks of the mouse, with the innumerable online retailers ranging from high-street multiples to high-end luxury retailers such as net-a-porter.com. New designers can now sell directly to consumers through the Internet, without any need of an intermediary.

Magazines and newspapers, long at the heart of the industry, have been quick to adapt and join the online world. Every leading magazine and newspaper now publishes its online version, alongside a torrent of new competition: free Internet magazines and Internet fashion blogs by the thousand.

The Internet has had a positive effect on fashion for the consumer, empowering them but also making them more demanding. Information and increasing choice means that retailers, brands and the media have to work harder to please an ever more impatient fashion-savvy public. ■

'It was time to take stock and re-evaluate after the extravagant fashion of the 1980s'

The New Age look was cool, calm and simple, and executed in pure white.

The dawn of a bright, white future

IDEA № 93
THE NEW PURITY

In 1990 the London-based Turkish designer Rifat Ozbek captivated critics and buyers with his all-white New Age collection, a refreshing series of loose separates influenced by clubbing, sport and streetwear. Ozbek reworked tracksuits and sports clothing into cool, comfortable clubwear, including sequined baseball caps, loose white hooded tops and pieces bearing slogans such as 'Nirvana'.

It was a fresh chapter in fashion, as had been Courrèges' Space Age collection in the 1960s. The Gulf War had shut off the lucrative markets of the Arab world, so it was a sobering time for the fashion houses. Ecological concerns were on people's minds. It was time to take stock and re-evaluate after the decorative consumption and extravagant fashion of the 1980s, with its often brash opulence. Ozbek's collection played to a clean, rehabilitative and calm spiritual mood. A less-is-more approach to fashion was to become one of the most important elements that defined 1990s style, particularly as it was so different from that of the previous decade. *i-D* magazine reported: 'In 1993, fashion has subjected itself to a reality check. Excessive flamboyance is now seen as a touch distasteful. Interest has shifted towards a movement that rejects gloss in favour of an acceptance of the political and economic turmoil of the times.'

Fashion saw a return to simple luxury separates, led by such designers as the American Zoran, who created capsule wardrobes in fine fabrics. Zoran concentrated on simplicity, perfecting the loose pyjama trouser and T-shirt, and kept accessories and fastenings to a minimum.

Throughout the final decade of the twentieth century, fashion quietened down its tone. Designers concentrated on sleek clothes, which were subtle, comfortable and, above all else, unshowy. ∎

Relaxed all-white pieces from the iconic 1990 New Age collection by Rifat Ozbek.

Muji T-shirts are pointedly unbranded, and Muji prides itself on its lack of aggressive marketing.

Just say no to the logo

IDEA № 94

THE ANTI-BRAND

How can a brand be unbranded? What, indeed, is an anti-brand? The 1990s saw the emergence of new companies whose philosophy was a reaction to the excesses of the 1980s. They began to build their names on the back of anti-consumerist ideals.

There was generally a new, moderating attitude to consumption in the 1990s, caused by an ailing worldwide economy. Fashion designers focused on low-key luxury, and bold logos came to be seen as vulgar.

In 2000 Naomi Klein published the influential book *No Logo*, chronicling the way in which brands had become more important than the products themselves, and taking a hard, critical look at the power of multinational corporations and our obsession with branding and consumption. Klein caught the mood of the time, and the anti-branding, anti-globalization movement went on to grow, with many fashion companies embracing its ideals. This paradoxically allowed them to build brands in a new way, but also encouraged them to take responsibility for their sourcing and manufacturing policies.

Today anti-branding is gaining momentum. The advent of the Internet has required companies to show more transparency, and those that are unethical or greedy risk becoming targets of global slur campaigns, which can be costly and damaging.

The Japanese company Muji went multinational in the late 1980s, offering simply designed clothing and interiors products. Muji prided itself on its lack of aggressive marketing and branding. A statement on the Muji website read: 'MUJI is not a brand. MUJI does not make products of individuality or fashion.' It launched a T-shirt with a blank space for the wearer to create his or her own logo.

In 2004 Adidas opened an unbranded store in London simply called 6 Newburgh Street. This no-nonsense approach aimed to convey authenticity to the consumer, in stark contrast to its heavily branded rivals.

Similarly, the multiple retailer American Apparel, selling mainly basic though fashion-led T-shirts and dresses in cotton jersey, vaunted its non-branded clothing and individually designed stores. The first shops opened in Canada and North America in 2003. All the clothing was made in the United States, and never in sweatshops abroad. The company used anti-corporate and anti-globalization ideas to market its products. Its advertising campaigns, featuring non-professional models, were carefully calculated to appeal to a new breed of questioning young shoppers.

Some argue that these anti-brand companies are merely using new marketing techniques to achieve the same goals as those corporations they profess to despise. Nonetheless, they tap into a desire on the part of those modern consumers who are increasingly asking questions about the products they buy, and demanding responsibility from their suppliers and manufacturers. And this consciousness has to be a positive thing. ∎

'A scruffy look of mismatched and layered clothes, rarely fitting perfectly'

High fashion dresses down

IDEA № 95
GRUNGE

Take a punk and a hippie, chew them up, roll them around your mouth and then spit them out. You have created grunge. Although a relatively small subcultural movement, grunge had an impact on fashion that was far larger than its original following. It tapped into the downbeat mood of the 1990s and into consumers' needs to buy into something 'real', a world away from the logo- and status-obsessed 1980s.

ABOVE: *The influential Perry Ellis Spring/Summer 1993 grunge show, designed by Marc Jacobs.*

OPPOSITE: *Grunge rock icon Kurt Cobain of Nirvana in Seattle, 1990.*

Grunge evolved in Seattle, a subgenre of American rock made famous by such bands as Pearl Jam and Nirvana. The word 'grunge' originated in the 1960s, when grungy meant dirty. Like the music it accompanied, grunge style was essentially anti-fashion, and about dressing down: a scruffy look of mismatched and layered clothes, usually oversized or undersized – rarely fitting perfectly. Kurt Cobain, the lead singer of Nirvana, epitomized the grunge look with his dishevelled hair, jeans, checked shirt and Converse shoes. The girls favoured short floral dresses teamed with heavy army boots, also pairing big jumpers with crumpled silk tops.

Grunge started on the street, but was quickly seized by such designers as Anna Sui, who incorporated the look into her catwalk collection for Spring/ Summer 1993. In 1992 Marc Jacobs had presented a grunge-inspired collection for Perry Ellis of skull caps, work boots, flannel shirts and silk dresses worn with cashmere thermals. *The New York Times* described it as 'a mess', and it was, perhaps unsurprisingly, Jacobs' last collection for Perry Ellis. More unpredictably, grunge was also interpreted by designers Christian Lacroix, Donna Karan for DKNY, Ralph Lauren, and Karl Lagerfeld for Chanel. However, designer ready-to-wear clients were reluctant to pay high prices for street-style clothes. It was not the 1980s, but they still wanted a little bit of luxury for their money. So grunge swiftly returned to the street – back where it belonged. ∎

Coleen McLoughlin in 2006 with her Yves Saint Laurent Muse bag, which was priced at over £1,000.

Waiting lists and four-figure price tags

IDEA № 96
THE STATUS HANDBAG

Status handbags are some of today's most conspicuous marks of wealth and consumption, with prices running to many thousands of pounds. A desirable designer bag often has a long waiting list of well-heeled customers anxious to buy it and flaunt their ownership.

Women's handbags in the 1980s were often made from newer and more economical materials than leather, and women got into the habit of combining different handbags with their various outfits.

By the 1990s clothing had become fashionably low-key (some might say boring) and canny designers realized that glamorous women wearing under-stated clothes would pay a great deal to acquire the perfect accessory by a luxury brand. By making only limited runs of their signature bags, they could generate enormous demand and long waiting lists.

The designer labels Prada, Dior, Fendi and Gucci commanded astro-nomical sums for their much sought-after handbags. Designer Marc Jacobs joined Louis Vuitton in 1997 and his injection of inspiration saw the company's sales of leather goods grow by nearly a third. The designers at Fendi scored particularly well with their Baguette bag, which tucks under the arm like a French loaf – a reputed 600,000 were sold in just three years, and it is still going strong. The Christian Dior Saddle bag, the Yves Saint Laurent Muse and the Chloé Paddington sent women running for their Amex cards.

By 2005 handbags were the best-selling items of women's fashion merchandise. This goldmine enticed companies without handbag lines, such as designers Narciso Rodriguez and Zac Posen, to rush in and launch their own accessories collections.

The major design houses continued to employ their classic bag shapes, but revived them with different materials and finishes from season to season. The more exotic finishes accounted for the five-figure price tags of some bags. Hermès continues to this day to sell the Kelly Bag, named after Grace Kelly and first launched in the 1950s, updating it in different finishes and materials. Karl Lagerfeld also updates the distinc-tive long-chained 2.55 bag for Chanel each year.

One of the hottest and most exclu-sive status bags is the Birkin, made by Hermès and named after the 1960s actress Jane Birkin. Both Martha Stewart and rapper Lil' Kim carried one for their court hearings. There is a two-year waiting list to buy them and they cost over $5,000. It is certainly a quiet way of making a bold statement in court. ∎

Grace Kelly announces her engagement to Prince Rainier of Monaco in 1956, carrying an Hermès bag. It was later named the Kelly Bag in her honour.

IDEA № 97

PERFORMANCE FABRICS

Fabrics and fibres can perform, as well as look fashionable – keep the wearer dry, protect from harmful bacteria or against UV rays, or even dose the body with vitamin C or moisturizer.

This revolutionary Prada raincoat from Autumn/Winter 2002 turns opaque in the rain.

Performance fabrics are synthetic technical fabrics that have been developed with a specific functional purpose in mind, often for the sports, military or medical industries. But it is not all about antibacterial or flame-retardant textiles: fashion designers have been quick to seize on some of the new fabrics for their collections. Versace and Issey Miyake were at the forefront of fabric technology during the 1980s, and by the 1990s designers were intrigued by the new ideas on offer from the major textile houses and textile fairs.

The fashion industry made full use of the new fabric technology, using some of its protective qualities in clothing. Junya Watanabe used a waterproof fabric that, rather than being coated to keep the rain out, trapped air and pushed water droplets to the surface. For his ski and cycle collections Ralph Lauren used Gore-Tex, which is breathable, windproof and waterproof. In sun-scorched Australia, Coolibar launched a range of clothing that blocked more than 97 percent of the sun's rays. Similarly, Evoluzione garments in treated cotton boasted a sunprotection factor of 40 and a promise to keep the body between five and ten degrees cooler. Dockers incorporated lined pockets in its trousers, which, it claimed, would shield users from mobile phone radiation. An extraordinary 2002 Prada innovation was a sheer raincoat that turned opaque in the rain.

To help stave off winter colds, Fuji Spinning Co. in Japan came up with a

T-shirt in 2001 that doses the wearer with vitamin C on contact with warm human skin. The company Cherie launched tights that moisturize the legs with aloe vera.

Fragrance has been popular in lingerie ranges. La Perla made sweetsmelling underwear by embedding particles of fragrance into the fabric. More extreme was Triumph's prototype anti-smoking bra, whose aromatherapy odours of jasmine and lavender were intended to stop the craving for nicotine.

For sportswear and underwear, the high-tech Coolmax fibre draws sweat away from the body towards a garment's surface, so the body can breathe and air will circulate.

And how about clothes that you never have to wash? Research into selfcleaning fabric suggests that cotton coated with titanium dioxide can use sunlight as a trigger to break down dirt. Now that could be a money-spinner if it ever came on to the market. ∎

'Triumph's prototype anti-smoking bra was intended to stop the craving for nicotine'

ABOVE AND RIGHT: *Sportswear by Adidas.*

Like mother, like daughter

IDEA № 98
ETERNAL YOUTH

By the end of the twentieth century, it was quite acceptable for three generations of women to wear the same style of clothing. Dress no longer had to be determined by the wearer's age, and a 70-year-old could shop at the same stores as her 18-year-old granddaughter.

Women of all ages were highly fashion-aware at the end of the 1990s. Healthy diet and exercise, an increasing rejection of smoking, and great advances in medicine had all led to women living longer. And also to looking younger: tremendous efforts were made to avoid looking old.

Cosmetics were continually being updated with new technology, and the creeping acceptance of cosmetic surgery allowed women, for a price, to retain their youthful good looks. With Botox treatment becoming widely available, it was goodbye to wrinkles and hello to smooth foreheads. Hair, eyelash and nail extensions and fake tan were marketed to cater to the illusion of eternal perfectibility.

Conversely, while the old sought to perpetuate their youth, the young increasingly aspired to dress like adults. Children's fashion ranges have encouraged the young to emulate adult trends, and precocious girls to mimic their pop icons. If children were not always treated like adults, they could at least dress like them. Today's pubescent girls are also physically and socially much more advanced than their early-twentieth-century counterparts. While the average age for the onset of menstruation in Victorian times was 16, it is today a mere 11.

The practice of children dressing as adults has a long and respectable history. Medieval and Renaissance portraits show small children dressed in all the extravagance of grown-up fashion. These often included 'ruffs, padded breeches, trailing sleeves, dragging skirts, high-heeled shoes and hats top-heavy with feathers and flowers', as Alison Lurie noted in *The Language of Clothes* (1981). It was not until the late eighteenth century that children were encouraged to wear loose fashions of their own that allowed them to run and play, instead of being dressed as small adults straight after infancy.

Life expectancy continues to grow in the West. With today's new babies expected to live beyond the age of 100, can it be long before the same fashions appeal across five generations? ∎

Siblings? No. Actress Demi Moore and her daughter Tallulah Belle Willis in 2007.

Dress no longer indicates age. Jade Jagger poses with her daughters Amba, 12, and Assisi, 15, in 2008.

'Hair, eyelash and nail extensions and fake tan were marketed to cater to the illusion of eternal perfectibility'

Fashion's green credentials

Eco campaigner and designer Katharine Hamnett on an Oxfam-sponsored visit to highlight the plight of cotton farmers in Mali, 2003.

IDEA Nº 99

ECO FASHION

The 1990s was a decade of great change, not least in consumers' awareness of climate change and other, interrelated environmental issues such as pesticide use, pollution and waste. As global warming became a more widely accepted challenge, so the fashion world started to respond with eco-friendly clothing and eco fashion.

Although the hippies embraced notions of sustainability as early as the 1960s, their impact on mainstream fashion was slight. 'Nobody wanted to know about fashion and ethics 20 years ago,' said Katharine Hamnett in 2008. Hamnett led the way, using environmentally friendly fabrics such as organic cotton, and eventually fair-trade and ecological fashion brands became more common. People Tree, for example, was set up in 1997 and sells fair-trade and organic clothing and accessories. The company works with organic producers in developing countries.

Second-hand clothing became known as vintage, and was suddenly chic. Expensive vintage stores opened up to cater for the demand. In 1992 Helen Storey started a high-fashion recycled label, entitled Second Life.

During the late 1990s the fashion and clothing manufacturing industries began to respond to fair-trade issues. In 1998 the Fair Labor Association developed a code of practices for clothing companies, resulting in a vital shift away from sweatshop labour and worker exploitation worldwide. Brands such as Nike and Sean John were exposed in the media for alleged bad practice, and many sweatshops in developing countries were shut down.

Today eco fashion is big business. Interest in organic natural fibres such as cotton, silk and linen has increased, and clothing ranges made from hemp, a highly sustainable crop, have come onto the market. Websites and brands promote recycled and reused clothes. The label Howies, founded in 1995, offers streetwear that can be recycled effectively after use and T-shirts using recycled cotton, while Worn Again designs trainers out of recycled materials. Denim ranges Ascension and

James Jeans both focus on using organic materials. More and more sustainable brands have been launched, such as Danish designer label Noir (2006). Bono's clothing range Edun promotes fairly traded, organic cotton and natural fibres. Topshop has collaborated with People Tree. Even Nike is expanding its ranges of clothing made from organic cotton and encourages the recycling of trainers at its stores.

Some high-end designers are also doing their bit, with Proenza Schouler and Diane von Furstenberg showing environmentally friendly clothing ranges. 'It's got to be fashion and not what people perceive as "organic fashion" – those hippie, oatmeal type of clothes,' says Hamnett. 'They have to be gorgeous clothes.' ■

*Recycled pleated polyester
dress, hand-painted and beaded
over a floral print, by Central
Saint Martins (London, UK)
graduate Davina Hawthorne,
Spring/Summer 2008.*

'Electrical and fabric engineers have started to embed electronics directly into textiles'

A dress with LED devices installed inside, designed by Swarovski and Hussein Chalayan, Tokyo, 2007.

The future is now

A Pioneer Corp employee shows the latest prototype in Japanese streetwear in 2002 – a hybrid of fashion and technology inspired by wearable PCs. The heatproof fabric display is embedded in the sleeve.

IDEA № 100

WEARABLE ELECTRONICS

Computers and telephones embedded into clothing is not a dream of the future. Wearable electronics are being developed right now, and are changing both the way that we communicate and use clothes. Some predict that we will come to rely on a favourite jacket, rather as we currently do a laptop or mobile phone, as an essential communication tool.

In 1922 Alfred Dunhill installed a light in its handbags, which switched on when the bag was opened. A little later, Elsa Schiaparelli designed handbags that played music. But recent technological changes have been far more ambitious than light and music.

The electronics company Philips collaborated with Levi Strauss in 1999 to bring out the ICD+ jacket, in which a mobile phone and an MP3 player sit in protective pockets and connect via integral wires to earphones in the jacket hood, allowing the wearer to switch between listening to music and taking a call. C'N'C Costume National developed bags that incorporated small strips of solar panels for recharging an MP3 or mobile. However, electronic devices in garments could look clunky – and there was always a big technical problem: how to wash the garments. The electronics had to be removed beforehand.

Motorcylists have long been grateful for the warmth generated inside their battery-heated jackets, vests and gloves, but in recent years electrical and fabric engineers have started to embed electronics directly into textiles, such as washable and stretchable electronic circuits. Softswitch and Burton Snowboards launched one of the first commercial electronic garments with an integrated fabric control pad, a 2002 snowboarding jacket with a flexible keypad built in to the jacket sleeve, operating a mini-disc player. Another snowboarding company, O'Neill, introduced the NavJacket, a ski jacket with built-in GPS on the sleeve. It also offered a jacket with an MP3-compatible entertainment system, operated by soft-touch remote controls woven into a sleeve, with a microphone in the collar for hands-free calls. Similarly, a sailing jacket by Gul had a textile control panel on the sleeve for an MP3 player hidden within.

Taking technology in a more fashion-driven direction, CuteCircuit produced a skirt whose colour and pattern could be changed by touch, and Hussein Chalayan played with clothes whose form and structure change by remote control (see Space Age, page 141).

As technology advances ever faster and communications become more portable, it seems inevitable that the clothes we wear will become increasingly complex and sophisticated. ∎

This lightweight silk Galaxy Dress by CuteCircuit from 2009 is embroidered with 24,000 paper-thin LEDs, and interspersed with over 4,000 hand-applied Swarovski crystals.

Further Reading

Books

David Bailey and Martin Harrison, *David Bailey: Archive One 1957–1969*, 1999

Hamish Bowles, *Yves Saint Laurent: Style*, 2008

Mariuccia Casadio, *Missoni (Made in Italy)*, 1998

Clifton Daniel, *20th Century Day by Day (DK Millennium)*, 1999

Christian Dior, *Dior by Dior*, 2007

Mick Farren, *The Black Leather Jacket*, 2008

Salvatore Ferragamo, *Shoemaker of Dreams: the autobiography of Salvatore Ferragamo*, 1972

Patty Fox, *Star Style: Hollywood Legends as Fashion Icons*, 1995

Neal Heard, *Trainers: Over 300 Classics, from Rare Vintage to the Latest Designs*, 2005

Tim Jackson and David Shaw, *The Fashion Handbook*, 2006

Naomi Klein, *No Logo*, 2000

Victor Margueritte, *La Garçonne*, 1922

Richard Martin, *Fashion and Surrealism*, 1989

Colin McDowell, *Galliano: Romantic, Realist and Revolutionary*, 1998

Patricia Mears and Steven Bluttal, *Halston*, 2001

PYMCA, Ted Polhemus, Jon Swinstead, and James Lange, *Unordinary People: British Youth Culture 1960–2009*, 2009

Ligaya Salazar, *Fashion V Sport*, 2008

Elsa Schiaparelli, *Shocking Life: The Autobiography of Elsa Schiaparelli*, 2007

Vivian Vale and Andrea Juno, *Modern Primitives: Investigation of Contemporary Adornment Rituals*, 1997

Louis Vuitton and Marc Jacobs, *Louis Vuitton: Art, Fashion and Architecture*, 2009

Claire Wilcox, *The Golden Age of Couture: Paris and London 1947–1957*, 2008

Anna Wintour and André Leon Talley, *Manolo Blahník Drawings*, 2003

Harriet Worsley, *Classics of Fashion*, 2002

Harriet Worsley, *Decades of Fashion*, 2006

Harriet Worsley, *The White Dress: Fashion Inspiration for Brides*, 2009

Websites

www.colette.fr

www.firstview.com

www.net-a-porter.com

www.style.com

www.thesartorialist.com

Fashion and costume museums

Victoria and Albert Museum (V&A)
Cromwell Road
South Kensington
London SW7 2RL
UK

Fashion Museum
Assembly Rooms
Bennett Street
Bath BA1 2QH
UK

MoMu
Antwerp Fashion ModeMuseum
Nationalestraat 28
B – 2000 Antwerpen
Belgium

Musée des Arts de la Mode
Palais du Louvre
107 rue de Rivoli
75001 Paris
France

Musée de la Mode et du Costume
Palais Galliéra
10 Avenue Pierre 1er de Serbie
75116 Paris
France

Lipperheidesche Kostümbibliothek
Kunstbibliothek
Staatliche Museen zu Berlin
Matthaikirchplatz 6
10785 Berlin
Germany

Costume Institute
Metropolitan Museum of Art
1000 5th Avenue at 82nd Street
New York
NY 10028-0198
USA

Museum at the Fashion Institute of Technology
7th Avenue at 27th Street
New York
NY 10001-5992
USA

Kobe Fashion Museum
9, 2-chome
Koyocho-naka
Higashinada
Kobe 658-0032
Japan

Galeria del Costume
Via della Ninna 5
50122 Florence
Italy

Museum Salvatore Ferragamo
Palazzo Spini Feroni
Via Tornabuoni 2
50123 Florence
Italy

Films

American Gigolo, directed by Paul Schrader, 1980. (The shoulder pad)

Blow Up, directed by Michelangelo Antonioni, 1966. (Raw photography)

Clash By Night, directed by Fritz Lang, 1952. (Jeans)

Coco Before Chanel, directed by Anne Fontaine, 2009. (Trousers for women)

Desperately Seeking Susan, directed by Susan Seidelman, 1985. (Pop stars)

The Devil Wears Prada, directed by David Frankel, 2006. (*Vogue*)

Dishonored, directed by Josef Von Sternberg, 1931. (The black leather jacket)

Do the Right Thing, directed by Spike Lee, 1989. (Hip hop, Trainers)

Dr. No, directed by Terence Young, 1962. (The bikini)

Foxy Brown, directed by Jack Hill, 1974. (Funk)

Intolerance, directed by D. W. Griffith, 1916. (False eyelashes)

Letty Lynton, directed by Clarence Brown, 1932. (The shoulder pad)

One Million Years B.C. directed by Don Chaffey, 1966. (The bikini)

Quadrophenia, directed by Franc Roddam, 1979. (Mods)

Rebel Without a Cause, directed by Nicholas Ray, 1955. (Jeans, Trainers)

Sabrina, directed by Billy Wilder, 1954. (Celebrities)

Shaft, directed by Gordon Parks, 1971. (Funk)

A Streetcar Named Desire, directed by Elia Kazan, 1951. (The T-shirt)

Superfly, directed by Gordon Parks, 1972. (Funk)

The Wild One, directed by László Benedek, 1953. (The black leather jacket)

Index

Page numbers in **bold** refer to pictures

Picture Credits

2 Martin Hayhow/AFP/Getty Images; 8 © The Bridgeman Art Library; 9 Photo by Tony Barson/WireImage /Getty Images; 10 (top) Photo by Arnaldo Magnani/Getty Images; 10 (bottom) Photo by Hulton Archive/Getty Images; 11 © Interfoto/ Lebrecht Music & Arts; 12 Photo by Mansell/Tim Life Pictures/ Getty Images; 13 Tony Barson/WireImage/Getty Images; 14 Photo by Hulton Archive/Getty Images; 15 Georges Lepape: © ADAGP, Paris and DACS, London 2010; 16 © Emmanuel Fradin/Reuters/Corbis; 17 © 2005 Roger-Viollet/Topfoto; 18 (top) Photo by Lipnitzki/Roger Viollet/Getty Images; 18 (bottom) Photo by Weegee (Arthur Fellig)/International Center of Photography/Getty Images; 19 Courtesy Agent Provocateur; 20 © Bettmann/Corbis; 21 After Sir George Hayter/V&A Images/Victoria & Albert Museum; 22 (top) SNAP/ Rex Features; 22 (bottom) Pierre-Philippe Marcou/AFP/Getty Images; 23 (left) © Bettmann/Corbis; 23 (right) Central Press/ Getty Images; 24 Condé Nast – Cecil Beaton/Trunk Archive; 25 (top) Courtesy EMAP; 25 (bottom) © Mary Evans Picture Library 2010; 26 (top) General Photographic Agency/ Getty Images; 26 (bottom) Clare Muller/PYMCA; 27 Waring Abbott/Getty Images; 28 The Art Archive/Royal Automobile Club London/NB Design; 29 Alan Band/Keystone/Getty Images; 30 (top) © Bettmann/Corbis; 30 (bottom) dpa Picture-Alliance GmbH; 31 Courtesy PETA; 32 Rob Loud/Getty Images; 33 (top) Slim Aarons/Getty Images; 33 (bottom) © Photo RMN – Ernest Bulloz; 35 Georges Lepape/Vogue © The Condé Nast Publications Ltd; 36 Joel Saget/AFP/Getty Images; 37 Courtesy John Galliano; 38 (left) Photo by Hulton Archive/Getty Images; 38 (right) Paul O'Doye/Getty Images; 39 Library of Congress, Prints & Photographs Division, Russell Patterson, LC-USZCN4-137; 40 © Bettmann/Corbis; 41 The Art Archive/ Kharbine-Tapabor/Coll. Galdoc-Grob; 42 © RA/Lebrecht Music & Arts; 43 (left) Bob Thomas/Popperfoto/Getty Images; 43 (right) Syndication International/Getty Images; 44 © Ullstein Bild/Topfoto; 45 Lee Miller/Getty Images; 46 © 2005 Roger-Viollet/Topfoto; 47 Courtesy Shaun Leane; 48 Robert Legon/Rex Features; 49 The Kobal Collection; 50 catwalking. com; 51(top) Kurt Hutton/Picture Post/Getty Images; 51 (bottom) Startraks Photo/Rex Features; 52 © CHANEL – Collection Denise Tual; 53 (left) The Kobal Collection/United Artists; 53 (right) akg-images; 54 © Man Ray Trust/Adagp – DACS/Telimage – 2010; 55 catwalking.com; 56 (top) Sipa Press/ Rex Features; 56 (bottom) Mark Large/Daily Mail/Rex Features; 57 Eugene Adebari/Rex Features; 58 © V&A Images/Victoria & Albert Museum; 59 catwalking.com; 60 (top) Courtesy Marc Jacobs; 60 (bottom) Courtesy Dior; 61 The Art Archive/Alfredo Dagli Orti; 62 Gjon Mili/Time Life Pictures/Getty Images; 63 (top) catwalking.com; 63 (bottom) The Art Archive/Kharbine-Tapabor; 64 The Kobal Collection; 65 (left) Mike Marsland/ WireImage/Getty Images; 65 (right) Everett Collection/Rex Features; 66 Dominique ISSERMANN for the No 5 advertising campaign in 2009 © CHANEL 2009; 67 © Chanel © Andy Warhol Foundation. From Andy Warhol serigraphies.; 68 Margaret Chute/Getty Images; 69 (top) Chris Moorhouse/ Getty Images; 69 (bottom) Popperfoto/Getty Images; 70 (top left) catwalking.com; 70 (top right) © Bata Shoe Museum, Toronto 2010; 70 (middle left) catwalking.com; 70 (middle) Getty Images; 70 (middle right) catwalking.com; 70 (bottom left) Courtesy Sergio Rossi; 70 (bottom right) © Interfoto/ Lebrecht Music & Arts; 71 catwalking.com; 72 Edward Steichen/© Corbis. All Rights Reserved; 73 © RA/Lebrecht Music & Arts; 74 © Steven Meisel/Art + Commerce/Courtesy Yves Saint Laurent; 75 akg-images; 76 (top) © Jerome Albertini/Corbis; 76 (bottom) Ron Galella/WireImage/ Getty Images; 77 © Roger Schall; 78 (top) LAPI/Roger Viollet/Rex Features; 78 (bottom) © John-Paul Pietrus; 79 Rex Features; 80 © RA/Lebrecht Music & Arts; 81 General Photographic Agency/Getty Images; 82 Terry Richardson/Art Partner; 83 (top) Giorgio Armani advertising campaign Autumn/Winter 1984–85 by Aldo Fallai; 83 (bottom) Sasha/Getty Images; 84 akg-images; 85 (top) John Kobal Foundation/Getty Images; 85 (bottom) akg-images; 86 Courtesy Monsoon; 87 (top)

Keystone/Getty Images; 87 (bottom) akg-images; 88 Image by Cecil Beaton © Condé Nast Archive/Corbis; 89 (left) © Philadelphia Museum of Art/Corbis; 89 (right) © Salvador Dali, Fundació Gala-Salvador Dalí, DACS, 2010; 90 (top) Photoshot. All right reserved; 90 (bottom) Michael Ochs Archives/Getty Images; 91 © Bata Shoe Museum, Toronto 2010; 92 (left) Eric Ryan/Getty Images; 92 (right) Berard: © ADAGP, Paris and DACS, London 2010; 93 catwalking.com; 94 Kurt Hutton/Getty Images; 95 Courtesy Advertising Archives; 96 catwalking.com; 97 (top) Peter Stackpole/Time & Life Pictures/Getty Images; 97 (bottom) © CinemaPhoto/ Corbis; 98 © Genevieve Naylor/Corbis; 99 Fred Ramage/Getty Images; 100 Peter Paul Hartnett/Rex Features; 101 (left) Fox Photos/Getty Images; 101 (right) Associated Newspapers/Daily Mail/Rex Features; 102 (left) Gavin Watson/PYMCA; 102 (right) Courtesy Dr Martens; 103 catwalking.com; 104 (top) Lichfield/ Getty Images; 104 (bottom) John Chillingworth/Getty Images; 105 © Anthea Simms; 106 (top) Roy Stevens/Time & Life Pictures/Getty Images; 106 (bottom) PA Archive/Press Association Images; 107 Jim Rakete/Photoselection; 108 The Kobal Collection/Danjaq/Eon/UA; 109 Keystone/Getty Images; 110 Rex Features; 111 © Condé Nast Archive/Corbis; 112 © Ullsteinbild/Topfoto; 113 Courtesy Advertising Archives; 114 John Pratt/Keystone Features/Getty Images; 115 © 2006 JapaneseStreets.com/Kjeld Duits; 116 Pascal Le Segretain/Getty Images; 117 (top) Getty Images; 117 (bottom) akg-images; 118 (top) Warner Bros/The Kobal Collection; 118 (bottom) © 2001 Topham Picturepoint; 119 Courtesy Katharine Hamnett & YOOX Group; 120 Courtesy Manolo Blahnik; 121 © Estate Guy Bourdin/Art + Commerce; 122 Courtesy of The Richard Avedon Foundation; 123 (top) © Henry Diltz/Corbis; 123 (bottom) Courtesy Advertising Archives; 124 (top) Keystone/ Getty Images; 124 (bottom) Ebet Roberts/Redferns/Getty Images; 125 (main) Courtesy Converse; 125 (top left) Courtesy Nike; 125 (top right) Courtesy Gola; 125 (bottom right) Courtesy Puma; 125 (bottom left) catwalking.com; 126 © Greg Gorman; 127 (top) Carlos Muina/Cover/Getty Images; 127 (bottom) © B.D.V./Corbis; 128 Terry O'Neill/Getty Images; 129 (main) © Ronald Wittek/dpa/Corbis; 129 (inset) © Deborah Feingold/Corbis; 130 Keystone/Getty Images; 131 (top) © Janette Beckman/PYMCA; 131 (bottom) The Kobal Collection/Curbishley-Baird; 132 Reg Lancaster/Getty Images; 133 Clive Arrowsmith/Celebrity Pictures; 134 catwalking.com; 135 (top) © Topfoto; 135 (bottom) Jim Smeal/WireImage/Getty Images; 136 (top) © Condé Nast Archive/Corbis; 136 (bottom) Everett Collection/Rex Features; 137 © Ronald Traeger; 138 akg-images; 139 (main) Rex Features; 139 (inset) Courtesy Advertising Archives; 140 © Peter Knapp; 141 Edward James/ Rex Features; 142 (top) Marc Hispard/© Condé Nast Archive/ Corbis; 142 (bottom) 2009 Getty Images; 143 Steve Lewis/Getty Images; 144 J. Emilio Flores/Corbis; 145 (top) © Anthea Simms; 145 (bottom) catwalking.com; 146 catwalking.com; 147 Hulton Archive/Getty Images; 148 V&A Images/Victoria & Albert Museum; 149 Courtesy Helen Storey; 150 Keystone/ Hulton Archive/Getty Images; 151 (left) George Stroud/Getty Images; 151 (right) © Norman Parkinson/Sygma/Corbis; 152 (top) Contrasto/eyevine; 152 (bottom) Gary Lewis/Polaris Images/eyevine; 153 James Whitlow Delano/Redux/eyevine; 154 McCarthy/Getty Images; 155 (top) Tim Graham/Getty Images; 155 (bottom) © Michael Ochs Archives/Corbis; 156 Everett Collection/Rex Features; 157 Gunnar Larsen/Rex Features; 158 Ilpo Musto/Rex Features; 159 (top) Alan Messer/ Rex Features; 159 (bottom) Peter Sanders/Redferns/Getty Images; 160 Berry Berenson © Condé Nast Archive/Corbis; 161 catwalking.com; 162 (top) Courtesy 'Against Malaria' Campaign; 162 (bottom) Francesco Scavullo, Vogue Magazine © Condé Nast Publications; 163 Terry O'Neill/Getty Images; 164 © Bettmann/Corbis; 165 © Bernd G. Schmitz/Corbis; 166 © Derek Ridgers; 167 David Dagley/Rex Features; 168 © Jacob Silberberg/Reuters/Corbis; 169 © Cardinale Stephane/Corbis/Sygma; 170 (top) © Derek Ridgers; 170 (bottom) © Ted Polhemus/PYMCA; 171 © Lynn Goldsmith/

Corbis; 172 © Josh Olins/Trunk Archive; 173 © Inez Van Lamsweerde and Vinoodh Matadin/Trunk Archive; 174 © Janette Beckman/Getty Images; 175 Courtesy Adidas; 176 Lynne Sladky/AP/Press Association Images; 177 (top) © James Lange/PYMCA; 177 (bottom) bigpicturesphoto.com; 178 © Anthea Simms; 179 © Jason Hetherington; 180 Studio Holle-Suppa; 181 Thierry Orban /Sygma/Corbis; 182 (top) Courtesy Stussy; 182 (bottom) Courtesy Staple Design; 183 Jeff Kravitz/Filmmagic/Getty Images; 184 © Billa/Everynight Images; 185 (top) © Derek Ridgers; 185 (bottom) © David Swindells/PYMCA; 186–187 Courtesy Benetton; 188 Ronald Stoops. Maison Martin Margiela A/W 2000–2001, Paris March 2000; 189 © Luc Roux/Corbis; 190 (top) Courtesy Net-a-Porter; 190 (bottom left) Courtesy The Sartorialist; 190 (bottom right) Courtesy John Galliano; 192 © Anne Menke/Trunk Archive; 193 Clive Dixon/Rex Features; 194 Courtesy Muji; 196 © Ian Tilton/Retna; 197 catwalking.com; 198 Chris Jackson/Getty Images; 199 © 2005 AP/Topfoto; 200 Stefano Rellandini/Reuters; 201 Courtesy Adidas; 202 Arnaldo Magnani/Getty Images; 203 Dave M. Benett/Getty Images; 204 Michael Dunlea/Rex Features; 205 Photo by Othello De Souza Hartley/Courtesy Davina Hawthorne; 206 © Kim Kyung Hoon/Reuters; 207 (top) Toshiyuki Aizawa/Reuters; 207 (bottom) © 2008 J.B. Spector/Museum of Science & Industry, Chicago/Courtesy of Cute Circuit.

Acknowledgements

An enormous thank you to Helen Rochester
and Susie May at Laurence King and to Heather
Vickers, Jon Allan and Kirsty Seymour-Ure for
all their hard work and patience. Thank you to
Jamie Lindsay and DW for their expert advice.

For Jessie Lindsay

LAURENCE KING

Published in 2011
by Laurence King Publishing Ltd
361–373 City Road
London EC1V 1LR

tel +44 20 7841 6900
fax +44 20 7841 6910

e-mail: enquiries@laurenceking.com
www.laurenceking.com

A catalogue record for this book is available from
the British Library.

ISBN-13: 978 1 85669 733 0

Designed by Two Sheds Design

Picture research by Heather Vickers

Printed in China

FRONTISPIECE: *Alexander McQueen's*
gold-painted fox-skeleton wrap,
seen at London Fashion Week,
February 2001.